# Use of Artificial Intelligence in Digital Transformation

# Use of Artificial Intelligence in Digital Transformation

**Prakhar Mittal**

ARCLER
PRESS

www.arclerpress.com

**Use of Artificial Intelligence in Digital Transformation**

*Prakhar Mittal*

**Arcler Press**
4164 Lakeshore Road
Burlington, ON L7L 1A4
Canada
www.arclerpress.com
Email: orders@arclereducation.com



ISBN: 978-1-77956-477-1 (Hardcover)

# ABOUT THE AUTHOR

**Prakhar Mittal** is a seasoned Product Development and Management Consultant with over 14 years of experience, including more than 10 years of international exposure. He holds an MBA from the prestigious Indian Institute of Management (IIM) Ahmedabad, one of the top business schools in Asia. Prakhar has successfully transitioned from an industry role to advising clients in the Life Sciences and Consumer Product sectors, where he specializes in digital transformation projects aimed at enhancing manufacturing processes and implementing cutting-edge digital innovations.

He is proficient in Supplier & Catalog Enablement, Innovation, Portfolio Project Management, BOM Management, Change Management, and New Product Introduction. He also has a strong understanding of software development, Agile methodologies, and Project Management principles.

Additionally, Prakhar excels in Business Process Assessment, As-Is and To-Be Process modeling, tools landscaping, pre-sales activities, proposal preparation, pitching, and responding to RFPs. He is adept at delivering manufacturing operations solutions and guiding comprehensive strategic initiatives.

# TABLE OF CONTENTS

# LIST OF FIGURES

# LIST OF TABLES

# PREFACE

In a world where technology is reshaping nearly every aspect of human life, artificial intelligence (AI) stands at the forefront of this transformation. The transformative power of AI accelerates the shift from traditional models to data-driven and highly adaptive ecosystems, enhancing agility and competitiveness. As AI continues to evolve, its role in digital transformation is expanding, encompassing everything from predictive analytics in decision-making to real-time personalization, advanced robotics, and enhanced cybersecurity, ultimately reshaping the modern business landscape and setting a new standard for operational excellence.

"*Use of Artificial Intelligence in Digital Transformation*" explores how AI is not just influencing but actively driving digital transformation across industries and sectors. This book provides a comprehensive exploration of AI's applications, benefits, challenges, and future potential in digitalizing and enhancing traditional and modern business functions. With each chapter, readers will gain insights into how AI enables innovative business models, improves customer experience, optimizes operations, refines marketing and sales, and enhances human resources, finance, healthcare, and cybersecurity.

Chapter 1 introduces readers to the fundamentals of AI and digital transformation. It covers essential topics such as the mechanics of AI, its historical evolution, and various applications from entertainment to healthcare. The chapter also discusses the ethical implications of AI, the governance required to ensure its responsible use, and the crucial role AI plays in digital transformation initiatives.

In Chapter 2, we shift focus to AI-driven business models. AI is fundamentally altering traditional business strategies and structures, creating new models that are data-driven, predictive, and customer-centric. This chapter explores how businesses harness AI to optimize decision-making, reduce operational costs, and enhance customer experiences.

The exploration continues in Chapter 3, where AI's role in customer service and experience is examined. AI technologies, such as big data analytics, recommendation systems, and conversational agents, are revolutionizing how businesses engage with customers. This chapter also tackles the challenges of humanizing AI-driven customer service, navigating complex customer issues, and balancing efficiency with personalization. The frameworks discussed will help businesses leverage AI to create meaningful and lasting customer relationships.

Chapter 4 explores AI's transformative impact on operations and supply chains. AI introduces end-to-end transparency, efficiency, and predictive capabilities that were previously unimaginable in supply chain management. From robotic process automation to demand forecasting and logistics, AI optimizes each link of the supply chain. This chapter also addresses ethical considerations such as data privacy, algorithmic bias, and job displacement, underscoring the need for a balanced approach that combines AI-driven automation with human judgment and responsibility.

Marketing and sales functions are experiencing their own AI-driven evolution, as discussed in Chapter 5. Here, AI empowers organizations to utilize predictive analytics for targeting and personalization, enabling more effective marketing strategies and improved ROI. This chapter highlights how AI helps companies understand consumer behavior, optimize supply chains, and improve cybersecurity. With a forward look into privacy concerns, this section also stresses the importance of maintaining consumer trust in the digital age.

The book then moves into the human resources and talent management in Chapter 6. AI offers HR departments tools to screen candidates, personalize employee retention strategies, and evaluate performance. This chapter considers the ethical challenges of AI in HR, including bias and transparency in algorithmic decision-making.

In Chapter 7, the focus shifts to financial services, where AI is driving innovations in fraud detection, cybersecurity, algorithmic trading, and financial planning. Fintech companies are embracing AI to improve accuracy, speed, and personalization in financial services, creating a more robust and customer-friendly financial ecosystem. This chapter discusses the current applications of AI in finance and envisions a future where AI continues to push the boundaries of financial technology.

Chapter 8, explores AI in healthcare. AI-powered systems are reshaping diagnostics, treatment personalization, patient monitoring, and healthcare operations. AI holds promise for improved patient outcomes. However, this chapter also considers the ethical and regulatory challenges, such as data privacy and algorithmic fairness, that accompany AI in such a sensitive field.

Finally, Chapter 9 examines AI in cybersecurity, a critical area in today's digital landscape. With AI-driven tools, organizations can detect anomalies, manage threats, and respond to incidents swiftly. This chapter covers the latest advancements in AI for cybersecurity, as well as the ethical and regulatory frameworks needed to navigate this evolving space.

This book is intended as a comprehensive guide for practitioners, students, and anyone interested in the transformative power of AI.

*–Author*

CHAPTER 1

# ARTIFICIAL INTELLIGENCE (AI) IN DIGITAL TRANSFORMATION: AN OVERVIEW

## Contents

# INTRODUCTION

To stay competitive in the fast-paced business world of today, organizations need to embrace digital transformation. However, what does "going digital" actually mean, and why is it so important? Leveraging technology to radically alter a company's operations and customer value delivery is known as digital transformation. It involves more than just implementing computers and cutting back on paper; it involves rethinking procedures and coming up with new ways to complete tasks. Consider how our lives have been transformed by smartphones. They have improved the convenience of information access, communication, and shopping. In a similar vein, digital transformation seeks to use technology to improve productivity, innovation, and development. Artificial Intelligence (AI) is a major force behind this change. As AI develops, computers will be able to learn, make choices, and recognize patterns similarly to humans. Businesses can benefit greatly from AI's ability to automate tedious tasks, make data-driven decisions, and customize customer experiences.

## 1.1. ARTIFICIAL INTELLIGENCE

The simulation of human intelligence processes by machines, particularly computer systems, is known as artificial intelligence (AI). Expert systems, natural language processing (NLP), speech recognition, and machine vision are a few applications of artificial intelligence.

Vendors have rushed to highlight how AI is incorporated into their goods and services as the buzz surrounding it has grown. A well-known technology like machine learning is frequently referred to as artificial intelligence.

In order to create and train machine learning algorithms, artificial intelligence requires specific hardware and software. Although there isn't just one programming language used in AI, Python, R, Java, C++, and Julia are all widely used by AI developers.

### 1.1.1. How Does AI Work?

Large volumes of labeled training data are typically ingested by AI systems, which then examine the data for correlations and patterns before using the patterns to forecast future states. For instance, an AI chatbot trained with text examples can produce natural conversations with humans, and an image recognition program trained on millions of examples can recognize and label objects in photos. Recent years have seen a rapid advancement in generative AI techniques, which now enable the creation of realistic text, images, music, and other media.

Programming AI systems focuses on cognitive skills such as the following:

- **Learning:** In order to turn data into information that can be used, this part of AI programming entails gathering data and developing rules, or algorithms. These algorithms give computers detailed instructions on how to carry out particular tasks.
- **Reasoning:** This aspect involves choosing the right algorithm to reach a desired outcome.
- **Self-Correction:** This aspect involves algorithms continuously learning and tuning themselves to provide the most accurate results possible.
- **Creativity:** This feature creates new images, text, music, ideas, and more using neural networks, rule-based systems, statistical methods, and other AI techniques.

### 1.1.2. Why Is AI Important?

The potential for AI to transform our way of life, work, and play makes it significant. It has been successfully applied in business to automate processes that have historically been completed by humans, such as quality control, fraud detection, lead generation, and customer service. AI can outperform humans in a variety of tasks in terms of accuracy and efficiency. It is particularly helpful for repetitive, meticulous tasks like going over a lot of legal documents to make sure all the pertinent fields are filled in. Large data sets can be processed by AI, which provides businesses with operational insights they might not have otherwise observed. The quickly growing number of generative AI tools is also becoming significant in domains like product design, marketing, and education.

In addition to contributing to an explosion in efficiency, advances in AI techniques have given some larger businesses access to completely new business opportunities. For instance, it would have been difficult to envision using computer software to match passengers with taxis on demand prior to the current wave of artificial intelligence, but Uber has achieved Fortune 500 status by doing just that.

Many of the biggest and most prosperous businesses in the world today, such as Alphabet, Apple, Microsoft, and Meta, rely heavily on AI to enhance their operations and outperform rivals. For instance, AI is essential to Google, an Alphabet subsidiary, and Waymo, a self-driving car startup, was once an Alphabet company. The transformer architecture that powers recent advances in natural language processing, like OpenAI's ChatGPT, was also created by the Google Brain research lab.

### 1.1.3. Differences among AI, Machine Learning, and Deep Learning

Though they have different meanings, the terms artificial intelligence, machine learning, and deep learning are frequently used synonymously, particularly in marketing materials from businesses. To put it succinctly, AI is the general notion of machines mimicking human intelligence; machine learning and deep learning are particular methods within this domain.

The term AI, which was first used in the 1950s, refers to a broad category of developing technologies, such as machine learning and deep learning, that seek to replicate human intelligence. Using past data as input, machine learning allows software to automatically identify patterns and forecast results. With the availability of large training data sets, this strategy became increasingly successful. Layered neural networks are used in deep learning, a branch of machine learning, to simulate the structure of the brain. It serves as the foundation for numerous significant discoveries and current developments in AI, such as ChatGPT and driverless cars (Figure 1.1).

**AI vs. machine learning vs. deep learning**

| | AI | Machine learning | Deep learning |
|---|---|---|---|
| **Optimal data volumes** | Varying data volumes | Thousands of data points | Big data: millions of data points |
| **Outputs** | Anything from predictions to recommendations to decision-making | Numerical value, like a classification or score | Anything from numerical values to free-form elements, like free text and sound |
| **How it works** | Machines are programmed to mimic human activity with human-like accuracy | Uses various types of automated algorithms that learn to model functions and predict future actions from data | Uses neural networks that pass data through many processing layers to interpret data features and relationships |
| **How it's managed** | Algorithms require human oversight in order to function properly | Algorithms are directed by data analysts to examine specific variables in data sets | Algorithms are largely self-directed on data analysis once they're put into production |

**Figure 1.1.** *AI vs machine learning vs deep learning.*

*Source: https://www.techtarget.com/searchenterpriseai/definition/AI-Artificial-Intelligence.*

### 1.1.4. Advantages and Disadvantages of Artificial Intelligence

AI technologies, especially deep learning models like artificial neural networks, are capable of processing vast amounts of data far more quickly and producing predictions that are more accurate than those made by humans. A human researcher would be overwhelmed by the massive amount of data generated every day, but AI applications that use machine learning can swiftly transform that data into useful knowledge. The cost of processing the massive volumes of data AI needs is one of its main drawbacks. Organizations must be aware of AI's potential to inadvertently or purposely produce biased and discriminatory systems as it is integrated into more goods and services.

### *1.1.4.1. Advantages of AI*

The following are some advantages of AI:

- **Excellence in Detail-Oriented Jobs:** Tasks involving the detection of minute patterns and connections in data that humans might miss are well suited for artificial intelligence. In oncology, for instance, AI systems have shown excellent accuracy in identifying early-stage cancers, including melanoma and breast cancer, by pointing out areas of concern for additional assessment by medical specialists.
- **Efficiency in Data-Heavy Tasks** The amount of time needed for data processing is significantly decreased by AI systems and automation tools. This is especially helpful in industries that rely heavily on routine data entry and analysis, as well as data-driven decision-making, such as finance, insurance, and healthcare. Predictive AI models, for instance, can process enormous amounts of data in the banking and finance industries to forecast market trends and assess investment risk.
- **Time Savings and Productivity Gains:** Robotics and AI have the potential to increase efficiency and safety in addition to automating tasks. For instance, in manufacturing, AI-powered robots are being utilized more and more to carry out repetitive or dangerous tasks as part of warehouse automation, which lowers the risk to human workers and boosts overall productivity.
- **Consistency in Results:** Modern analytics tools process large amounts of data consistently while utilizing AI and machine learning, allowing them to continuously learn and adjust to new information. AI applications, for instance, have produced dependable and consistent results in language translation and legal document review.
- **Customization and Personalization:** By personalizing interactions and the way content is delivered on digital platforms, AI systems can improve user experience. For instance, AI models examine user behavior on e-commerce platforms to suggest products that are personalized for each user, thereby boosting customer satisfaction and engagement.
- **Round-the-Clock Availability:** AI systems don't require breaks or sleep. AI-powered virtual assistants, for instance, can offer

continuous, round-the-clock customer support even in the face of a high volume of interactions, speeding up response times and cutting expenses.

- **Scalability:** AI systems are scalable, able to manage increasing volumes of data and work. This makes AI a good fit for applications like business analytics and internet search where workloads and data volumes can increase rapidly.
- **Accelerated Research and Development:** AI has the potential to accelerate R&D in industries like materials science and pharmaceuticals. AI models can assist researchers in finding new medications, materials, or compounds more quickly than with conventional techniques by quickly simulating and analyzing a wide range of potential scenarios.
- **Sustainability and Conservation:** Monitoring environmental changes, forecasting future weather, and overseeing conservation initiatives are all being done more and more with AI and machine learning. For instance, machine learning models can analyze sensor data and satellite imagery to monitor endangered species populations, pollution levels, and wildfire risk.
- **Process Optimization:** AI is used in many different industries to automate and streamline complicated processes. AI models, for instance, can predict bottlenecks and find inefficiencies in manufacturing processes. In the energy sector, they can also forecast demand for electricity and distribute supply in real time.

### *1.1.4.2. Disadvantages of AI*

The following are some disadvantages of AI:

- **High Costs:** AI development can be highly costly. Developing an AI model necessitates a large initial investment in software, computational power, and infrastructure in order to train the model and store its training data. Model inference and retraining come with additional recurring expenses after initial training. Costs can therefore mount up rapidly, especially for sophisticated, intricate systems like generative AI applications; according to OpenAI CEO Sam Altman, the company's GPT-4 model training cost more than $100 million.
- **Technical Complexity:** It takes a lot of technical expertise to develop, run, and troubleshoot AI systems, particularly in real-world production settings. This knowledge is frequently different from

what is required to create software that isn't AI. For instance, creating and implementing a machine learning application is a multi-step, intricate, and extremely technical process that includes parameter tuning, model testing, algorithm selection, and data preparation.

- **Talent Gap:** The issue of technical complexity is exacerbated by the fact that, despite the increasing demand for professionals with AI and machine learning training, there is a notable dearth of these specialists. Despite the growing interest in AI applications, many organizations are finding it difficult to find enough qualified workers to staff their AI initiatives due to the gap between the supply and demand of AI talent.
- **Algorithmic Bias:** The biases in training data are reflected in AI and machine learning algorithms, and when AI systems are implemented at scale, the biases also increase. By encoding training data into reinforceable and pseudo-objective patterns, AI systems can occasionally even magnify subtle biases. As a well-known illustration of the wider gender disparities in the tech sector, Amazon created an AI-driven hiring tool to automate the process that unintentionally favored male applicants.
- **Difficulty with Generalization:** AI models frequently perform exceptionally well on the particular tasks for which they were trained but poorly when asked to handle unfamiliar situations. AI's utility may be limited by this rigidity since new tasks may necessitate the creation of a completely new model. For instance, without a lot of extra training, an NLP model trained on English-language text might not perform well on text in other languages. Although efforts are being made to enhance models' capacity for generalization, also referred to as domain adaptation or transfer learning, this issue is still unresolved.
- **Job Displacement:** As AI models' capabilities advance and businesses increasingly seek to use AI to automate workflows, there is growing concern that AI may result in job losses if companies replace human workers with machines. For instance, some copywriters claim that ChatGPT and other large language models (LLMs) have supplanted them. Concerns regarding reskilling and economic inequality are raised by the possibility that broad AI adoption will also lead to the creation of new job categories that do not overlap with the jobs that are being eliminated.
- **Security Vulnerabilities:** A variety of cyberthreats, such as adversarial machine learning and data poisoning, can affect AI

systems. For example, hackers can take private training data out of an AI model or fool AI systems into generating harmful or inaccurate results. This is especially worrisome for security-sensitive industries like government and finance.

- **Environmental Impact:** The network infrastructures and data centers that support AI model operations use a lot of water and energy. As a result, AI model training and operation have a big effect on the climate. Large generative models, which demand a lot of processing power for training and continuous use, raise particular concerns about AI's carbon footprint.
- **Legal Issues:** AI poses difficult privacy and legal liability issues, especially in light of the rapidly changing regulatory environment that varies by jurisdiction. For instance, there are significant privacy concerns when using AI to evaluate and decide on personal data, and it is still unknown how courts will perceive authorship of content produced by LLMs trained on copyrighted works.

### 1.1.5. Strong AI vs. Weak AI

Narrow (or weak) AI and general (or strong) AI are the two broad categories into which AI can be divided.

- **Narrow AI:** This type of AI describes models that have been trained to carry out particular tasks. Without the capacity to learn beyond its original programming or generalize widely, narrow AI functions only within the parameters of the tasks it is designed to complete. Virtual assistants like Apple Siri and Amazon Alexa, as well as recommendation engines like those on streaming services like Spotify and Netflix, are examples of narrow artificial intelligence.
- **General AI:** The term artificial general intelligence (AGI) is more frequently used to describe this kind of AI, which does not yet exist. AGI has the potential to accomplish any intellectual task that a human can. In order to accomplish this, AGI would need to be able to use reasoning in a variety of contexts to comprehend challenging issues that it was not designed to address. This would therefore necessitate the application of fuzzy logic, a concept in artificial intelligence that deals with gradations of uncertainty and gray areas rather than binary, black-and-white results.

Notably, AI experts continue to vigorously debate both the possibility of creating AGI and its implications. Even the most sophisticated AI technologies available today, like ChatGPT and other exceptionally competent LLMs, are unable to generalize across a range of scenarios and do not exhibit cognitive capacities comparable to those of humans. For instance, ChatGPT is limited to its original programming and cannot perform tasks like complex mathematical reasoning because it is designed for natural language generation.

### 1.1.6. Types of AI

From the widely used task-specific intelligent systems of today to the as-yet-undiscovered sentient systems, artificial intelligence can be divided into four categories.

The categories are as follows:

1. **Reactive Machines:** These AI systems are task-specific and lack memory. One such is the IBM chess program Deep Blue, which defeated Russian grandmaster Garry Kasparov in the 1990s. Although Deep Blue lacked memory, it was still able to recognize pieces on a chessboard and predict outcomes, but it was unable to draw lessons from its past to guide its future actions.
2. **Limited Memory:** Since these AI systems are sentient, they can draw lessons from the past to guide their decisions in the future. This is how some of the decision-making processes in autonomous vehicles are built.
3. **Theory of Mind:** Theory of mind is a term used in psychology. In terms of artificial intelligence, it describes a system that has emotional intelligence. In order for AI systems to become essential components of traditionally human teams, they must possess the ability to predict behavior and infer human intentions.
4. **Self-Awareness:** AI systems in this category are conscious because they possess a sense of self. Self-aware machines are aware of their own condition. There isn't any AI like this yet.

### 1.1.7. Examples of AI Technology, and How Is It Used Today

AI technologies can improve the functionality of current tools and automate a range of tasks and processes, which can have a significant impact on many facets of daily life. Here are a few well-known instances.

#### *1.1.7.1. Automation*

AI expands the scope, complexity, and quantity of tasks that can be automated, thereby improving automation technologies. One such is robotic process automation (RPA), which is the automation of data processing tasks that are repetitive and rule-based and are typically carried out by humans. Integrating AI and machine learning capabilities allows RPA to handle increasingly complex workflows, as AI assists RPA bots in adapting to new data and responding dynamically to process changes.

### *1.1.7.2. Machine Learning*

The science of teaching computers to learn from data and make decisions without having to be specifically programmed to do so is known as machine learning. Deep learning, a branch of machine learning, is essentially an enhanced version of predictive analytics that makes use of complex neural networks. Three broad categories can be used to group machine learning algorithms: reinforcement learning, unsupervised learning, and supervised learning.

- **Supervised Learning** Trains models on labeled data sets, enabling them to accurately recognize patterns, predict outcomes or classify new data.
- **Unsupervised Learning:** Trains models to sort through unlabeled data sets to find underlying relationships or clusters.
- **Reinforcement Learning:** Takes a different approach, in which models learn to make decisions by acting as agents and receiving feedback on their actions.

Additionally, there is semi-supervised learning, which blends elements of unsupervised and supervised methods. This method reduces the need for labeled data, which can be time and labor intensive to obtain, while increasing learning accuracy by using a smaller amount of labeled data and a larger amount of unlabeled data.

### *1.1.7.3. Computer Vision*

AI's field of computer vision focuses on teaching machines to understand the visual world. Through the use of deep learning models to analyze visual data from cameras and videos, computer vision systems can be trained to recognize and categorize objects and then make decisions based on those analyzes. The main goal of computer vision is to use AI algorithms to mimic or enhance the human visual system.

Applications for computer vision are numerous and include autonomous cars, medical image analysis, and signature identification. While computer vision and machine vision are sometimes used interchangeably, machine vision refers specifically to the application of computer vision to the analysis of camera and video data in industrial automation contexts, such as manufacturing production processes.

### *1.1.7.4. Natural Language Processing*

NLP is the term used to describe how computer programs process human language. NLP algorithms are capable of speech recognition, sentiment analysis, translation, and other tasks involving the interpretation and interaction of human language. Spam detection, which determines whether an email is spam by analyzing its subject line and body, is among the earliest and most well-known applications of natural language processing. Advanced NLP applications include LLMs like Claude from Anthropic and ChatGPT.

### *1.1.7.5. Robotics*

The engineering discipline of robotics is concerned with the creation, maintenance, and use of automated devices known as robots. These machines are designed to mimic and replace human actions, especially those that are laborious, hazardous, or difficult for people to carry out. Applications for robotics include manufacturing, where machines carry out dangerous or repetitive assembly-line jobs, and exploration missions in far-off, hard-to-reach places like space and the deep sea. Robots' capabilities are greatly increased by the integration of AI and machine learning since it allows them to adapt to new circumstances and data and make more intelligent decisions on their own. Robots equipped with machine vision capabilities, for instance, can be trained to sort items according to color and shape on a production line.

### *1.1.7.6. Autonomous Vehicles*

Self-driving cars, also referred to as autonomous vehicles, are able to sense and navigate their surroundings with little to no assistance from humans. Radar, GPS, and various AI and machine learning algorithms, like image recognition, are among the technologies that these cars rely on. In order to make well-informed decisions about when to brake, turn, and accelerate; how to stay in a specific lane; and how to avoid unforeseen obstacles, such as pedestrians, these algorithms learn from real-world driving, traffic, and map data. The ultimate goal of an autonomous vehicle that can completely replace a human driver has not yet been accomplished, despite significant technological advancements in recent years.

### *1.1.7.7. Generative AI*

Machine learning systems that can produce new data from text prompts—most frequently text and images, but also audio, video, software code, and even genetic sequences and protein structures—are referred to as generative AI. These algorithms are able to produce new content that resembles the training data by gradually learning the patterns of the kinds of media they will be asked to produce through training on large data sets. Following the release of widely accessible text and image generators like ChatGPT, Dall-E, and Midjourney in 2022, generative AI experienced a sharp increase in popularity and is now being used more frequently in business contexts. Although the capabilities of many generative AI tools are impressive, they also bring up issues that are still up for debate in the tech industry, like copyright, fair use, and security.

## 1.1.8. Applications of AI

Artificial Intelligence has penetrated numerous industry sectors and research domains. Here are a few of the most noteworthy instances.

### *1.1.8.1. AI in Healthcare*

AI is used in the healthcare industry for a variety of tasks, with the main objectives being lower systemic costs and better patient outcomes. Using machine learning models trained on massive medical data sets to help medical professionals diagnose patients more accurately and quickly is one important application. AI-driven software, for instance, can evaluate CT scans and notify neurologists of possible strokes. Virtual health assistants and chatbots on the internet can help patients with general medical information, appointment scheduling, billing clarification, and other administrative duties. AI algorithms for predictive modeling can also be used to stop the spread of pandemics like COVID-19.

### *1.1.8.2. AI in Business*

AI is being incorporated more and more into a range of business operations and sectors with the goal of enhancing productivity, customer satisfaction, strategic planning, and decision-making. Many of the data analytics and customer relationship management (CRM) platforms used today, for instance, are powered by machine learning models, which assist businesses in understanding how to best serve customers by personalizing offerings and providing more precisely tailored marketing.

Additionally, chatbots and virtual assistants are used in mobile applications and business websites to offer 24/7 customer support and respond to frequently asked queries. Furthermore, an increasing number of businesses are investigating the potential of generative AI tools, like ChatGPT, to automate processes like computer programming, product design and ideation, and document drafting and summarization.

### *1.1.8.3. AI in Education*

There are several possible uses for AI in educational technology. It can automate certain grading procedures, freeing up teachers' time for other duties. In addition to evaluating student performance and adjusting to each student's unique needs, AI tools can also personalize learning experiences and let students work at their own pace. AI tutors may also offer students extra assistance to help them stay on course. Additionally, the technology may modify the traditional role of educators by influencing the places and methods in which students learn. With ChatGPT and Google Gemini's growing capabilities, educators may find it easier to create lesson plans and engage students in novel ways. The introduction of these tools, however, also compels educators to reevaluate homework assignments, assessments, and plagiarism guidelines, particularly in light of the unreliability of current AI detection and watermarking systems.

### *1.1.8.4. AI in Finance and Banking*

AI helps banks and other financial institutions make better decisions when it comes to lending money, establishing credit limits, and spotting investment possibilities. Furthermore, advanced AI and machine learning-driven algorithmic trading has revolutionized the financial markets by enabling trades to be executed at speeds and efficiencies that far outpace the capabilities of human traders working manually. The field of consumer finance has also been affected by AI and machine learning. For instance, banks use AI chatbots to answer routine transactions and customer inquiries that don't need for human assistance, as well as to tell clients about services and offerings. Similar to this, Intuit's TurboTax e-filing product has generative AI features that let users receive tailored advice based on information like their tax profile and the local tax code.

### *1.1.8.5. AI in Law*

AI is revolutionizing the legal industry by automating labor-intensive processes like document review and discovery response, which can be tiresome and time-consuming for paralegals and attorneys. These days, law firms use AI and machine learning for a range of tasks, such as NLP to interpret and react to discovery requests, computer vision to classify and extract information from documents, and analytics and predictive AI to analyze data and case law. This integration of AI not only increases productivity and efficiency but also frees up human lawyers to focus on more creative, strategic work that AI is less equipped to do and spend more time with clients. Businesses are investigating employing LLMs to draft standard documents like boilerplate contracts in light of the growing use of generative AI in the legal field.

## 1.1.9. AI in Entertainment and Media

AI is used in the media and entertainment industry for fraud detection, distribution, content recommendations, and targeted advertising. Businesses can use the technology to optimize content delivery and customize the experiences of their audience members. Another popular topic in the field of content creation is generative AI. These tools are already being used by advertising professionals to edit advertising photos and produce marketing collateral. Their application is more debatable, though, in fields like visual effects and screenplay writing for movies and television shows, where they boost productivity while simultaneously endangering the livelihoods and intellectual property of people working in creative fields.

### *1.1.9.1. AI in Journalism*

AI can improve workflows in journalism by automating repetitive processes like proofreading and data entry. By using machine learning models to sift through massive data sets, investigative, and data journalists can also use AI to find and research stories. This allows them to uncover hidden connections and trends that would take a lot of time to find manually. For instance, five journalism finalists for the 2024 Pulitzer Prizes revealed that they used AI in their reporting to carry out tasks like examining enormous amounts of police data. Although the use of conventional AI tools is becoming more widespread, the application of generative AI to journalistic writing is controversial because it raises questions about ethics, accuracy, and dependability.

### *1.1.9.2. AI in Software Development and IT*

Numerous IT, DevOps, and software development processes are automated with the help of AI. AI-powered monitoring tools can help identify possible anomalies in real time based on historical system data, and AIOps tools enable predictive maintenance of IT environments by analyzing system data to forecast potential issues before they occur. The use of generative AI tools, like GitHub Copilot and Tabnine, to generate application code in response to natural language prompts is also growing. Although there has been early interest in and promise for these tools among developers, it is unlikely that they will completely replace software engineers. Rather, they are helpful tools for increasing productivity that automate monotonous work and boilerplate code writing.

### *1.1.9.3. AI in Security*

Buyers should exercise caution because AI and machine learning are popular buzzwords in security vendor marketing. Nevertheless, AI is a helpful tool for a number of cybersecurity tasks, such as behavioral threat analytics, anomaly detection, and lowering false positives. Machine learning, for instance, is used by businesses to identify possible threats and suspicious activity in security information and event management (SIEM) software. AI tools can notify security teams of new and emerging attacks, frequently far sooner than human employees and earlier technologies could, by analyzing large amounts of data and identifying patterns that resemble known malicious code.

### *1.1.9.4. AI in Manufacturing*

With recent developments centered on collaborative robots, or cobots, manufacturing has been at the forefront of integrating robots into workflows. Cobots are more compact, adaptable, and made to work alongside humans than traditional industrial robots, which were programmed to carry out specific tasks and operated independently from human workers. These multitasking robots are capable of performing a wider range of jobs, such as assembly, packaging, and quality control, in factories, warehouses, and other workspaces. Specifically, employing robots to carry out or support humans in physically taxing and repetitive jobs can increase worker productivity and safety.

### *1.1.9.5. AI in Transportation*

AI is used in automotive transportation to manage traffic, lessen congestion, and improve road safety in addition to its basic role in operating autonomous vehicles. AI can forecast flight delays in the aviation industry by examining data points like weather and air traffic patterns. AI can improve safety and efficiency in international shipping by automatically monitoring vessel conditions and optimizing routes.

AI is taking the place of conventional methods in supply chains to forecast demand and improve the accuracy of forecasts regarding possible disruptions and bottlenecks. The COVID-19 pandemic brought to light the significance of these capacities since it caught many businesses off guard with its effects on the global supply and demand of goods.

## 1.1.10. Augmented Intelligence vs. Artificial Intelligence

Because of the term's strong ties to popular culture, the general public may have inflated expectations about how artificial intelligence will affect daily life and the workplace. An alternative term, augmented intelligence, has been proposed to distinguish between fully autonomous systems found in science fiction, such as Skynet from the Terminator movies, and machine systems that assist humans. Examples of these systems include HAL 9000 from 2001: A Space Odyssey.

The two terms can be defined as follows:

- **Augmented Intelligence:** The phrase "augmented intelligence," with its more ambiguous meaning, implies that the majority of AI applications are meant to supplement human abilities rather than to replace them. These specialized AI systems mainly enhance goods and services by carrying out particular functions. Examples include emphasizing crucial information in court filings or automatically surfacing significant data in business intelligence reports. The swift uptake of ChatGPT and Gemini among diverse sectors suggests an increasing readiness to employ artificial intelligence to bolster human judgment.
- **Artificial Intelligence:** To better manage public expectations and make the distinction between current use cases and the goal of achieving AGI clear, the term AI would be reserved in this framework for advanced general AI. The idea of AGI is closely linked to the idea of the technological singularity, which is a future in which artificial superintelligence vastly exceeds human cognitive capacities and has the potential to drastically alter reality. Although science fiction has long relied on the singularity, some AI developers are currently actively working toward the development of AGI.

### 1.1.11. Ethical Use of Artificial Intelligence

Businesses can take advantage of many new functionalities offered by AI tools, but there are serious ethical concerns associated with their use. For better or worse, AI systems rely heavily on the data they are trained on because they reinforce the knowledge they already possess. Due to the fact that human beings choose the training data, bias is inevitable and needs to be properly watched over. The use of generative AI raises additional ethical concerns. Although these tools are useful for many legitimate applications, they can also be used to create harmful content, such as deepfakes, and misinformation by producing extremely realistic and convincing text, images, and audio.

As a result, anyone wishing to apply machine learning to production systems in the real world must consider ethics when training AI systems and work to eliminate bias. This is particularly crucial for opaque AI algorithms like deep learning's intricate neural networks. Responsible AI is the creation and application of AI systems that are secure, law-abiding, and advantageous to society. It is motivated by worries about unintended consequences, lack of transparency, and algorithmic bias. Although the idea is based on well-established AI ethics theories, it gained popularity as generative AI tools became more accessible and, with them, more worrisome risks. By incorporating ethical

AI principles into corporate strategy, organizations can reduce risk and increase public confidence.

A developing field of interest in AI research is explainability, or the capacity to comprehend the decision-making process of an AI system. One potential barrier to applying AI in sectors with stringent regulatory compliance requirements is its lack of explainability. Fair lending laws, for instance, mandate that U. S. financial organizations to provide loan and credit card applicants with an explanation of their credit-issuing decisions. However, when AI systems make these kinds of choices, the minute relationships between thousands of variables can lead to an opaque decision-making process known as a "black box."

In summary, AI's ethical challenges include the following:

- **Bias** due to improperly trained algorithms and human prejudices or oversights.
- **Misuse** of generative AI to produce deepfakes, phishing scams and other harmful content.
- **Legal Concerns**, including AI libel and copyright issues.
- **Job Displacement** due to increasing use of AI to automate workplace tasks.
- **Data Privacy Concerns**, particularly in fields such as banking, healthcare, and legal that deal with sensitive personal data.

## 1.1.12. AI Governance and Regulations

The use of AI tools is currently unregulated, despite possible risks, and many laws already in place only indirectly rather than directly address AI. For instance, as was already mentioned, financial institutions are required by US fair lending laws like the Equal Credit Opportunity Act to inform prospective customers of their credit decisions. This restricts the use of deep learning algorithms by lenders, as these algorithms are inherently opaque and unexplainable.

The European Union has approached the topic of AI governance with initiative. Many consumer-facing AI applications are affected in terms of functionality and training by the stringent limitations imposed by the EU's General Data Protection Regulation (GDPR) on the use of consumer data by businesses. Furthermore, in August 2024, the EU AI Act came into force with the objective of creating a thorough legal framework for the development and application of AI. Depending on how risky an AI system is, the Act applies different levels of regulation; critical infrastructure and biometrics are given more attention than others. Even though the US is improving, there is currently no country-specific federal legislation similar to the EU's AI Act. Legislators still haven't passed any comprehensive AI legislation, and the federal regulations that are in place now concentrate on risk management and particular use cases. State initiatives also play a part in this. Having said that, the stricter laws in the EU may wind up establishing de facto guidelines for US-based multinational corporations, much like the GDPR changed the global data privacy scene.

Regarding specific developments in US AI policy, in October 2022 the White House Office of Science and Technology Policy released a Blueprint for an AI Bill of Rights that offered advice to companies on how to deploy moral AI systems. In a report published in March 2023, the US Chamber of Commerce also urged regulations pertaining to AI, highlighting the necessity of a well-rounded strategy that promotes competition while addressing risks.

A more recent executive order on the subject of responsible and safe AI development was issued by President Biden in October 2023. The order, among other things, required developers of strong AI systems to disclose the results of safety tests and federal agencies to take specific steps to evaluate and manage AI risk. Given that Donald Trump and Kamala Harris have advocated for different approaches to tech regulation, the outcome of the next US presidential election is also anticipated to have an impact on future AI regulation.

It will be difficult to create laws governing AI, in part because the field encompasses a wide range of technologies used for diverse purposes and in part because such regulations may impede the advancement and development of AI and lead to industry backlash. Further impediments to the formation of meaningful regulations include the rapid evolution of AI technologies and their lack of transparency, which makes it challenging to comprehend how algorithms arrive at their conclusions. Furthermore, new applications and technological advancements like ChatGPT and Dall-E can quickly make laws that are currently in place obsolete. Laws and other regulations, of course, are unlikely to stop bad actors from utilizing AI for destructive ends.

### 1.1.13. History of AI

Since ancient times, people have entertained the idea that inanimate objects could possess intelligence. The Greek god Hephaestus was portrayed in myths as sculpting robot-like attendants from gold, and Egyptian engineers created god statues that were animated by secret mechanisms that were controlled by priests.

The mathematician René Descartes, the statistician Thomas Bayes, the Spanish theologian Ramon Llull in the 13$^{th}$ century, and the Greek philosopher Aristotle all employed the logic and instruments of their respective eras to characterize human thought processes as symbols. Their contributions established the groundwork for AI ideas like logical reasoning and general knowledge representation.

The work that laid the groundwork for the modern computer was produced in the late 19th and early 20th centuries. Charles Babbage, a mathematician at Cambridge University, and Augusta Ada King, Countess of Lovelace, created the Analytical Engine, the first programmable machine, in 1836. Babbage laid out the blueprints for the first mechanical computer, but Lovelace, who is frequently credited as the first computer programmer, anticipated that the device would be able to do anything that could be explained algorithmically, not just basic calculations.

Important advancements in computing during the 20th century influenced the development of artificial intelligence. The idea of a universal machine that could mimic any other machine was first proposed in the 1930s by British mathematician and World War II codebreaker Alan Turing. His theories played a pivotal role in the advancement of digital computers and, ultimately, artificial intelligence.

### *1.1.13.1. 1940s*

John Von Neumann, a Princeton mathematician, developed the stored-program computer architecture, which is based on the notion that a computer's memory can store both the program and the data it processes. The groundwork for neural networks and other upcoming advancements in artificial intelligence was laid by Warren McCulloch and Walter Pitts' mathematical model of artificial neurons.

### *1.1.13.2. 1950s*

Scientists started putting their theories about machine intelligence to the test when they developed modern computers. Turing developed a technique in 1950 that he named the imitation game but is now more widely known as the Turing test to assess if a computer is intelligent. This test measures how well a computer can persuade interrogators that the responses it provided to their queries were created by a human.

A summer conference at Dartmouth College in 1956 is frequently cited as the start of the modern field of artificial intelligence. Ten prominent figures in the field, including AI pioneers Marvin Minsky, Oliver Selfridge, and John McCarthy—who is recognized for coining the term artificial intelligence—attended the conference, which was supported by the Defense Advanced Research Projects Agency. Herbert A. and computer scientist Allen Newell were also present. Simon is a political scientist, cognitive psychologist, and economist.

The two introduced their ground-breaking Logic Theorist, sometimes referred to as the first AI program, which was a computer program that could prove specific mathematical theorems. The General Problem Solver algorithm was developed by Newell and Simon in 1957, a year later. Although it was unable to solve more complicated problems, it did provide the groundwork for the development of more advanced cognitive architectures.

### *1.1.13.3. 1960s*

Following the Dartmouth College conference, pioneers in the nascent field of AI forecasted the imminent arrival of human-created intelligence on par with the human brain, garnering significant backing from both the government and industry. Indeed, substantial advancements in AI have been produced by nearly 20 years of well-funded basic research. McCarthy created Lisp, a language still in use today that was first created for AI programming. Eliza, a pioneering NLP program created by MIT professor Joseph Weizenbaum in the middle of the 1960s, served as the model for modern chatbots.

### *1.1.13.4. 1970s*

Due to the complexity of the issue and limitations in computer processing and memory, achieving AGI proved elusive rather than imminent in the 1970s. As a result, corporate and governmental support for AI research declined, resulting in the first AI winter, a period of inactivity that lasted from 1974 to 1980. Funding and interest in the emerging field of artificial intelligence significantly decreased during this time.

### *1.1.13.5. 1980s*

A new wave of AI enthusiasm was sparked in the 1980s by research on deep learning techniques and industry adoption of Edward Feigenbaum's expert systems. Expert systems have been used for financial analysis and clinical diagnosis. They replicate the decision-making of human experts by using rule-based programs. However, the resurgence of AI was short-lived, as industry and government support collapsed again due to the high cost and limited capabilities of these systems. Known as the "second AI winter," this period of decreased interest and investment persisted until the mid-1990s.

### *1.1.13.6. 1990s*

The mid-to late 1990s saw an AI renaissance driven by increases in computational power and an explosion of data, which laid the groundwork for the amazing advancements in AI that we see today. Big data along with more processing power drove advances in NLP, computer vision, robotics, machine learning, and deep learning. When Deep Blue defeated Kasparov in 1997, it made history as the first computer program to defeat a world chess champion.

#### *1.1.13.7. 2000s*

Additional developments in NLP, speech recognition, computer vision, deep learning, machine learning, and other fields led to the creation of goods and services that have influenced modern life. The introduction of Google's search engine in 2000 and Amazon's recommendation engine in 2001 are two significant developments. The 2000s also saw the introduction of Facebook's facial recognition technology, Microsoft's speech recognition system for audio transcription, and Netflix's movie recommendation system. Google began working on its Waymo autonomous vehicle project, and IBM introduced its Watson question-answering system.

#### *1.1.13.8. 2010s*

The years 2010–2020 saw a continuous flow of advancements in AI. These include the introduction of voice assistants like Apple's Siri and Amazon's Alexa, IBM Watson's Jeopardy victories, the development of car self-driving features, and the application of AI-based systems that accurately detect cancer. In addition, Google introduced TensorFlow, an open-source machine learning framework that is frequently used in AI development, marking the creation of the first generative adversarial network. The revolutionary AlexNet convolutional neural network, which debuted in 2012 and greatly advanced image recognition while popularizing the use of GPUs for AI model training, marked a significant turning point in the field. The world Go champion Lee Sedol was defeated in 2016 by Google DeepMind's AlphaGo model, demonstrating AI's capacity to win intricate strategic games. The previous year saw the establishment of the research lab OpenAI, which would advance NLP and reinforcement learning significantly in the latter half of that decade.

#### *1.1.13.9. 2020s*

So far, generative AI—which can create new content in response to a user's prompt—has taken center stage in this decade. These prompts can be any type of input that the AI system can process, including text, images, videos, music, and design blueprints. Essays, explanations of how to solve problems, and realistic illustrations created from images of individuals are examples of output content. The third version of OpenAI's GPT language model was released in 2020, but public awareness of the technology did not increase until 2022. With the release of the image generators Dall-E 2 and Midjourney in April and July of that year, respectively, the generative AI wave got underway. When ChatGPT was made available to the general public in November of that year, the anticipation and hype peaked. Soon after ChatGPT was released, rival LLM chatbots like Google's Gemini and Anthropic's Claude were introduced by OpenAI's rivals. In 2023 and 2024, audio and video generators like Runway and ElevenLabs came next. As seen by its persistent propensity to hallucinate and its ongoing quest for useful, affordable applications, generative AI technology is still in its infancy. However, these advancements have introduced AI into the public discourse in a novel way, arousing both curiosity and caution.

## 1.1.14. AI Tools and Services: Evolution and Ecosystems

AI services and tools are developing quickly. The 2012 AlexNet neural network, which ushered in a new era of high-performance AI built on GPUs and large data sets, is responsible for many of the innovations that occur today. The most significant development was the realization that neural networks could be trained in parallel on many GPU cores with enormous volumes of data, which made the training process more scalable.

The development of algorithmic breakthroughs at companies such as Google, Microsoft, and OpenAI in the twenty-first century has resulted in a symbiotic relationship with the hardware innovations led by infrastructure providers such as Nvidia. These advancements have allowed for the execution of ever-larger AI models on a greater number of connected GPUs, leading to revolutionary gains in scalability and performance. Working together, these luminaries of AI made ChatGPT and dozens of other ground-breaking AI services successful. These are a few instances of the technological advancements propelling the development of AI products and services.

### *1.1.14.1. Transformers*

Google took the lead in developing a method that was more effective for distributing AI training across sizable clusters of GPU-equipped commodity PCs.

The discovery of transformers, which automate many steps in the process of training AI on unlabeled data, was made possible as a result of this. Google researchers presented a novel architecture that leverages self-attention mechanisms to enhance model performance on a variety of natural language processing tasks, including translation, text generation, and summarization, in their 2017 paper Attention Is All You Need. This transformer architecture was crucial to the creation of ChatGPT and other modern LLMs.

### *1.1.14.2. Hardware Optimization*

Algorithmic architecture and hardware play equal roles in creating scalable, effective, and efficient artificial intelligence. Originally intended for graphics rendering, GPUs are now necessary for processing large amounts of data. Complex AI model training has been accelerated by tensor processing units and neural processing units, which are specifically made for deep learning. For the most popular algorithms, vendors such as Nvidia have optimized the microcode to run in parallel across multiple GPU cores. Additionally, chipmakers are collaborating with big cloud providers to offer AI as a service (AIaaS) through IaaS, SaaS, and PaaS models, thereby increasing accessibility to this capability.

### *1.1.14.3. Generative Pre-trained Transformers and Fine-tuning*

Over the past few years, the AI stack has rapidly evolved. Businesses used to have to start their AI models from scratch when training them. Generative pre-trained transformers (GPTs) are now offered by companies like OpenAI, Nvidia, Microsoft, and Google. These GPTs can be adjusted for particular tasks with significantly less money, time, and effort.

### *1.1.14.4. AI Cloud Services and AutoML*

A significant obstacle impeding enterprises' effective use of AI is the intricacy of data science and data engineering tasks needed to integrate AI capabilities into new or current applications. Leading cloud providers are introducing branded AIaaS solutions to expedite model development, application deployment, and data preparation. Prominent instances comprise Amazon AI, Google AI, Microsoft Azure AI and Azure ML, IBM Watson, and the AI functionalities offered by Oracle Cloud. In a similar vein, many stages of ML and AI development can be automated with the help of automated machine learning (AutoML) platforms offered by major cloud providers and other vendors. AutoML tools increase deployment efficiency and democratize AI capabilities.

### *1.1.14.5. Cutting-edge AI Models as a Service*

Top AI model developers additionally provide state-of-the-art models on top of these cloud services. OpenAI offers a number of LLMs that are provisioned via Azure and optimized for chat, NLP, multimodality, and code generation. By offering AI infrastructure and foundational models optimized for text, images, and medical data across all cloud providers, Nvidia has adopted a more cloud-agnostic strategy. A lot of smaller companies also provide models that are tailored for different use cases and industries.

## 1.2. DIGITAL TRANSFORMATION

The integration of digital technology through the conversion of all manual and semi-manual business processes into fully digital ones is known as digital transformation, or DT.

With the introduction of new technologies in recent years, not only have our everyday lives drastically changed, but so have businesses. This change has accelerated, particularly in the wake of the Covid-19 pandemics. Businesses who could adjust to this new normal and were ready for it gained a competitive edge over their rivals. Digitalization has made it necessary for many business areas to transform their companies (Vial G, 2019). The use of digital technologies to develop innovative business processes, cultural norms, and consumer behaviors in order to adjust to a new business environment is known as digital transformation, or DT. DT is a team effort that requires participation from every department within the company. Major alterations to traditional industry practices are brought about by this all-encompassing transformation (Dehning et al., 2003). According to Wade M. and Shan J. 2020, the primary technologies that improve DT are social media, mobile technologies and apps, business analytics and applications, Internet of Things (IoT), communication, and data sharing environments, and collaboration apps. However, DT is changing the entire organizational structure of the business to become more digital in addition to implementing these new digital technologies. The four phases of digital transformation are: process transformation, business model transformation, domain transformation, and culture transformation. For the transformation to go smoothly, determining the areas for improvement and evaluating the DT readiness level are crucial. The primary monitoring areas in Li et al.'s DT monitoring index are "transformation stages," "single-domain digitalization," "integration and interconnection, and collaboration," and "interaction and mode innovation" (Li et al., 2021).

The success of DT is influenced by a number of factors, even though it has become essential and businesses must and want to go digital. The primary obstacles to a successful DT include financing issues with the entity's current digital capabilities, issues with human resources, and technical issues. The DT of fintech companies was the main focus of Saraji et al. (Saraji et al., 2021). "Difficulty in coordination and collaboration" and "resistance to change" are the challenges identified in this study. Liu et al. investigated the relationship between DT performance and adaptation capacity and demonstrated that it differs across industries with varying degrees of technological sophistication (Liu et al., 2021).

The phrase "Industrial Revolution," or "Industrial 4.0," was initially used at the 2011 Hannover Fair in Germany. The integration of industrial activities, information technology, and technology that results from fusing the latest advancements in informatics with industry technologies is known as Industry 4.0, a DT process. Businesses must adapt to the changes brought about by the industrial revolutions and make new investments in their organizational structures if they want to keep their competitive edge in the globalizing market. Due to DT, companies are now investing in areas like the Internet of Things, big data and analytics, artificial intelligence, cyber security, cloud computing, autonomous systems, and wired and wireless communication infrastructure, all of which fall under the purview of Industry 4.0.

Four significant industrial revolutions throughout history are shown in Figure 1.2. The characteristics of industrial revolutions can be summed up as follows.

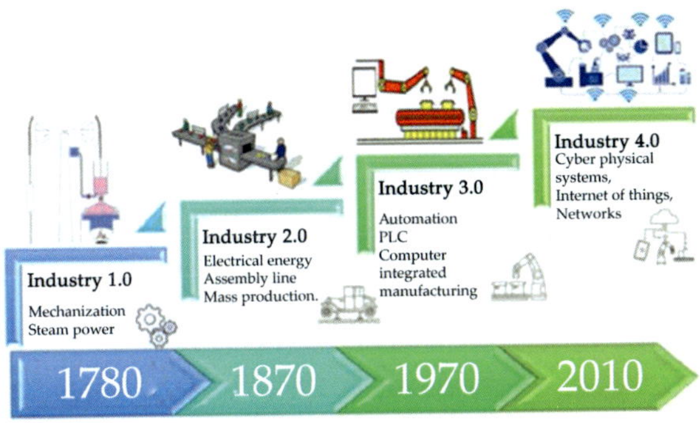


**Figure 1.2.** *Industrial revolution.*

*Source: Cengiz Kahraman and Elif Haktanır. Intelligent Systems in Digital Transformation: Theory and Applications. Springer. https://doi.org/10.1007/978-3-031-16598-6.*

- **Industry 1.0 Mechanization:** The first industrial revolution is thought to have begun with the invention of the steam engine. The use of steam engines in the manufacturing of water- and steam-powered machinery began in the 1780s, when they were invented. Large forces that are impossible to generate with human strength can now be produced, and products that are difficult or take a long time to produce can now be produced quickly.
- **Industry 2.0 Mass Production:** The second industrial revolution is thought to have been brought about by the widespread use of electric motors in manufacturing. The logic of the production line was enhanced after the 1870s by Henry Ford's design and the widespread use of electricity in mass production. As a result, production quantities increased and production times decreased.

- **Industry 3.0 Automation:** The third industrial revolution is thought to have begun with the advent of production automation. The production was given a new dimension by the automation system, which was developed in the 1970s by combining various technologies, including computer, software, hydraulic, pneumatic, electrical, and electronic. During this time, production quality and efficiency have improved thanks to the use of computer-controlled machinery and programmable logic controller technology.
- **Industry 4.0 Smart Factories:** Industry 4.0 is the production phase where human intervention is kept to a minimum and all systems and machines utilized in production are able to communicate with one another. The fundamental components of Industry 4.0 are represented as cyber-physical systems, the Internet of Things, and networks. Industry 4.0's fundamental elements are defined as virtualization, autonomous management, interoperability, and real-time capability.

Five fundamental functions can be used to describe a production process: (i) force needed for production; (ii) quantity needed for production; (iii) direction needed for force required for production; (iv) communication and panning; and (v) initial setup and maintenance. Prior to the industrial revolution, human labor was used to carry out all of these tasks.

During the first industrial revolution, steam engines replaced laborers as the primary source of production force. Human labor was used to complete the remaining production tasks.

The second industrial revolution saw the development of mass production logic as well as the switch from steam power to electric power. The third industrial revolution saw the transfer of force direction and control to computer numerically controlled systems, along with an increase in production quantities and quality through automation of production processes.

The handling, direction, and control of the residual force were thus delegated to mechanical systems. The production working environment's communication and production planning functions were moved to cyber systems with the advent of the fourth industrial revolution. Therefore, the goal is to retrieve the raw material from the warehouse, move it to the workbench, process it there, and then deliver it to the client via the network of communication between the machines.

The European Commission unveiled Industry 5.0 in 2021, offering a vision of an industry that goes beyond productivity and efficiency. Industry 5.0 is defined as value-driven, which propels technological transformation for a specific goal, in contrast to Industry 4.0, which is technology-driven. The last tasks completed by humans after the fourth industrial revolution were maintenance and the initial setup of the production systems. In the future, the industry will experience its fifth revolution (Industry 5.0) when these tasks are transferred to humanoid robots. The changes in production systems brought about by the industrial revolutions are displayed in Table 1.1.

**Table 1.1.** *Improvements Provided by Industrial Revolutions in Production Systems*

| **Components of Production Systems** | **Before Industry Revolution** | **Industry 1.0** | **Industry 2.0** | **Industry 3.0** | **Industry 4.0** | **Industry 5.0** |
|---|---|---|---|---|---|---|
| Source of power/force | Human | Steam | Electrical | Electrical | Electrical | Electrical |
| Quantity of production | Handmade | Custom-made | Mass production | Mass production | Mass production | Mass production |
| Motion-force control | Human | Human | Human | Machine | Machine | Machine |
| Communication and planning | Human | Human | Human | Human | Cyber physical systems Networks | Cyber physical systems Networks |
| Initial installation and maintenance | Human | Human | Human | Human | Human | Humanoid Robots |

*Source: Cengiz Kahraman and Elif Haktanır. Intelligent Systems in Digital Transformation: Theory and Applications. Springer. https://doi.org/10.1007/978-3-031-16598-6.*

## 1.3. THE ROLE OF ARTIFICIAL INTELLIGENCE IN DIGITAL TRANSFORMATION

Digital transformation (DX) and AI are related concepts. Organizations and thought leaders will probably still be talking about both working together even if they only mention one. In summary, AI will drive the next stage of DX projects and software, opening up possibilities and enabling advancements that were not previously achievable. We must first define AI in relation to the idea of DX, as there are many different definitions of it depending on the context and application (Figure 1.3).

**Figure 1.3.** *Role of artificial intelligence in digital transformation.*

*Source: https://www.ptc.com/-/media/Images/blog/post/corporate/ai-role-transformation-900.jpg.*

AI and Digital Transformation have become essential elements that are changing the business landscape in the ever-evolving business environment. Figure 1.4 displays the size and technologies of the global market for digital transformation.

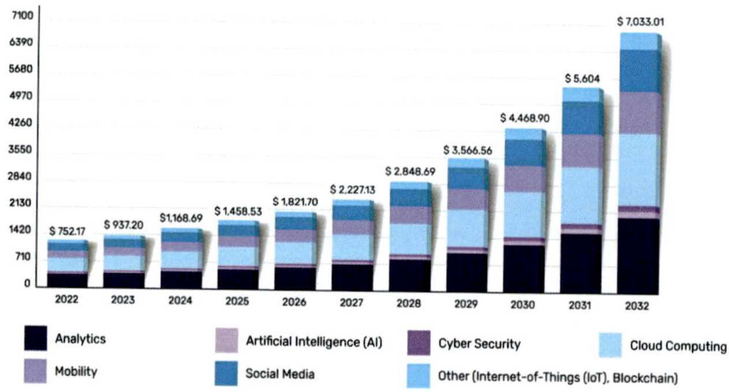


**Figure 1.4.** *Global digital transformation market size in USD Billion (2022–2032).*

*Source: https://www.vlinkinfo.com/blog/artificial-intelligence-in-digital-transformation/.*

As a result of technological advancements, organizations are increasingly looking to use AI to improve operational efficiency, glean insightful information from data, and provide outstanding customer service. This convergence of AI and business processes has sparked a shift in perspective, enabling companies to rethink their value propositions, customer interactions, and operational strategies, thereby ushering in a new era of digital transformation. There are many opportunities at the nexus of AI and digital transformation, from improved customer experiences and creative business models to more efficient operations and higher productivity. However, there are a number of challenges associated with integrating AI. A clear vision, a strategic approach to integrating AI into digital transformation, and a deep understanding of both AI and digital transformation are necessary for successful implementation. This change requires overcoming a learning curve, addressing ethical issues, and continuously adjusting to the rapidly evolving technological environment.

### 1.3.1. What Is Artificial Intelligence (AI) in Digital Transformation?

Instead of machines mimicking human thought processes, AI uses complex algorithms designed for particular tasks with clearly defined inputs. For example, AI in digital transformation doesn't think for itself; instead, it works within preset parameters. AI-powered processes, in contrast to traditional automation, are excellent at adjusting to new data and unforeseen changes. Their key advantage is their capacity to learn from both achievements and setbacks, which allows for proactive data analysis to foresee problems and self-correction. AI works best when faced with complex problems or circumstances that are not governed by predetermined rules, in contrast to standard automation, which flourishes in established processes. Depending on the situation, AI can evaluate a set of inputs and either automatically carry out or suggest the best course of action. Artificial narrow intelligence is what we mean most frequently when we talk about AI in relation to engineering and manufacturing. Sophisticated algorithms created for a predetermined task with a known set of inputs are the problem, not machines thinking like humans. For example, artificial narrow intelligence created for CAD applications will never "think" outside of those precise, previously mentioned bounds. AI-powered processes, in contrast to conventional automation, are able to respond to fresh data or unforeseen developments. Its greatest advantage is that. AI algorithms can learn from both successes and failures without being constrained by preset outputs. They can self-correct and use data analysis to identify impending problems before they arise (Figure 1.5).

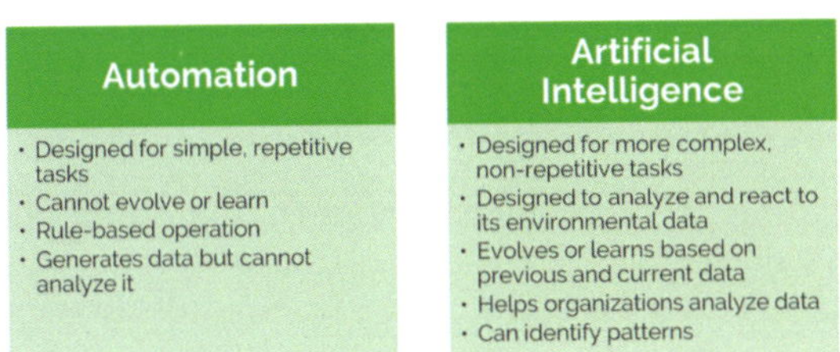


**Figure 1.5.** *Automation vs artificial intelligence.*

*Source: https://www.ptc.com/en/blogs/corporate/artificial-intelligence-digital-transformation.*

From a different angle, automation offers the best value when used in a process that already exists and is clearly defined, like well-established production lines. Automation procedures are always controlled by the user within a predetermined set of inputs. On the other hand, AI works best when attempting to solve problems that are more complicated or not predetermined by rules. If an AI receives a set of inputs from the user, it will either analyze the data and recommend the best course of action or, depending on the circumstances, carry it out automatically.

## 1.3.2. Benefits of AI in Digital Transformation

The financial success of a company must be taken into account when evaluating any technology, including AI. Businesses are already looking to implement DX initiatives in highly regulated environments where the results can be evaluated in relation to financial performance. Saying that this process is improved by using DX technology is insufficient. In order to determine precisely how and why their investments are affecting their workflows, organizations should be measuring. With this way of thinking, uncertainty is eliminated, enabling executives to act and speak with more assurance about the company's direction. Keeping this in mind, we have determined four important, quantifiable advantages of AI in DX projects (Figure 1.6).

**Figure 1.6.** *Benefits of AI in digital transformation.*

*Source: https://www.vlinkinfo.com/blog/artificial-intelligence-in-digital-transformation/.*

### *1.3.2.1. More Effective Decision-Making*

Contrary to many movies and television shows, important decisions cannot be made purely based on intuition. To arrive at the best decision, even an experienced leader needs access to all pertinent data. Since time is a constant consideration, this choice must frequently be made quickly. AI can assist in locating and emphasizing crucial data about workflow optimization, product performance, and forecasted results. For example, using the data at hand, a well-defined program can perform millions of simulations to estimate the performance of a new product during the first six months of its lifecycle. Decision-makers can more accurately estimate and predict the time and resources they will need to proceed, assess what work remains to be done, and spot potential problems with the help of information like this.

### *1.3.2.2. Increased Profitability*

While AI cannot replace human judgment, it can be a very useful tool for time-to-value optimization.

The need to more reliably deliver functional products that satisfy all regulations within a predetermined (and typically dwindling) time frame is a constant challenge for manufacturers. Whether it is through simulations, fact-checking against existing proprietary data, or helping identify issues before they arise, AI aids in the optimization of product timelines. These and other time-consuming tasks can be fully automated by AI software, which reduces the resources required and boosts profit margins while freeing up human resources to focus on the more cerebral aspects of product development.

### *1.3.2.3. Enhanced Analytics*

Large and intricate data sets that originate from different sources and places can exist. In the past, gathering, processing, and analyzing this data required a significant amount of manpower and time.

Although humans should always play a crucial role in the final analysis, AI can quickly and efficiently streamline every step of the process, providing data results in a much shorter amount of time.

AI may be crucial to providing timely actionable insights for global manufacturers with a large number of assets dispersed across the globe.

### *1.3.2.4. Holistic View of the Customer*

Data is the foundation of the digital world, and its nature and source are ever-evolving. Cookies and other similar tools were once used by businesses to better understand the behavior of their customers.

But these days, cookie usage has sharply decreased due to privacy concerns and other factors, so businesses will need new tools to better understand how their customers are acting. This next iteration—AI-enhanced software—can and probably will help decision makers see their customers in a way that is perhaps more complete and accurate than cookies were able to.

## 1.3.3. How AI Improves Digital Transformation?

### *1.3.3.1. Data Analysis and Insights*

AI in digital transformation swiftly and precisely processes and analyzes enormous volumes of data. Patterns, trends, and correlations in data that may be difficult for conventional analytics tools to find can be found using machine learning algorithms and data analytics services. Making better decisions is made possible by this capability, which gives businesses a deeper understanding of their operations, consumer behavior, and market trends.

### *1.3.3.2. Customer Experience Enhancement*

Chatbots and virtual assistants are examples of AI-powered solutions that greatly enhance consumer interactions. These systems can comprehend and react to human language thanks to NLP, which improves the general customer experience. By providing pertinent content and services based on user preferences, AI-powered personalized recommendation engines in digital transformation help to increase customer satisfaction.

### *1.3.3.3. Automation and Operational Efficiency*

Automation powered by AI transcends conventional rule-based procedures. Automation systems can become more flexible and effective by adapting and learning from experience thanks to machine learning algorithms. It improves operational workflows, lessens the need for manual labor, and enables businesses to increase process efficiency.

### *1.3.3.4. Decision Support and Predictive Analytics*

AI's contribution to the digital transformation enables more sophisticated analytics and predictive modeling, which improve decision-making. AI systems can help with forecasting, risk management, and strategic planning by evaluating historical data and finding trends. It provides decision-makers with insightful information that enables them to make well-informed decisions that support organizational objectives.

### *1.3.3.5. Proactive Problem Solving*

AI systems can be proactive, in contrast to traditional systems that follow preset rules. They enable businesses to foresee obstacles and opportunities by continuously analyzing data in real-time. Proactively addressing problems before they become critical and quickly adapting to changing conditions help businesses become more resilient.

### 1.3.3.6. Intelligent Automation in Processes

By adding intelligence to repetitive procedures, AI plays a part in digital transformation that improves automation. It entails adjusting to shifting circumstances and automating difficult decision-making processes. In addition to speeding up procedures, intelligent automation increases precision and lowers errors, resulting in more dependable and effective operations (Figure 1.7).

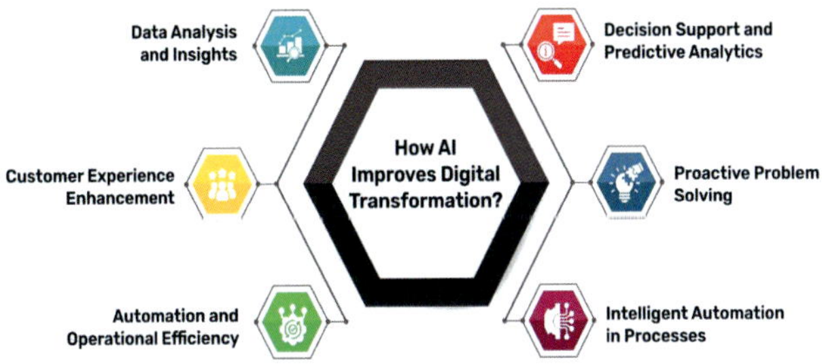


**Figure 1.7.** *How AI improves digital transformation.*

*Source: https://www.vlinkinfo.com/blog/artificial-intelligence-in-digital-transformation/.*

## 1.3.4. How AI Drives Digital Transformation Initiatives

With these advantages, it should come as no surprise that AI is driving DX initiatives across a variety of industries and will continue to do so. To provide a clearer example, let's examine two specific areas where AI is useful: automation and data analytics.

### 1.3.4.1. Automation

The quality of the program that controls automation has always been its determining factor. Indeed, some assembly processes can be automated by a machine, but if the machine is unaware of its connection to a larger assembly line or which process it is in charge of, work will abruptly stop. Automation has long been guided by software, and AI initiatives like machine learning have been improving automation for years. This trend is only expected to continue. A key component of DX is automation since it frequently leads to visibility. A business can see the average completion time, average downtime, and other important details once they have automated a process and fully understand it. Applying a well-designed AI application, like machine learning, can help you better understand this data, identify bottlenecks, and determine why and when downtime occurs most frequently—not just for a single automated system, but for the entire ecosystem. Yes, software is the source of this data, but so are IoT sensors, edge computing devices, service reports, and numerous other areas that are already commonly reliant on DX technology. Organizations can gain even more advantages by integrating the appropriate AI tools into their current DX deployments.

#### *1.3.4.2. Data Analytics*

As previously stated, data analytics and artificial intelligence are a great match. Numerous sources provide crucial information, even prior to the product's release into the market. Businesses can begin to fully leverage the power of the digital thread—a connected closed loop of data derived from a product at every stage of its lifecycle, from design to end-of-life service—with the aid of artificial intelligence. Unprecedented levels of product understanding and PLM optimization opportunities are made possible by this abundance of information. However, data from so many sources needs to be combined as soon as possible, and AI is just faster than humans at doing so. AI can display all pertinent information to help it make the best choice, even if it doesn't understand what it's looking at.

### 1.3.5. Real-World Use Cases of AI and Digital Transformation

Although they are aware of the benefits of technology, decision makers are typically convinced by its usefulness. Artificial Intelligence is a useful tool that many organizations are already utilizing to enhance their internal processes and expand their offerings. It is not a solution that will take years or even months to implement. Here are three brief instances of how AI is being used in DX projects to boost operational effectiveness:

#### *1.3.5.1. Customer Service*

The most popular type of AI customer service that most people think of is chatbots, which are nothing new. Although they are frequently very limited and only match a customer's query to one of many pre-programmed answers, chatbots can be useful. These presets can answer a lot of customer questions, but not nearly all of them, because they are frequently created from the most popular Q&A. On the other hand, large language models, like ChatGPT, are more sophisticated. There are no presets in these new models. Rather, a large language model's worth is frequently linked to the data it uses. Even though ChatGPT is impressive, it cannot distinguish fact from fiction, so the source of its model directly affects how reliable it is. A massive language model that gathers data from the internet might not be beneficial because real solutions could be muddled by contradicting and inaccurate information. Nevertheless, much more specialized language models can be trained using this new type of generative AI. For example, PTC might develop a ChatGPT-like application that pulls data exclusively from PTC and associated websites. As a result, its knowledge is far more likely to be accurate because it is only searching authorized sources for information. This new generation of chatbots will be able to respond immediately to customer inquiries. Although it is still far from ideal, the system is a big improvement over previous preset-based chatbot models.

#### *1.3.5.2. Manufacturing*

Since there are numerous subsectors within manufacturing in its widest sense, as well as numerous applications for AI, we'll concentrate on smart manufacturing for the sake of conciseness. As the name implies, smart manufacturing is the integration of intelligent, networked technology, such as artificial intelligence, into various aspects of conventional manufacturing. Failure prediction, for example, involves anticipating when and where equipment will malfunction so that technicians are better prepared and armed. Organizations that lack failure prediction are only able to respond to outages, which frequently results in longer periods of inactivity and higher costs for each and every failure. Although failure predictions can be calculated by humans, it is a labor-intensive process. In smart manufacturing, AI can quickly read and analyze data and provide human operators with reliable warnings about the location and timing of machine failures. This significantly raises first-time-fix rates and enables businesses to be more proactive and strategic in their maintenance operations.

#### *1.3.5.3. Healthcare*

Preventive maintenance reduces manufacturing costs. Cutting-edge, AI powered healthcare analytics can enhance preventative healthcare and save lives by resolving issues before they become life-threatening. AI is able to quickly evaluate millions of X-rays, assisting in the identification of problems that even highly qualified technicians could overlook. This also applies to ultrasounds, CAT scans, and pretty much any other type of data. All of it can be compared to a far broader set of outcomes for analysis, which enables medical professionals to identify trends and create more informed treatment plans.

### 1.3.6. Future of AI in Digital Transformation

AI's role in the digital transformation has enormous potential. Automation, efficiency, and innovation will all be accelerated by AI in various industries. Business processes will be redefined by improved data analytics, predictive capabilities, and personalized user experiences. The incorporation of AI into decision-making procedures and its quick adaptation to changing trends will be essential. To maximize productivity, human-AI collaboration will be prioritized. Strong security protocols and ethical considerations will be essential. In general, AI is expected to be a revolutionary force that will lead organizations into a future that is more technologically sophisticated, intelligent, and adaptable.

## 1.3.7. Examples of AI-Influenced Digital Transformation

### *1.3.7.1. Conversational AI for Better Customer Service*

Basic chatbots to sophisticated virtual customer assistants are the evolution of conversational AI. A simple FAQ bot uses machine learning to deliver pertinent answers to users' frequently asked questions by requesting keywords. AI personal assistant apps, such as Google Assistant, Apple's Siri, and Amazon's Alexa, answer complex, personalized queries and help users complete tasks or place orders. Highly developed virtual assistants, like Microsoft Power Virtual Agents, are able to understand contextual information like the type of customer and the issue at hand and use that information to intelligently route incoming requests to the appropriate bot.

### *1.3.7.2. Better Customer Relationships with AI-Powered CRMs*

By combining information from sources like web searches, order histories, and product reviews, AI in digital transformation provides sales teams with a thorough customer overview. This knowledge facilitates better engagement, comprehension of customer needs, and automation of repetitive CRM tasks. They were using AI to process customer input and offer wise brand recommendations for CRM software such as Sugar CRM, Siebel, Salesforce integration solution, and Zoho. With ASOS correctly predicting customer lifetime spending and OTTO employing ML-trained algorithms for precise stock management and 90% accurate predictions of upcoming purchases over the next month, Amazon's AI recommendation engine customizes its approach for a variety of personality types.

### *1.3.7.3. Intelligent Assistants Help Close Deals Faster*

Google's Nespresso Assistant is an example of advanced sales assistant software that uses a three-step process to predict customer preferences consist of:

- Intelligent assistants pose focused questions to help buyers pinpoint their desires or requirements.
- AI-driven systems employ algorithms to identify and present buyers with suitable products.
- The intelligent system assists buyers in completing sales.

The low-touch model of AI-guided sales, which converts leads with little human intervention, is what makes it so appealing. This strategy is the fastest-growing trend in modern sales, with 60% of sophisticated companies expected to implement it by 2025.

### *1.3.7.4. AI for Data Collection & Predictive Analytics*

Imagine being able to predict the future of your business to prevent mistakes and automate processes for higher profitability in advance. AI does this with the help of machine learning and programs like SAS Advanced Analytics. By analyzing business data, this software finds areas for improvement and highlights the most appealing products and marketing tactics. Integrated features consist of:

- Anomaly detection, pinpointing ineffective marketing strategies, and eliminating features that deter potential customers.
- Sentiment analysis, gauging social media opinions about your brand for product enhancement.
- Predictive analytics for fraud detection, attrition, turnover, and retention projections.

By enabling businesses to make educated decisions, this clever software promotes expansion and reduces risks.

### *1.3.7.5. Detecting Security Problems with AI*

Companies use AI and machine learning development services to improve cybersecurity and physical security while preserving intellectual property (Figure 1.8). Examples include:

- Security Screening;
- Security & Crime Prevention;
- Endpoint Protection;
- Sophisticated Cyber Protection.

**Figure 1.8.** *5 Examples of AI influenced digital transformation.*

*Source: https://www.vlinkinfo.com/blog/artificial-intelligence-in-digital-transformation/.*

## REFERENCES

1. Bartodziej, C. J. (2017). *The Concept Industry 4.0: An Empirical Analysis of Technologies and Applications in Production Logistics*. Springer Gabler.
2. Chen, C. L., Lin, Y. C., Chen, W. H., Chao, C. F., & Pandia, H. (2021). Role of government to enhance digital transformation in small service business. *Sustainability, 13*, 1028.
3. Ciaramella, A., & Ciaramella, M. (2024). *Introduction to Artificial Intelligence: From Data Analysis to Generative AI* (1st ed.). Intellisemantic Editions.
4. De Propris, L., & Bailey, D. (2020). *Industry 4.0 and Regional Transformations*. Routledge Taylor & Francis Group.
5. Dehning, B., Richardson, V. J., & Zmud, R. W. (2003). The value relevance of announcements of transformational information technology investments. *Management Information Systems Quarterly, 27*(4), 637–656.
6. Ertel, W. (2017). *Introduction to Artificial Intelligence* (2nd ed.). Springer.
7. Hess, T., Matt, C., Benlian, A., & Wiesböck, F. (2016). Options for formulating a digital transformation strategy. *MIS Quarterly Executive, 15*, 103–119.
8. Kane, G., Palmer, D., & Phillips, A. N. (2015). Is your business ready for a digital future? *MIT Sloan Management Review, 56*, 37–44.
9. Li, J., Dou, K., Wen, S., & Li, Q. (2021). Monitoring index system for sectors' digital transformation and its application in China. *Electronics, 10*, 1301.
10. Liu, J., Yang, W., & Liu, W. (2021). Adaptive capacity configurations for the digital transformation: A fuzzy-set analysis of Chinese manufacturing firms. *Journal of Organizational Change Management, 34*(6), 1222–1241.
11. Luger, G., & Stubblefield, W. (2004). *Artificial Intelligence: Structures and Strategies for Complex Problem Solving* (5th ed.). Benjamin/Cummings.
12. Nilsson, N. (1998). *Artificial Intelligence: A New Synthesis*. Morgan Kaufmann.
13. Rich, E., Knight, K., & Nair, S. B. (2010). *Artificial Intelligence* (3rd ed.). Tata McGraw Hill India.
14. Russell, S. J., & Norvig, P. (2003). *Artificial Intelligence: A Modern Approach* (2nd ed.). Prentice Hall.
15. Russell, S. J., & Norvig, P. (2021). *Artificial Intelligence: A Modern Approach* (4th ed.). Pearson.

16. Saraji, M. K., Streimikiene, D., & Kyriakopoulos, G. L. (2021). Fermatean fuzzy CRITIC-COPRAS method for evaluating the challenges to industry 4.0 adoption for a sustainable digital transformation. *Sustainability, 13*(17), 9577.
17. Sarvari, P. A., Ustundag, A., Cevikcan, E., Kaya, I., & Cebi, S. (2018). Technology roadmap for industry 4.0. In *Industry 4.0: Managing the Digital Transformation* (pp. 95–106). Springer Series in Advanced Manufacturing. Springer.
18. Vial, G. (2019). Understanding digital transformation: A review and a research agenda. *Journal of Strategic Information Systems, 28*(2), 118–144.
19. Wade, M., & Shan, J. (2020). Covid-19 has accelerated digital transformation, but may have made it harder not easier. *MIS Quarterly Executive, 19*(3), 213–220.
20. Xu, X., Lu, Y., Vogel-Heuser, B., & Wang, L. (2021). Industry 4.0 and Industry 5.0—Inception, conception and perception. *Journal of Manufacturing Systems, 61*, 530–535.
21. Zimmermann, A., Schmidt, R., Sandkuhl, K., & Masuda, Y. (2021). Architecting intelligent digital systems and services. In A. Zimmermann, R. Howlett, & L. Jain (Eds.), *Human Centred Intelligent Systems* (Vol. *189*, pp. 129–137). Springer.

# CHAPTER 2

# AI-DRIVEN BUSINESS MODELS

## Contents

# INTRODUCTION

AI-driven business models leverage artificial intelligence technologies to optimize operations, enhance customer experiences, and create new revenue streams. These models are reshaping industries by using machine learning, natural language processing, and data analytics to automate processes and make data-driven decisions at scale. For instance, companies in e-commerce utilize AI for personalized recommendations, dynamic pricing, and inventory management, increasing both efficiency and customer satisfaction.

The impact of AI has once again been a topic of discussion thanks to an AI chatbot that was developed using the GPT-3 deep learning language model. Businesses require suitable business models (BMs) to effectively extract value from AI applications. These BMs comprise the "architecture of the firm's mechanisms for creating, delivering, and capturing value." By pushing the limits of human-machine interactions, GPT-4, the successor to GPT3, has made it possible to create novel BMs that contradict established models (Kanbach et al., 2023). Midjourney, an image-generation tool, and other generative AI tools like Bard, Gemini, or Claude, which are complex large language models, highlight the rapidly increasing applicability of generative AI in a variety of fields (McKinsey, 2023).

As a result, more businesses are utilizing AI technology, and managers are attempting to determine which BMs have the greatest potential. AI has a wide range of possible applications in business processes as a result. Decision-making processes are optimized and their accuracy and reliability are increased through data-driven decision making, which is an example of a practical application of AI. To improve its operational efficiency and decision-making, eBay, for example, successfully implemented machine translation. This led to significant changes to the data used in decision-making and the overall BM. In a similar vein, Vodafone improved customer service through a variety of channels by incorporating AI-driven data analysis into its business model, which led to the customization of goods and services. In line with Lee et al. (2019), over 70% of business executives conclude that AI will open doors for new BMs, and over 80% of business executives think it will help companies maintain or gain a competitive advantage. To take advantage of AI's potential for value creation, established businesses must engage in business model innovation (BMI) in order to use and implement AI in business processes (Mariani et al., 2023). "Designed, novel, and nontrivial changes to the key elements of a firm's BM and/or the architecture linking these elements" is how BMI is defined.

To speed up AI adoption across the entire organization and AI-driven BMI, most business leaders, however, likewise feel unprepared. Most businesses are unable to successfully implement AI because they lack the necessary skills and knowledge, which prevents them from moving past concept stage in their AI initiatives.

The complex nature of AI's challenges for management and businesses has led to a wide range of research on AI-driven BMI. Notwithstanding its wide focus on technology, management research addresses managerial issues such as the adoption and application of AI, which frequently calls for adjustments to organizational culture because of employee resistance.

Additionally, BMI and AI applications force managers and staff to embrace new practices and develop new competencies. Broadly speaking, new management skills are needed to address the growing ethical issues, regulatory ambiguity, and uncertainties surrounding the use of AI. These unique needs call for both the innovation of existing BMs and the creation of new ones. The current literature is ambiguous about how BMs evolve and how managers must (re)configure their BMs to generate and reap the benefits of AI as a result of these quirks and difficulties. Analytically speaking, descriptive elaborations of AI-driven BMs have been a common feature of recent research on AI-driven BMI. Additionally, although researchers have examined the phenomenon from a variety of perspectives and conceptual frameworks, they have mostly concentrated on a single AI implication or a particular sector or division, which has resulted in conflicting, fragmented, and disparate opinions on AI-driven BMI. Numerous studies mostly concentrate on technical issues like data requirements, data security, and AI adoption and implementation. These studies frequently examine research questions unique to AI within the framework of BMI. This technology focus produces a disjointed body of research regarding the management of AI-driven BMI, even though it provides insightful information about the organizational challenges of using AI. However, BMI frequently serves as an evolutionary "byproduct" of the application of AI. This brings up the second flaw in the research that has already been done: the literature on AI-driven BMI covers everything from creating disruptive AI-driven BMI to using AI to boost an existing BM's efficiency. Since research themes cover varying degrees of the scope of AI-driven BMI, the current body of research in this area impedes a comprehensive understanding of AI-driven BMI management. Conceptually, some studies use static research methods to identify the components, obstacles, and difficulties of AI-driven BMI, while other studies look at AI-driven BMI from the standpoint of a dynamic process.

## 2.1. ARTIFICIAL INTELLIGENCE (AI) IN BUSINESS

In business, artificial intelligence refers to the application of AI technologies like computer vision, natural language processing, and machine learning to enhance operational efficiency, increase worker output, and create value for the company.

Numerous business operations are impacted by artificial intelligence, which is the creation of computer programs and machine learning that simulate human intelligence's capacity for problem-solving and judgment. Artificial intelligence (AI) is used by businesses to enhance data analysis and decision-making, enhance customer experiences, create content, optimize IT operations, and improve sales, marketing, cybersecurity, and other areas. New business applications appear as AI technologies advance and change (Figure 2.1).

**Figure 2.1.** *AI in business: Moving to better performance.*

*Source: https://www.manutan.com/blog/medias/files/856_ILLUSTRATION_0.jpeg.*

A human workforce can be assisted by artificial intelligence in streamlining processes and increasing the effectiveness of corporate operations. These improvements are achieved in a number of ways, such as by employing AI to automate monotonous tasks, produce information using machine learning algorithms, swiftly process enormous volumes of data sets and derive insightful information, and forecast future events using data analysis. Numerous forms of business automation, such as enterprise and process automation, are powered by AI systems, which help to lower human error and free up human workers for higher-level tasks. In order to support business operations, these systems rely on business data and make use of technologies such as deep learning, machine learning, and natural language processing (NLP). Integrating AI into business functions requires a baseline understanding of the following components:

1. **Machine Learning Algorithms:** A subset of artificial intelligence, these algorithms are used to classify or predict data based on input. These algorithms can be trained to find patterns, anomalies, or forecast future sales revenue using training data sets. Large datasets can be mined using machine learning algorithms to find important

insights that can help businesses make better decisions in the real world. Data that has been labeled—that is, classified by a human expert prior to processing—benefits machine learning algorithms.

2. **Deep Learning:** A branch of machine learning called deep learning makes it possible to automate processes without the need for human involvement. Deep learning is essential to facial recognition, chatbots, virtual assistants, and fraud prevention technologies. Deep learning models are able to forecast future behavior by analyzing data pertaining to user behavior. Deep learning models require less human intervention and are more accurate at extracting information from unstructured data, like text and images, than general machine learning.

3. **Natural Language Processing (NLP):** A subfield of artificial intelligence known as "natural language processing" "allows computers and digital devices to recognize, understand, and generate text and speech." NLP is the engine behind chatbots for customer service, digital assistants, and voice-activated gadgets like GPS units. When combined with deep learning models and machine learning algorithms, NLP enables systems to glean insights from unstructured data that is text- or voice-driven.

4. **Computer Vision:** A branch of artificial intelligence called computer vision enables computer systems to gather data from digital photos, videos, and other visual inputs. 5 To learn and recognize particular components of digital imagery, computer vision employs both machine learning and deep learning algorithms. There are currently many uses for computer vision, and as the technology develops, so do the applications. Production lines, for instance, can use computer vision to identify small flaws in the manufacturing process.

Enterprise-grade AI can be integrated to improve data analysis, business strategy, and decision-making, relieve human workers of repetitive manual tasks, and streamline organizational procedures. In order to accomplish this, businesses need to have an infrastructure that supports AI technology and handles data appropriately. A robust framework for data governance keeps data safe from breaches and accessible to all pertinent parties.

Furthermore, it facilitates the application of advanced data analytics. Large-scale data management is facilitated by this framework's incorporation of multi-cloud and hybrid cloud environments, as well as a digital transformation. After putting these systems in place, a company can start developing training models to teach AI technologies and mining data for insights.

### 2.1.1. Importance of Artificial Intelligence in Business

One of the most amazing technologies that will change people's lives in practically every aspect of contemporary society is artificial intelligence. Numerous companies have already seized the substantial development opportunities presented by this technology. AI is the collective term for a number of technologies that enable machines to perceive, learn, comprehend, and act to enhance human abilities. AI has the capacity to learn and process enormous volumes of data, which will improve and revolutionize operations across a variety of industries. AI technology can anticipate needs and make pertinent and well-informed decisions after a certain amount of learning and comprehension. AI will make decisions after analyzing data, in contrast to business intelligence technology, which analyzes data and leaves the decision-making to humans.

So, here are the various ways in which Artificial Intelligence is important in business:

- **Saving Time and Money:** Machines are more productive than people when it comes to working. AI systems are able to work around the clock without getting bored. Additionally, unlike humans, they are not required to sleep or take breaks. This indicates that they are completely trustworthy whenever you choose to collaborate with them. You can ask them to alert you to important events whenever you'd like. Large volumes of data can be analyzed by artificial intelligence machines in a matter of seconds. As long as they have pertinent information, they typically make decisions faster. Therefore, this technology is incredibly a time-saver and works effectively than humans would do.
- **Generate Business Insights to Make Smart Decisions:** Data is a valuable resource for any business in the modern economy. However, your business data will be worthless if you are unable to understand it. AI systems are effective at processing data quickly and producing pertinent responses to any queries that may come up in the workplace. Based on what they discover, they provide precise forecasts and client needs. No human will be as quick or flawless as AI predictive analytics technology.
- **Improving Customer Experience:** AI-powered chatbots enable companies to offer round-the-clock customer support. AI has made it possible for businesses to automate phone calls, emails, and online chats. AI has the advantage of being able to communicate with numerous clients at once and efficiently answer their inquiries on

websites or applications. The OracleCMS offers the best customer management solutions in Australia if you want to improve customer interactions in your company.

- **AI Technology Enhances Productivity:** Your employees are more likely to concentrate on doing their best work when you take things off of their to-do list. Because AI will do the majority of the work, you won't need to give your staff a ton of work to do. This increases productivity by enabling your employees to focus on their areas of expertise. AI will provide real-time support if your company communicates with clients continuously throughout the day. For instance, AI can provide passengers with crucial travel information in the travel sector, which handles millions of thousands of passengers daily.
- **Reducing Errors:** Artificial intelligence is far more accurate than humans, even though it is not perfect. The accuracy of AI technology typically falls between 99% and 100%, even in highly urbane systems. Cash flow forecasting is the most labor-intensive and prone to human error process in any organization. Without the need for human intervention, AI technology can aid in improving cash flow forecasting accuracy. This increases the likelihood of success for the company.

With its many advantages that can greatly affect risk management, revenue growth, and brand awareness, AI has become a crucial component of contemporary business operations. Businesses can improve decision-making skills, obtain insightful information from data, and streamline procedures by implementing AI technologies. This is a thorough examination of the value of AI in business and how it can be used to accomplish a range of strategic goals (Figure 2.2).

**Figure 2.2.** *Advantages of artificial intelligence in business processes.*

*Source: https://www.clavistechnologies.com/wp-content/uploads/2020/04/ai-business-processes.jpg.*

#### 2.1.1.1. Increasing Brand Awareness

AI is essential for increasing brand recognition through targeted marketing tactics. Businesses can create targeted marketing campaigns by analyzing consumer behavior, preferences, and purchase patterns through the use of AI-powered tools like machine learning algorithms and predictive analytics. This degree of customization strengthens relationships with consumers and boosts the efficacy of marketing campaigns. AI-powered chatbots and virtual assistants can also offer real-time customer support, which raises brand engagement and loyalty even further.

#### 2.1.1.2. Improving Revenue

AI enables companies to use automation and sophisticated analytics to streamline their revenue-generating and sales processes. Businesses can modify their pricing strategies and inventory levels by using predictive analytics models, which can forecast customer demand. Additionally, by tailoring product offers to each customer's unique preferences, AI-driven recommendation systems can enhance the likelihood of cross-selling and upselling. Moreover, AI-driven sales forecasting systems can offer precise insights into potential revenue streams, enabling companies to plan their resource allocation and expansion plans.

#### 2.1.1.3. Risk Management

AI presents significant advantages in risk management as it can be used to detect possible threats and reduce operational risks. Massive data sets can be analyzed by machine learning algorithms, which can then look for patterns or anomalies that point to fraud. This proactive strategy improves overall security measures while protecting businesses from monetary losses. Furthermore, market trends and outside variables that could endanger the company can be evaluated by AI-based predictive modeling, allowing for the proactive implementation of risk-reduction plans.

#### 2.1.1.4. Operational Efficiency

AI technologies enhance operational efficiency by streamlining workflows and automating tedious tasks.

AI-powered robotic process automation (RPA) can take care of routine administrative duties, freeing up human resources to concentrate on more intricate and important tasks. AI-driven tools for process optimization can also find inefficiencies in company operations and recommend changes to boost productivity.

#### *2.1.1.5. Data-Driven Decision Making*

AI gives companies the ability to use big data to make well-informed decisions. AI-powered advanced analytics tools are capable of processing massive amounts of both structured and unstructured data to extract insightful information. These insights help firms make data-driven decisions that spur growth and innovation by pointing out market trends, customer behavior patterns, and operational inefficiencies. In conclusion, it is impossible to exaggerate the significance of AI in business. AI provides a plethora of advantages that are critical for remaining competitive in the fast-paced business world of today, from boosting revenue generation through sophisticated analytics and automation to raising brand awareness through tailored marketing strategies.

### 2.1.2. Why Should Companies Use AI?

In the twenty-first century, business processes are characterized by a high degree of complexity, involving tasks that are too stressful and inefficient for humans to perform. The era of data has taken over business in the modern world. Data can provide businesses with insightful information about tactics that can significantly boost growth.

### 2.1.3. The Growth of Artificial Intelligence for Business

More data is available to businesses today than ever before. As per Forbes, there was a 5000% surge in the generation and utilization of data from 2010 to 2020. Businesses can now gather user data to support their decision-making with the aid of developing technologies.

In the past few years, many companies have wholeheartedly embraced AI in their efforts to make better use of the data they are already collecting. Consider the following:

- The global AI market size was worth $62 billion in 2020, and is expected to have an annual growth rate of 40.2% from 2021 to 2028, according to Grand View Research;
- 56% of respondents in McKinsey's "The state of AI in 2021" survey report adopting AI, up from 50% of respondents in 2020;
- Accenture's report on AI found that 84% of C-suite executives think leveraging AI will help them achieve their growth objectives.

These statistics show that AI is no longer an experimental technology only used by select brands. For many companies around the world, it has become a core part of their operations.

### 2.1.4. Key Benefits of AI for Business

Businesses are experiencing real advantages from integrating artificial intelligence technologies into their operations, which should result in substantial financial gains. 87% of organizations believe AI and machine learning will help them grow revenue, boost operational efficiency and improve customer experiences, according to research firm Frost & Sullivan's "Global State of AI, 2022" report. Those are only a few of the benefits AI can deliver.

Here are 12 advantages the technology brings to organizations across various industry sectors.

#### *2.1.4.1. Better Decisions*

Businesses are using AI more and more to make data-driven decisions, or, to use the business jargon of the day, insights from their data. When they do so, they discover that they actually make better, more accurate decisions as opposed to ones that are influenced by biases and preferences or based on personal instincts.

Kavita Ganesan, strategist, adviser, and founder of Opinosis Analytics, gave an example of a company that used AI to help it sift through 42,000 employees' survey responses. Instead of giving employees check-the-box options to rank, the technology analyzed narrative responses and presented summarized findings, allowing company officials to effectively understand what employees wanted most.

#### *2.1.4.2. Efficiency and Productivity Gains*

According to Adnan Masood, chief AI architect at UST, a provider of digital transformation solutions, enterprises can also benefit greatly from increased productivity and efficiency. According to Masood, AI enables businesses to complete tasks at a rate and volume that is just not achievable for humans. This includes using AI for search, data analysis, software development, and the execution of particular business procedures.

According to Masood, AI not only operates at a scale beyond human capability but also frees workers from labor-intensive manual tasks, increasing productivity and enabling them to execute higher-level tasks that are limited to human performance. Using software development as an example, he emphasized how AI can generate test data to validate code, freeing up developers to concentrate on more interesting tasks. This enables businesses to maximize the potential of their human capital while reducing the costs associated with carrying out repetitive, routine tasks that can be handled by technology.

### 2.1.4.3. Improved Speed of Business

According to Seth Earley, CEO of Earley Information Science and author of The AI-Powered Enterprise, AI accelerates business processes in the digital age. According to him, it's all about accelerating the enterprise's clock. AI essentially makes it possible for cycles to be shorter and reduces the amount of time needed to go from one stage to the next, like from design to commercialization. This shorter timeline results in a better and faster return on investment.

### 2.1.4.4. New Capabilities and Business Model Expansion

According to experts, executives can use AI to expand their business models. They noted that as organizations integrate data, analytics, and intelligence into their operations, they are discovering new opportunities. Companies that make autonomous vehicles, for instance, might use the mountains of data they gather to find new insurance-related revenue streams, and insurance companies might use AI to leverage their massive data stores to enter the fleet management market.

### 2.1.4.5. Personalized Customer Services and Experiences

According to Brian Jackson, principal research director at Info-Tech Research Group, AI uses data analysis and learning to produce highly personalized and customized experiences and services. The most obvious examples, according to him, come from the consumer sector, where retailers and streaming services like Netflix employ intelligent systems to analyze purchasing trends, individual customer data, and bigger data sets to figure out what each customer wants at any given time to fit their needs, interests, and personal style. But AI also provides that personalization in many other domains, like healthcare, where it tailors treatments, and in the workplace, where it accommodates each worker's unique needs.

### 2.1.4.6. Improved Services

AI makes technology interactions easier, more natural, more precise, and better overall, according to Mike Mason, chief AI officer of consulting thought works. Mason clarified that the AI is capable of comprehending both unstructured data and unstructured queries. To put it another way, the technology can comprehend a user's request even if it is made in simple, conversational language. It can also interpret every detail of every listing, including the narrative notes that real estate agents have added. Finally, it can provide the user with a highly precise and customized list of properties that match their needs.

### 2.1.4.7. Improved Monitoring

According to experts, organizations can implement near-instantaneous monitoring capabilities to alert them to issues, recommend actions, and, in some cases, initiate a response, thanks to AI's ability to process massive amounts of data in real time. For instance, AI can forecast maintenance requirements and identify issues based on data collected by devices on factory equipment. This stops expensive maintenance from being done because it's needed rather than scheduled, and it also prevents disruptive breakdowns. The monitoring powers of AI can also be useful in other domains, like enterprise cybersecurity operations, where a lot of data needs to be understood and analyzed.

### 2.1.4.8. Better Quality and Reduction of Human Error

When AI technologies are integrated into operations, organizations can anticipate a decrease in errors and increased adherence to established standards. Furthermore, the combination of AI and machine learning with robotic process automation—a technology that automates repetitive, rule-based tasks—not only speeds up processes and lowers errors, but it can also be trained to become more intelligent and take on larger tasks. AI enhances the value proposition because it reduces errors and produces better quality, according to Earley. When AI is used for financial reconciliation, for instance, the results are almost always error-free, but when human employees handle even a portion of the reconciliation, errors can still occur.

### 2.1.4.9. Better Talent Management

AI is being used by businesses to enhance many facets of talent management, from eliminating bias in corporate communications to expediting the hiring process. Furthermore, by effectively sourcing, screening, and identifying top-tier candidates, AI-enabled processes can impact workforce productivity in addition to saving businesses money on hiring. Companies are also using chatbots to mentor staff members and give job candidates a personalized experience as natural language processing tools have improved. AI tools can also measure employee satisfaction, recognize, and manage top performers, calculate fair compensation, and create more engaging and personalized work environments with fewer tedious, repetitive tasks.

### 2.1.4.10. More Innovation

Experts stated that workers at all levels are beginning to use AI tools to support their increased creativity and innovation as they grow more at ease and self-assured when interacting with AI. In her book, Ganesan detailed how a chain of restaurants leveraged technology to power a smartphone app that lets users create custom cocktails based on their tastes in food and drink. The tool creates the recipe and sends it to a human bartender for mixing and serving. Other industries, like the consumer goods industry for new product development and the healthcare sector for drug discovery, use AI to support research and development (R&D) efforts.

### *2.1.4.11. Increased Profitability*

Organizations will see increased productivity, lower costs, higher efficiency, and possibly new growth opportunities as they use AI in more areas of the enterprise, such as personalizing services, supporting innovation, and helping with risk management. Taken together, that can deliver higher profitability, said Sreekar Krishna, U.S. leader of AI at professional services firm KPMG. "On the revenue side, it's potential is exponential: You can keep growing as long as you're bringing value to customers."

### *2.1.4.12. Industry-Specific Improvements*

In addition to the benefits listed above, AI can fuel the following industry-specific improvements:

- Retailers can leverage AI to improve pricing calculations for maximum returns, improve supply chain efficiency, and more effectively target their marketing campaigns. AI assists retail businesses in anticipating customer needs and determining the right amount of staffing.
- The technology enables the pharmaceutical industry to make predictions and analyze drug discovery data in ways that traditional technologies cannot.
- The financial industry can use AI to strengthen its fraud detection efforts.

It's crucial to keep in mind that businesses are facing difficulties as they figure out how to use AI to their advantage. Concerns include talent shortages, AI bias, government regulation of AI, and data management needed for machine learning projects. Additionally, without the necessary infrastructure and talent to apply AI, financial gains may prove elusive.

## 2.1.5. Challenges

Artificial intelligence is being used in business in more and more ways. However, a few crucial elements that restrict the application of AI technologies in business pose a threat to this growth.

1. **Data Scarcity:** The adoption of artificial intelligence is still difficult in some ways, despite the wealth of data that businesses have access to today. Large volumes of data are needed to train the model in machine learning, which underpins the majority of artificial intelligence applications in business. This restricts the application of AI in new business domains where data is not yet available. Because most AI applications involve supervised training on labelled data, the vast majority of the enormous amount of data we possess is often unstructured and unlabeled. This presents a challenge to the application of artificial intelligence in business.
2. **Algorithm Bias:** Due to the AI face recognition software's racial, ethnic, and gender biases, Microsoft, and Amazon have recently stopped selling it to law enforcement agencies. This demonstrates a significant AI challenge by showing how poorly an algorithm may perform when trained on skewed data. Such biases will eventually be adequately addressed by AI systems, but for the time being they seriously jeopardize the acceptance of AI in certain application domains.

Other challenges include:

- Limitations in current computing capability;
- Issues of threats to data security and privacy (since the use of AI involves the collection of sensitive information of people).

## 2.2. DEFINING AI-DRIVEN BUSINESS MODELS

AI is being incorporated into business models, which is a major shift in how businesses function and plan. The use of AI technologies to improve, innovate, or create new aspects of a company's operations, goods, or services is what defines AI-driven business models.

The ability to use data and machine learning (ML) technologies to build more intelligent, responsive, and efficient business processes is what sets AI-driven business models apart. The role of AI and ML in digital transformation, specifically in the manufacturing sector, is covered by Ahmed and Miskon (2020). They highlight how AI-driven models can improve decision-making processes and obtain quick insights by leveraging massive datasets produced by the integration of devices in the Internet of Things (IoT) environment. In industries like manufacturing, where integrating intelligent and integrated systems is essential, this strategy is critical to achieving resilience and efficiency (Ahmed and Miskon, 2020). Artificial intelligence-driven models are transforming conventional production paradigms in the field of customized manufacturing. Wan et al. (2020) examine how AI is being used in factories that produce customized goods, emphasizing how AI technologies allow manufacturing systems to extract process knowledge and adapt to external needs. This covers the creation of networked collaboration, extended service models, and intelligent production models. The self-perception, operations optimization, dynamic reconfiguration, and intelligent decision-making capabilities of the AI-driven customized manufacturing factory define it. These traits highlight how AI is revolutionizing manufacturing, leading to more adaptable and effective production techniques (Wan et al., 2020).

Another viewpoint on AI-driven business models is offered by the incorporation of AI in customer service, particularly in the e-commerce industry. Ping (2019) focuses on the concepts of AI customer service in e-commerce, demonstrating how AI can support human agents, improving productivity and service quality. The shortcomings of traditional models, such as their inefficiency and limited availability, have led to the integration of AI in customer service. By utilizing technologies like chatbots and automated response systems, AI-driven customer service models in e-commerce are distinguished by their capacity to deliver individualized and effective service (Ping, 2019) (Figure 2.3).

**Figure 2.3.** *AI-driven business models.*

*Source: https://media.licdn.com/dms/image/D5612AQGK31xCEAusyA/article-cover_image-shrink_720_1280/0/1703702263415?e=2147483647&v=beta&t=RcMZkzAGdUNfuPpRMAaR2Q-SGxK6zEMAvMNMjkC7ycI.*

The transition from conventional, frequently inflexible business processes to more dynamic, data-driven, and customer-centric methods characterizes the evolution of business models in the AI era. The capabilities of AI, ML, and IoT are combined in AI-driven business models to produce systems that are resilient, effective, and able to learn and adapt continuously. This development represents a shift toward more intelligent, responsive, and customized business operations that meet the unique demands of the market and customers.

Rethinking traditional business practices is necessary when integrating AI with traditional business strategies. AI-driven models create new value propositions and competitive advantages by often redefining traditional strategies rather than just supplementing them. AI technologies are used to improve operational efficiency, customer engagement, and innovation in a variety of sectors, including manufacturing and customer service.

AI-driven business models, which employ AI and ML to innovate and enhance different facets of business operations, mark a dramatic change in the business environment. AI integration is changing conventional business models in a variety of industries, including manufacturing and customer service, and resulting in more intelligent, flexible, and efficient business processes.

### 2.2.1. Characteristics of AI-Driven Business Models

Many industries are changing as a result of AI-driven business models that incorporate cutting-edge AI technologies into their fundamental operations and strategies. These models can be distinguished from conventional business models by a number of important characteristics.

Focusing on using AI to improve operational efficiency and decision-making is one of the main traits of AI-driven business models. Metelskaia et al. (2018) provide a business model canvas that highlights the essential components of AI-driven business models and is especially made for AI solutions. AI-tailored value propositions, multi-sided platforms for customer segments, automated services for customer relationships, and social network integration in marketing channels are some of the elements that make up this canvas. The canvas also stresses the value of investors as important collaborators and the importance of human resources and research and development (R&D) as vital resources. This framework highlights AI's distinct value-creating capabilities and illustrates how AI-driven business models are built differently from conventional models (Metelskaia et al., 2018).

AI-driven business models are especially revolutionary in the healthcare sector. Value creation, customer delivery, and market communication are three distinctive design components that Kulkov (2023) identifies in his analysis of next-generation business models for AI start-ups in the healthcare industry. The various ways AI can be incorporated into healthcare business models are demonstrated by these components, which are framed within 16 distinct models and three overarching design themes. This study emphasizes how AI is helping to develop new healthcare value propositions, like efficient patient care and personalized medicine, and how crucial AI is to conveying and delivering these benefits to the market (Kulkov, 2023).

The use of AI-driven business models in customized manufacturing is one of their other important features. Wan et al. (2020) talk about how AI is being used in factories that produce customized goods, with an emphasis on networked collaboration, intelligent production, and extended service models. These factories stand out for their ability to perceive themselves, optimize operations, reconfigure dynamically, and make intelligent decisions. By incorporating AI technologies, manufacturing systems can become more flexible and efficient in production by extracting process knowledge and adapting to external demands. This research shows how AI-driven models can change conventional manufacturing procedures into systems that are more responsive and nimbler (Wan et al., 2020).

AI-driven business models can be identified by their creative application of AI to develop novel value propositions, improve operational effectiveness, and revolutionize established business procedures. By utilizing AI's special abilities to analyze data, learn on its own, and make deft decisions, these models help businesses operate in a more responsive and dynamic manner. The application of AI in a variety of industries, such as manufacturing and healthcare, demonstrates the revolutionary potential of these models and presents fresh chances for development and innovation.

AI-driven business models are characterized by their emphasis on using AI to improve decision-making, operational effectiveness, and the development of new value propositions.

These models show how AI is having a revolutionary effect on the contemporary business landscape by introducing novel ways to incorporate AI into business operations, thereby reshaping industries.

## 2.2.2. Evolution of Business Models in the AI Era

A new era in business has been brought about by the introduction of AI, which has drastically changed conventional business models and introduced novel paradigms. A move toward more data-driven, customer-centric, and technologically sophisticated methods characterizes this evolution.

The evolving nature of human-machine interaction and its implications for competitive business strategies are important aspects of this evolution. Delbufalo, Di Bernardo, and Risso (2022) examine how people interact with machines in the digital age and stress the necessity for companies to balance artificial and human intelligence. They contend that sustainable business practices that successfully combine AI's mechanical thinking and human creativity are what will make companies competitive in the AI era. In decision-making processes, where AI can offer data-driven insights and humans can contribute with creative and strategic thinking, this integration is essential. The study emphasizes how crucial it is to redefine business models to account for roles involving AI and human intelligence in order to keep companies competitive and innovative.

AI's function in social interaction and brand engagement is another aspect of how business models are changing. The digital age's effects of brand algorithms and social interaction, with an emphasis on how AI and related technologies change marketing tactics and customer interactions. Big data, AI and the IoT are the main forces behind the revolution in communication and interactions between people, goods, and brands. The study emphasizes the impact of AI-mediated algorithms on customer engagement and value creation, emphasizing the move toward more interactive and personalized marketing strategies. The way that business models are evolving shows that AI and digital transformation play a major role in establishing and preserving customer relationships.

The convergence of 5G technology and AI is redefining business models and propelling digital transformation in a number of industries. The creation of fresh, cutting-edge services and applications, like improved image recognition and complex natural language AI systems, is being encouraged by this synergy. These technological developments are creating new avenues for customer contact and service delivery in addition to optimizing operational procedures. The combination of 5G and AI signals a move toward more intelligent, flexible, and networked business models that take advantage of 5G networks' extensive and fast capabilities to the fullest extent possible.

The increasing integration of technology and AI in various business operations is a hallmark of the evolution of business models in the AI era. This transformation is characterized by a move toward more data-driven decision-making, improved human-machine interaction, and creative customer engagement and marketing strategies. This evolution is accelerated by integrating AI with other cutting-edge technologies like 5G, which creates more flexible, effective, and customer-focused business models.

### 2.2.3. The Intersection of AI and Traditional Business Strategies

The amalgamation of AI with conventional business tactics signifies a significant transformation in the business environment, amalgamating the advantages of AI with conventional business methodologies. New paradigms for innovation, strategy formulation, and competitive advantage are being created by this intersection. The combination of AI and learning analytics is transforming conventional business models and strategies in the education technology (EdTech) industry. Alam and Mohanty (2022) talk about how learning analytics and AI are being utilized in EdTech businesses to create customized learning experiences. This integration represents a move away from conventional educational models and toward more individualized, data-driven strategies. The study emphasizes the need for a deeper understanding of data and its potential to improve learning experiences, as well as the obstacles and driving forces behind this shift. This example shows how creative, data-driven approaches can be used to integrate AI into established industries like education and transform them.

The wider effects of AI in business are discussed by Wisniewski (2020), who emphasizes the necessity for leaders and decision-makers of the future to comprehend AI and incorporate it into their plans. The incorporation of AI into business curricula, with a focus on the significance of training leaders capable of navigating the intricacies of AI and its business implications. This strategy reflects the need for a new generation of business leaders who are skilled at incorporating AI into conventional business models and strategies as well as the growing understanding of AI's strategic significance. The study emphasizes how AI has the power to fundamentally alter business practices and business education.

The work of Fenwick, Vermeulen, and Corrales (2018) investigates how businesses and governments are responding to artificial intelligence, especially in light of dynamic regulation and innovation ecosystems. They talk about how companies and authorities are adjusting to the difficulties brought about by disruptive artificial intelligence technologies. The study emphasizes the value of innovation ecosystems and dynamic regulation in fostering collaborations between well-established businesses and startups with an AI focus. This strategy for mitigating AI's effects points to a strategic alignment between AI's innovative potential and established business procedures. The study offers information on how companies can use AI to their advantage by strategically managing its disruptive nature.

A synergistic fusion of innovation and tried-and-true methods characterizes the intersection of AI and traditional business strategies. Many industries, including education and more general business practices, are changing as a result of this integration. Understanding and utilizing AI's potential within the framework of established business models, preparing the next generation of leaders for this new environment, and modifying legal and policy frameworks to account for AI's disruptive potential are all crucial (Figure 2.4).

**Figure 2.4.** *AI and traditional business strategies.*

*Source: https://cdn.westmonroe.com/-/media/west-monroe-images/client-stories-images/amoderndataplatform_2504x1440hero.png?cx=0.5&cy=0.5&cw=1176&ch=848&hash=29F386B0E506FF2A12BD620D75633AF2.*

## 2.3. BETTER DECISION-MAKING AND DATA ANALYSIS

AI can analyze massive amounts of data, identify patterns, and predict outcomes, which can enhance data analysis and commercial decision-making. Companies can use AI to gain insights that aren't always evident to humans and then use those insights to inform more informed decisions. AI can be used, for example, in the healthcare industry to analyze medical imaging and patient data to help doctors diagnose patients and develop treatment plans. This could lead to more precise diagnosis and better patient outcomes. AI is useful in the finance industry for risk assessment and fraud detection. AI can help stop financial losses by sifting through enormous amounts of financial data to identify patterns that may indicate fraud. AI can also be used to identify market trends and opportunities, which can help businesses make better decisions and stay ahead of the competition.

In general, using AI for data analysis and decision-making may help businesses make better decisions, reduce the likelihood of errors and monetary losses, and stay competitive in their respective industries.

### 2.3.1. Enhanced Customer Experience

AI can enhance the customer experience by providing personalized and prompt customer service. AI-powered chatbots and virtual assistants can respond to frequently asked customer questions, freeing up customer service representatives to deal with more complex issues. Chatbots can be programmed to recommend products, answer commonly asked questions, and even make reservations or purchases for users. This could improve customer satisfaction and reduce wait times. AI can also be used to customize the customer experience. By examining consumer data, AI may generate tailored product recommendations and promotions that are tailored to the preferences and actions of individual customers. This could lead to a rise in repeat business and customer loyalty. AI can also be used to gather consumer feedback through sentiment analysis and surveying. This can help businesses pinpoint areas that need improvement and make changes to improve the customer experience. Overall, by using AI to provide individualized and responsive customer care, businesses may improve customer satisfaction, loyalty, and their capacity to compete in the market.

### 2.3.2. Reduced Operational Costs

AI can help businesses reduce operating costs by automating tedious tasks and optimizing workflows. For example, an Accenture report claims that by 2035, AI can double economic growth rates and boost labor productivity by as much as 40%. By automating processes like data entry, assembly-line work, and quality control, businesses can reduce their human labor costs and save money. By evaluating data and identifying areas for improvement, AI may also enhance workflows. This could lead to increased efficiency and less waste, further reducing operating costs. For example, the logistics industry can use AI to reduce transportation costs and optimize delivery routes. By analyzing data on traffic patterns, weather, and other factors, AI can identify the best routes and modes of transportation.

All things considered, by automating processes and optimizing workflows, AI may significantly reduce operating costs for companies, enabling them to function more efficiently and preserve their competitiveness in the market.

### 2.3.3. AI-Driven Industries

Numerous industries are feeling the effects of artificial intelligence. According to a PwC analysis, industries like healthcare, manufacturing, and transportation are among those that AI is most likely to drastically disrupt. AI is being used in the healthcare industry to identify patterns in patient data, evaluate medical images, and recommend treatments. For example, AI-powered algorithms can analyze mammograms to detect breast cancer early, improving patient outcomes. The industrial sector is using AI to improve quality assurance, reduce costs, and streamline production processes. AI-powered robots, for example, could perform assembly and packaging tasks, reducing labor costs and increasing productivity. AI is being used in the transportation industry to improve safety, reduce costs, and optimize delivery routes. For example, self-driving cars are developing AI-powered sensors and algorithms to navigate roads and avoid collisions. All things considered, artificial intelligence is revolutionizing a variety of industries, and this trend is most likely to continue in the years to come, resulting in improved efficacy, productivity, and results.

### 2.3.4. Healthcare

AI has the potential to completely change the healthcare sector in a number of ways, including by automating administrative tasks, cutting costs, and improving diagnosis and treatment. One industry that has already adopted AI is medical imaging. AI algorithms may analyze medical images such as X-rays, CT scans, and MRI scans to look for anomalies and help with diagnosis. For example, extremely precise AI-powered mammography breast cancer detection algorithms have been developed. AI is also being used in the field of drug discovery.

Through the analysis of vast amounts of data regarding chemicals and their interactions with the human body, AI systems are able to identify potential therapeutic candidates and forecast their efficacy. This might speed up the search for new drugs and the time it takes for cutting-edge medications to reach the market. AI can also be used to improve patient outcomes by developing customized treatment plans. By analyzing patient data such as medical history, genetics, and lifestyle factors, AI algorithms can identify the most appropriate treatment options for individual patients.

### 2.3.5. Retail

Using AI to forecast future product demand allows retailers to modify their inventory levels. AI is also being used to improve personalization and product recommendations. By examining customer information like demographics, search, and purchase histories, and other data, AI algorithms can determine which products are most likely to appeal to each individual customer. This could help retailers increase their customer base and revenue. Finally, AI is being used to improve in-store experiences. AI-capable robots and kiosks can assist consumers with product identification, feature, and pricing information, and payment processing. This can increase overall customer satisfaction and reduce wait times. All things considered, artificial intelligence is transforming the retail industry by improving the in-store atmosphere, optimizing the supply chain, facilitating better product recommendations and customization, and improving the consumer shopping experience.

### 2.3.6. Manufacturing

AI is transforming the manufacturing industry in a number of ways. One of the most important uses of AI in manufacturing is predictive maintenance. By evaluating data from sensors and other sources, AI systems are able to predict when machines are likely to break down and plan maintenance beforehand. Production may increase and downtime may decrease as a result. AI is also used in production process optimization. AI algorithms can analyze data from industrial processes to find inefficiencies and suggest fixes. Businesses can save money, increase output, and decrease waste by doing this. AI is also being applied to manufacturing to enhance quality control (Figure 2.5).

**Figure 2.5.** *Implementing AI-driven automation in manufacturing industry.*

*Source: https://www.pranathiss.com/blog/wp-content/uploads/Implementing-AI-driven-automation-in-Manufacturing-and-Industry.png.*

## 2.4. PREDICTIVE ANALYTICS

Predictive analytics is a subset of data analytics that analyzes historical data and forecasts future results using statistical methods and machine learning algorithms. It is done by looking for connections, patterns, and trends in data sets that can be utilized to forecast future events.

Predictive analytics has applications across a wide range of industries, including:

- **Marketing:** Increase conversion rates, customize offers and marketing messaging, and find new clients with predictive analytics.
- **Predictive:** Analytics can be applied in the healthcare sector to identify patients at risk for specific illnesses or conditions, forecast readmission rates following discharge, and enhance patient outcomes in general.

- **Finance:** Finding patterns in financial data through predictive analytics can help identify high-risk loans, spot fraud, and predict market trends.
- **Manufacturing:** Predictive analytics can improve production process optimization, downtime reduction, and quality control.
- **Transportation:** Route optimization, safety enhancement, and fuel consumption reduction are all possible with predictive analytics.

Data preparation, data inquiry, data visualization, model selection, model training, testing, and validation are often among the steps in predictive analytics processes. Numerous methods, including neural networks, decision trees, random forests, and linear regression, can be used to develop predictive models. Predictive analytics is a potent tool that could help businesses make better decisions, become more efficient, and obtain a competitive edge in today's data-driven environment.

### 2.4.1. Chat Bot's And Virtual Assistants

Virtual assistants and chatbots are two instances of conversational AI systems that converse with users and reply to their questions or requests through the use of NLP and machine learning. Computer programmers that can mimic conversations between human users via text or voice messaging are known as chat bots. They are helpful for many purposes, such as individual productivity, customer service, and e-commerce. Chatbots are a useful tool for businesses to automate customer service procedures and offer round-the-clock customer support. They can also be used to adjust marketing messaging and offer suggestions according to the tastes and actions of customers. On the other hand, virtual assistants are AI-powered digital assistants that can help users with a variety of tasks, such as making appointments, sending out reminders, and responding to inquiries. Users can communicate with them using natural language commands because they can be integrated with smart phones, smart homes, and other digital devices. Virtual assistants can help users handle their everyday responsibilities more effectively.

Personalized recommendations can also be given by these assistants based on the users' preferences and actions. Chatbots and virtual assistants use NLP and machine learning algorithms to identify speech patterns, comprehend user intent, and respond to user inquiries in a conversational and natural way. They can also improve their ability to meet client demands by learning from previous interactions and honing their responses through practice. Chat bot's and virtual assistants are generally effective technologies that can help firms improve user personalization, streamline processes, and boost customer engagement.

## 2.4.2. Personalization

The process of tailoring experiences, goods, and services to a customer's unique requirements and preferences is known as personalization. The foundation of personalization is the notion that each client is distinct and that companies can obtain a competitive edge by offering solutions that are specifically customized to each individual's needs.

Personalization has advantages in many fields and applications, including ecommerce, marketing, healthcare, and finance. Examples of personalization include:

- **Suggestions for Products:** E-commerce websites can use customer data, such as past purchascs and browsing habits, to providc personalized product recommendations that are more likely to fit each user's preferences.
- **Material Personalization:** Websites and social media platforms can recommend personalized content, like news articles, videos, or social network posts, based on information about users' interests and behavior.
- **Personalized Marketing:** Businesses may generate tailored marketing messages and offers that are more likely to appeal to each customer's unique preferences by using data on consumer demographics, interests, and behavior.
- **Personalized Healthcare:** Medical professionals can create personalized treatment plans by gathering information on a patient's genetics, medical history, and lifestyle.

Machine learning algorithms, which can evaluate vast volumes of data and identify patterns and relationships that can be utilized to produce customized forecasts and recommendations, are typically what make personalization possible. By learning from past interactions, machine learning algorithms are able to adjust when customer preferences change over time.

All things considered, personalization is a powerful tool that businesses can use to increase customer engagement, loyalty, and gain a competitive edge by offering solutions that are specifically designed to meet the needs and preferences of each individual customer. The use of technology to automate repetitive or manual tasks, improve workflows, and reduce the need for human interaction in business processes is known as process automation.

Numerous industries and applications, such as manufacturing, banking, healthcare, and customer service, can benefit from automation. Process automation includes, for instance:

- **Robotic Process Automation (RPA):** RPA is the use of software robots to automate repetitive tasks like data entry, invoice processing, and answering customer service inquiries. RPA can boost output, reduce mistakes, and free up employees' time so they can focus on more challenging tasks.
- **Business Process Management (BPM):** BPM is the process of using software tools to model, assess, and optimize business processes. Businesses can find inefficiencies in their processes, automate tedious tasks, and boost productivity with the help of business process management (BPM).
- **Machine Learning (ML) and Artificial Intelligence (AI):** These two technologies can be used to automate decision-making tasks like consumer segmentation, fraud detection, and predictive maintenance. ML and AI algorithms are capable of analyzing large data sets, and on the basis of the patterns and correlations found in the data, they can make predictions.

Process automation enables businesses to improve output, reduce costs, and improve the quality of their products and services. Furthermore, automation can free up workers to focus on more strategic tasks like innovation and corporate growth. Organizations must carefully consider the potential effects of automation on their workforce in order to ensure that they have a plan in place to reskill and upskill individuals who may be impacted by it.

## 2.5. EXAMPLES OF SUCCESSFUL AI-DRIVEN BUSINESSES

Here are some examples of successful AI-driven businesses:

### 2.5.1. Amazon

Among the biggest online retailers globally, Amazon is a multinational technology company headquartered in Seattle, Washington. Jeff Bezos established the business in 1994, initially operating as an online bookshop. Amazon is a modern marketplace that provides a vast array of goods and services, such as digital streaming, cloud computing, artificial intelligence, and e-commerce. Amazon has used AI in many ways to change the way consumers shop online. For example, the business uses AI to customize product recommendations according to a client's past browsing and purchases. Amazon boosts sales and enhances the shopping experience by making it easier for customers to find products they are more likely to be interested in. Amazon leverages AI not only for customization but also for supply chain optimization and warehouse automation. The company has created a range of AI-powered robots and drones that can move goods around warehouses more accurately and efficiently than human workers. The Echo smart speaker, which uses Alexa, the company's voice-activated assistant, is one of Amazon's AI-powered products. Because of the success of its consumer devices, the Echo and Alexa, Amazon has made a name for itself in the expanding smart home technology sector. Generally speaking, Amazon's use of AI has aided the company in boosting output, customizing customer experiences, and developing innovative, previously impractical business models. By continuing to invest in artificial intelligence, Amazon is likely to maintain its position as a leader in e-commerce innovation.

## 2.5.2. Netflix

On-demand viewing of TV shows, movies, documentaries, and other media is available to subscribers of the Netflix video streaming service. Founded in 1997 by Reed Hastings and Marc Randolph, the company started out as a DVD-by-mail service. Currently, Netflix boasts over 200 million members in over 190 countries. Netflix employs AI in a number of ways to enhance its content distribution system and personalize the user experience. For example, the business offers each user tailored content recommendations by using AI algorithms to analyze user comments and viewing habits. To make recommendations that are more likely to be of interest to the user, these algorithms take into account the user's viewing history, preferences, and time of day. In addition to customization, Netflix uses AI to optimize its content delivery network, reducing buffering and ensuring a high-quality viewing experience. The company uses machine learning algorithms to analyze network performance and then makes real-time adjustments to video quality based on the user's device capabilities and internet connection speed.

## 2.5.3. UBER

Uber is a ride-sharing business that uses a mobile app to link drivers and passengers. Since its founding in 2009 by Travis Kalanick and Garrett Camp, the business has grown to operate in over 700 cities across the globe. Uber uses AI in a number of ways to streamline operations and enhance the user experience for both drivers and passengers. For example, the business optimizes its pricing and routing algorithms and estimates rider demand using machine learning algorithms. This makes it possible to match drivers and passengers quickly and effectively and ensures that drivers receive fair compensation for their labor. Uber employs AI in addition to optimization to increase driver security. The business has created Real-Time ID Check, a facial recognition system driven by AI, which verifies drivers before they pick up passengers. This increases passenger and driver safety by lowering fraud. AI has also been utilized by Uber to create new business prospects. For instance, the business introduced Uber Eats, a service that uses AI algorithms to predict and enhance the promptness of food deliveries. The business has also made investments in the technology that will eventually enable driverless cars to take the place of human drivers. All things considered, Uber's application of AI has transformed the transportation sector and opened up new business prospects. It is expected that Uber's ongoing investments in AI will support the company's continued leadership in innovation.

### 2.5.4. ZILLOW

Users can purchase, sell, rent, and finance homes on Zillow, an online real estate marketplace. Rich Barton and Lloyd Frink started the business in 2006, and it has since grown to rank among the most popular real estate websites globally, drawing in over 200 million monthly visitors. Zillow employs AI in a number of ways to enhance user experience and give users more precise and tailored information. For example, the business uses machine learning algorithms to calculate real estate prices and to give clients a Zestimate, which is an estimate of a house's worth derived from a variety of data sources, including neighborhood statistics, recent sales, and other variables. Zillow employs AI to increase the accuracy of its real estate listings in addition to using it for valuations. The business has created an AI system that recognizes and classifies information in property photos, such as the number of bedrooms and bathrooms, using computer vision. This ensures real estate listings are more accurate and thorough, which can enhance user experience and shorten the time it takes to sell a home. Through initiatives like its Instant Offers campaign, Zillow has also leveraged AI to create new business opportunities. Through the use of AI, this project links homeowners with investors who are ready to purchase their homes swiftly and without the inconvenience of conventional home selling processes. In general, Zillow has benefited from using AI to enhance user experience, give users more precise and personalized data, and open up new business opportunities. Zillow is probably going to stay at the forefront of innovation in the real estate sector if it keeps investing in AI.

## 2.6. FUTURE PROSPECTS OF AI-DRIVEN BUSINESSES

Given the wide range of industries AI can revolutionize and the way it will change how businesses function, the future of AI-driven enterprises is extremely bright.

Here are a few reasons why:

- **Enhanced Efficiency:** AI has the potential to automate repetitive and time-consuming tasks, freeing up employees to focus on more challenging and creative tasks. This could lead to increased productivity, profitability, and effectiveness.
- **Enhanced Personalization:** AI may assist firms in tailoring their goods and services to specific clients, improving customer satisfaction and loyalty.
- **Better Decision Making:** Using AI, firms can analyze vast volumes of data and come to more educated conclusions, which will improve business outcomes.
- **New Business Models:** AI can create new business models that were previously unimaginable, such driverless vehicles, personalized product recommendations, and predictive maintenance.
- **Competitive Advantage:** AI can give companies an advantage over their rivals by allowing them to work more effectively, offer better consumer experiences, and make more informed decisions.

All things considered, businesses that use AI have a very promising future. As AI advances and becomes more accessible, companies of all sizes will be able to use it to improve operations and create new revenue streams. Businesses must carefully consider the ethical implications of AI and allot the necessary resources to ensure that their use of the technology is both sustainable and moral.

### 2.6.1. Integration with Other Emerging Technologies

AI is expected to combine with other cutting-edge technologies in the future to produce innovative and novel applications across a range of sectors. Here are some instances of how AI might be used with other cutting-edge technologies:

- **Internet of Things (IoT):** AI and IoT devices can be used to build more intelligent and automated systems. For example, AI algorithms may examine data from Internet of Things sensors to predict maintenance needs, maximize energy efficiency, and increase overall efficacy.
- **Blockchain:** Blockchain technology and artificial intelligence together could improve the security and transparency of data exchange. For example, blockchain data can be analyzed by AI algorithms to identify fraud or other anomalies.

- **Augmented Reality (AR):** By combining AI and AR technology, users can have more individualized and immersive experiences. AI systems, for instance, might examine user data to offer tailored recommendations or improve the AR experience.
- **5G Networks:** 5G networks can process data more rapidly and intelligently by incorporating AI. For example, AI algorithms used for real-time data analysis and decision-making can produce more effective and efficient systems.

The integration of AI with other emerging technologies is generally expected to yield innovative and creative applications across multiple industries. Organizations will need to be aware of the latest developments and prepared to incorporate AI with these technologies in order to remain competitive and provide the greatest customer experiences as these technologies advance.

### 2.6.2. Increased Automation and Autonomy

Among AI's primary benefits are increased automation and autonomy. Artificial Intelligence has the capability to automate numerous repetitive and ordinary tasks, allowing humans to focus on more demanding and innovative tasks. It might also enable machines to function independently and form opinions without the need for human input.

Numerous advantages for firms can result from increased automation and autonomy, including:

- **Increased Productivity:** Automation and autonomy can increase the accuracy and speed of many corporate processes, resulting in increased productivity.
- **Lower Labor Costs:** Businesses can cut labor costs and save money by automating regular processes.
- **Increased Safety:** The employment of autonomous systems lowers the chance of worker injury or death in hazardous or dangerous areas. Better and more informed decision-making is made possible by autonomous systems' ability to analyze vast volumes of data and make judgments in light of that data.
- **New Business Models:** New business models that weren't previously feasible, like autonomous cars or drones for delivery and transportation, can be made possible by automation and autonomy.

Nevertheless, there are possible risks and challenges associated with increased automation and autonomy. For example, the use of autonomous systems, such as self-driving cars, may raise ethical concerns, and concerns about job loss may arise if more work is automated. Organizations must thus carefully balance the potential risks and benefits of increased automation and autonomy in order to make sure that their use of AI is morally righteous and long-lasting.

### 2.6.3. Potential for Disruption in Traditional Industries

The potential for disruption in well-established industries is among the most significant consequences of AI-driven organizations. AI has the potential to transform many different industries by improving decision-making, automating procedures, and creating new business models. Listed below are a few sectors that AI could potentially disrupt:

- **Industrial:** AI has the potential to increase the automation and efficiency of industrial processes, which will boost output and reduce expenses. Robots with AI capabilities, for instance, can be used for product assembly and quality control inspections.
- **Retail:** AI can offer more customized shopping experiences, boosting client loyalty and satisfaction. For example, using data from past purchases or browsing patterns, AI algorithms can be used to suggest products to consumers.
- **Treatment:** By enabling more individualized and accurate treatment, AI can enhance patient outcomes. For example, AI algorithms can be used to analyze medical photos, recognize diseases, or develop personalized treatment plans for each patient.
- **Transportation:** AI has the potential to create autonomous and more efficient transportation systems, which would save costs and increase safety. For example, delivery and transportation can be handled by drones or self-driving cars.
- **Finance:** AI can improve investment selection and lower risk by assisting with more precise and effective financial analysis. AI algorithms, for instance, can be used to evaluate financial data and suggest investments.

AI has the potential to completely transform many business processes, which poses a serious risk of upending traditional industries. This might lead to new business opportunities, but it might also have negative social and economic effects, like job losses. Organizations must thoroughly assess the possible impacts of AI on their sector and take the necessary safety measures to guarantee that the shift to AI-driven operations is morally and sustainably done.

## REFERENCES

1. Agbaji, A. L. (2021). Leadership and managerial decision-making in an AI-enabled oil and gas industry. https://doi.org/10.2118/207613-MS.
2. Ahmed, S., & Miskon, S. (2020). IoT-driven resiliency with artificial intelligence, machine learning and analytics for digital transformation. In *2020 International Conference on Decision Aid Sciences and Application (DASA)* (pp. 1205–1208).
3. Alam, A., & Mohanty, A. (2022). Business models, business strategies, and innovations in EdTech companies: Integration of learning analytics and artificial intelligence in higher education. In *2022 IEEE 6th Conference on Information and Communication Technology (CICT)* (pp. 1–6). IEEE.
4. Bahador, M. H., & Ibraim, S. S. (2021). Technology innovations toward sustainable growth of small and medium enterprise (SMEs): Aftermath COVID-19 pandemic. *International Journal of Academic Research in Business and Social Sciences, 11*, 1235–1241.
5. Bhatt, K., & Kumar, S. M. (2022). Reindustrialization using industry 4.0 maturity models in MSMEs and tenets of digital transformation phases. In *2022 Fourth International Conference on Emerging Research in Electronics, Computer Science and Technology (ICERECT)* (pp. 1–6). IEEE.
6. Breidbach, C. F., & Maglio, P. (2020). Accountable algorithms? The ethical implications of data-driven business models. *Journal of Service Management, 31*(2), 163–185.
7. Bulatnikov, V., & Constantin, C. P. (2021). Systematic analysis of literature on the marketing of healthcare systems: Challenges for Russian and Romanian healthcare systems. *Healthcare, 9*(6), 656.
8. Cao, L. (2021). Artificial intelligence in retail: Applications and value creation logics. *International Journal of Retail & Distribution Management, 49*(7), 958–976.
9. Coltey, E., Alonso, D., Vassigh, S., & Chen, S. C. (2022). Towards an AI-driven marketplace for small businesses during COVID-19. *SN Computer Science, 3*(6), 441.
10. Crockett, K. A., Colyer, E., Gerber, L., & Latham, A. (2021). Building trustworthy AI solutions: A case for practical solutions for small businesses. *IEEE Transactions on Artificial Intelligence, 2*(1), 1–1.
11. Enholm, I. M., Papagiannidis, E., Mikalef, P., & Krogstie, J. (2022). Artificial intelligence and business value: A literature review. *Information Systems Frontiers, 24*(5), 1709–1734.

12. Escajeda, H. G. (2018). Legal education: A new growth vision: Part I–The issue: Sustainable growth or dead cat bounce: A strategic inflection point analysis. *Nebraska Law Review, 97*, 628.

13. Fang, J. (2023). Research on the design of business models and transformation management of new entrepreneurial ventures driven by artificial intelligence. *BCP Business & Management, 49*, 36–41.

14. Fenwick, M., Vermeulen, E. P., & Corrales, M. (2018). Business and regulatory responses to artificial intelligence: Dynamic regulation, innovation ecosystems and the strategic management of disruptive technology. In *Robotics, AI and the Future of Law* (pp. 81–103). Springer.

15. Gomes, P., Verçosa, L., Melo, F., Silva, V., Filho, C. B., & Bezerra, B. (2022). Artificial intelligence-based methods for business processes: A systematic literature review. *Applied Sciences, 12*(5), 2314.

16. Hahn, C., Traunecker, T., Niever, M., & Basedow, G. N. (2020). Exploring AI-driven business models: Conceptualization and expectations in the machinery industry. In *2020 IEEE International Conference on Industrial Engineering and Engineering Management (IEEM)* (pp. 567–570). IEEE.

17. Huang, J., Beling, P., Freeman, L., & Zeng, Y. (2021). Trustworthy AI for digital engineering transformation. *Journal of Integrated Design and Process Science, 25*(1), 1–7.

18. Ilieva, R., Ivanova, M., Peycheva, T., & Nikolov, Y. (2021). Modelling in support of decision making in business intelligence. In *Integration Challenges for Analytics, Business Intelligence, and Data Mining* (pp. 115–144).

19. John, M. M., Olsson, H. H., & Bosch, J. (2023). Towards an AI□driven business development framework: A multi□case study. *Journal of Software: Evolution and Process, 35*(6), e2432.

20. Kanbach, D. K., Heiduk, L., Blueher, G., Schreiter, M., & Lahmann, A. (2023). The GenAI is out of the bottle: Generative artificial intelligence from a business model innovation perspective. *Review of Managerial Science, 18(3)*.

21. Kulkov, I. (2023). Next-generation business models for artificial intelligence start-ups in the healthcare industry. *International Journal of Entrepreneurial Behavior & Research, 29*(4), 860–885.

22. Kutz, J., Neuhüttler, J., Spilski, J., & Lachmann, T. (2022). Implementation of AI technologies in manufacturing – success factors and challenges. *AI & Society, 37*(2), 445–463.

23. Mariani, M. M., Machado, I., & Nambisan, S. (2023). Types of innovation and artificial intelligence: A systematic quantitative literature review and research agenda. *Journal of Business Research, 155*, 113364.
24. Marrone, T., & Testa, P. (2022). Brand algorithms and social engagement in the digital era. *The Human Side of Service Engineering, 62*, 62.
25. McKinsey. (2023). The economic potential of generative AI: The next productivity frontier. Retrieved from: https://www.mckinsey.com/capabilities/mckinsey-digital/our-insights/the-economic-potential-of-generative-ai-the-next-productivity-frontier#introduction (accessed on 1 November 2024).
26. Metelskaia, I., Ignatyeva, O., Denef, S., & Samsonowa, T. (2018). A business model template for AI solutions. In *Proceedings of the International Conference on Intelligent Science and Technology* (pp. 35–41).
27. Mishra, S., & Tripathi, A. R. (2021). AI business model: An integrative business approach. *Journal of Innovation and Entrepreneurship, 10*(1), 18.
28. Nortje, M. A., & Grobbelaar, S. S. (2020). A framework for the implementation of artificial intelligence in business enterprises: A readiness model. In *2020 IEEE International Conference on Engineering, Technology and Innovation (ICE/ITMC)* (pp. 1–10). IEEE.
29. Pfau, W., & Rimpp, P. (2021). AI-enhanced business models for digital entrepreneurship. In *Digital Entrepreneurship: Impact on Business and Society* (pp. 121–140).
30. Ping, N. L. (2019). Constructs for artificial intelligence customer service in E-commerce. In *2019 6th International Conference on Research and Innovation in Information Systems (ICRIIS)* (pp. 1–6). IEEE.
31. Popa, A., Amaba, B., & Daniels, J. (2021). A framework of best practices for delivering successful artificial intelligence projects: A case study demonstration. In *SPE Annual Technical Conference and Exhibition* (p. D021S022R002). SPE.
32. Rojas, A., & Tuomi, A. (2022). Reimagining the sustainable social development of AI for the service sector: The role of startups. *Journal of Ethics in Entrepreneurship and Technology, 2*(1), 39–54.
33. Sai, B., Thanigaivelu, S., Shivaani, N., Babu, S., & Ramaa, A. (2022). Integration of chatbots in the procurement stage of a supply chain. In *2022 6th International Conference on Computation System and Information Technology for Sustainable Solutions (CSITSS)* (pp. 1–5). IEEE.

34. Thomas, A. (2020). Convergence and digital fusion lead to competitive differentiation. *Business Process Management Journal, 26*(3), 707–720.
35. Turktarhan, G., Aleong, D. S., & Aleong, C. (2022). Re-architecting the firm for increased value: How business models are adapting to the new AI environment. *Journal of Global Business Insights, 7*(1), 33–49.
36. Wan, J., Li, X., Dai, H. N., Kusiak, A., Martinez-Garcia, M., & Li, D. (2020). Artificial-intelligence-driven customized manufacturing factory: Key technologies, applications, and challenges. *Proceedings of the IEEE, 109*(4), 377–398.
37. Whitfield, S., & Zborowski, M. (2019). SPE offshore Europe industry emerges as revitalized, digitally motivated. *Journal of Petroleum Technology, 71*(11), 48–52.
38. Wisniewski, H. S. (2020). What is the business with AI? Preparing future decision-makers and leaders. *Technology & Innovation, 21*(4), 1–14.
39. Zarifis, A., Holland, C. P., & Milne, A. (2019). Evaluating the impact of AI on insurance: The four emerging AI-and data-driven business models. *Emerald Open Research, 1*, 15.

CHAPTER 3

# AI IN CUSTOMER SERVICE AND EXPERIENCE

## Contents

# INTRODUCTION

Customer experience has emerged as a critical determinant of organizational success in the modern business environment. Although companies have historically prioritized product-centric models, there has been a noticeable shift in favor of customer-centric strategies. A company's bottom line is greatly impacted by providing a superior customer experience, which is a key factor in fostering customer loyalty, retention, and lifetime value (Homburg et al., 2017).

The term "customer experience" refers to all of the interactions that take place between a consumer and a brand, from the initial introduction to the brand to the post-purchase assistance. Businesses must innovate and improve their customer experience strategies in response to changing consumer expectations. Businesses that put the customer experience first beat their rivals in terms of revenue growth and customer satisfaction, per a Forrester Research study.

The importance of the customer experience has increased with the rise of social media and digital platforms. Thanks to the widespread dissemination of customer experiences, clients can now affect the opinions and choices of other possible clients. The increased level of transparency calls for proactive management and enhancement of the customer experience. Furthermore, studies show that increased customer advocacy, brand reputation, and repeat business are all correlated with positive customer experiences.

The application of artificial intelligence (AI) has become a game-changing tool for improving customer experience. These technologies improve customer journeys by enabling businesses to provide personalized, real-time interactions, automate repetitive tasks, and anticipate customer needs. Artificial intelligence (AI)-powered chatbots and virtual assistants, for example, offer prompt assistance, enhancing customer satisfaction and response times.

There are also a lot of operational advantages to using AI in customer service. Businesses can increase productivity, cut expenses, and better allocate resources by automating customer service procedures. Additionally, businesses can continuously improve their customer experience strategies by using artificial intelligence tools to analyze large amounts of customer data and generate insightful information (Wirtz et al., 2019)

Even with these benefits, there are still difficulties when incorporating AI into customer experience. Businesses need to take serious measures to address issues like data security and privacy, transparency, and ethical considerations in AI applications. Additionally, a significant investment in talent and technology as well as a cultural shift toward innovation and customer centricity are necessary for the successful implementation of AI-driven customer experience solutions. Research and development in this field will continue to influence how customers interact with businesses in the future and present new opportunities for meaningful and successful customer engagement. Prospective advancements, like sophisticated predictive analytics and increasingly natural AI interactions, hold the potential to significantly transform the customer experience domain.

We investigate how artificial intelligence might enhance customer support. In particular, the ability of AI-driven technologies to provide tailored solutions, improve customer satisfaction, and expedite general customer service processes and experiences is investigated.

## 3.1. EVOLUTION OF ARTIFICIAL INTELLIGENCE FROM A CUSTOMER EXPERIENCE PERSPECTIVE

The way businesses interact with their customers has changed significantly as a result of the development of artificial intelligence in customer experience. AI technologies have developed over time from simple rule-based systems to sophisticated solutions that use deep learning and machine learning to provide incredibly effective and individualized customer service.

### 3.1.1. Historical Development of AI in Customer Service

The inception of AI can be traced back to Alan Turing's seminal 1950 paper, "Computing Machinery and Intelligence." In this work, Turing posed the pivotal question: "Can machines think?" and introduced the Turing Test as a benchmark for assessing machine intelligence. The Turing Test establishes a rigorous standard for AI advancement, aiming for machines capable of replicating human-like dialogue and logical thinking to the extent that they are indistinguishable from humans (Turing, 1950).

The field of artificial intelligence started to take shape in the 1950s. The 1956 Dartmouth Conference, a crucial occasion that formally established artificial intelligence as a field of study, was an important turning point. Prominent thinkers gathered here with a common vision of machines carrying out tasks that have historically required human intelligence. Early artificial intelligence (AI) programs from this era, like Arthur Samuel's checkers-playing program, demonstrated how machines could learn and improve performance through experience. Joseph Weizenbaum unveiled ELIZA, a cutting-edge artificial intelligence program created to mimic human speech, in 1966. The foundation for future customer service applications was laid by ELIZA's ability to simulate the role of a Rogerian psychotherapist, demonstrating AI's capacity for human-like conversation. Expert systems were developed in the 1970s with the goal of using rule-based logic to simulate human experts' decision-making processes. One notable example of this technology was MYCIN, which was created at Stanford University and focused on identifying bacterial infections and suggesting treatments. The development of expert systems such as MYCIN demonstrated how artificial intelligence could be used practically in specialized fields, especially those where expert knowledge was crucial. In order to provide precise and thorough answers to customer questions, AI has been applied in customer service in recent years. This integration of knowledge from multiple domains includes product details and industry-specific information.

Machine learning emerged in the 1980s as a result of the development of algorithms that let computers learn from data without the need for explicit programming. The development of back propagation algorithms for neural network training also occurred during this time, which was a major breakthrough that improved computers' capacity for pattern recognition and prediction. These developments laid the foundation for complex AI applications in customer service, enabling systems to handle challenging jobs and gradually improve performance.

With the advent of support vector machines (SVMs) and significant advancements in natural language processing, the 1990s were a pivotal decade in the development of artificial intelligence. SVMs improved service delivery by introducing a reliable method for classification and regression tasks. They are essential to the thorough analysis of customer data. At the same time, significant advancements in natural language processing (NLP) technologies enabled machines to better understand and generate human language. The creation of more user-friendly customer support interfaces was greatly aided by this advancement. Furthermore, improvements in NLP technologies have made it possible for machines to comprehend and produce human language more effectively, which is an essential advancement for designing user-friendly customer support interfaces. A major advancement in artificial intelligence was marked in 1997 when IBM's Deep Blue defeated world chess champion Garry Kasparov, marking a historic milestone. This achievement demonstrated the speed at which AI systems are developing and the potential for AI to outperform humans in handling challenging problem-solving tasks.

Significant progress in artificial intelligence was made in the early 2000s, especially with the introduction of increasingly complex natural language processing methods. Improved text analysis and speech recognition were the outcomes of the application of statistical techniques in language processing, such as hidden Markov models. These advancements were crucial in enhancing interactions with customer service.

Deep learning, a branch of machine learning that makes use of multi-layered neural networks, gained popularity during the 2010s. The development of increasingly sophisticated AI systems was aided by algorithms such as convolutional and recurrent neural networks, CNNs, and RNNs, which produced notable improvements in speech and picture recognition. These advancements were essential in the development of advanced chatbots and virtual assistants driven by AI that could manage challenging customer support tasks. A significant advancement came with the release of virtual assistants, such as Apple's Siri in 2011. Siri paved the way for more interactive and user-focused customer service applications by utilizing cutting-edge speech recognition and natural language processing technologies to converse with users in natural language.

In a similar vein, IBM's Watson, which gained notoriety for winning the game show Jeopardy! in 2011, demonstrated how AI can comprehend and process natural language questions extremely well, highlighting the applicability of AI in the field of customer service. The triumph of Google's AlphaGo over Lee Sedol, the world champion go player, in 2016 brought to light the exceptional capacities of deep learning and reinforcement learning in handling intricate games with wide decision spaces. This accomplishment demonstrated AI's ability to handle complex problems and improve decision-making procedures relevant to enhancing customer service. Thanks to open-source platforms like TensorFlow and PyTorch, AI is now widely available, allowing many businesses to incorporate AI into their customer service strategies. With the help of these tools, businesses can now create and implement AI models more effectively, which promotes innovation and improves customer interactions by offering individualized and expedited service. Concerns about accountability and transparency in AI applications have been successfully addressed by advances in explainability and ethics in AI. These advancements have enabled companies to adopt efficient AI solutions while maintaining regulatory compliance and building trust.

Artificial intelligence systems' capabilities underwent a significant change with the advent of Large Language Models (LLMs) in the early 2020s. The performance of AI-driven chatbots was significantly enhanced by these models, which are renowned for their capacity to comprehend contextual cues and generate text that resembles human writing. Customer satisfaction and engagement increased as a result of this advancement, which enabled chatbots to manage more complex and contextually sensitive interactions. Businesses are now able to provide highly customized services, strengthening customer satisfaction and loyalty, thanks to AI's capacity to process enormous volumes of real-time customer data. As companies looked for scalable and effective ways to handle the spike in online interactions and support needs, the COVID-19 pandemic accelerated the adoption of AI in customer service. By 2024, AI technology is still developing thanks to continuous research and development that aims to increase the range of attainable objectives. Conversational AI, sentiment analysis, and emotion recognition developments have the potential to further revolutionize customer service by improving the effectiveness, empathy, and intuitiveness of interactions.

The development of AI in customer service over time demonstrates a consistent commitment to enhancing customer interactions through technological innovation. The development of AI has profoundly changed how companies interact with their customers, from Turing's groundbreaking theoretical work to today's AI-driven chatbots. This has improved operational efficiency, personalization, and the customer experience as a whole.

### 3.1.2. Recent Advancements in Artificial Intelligence

The customer service industry has seen substantial changes as a result of the last ten years' rapid advancements in artificial intelligence technologies. These developments have given companies the ability to enhance client experiences by facilitating faster, more efficient, and more individualized interactions.

One significant development in the field of customer service is the emergence of advanced natural language processing and conversational artificial intelligence technologies. These advancements have made it easier to create chatbots and virtual assistants that are intelligent enough to understand and respond to natural language inquiries from customers. As an illustration, Google's BERT (Bidirectional Encoder Representations from Transformers) model has significantly improved AI systems' ability to understand the context and nuances of consumer queries, leading to more accurate and relevant responses. Similarly, by providing logical and contextually appropriate answers, OpenAI's GPT-3 and the more recent GPT-4 have raised the bar for conversational AI.

Customer service advancements have been significantly impacted by machine learning algorithms. Through the analysis of vast amounts of customer data, machine learning models are able to precisely predict the needs and preferences of customers, allowing businesses to offer proactive support and tailored recommendations. Qualified, for instance, uses AI to evaluate website visitor data and interact with potential clients through tailored chats, increasing lead generation and conversion rates. Similar to this, Intercom uses machine learning to automate customer service, providing prompt answers to frequently asked questions while freeing up human agents to handle trickier problems.

Technologies for sentiment analysis and emotion recognition are now essential for understanding consumer sentiments and emotions expressed through voice, text, and facial expressions. Businesses can now evaluate customer satisfaction and tailor responses with the help of these AI-powered technologies. For example, IBM Watson's Tone Analyzer can recognize emotions like happiness, rage, and sadness in customer communications, helping service representatives respond with empathy. Similar to this, Microsoft's Azure Cognitive Services offer sentiment analysis APIs that can quickly determine the tone of client reviews, enabling prompt and suitable responses.

By effectively managing repetitive and time-consuming tasks, automation—primarily through robotic process automation, or RPA—has dramatically changed customer service operations. RPA bots are capable of handling a wide range of tasks, such as handling regular enquiries, managing customer data, and processing transactions. Consequently, this enables human agents to focus on more complex problems. Notable RPA solutions from Automation Anywhere and UiPath have been crucial in improving accuracy, speeding up response times, and organizing customer support processes. Moreover, Glean uses AI to streamline knowledge management and retrieval procedures, giving customer support teams fast access to the data they need to address client issues.

Businesses now provide seamless, individualized customer experiences thanks to the integration of artificial intelligence with CRM systems. CRM systems with AI capabilities, like Microsoft Dynamics 365 and Salesforce Einstein, use AI to examine consumer interactions across various channels, spot trends, and provide useful information. These systems predict sales opportunities, segment customers automatically, and offer suggestions for customer engagement. Businesses can make sure that customer interactions are timely, personalized, and well-informed thanks to this integration. By using automated data entry and predictive lead scoring, HubSpot's AI-powered CRM improves customer engagement.

Customer service is now much more accessible and efficient thanks to voice recognition and speech-to-text technologies. Real-time transcription of customer calls and voice commands is made possible by AI-powered voice recognition systems that accurately translate spoken language into text, like Google's Speech0to-Text and Amazon Transcribe. Customer service representatives are better equipped to recognize and quickly respond to the needs of their customers thanks to these technologies. Additionally, voice recognition technology optimizes the processing of customer inquiries and support requests and is essential to the operation of virtual assistants and Interactive Voice Response (IVR) systems.

Customer feedback gathering and analysis are essential to the ongoing improvement of customer service. Large amounts of feedback data can be processed by AI-powered survey analysis tools, making it possible to find recurring themes, sentiments, and areas that need improvement. Prominent platforms like Qualtrics and SurveyMonkey use AI algorithms to evaluate open-ended survey answers, providing companies with deeper understanding of consumer attitudes and experiences. These insights enable businesses to improve their customer service strategies by making data-driven decisions.

The ethical ramifications and the requirement for Explainable AI (XAI) decisions have become more prominent as AI becomes more integrated into customer service. Establishing frameworks and rules to guarantee the accountability, transparency, and fairness of AI systems is the main goal of research in AI ethics. By making AI decisions easier for users to understand and interpret, explainable AI techniques increase user confidence in AI-powered customer support systems.

Neural machine translation (NMT) models are used by Google Translate and Microsoft Translator to provide precise and appropriate translations in real-time. This feature increases accessibility and customer satisfaction by enabling businesses to communicate with customers in the language of their choice.

## 3.2. ROLE OF AI IN CUSTOMER SERVICE

By automating repetitive tasks, offering individualized support, and speeding up response times, artificial intelligence is changing the paradigms of customer service. Here, we look at the different ways AI can be used in customer service, beginning with the revolutionary possibilities it offers and moving on to a review of AI-powered frameworks and applications.

### 3.2.1. Opportunities for AI-Driven Solutions in Customer Service

Companies have to deal with the twin challenges of meeting ever-increasing customer demands and answering ever-more-complex questions. AI-powered solutions give businesses a competitive edge by allowing them to automate repetitive tasks, optimize workflows, and offer proactive support. The different subcategories of AI applications in customer service are outlined in Table 3.1, along with real-world examples, important performance indicators, and the particular AI technologies that are being used.

#### *3.2.1.1. Enhanced Efficiency and Agent Productivity*

By handling common questions and tasks, the use of AI technologies—such as chatbots and process automation—has been shown to greatly increase customer service efficiency. Consequently, this enhances overall productivity and speeds up response times by freeing up human agents to focus on solving more complicated problems. After integrating AI, a Brazilian commercial bank's interaction volumes and service attendance significantly increased, indicating significant productivity and efficiency gains, according to research on the adoption of AI in that bank. Furthermore, through the optimization of various business processes, AI-enabled service operations have demonstrated notable improvements in customer satisfaction and service delivery. (Chung, M. et al., 2020)

### *3.2.1.2. Personalized Customer Interactions*

AI-driven systems can understand individual customer preferences and behaviors by analyzing large datasets, which enables businesses to provide highly customized experiences. Customer satisfaction can be increased by this degree of personalization because it makes interactions more interesting and relevant. By tailoring services or goods to meet particular customer needs, AI integration with CRM systems improves personalization. Moreover, the ability of AI to provide tailored solutions and recommendations greatly increases customer engagement and loyalty (Xu et al., 2020).

**Table 3.1.** *Opportunities, Applications, and Technologies of AI-Driven Customer Service*

| **Opportunity Area** | **Practical Implementations** | **Key Performance Indicators (KPIs)** | **Artificial Intelligence Technologies Used** |
|---|---|---|---|
| Operational Efficiency Enhancement | Sort and prioritize inquiries, Automate manual load to increase productivity | Average Handling Time (AHT), Customer Satisfaction (CSAT) | Natural Language Processing, Robotic Process Automation |
| Faster Response Time and Issue Resolution | Configure chatbots to handle FAQs and provide immediate responses to customers | First Response Time (FRT), First Contact Resolution (FCR), Average Time to Resolution (TTR) | Chatbots, Natural Language Understanding |
| Workflow Automation | Automate follow-up emails and other repetitive tasks to streamline processes | Task Completion Rate, Operational Efficiency | Robotic Process Automation, AI Workflow Engines |
| Enhanced Escalation Management | Intelligently route complex queries to specialized agents | Escalation Rate, Resolution Time for escalated issues | AI Routing Algorithms, Machine Learning |

| | | | |
|---|---|---|---|
| Personalized Interactions and Recommendations | Provide customized product recommendations based on customer data | Customer satisfaction, Repeat purchase rate | Recommender Systems, Collaborative Filtering |
| Self-Service Options | AI-driven online troubleshooting guides to empower customers | Self-service usage rate, Resolution rate | Large Language Models, Chatbots, Natural Language Processing |
| AI-Driven Loyalty Programs | Offer personalized loyalty rewards and discounts | Customer retention rate, Loyalty program engagement | Machine Learning, Predictive Analytics |
| Improved Customer Insights | Create comprehensive customer profiles, analyze customer sentiment | Sentiment accuracy, Customer satisfaction | Sentiment Analysis, NLP, Machine Learning |
| Proactive Customer Support | Notify customers about potential issues proactively | Mean Time to Resolve, Customer satisfaction | Predictive Analytics, Machine Learning |
| Customer Feedback Analysis | Deploy AI to analyze survey data for actionable insights | Continuous Learning, Feedback processing time | Text Analytics, Machine Learning |
| Scalability and 24/7 Availability | AI-powered virtual assistants round-the-clock | Agent productivity, Service Reliability | Virtual Assistants, Natural Language Processing |

*Source: https://www.researchgate.net/figure/Opportunities-applications-and-technologies-of-AI-Driven-Customer-Service_tbl1_381224987.*

### *3.2.1.3. Proactive Customer Support*

A proactive approach is made possible by the incorporation of AI into customer support operations, which anticipates and resolves problems before they arise. By offering proactive solutions, this predictive capability helps to prevent issues and improve customer satisfaction. Notably, by anticipating client needs and responding quickly, AI-powered service operations have the potential to significantly improve service delivery and customer satisfaction. Additionally, AI chatbots play a key role in providing prompt and effective customer service, which lessens the need for human intervention.

#### *3.2.1.4. Scalability and 24/7 Availability*

Scalability and continuous availability are provided by AI systems, which can handle significant customer interactions and run around-the-clock. This guarantees continuous availability of customer service, improving customer satisfaction and service reliability. For instance, AI-powered chatbots can respond to consumer questions 24/7, ensuring that clients receive help promptly. Especially in sectors with high volumes of customer interactions, the ability to offer ongoing support promotes customer engagement and trust.

#### *3.2.1.5. Improved Customer Insights and Data Collection*

AI is a key component in facilitating the gathering and examination of data from consumer interactions, which produces insightful information about the preferences and actions of the consumer. These insights play a crucial role in helping businesses improve their offerings in terms of goods and services, customer experience, and strategy. Businesses can find patterns and trends that help them make better decisions and enable more efficient customer relationship management by utilizing AI-driven analytics. Businesses can obtain deeper insights into customer needs and preferences by leveraging AI's ability to process and analyze large datasets. This leads to the development of more impactful marketing and service strategies. Table 3.1 illustrates the wide range of potential applications of AI-driven solutions in customer service. AI technologies are changing the face of customer service, from improving customer interactions with proactive support and personalized recommendations to increasing operational efficiency through automation. Customer service operations will be more effective, responsive, and able to provide outstanding experiences if these AI-driven solutions are strategically implemented.

### 3.2.2. AI-Powered Applications and Frameworks

We examine particular AI innovations that are revolutionizing customer support. These technologies make use of AI developments to boost efficiency and personalization, improve customer interactions, offer security, and offer analytical insights. Every technology has useful applications that take advantage of important opportunities to increase operational efficacy and customer satisfaction. Businesses can take advantage of AI's potential in customer service by comprehending and utilizing these technologies.

#### *3.2.2.1. Natural Language Technologies*

Because natural language technologies allow machines to understand and react to human language naturally, they are essential to the transformation of customer service. These technologies include a variety of techniques and instruments that enable smooth communication between automated systems and clients, improving both the client experience and operational effectiveness. LLMs and Natural Language Processing (NLP) and Understanding (NLU) are essential elements of natural language technologies.

### *3.2.2.1.1. Natural Language Processing (NLP) and Understanding (NLU)*

NLP and NLU are fundamental technologies that allow automated systems to comprehend and process customer inquiries with accuracy. NLP is the process of analyzing and synthesizing natural language data using computational methods. As a result, machines can now read, decode, and comprehend human language. By concentrating on the machine's comprehension of the meaning and context of the words, NLU goes one step further. For interactions to be meaningful and productive, this is essential.

The accuracy of automated responses in customer service is greatly improved by the combination of NLP and NLU. For example, chatbots with sophisticated NLP can comprehend a variety of linguistic subtleties and comprehend complex sentences, which allows them to respond to customer inquiries with greater precision and relevance. This feature enhances the general customer experience by lowering miscommunications.

Managing support tickets is a common way that NLP and NLU are used in customer service. Through the use of these technologies, automated systems are able to classify and rank tickets according to their content, sending them to the relevant departments for handling.

### *3.2.2.1.2. Large Language Models*

The development of conversational agents is ushered in by LLMs, which greatly improve the caliber and consistency of consumer interactions. By using deep learning methods and large training datasets, LLMs can generate responses that are relevant and fluent, just like those of a human.

One significant advantage of LLMs is their ability to understand and produce text in a specific context, which promotes more organic and interesting interactions. For instance, an LLM-powered chatbot can skillfully handle a variety of subjects and provide thorough answers that closely resemble human speech. This quality is especially helpful in the field of customer service, where keeping a friendly and understanding manner is essential to guaranteeing client satisfaction. LLMs are also excellent at providing individualized interactions. These models can customize responses to meet specific needs and preferences by analyzing past interactions and customer data, creating a customized experience. Because customers feel understood and appreciated, this kind of personalized engagement has the potential to increase consumer engagement.

### *3.2.2.2. Customer Interaction Technologies*

By enabling direct communication between automated systems and customers, customer interaction technologies are essential to contemporary customer service. By providing instant assistance and raising general customer satisfaction, these technologies greatly increase the effectiveness and caliber of customer interactions. Table 3.2 lists the features and capabilities of chatbots, virtual assistants, and voice assistants—three essential elements of customer interaction technologies.

**Table 3.2.** *Comparison of the Features and Capabilities of Chatbots, Virtual Assistants, and Voice Assistants*

| Feature | Chatbots | Virtual Assistants | Voice Assistants |
|---|---|---|---|
| Interaction Complexity | Handles simple, predefined queries | Manages complex, multistep interactions | Handles spoken queries, including complex interactions |
| Personalization | Limited, generic responses for all users | High, tailored responses based on user data | High, with responses tailored based on voice recognition and user data |
| Learning Capabilities | Requires manual updates for new queries | Learns and adapts from interactions over time | Learns and adapts from voice interactions over time |
| Engagement Level | Reactive, responds only to customer queries | Proactive, can initiate interactions based on behavior | Proactive, can initiate interactions based on context and behavior |
| Use Cases | FAQ handling, basic customer support | Detailed support, personalized recommendations | Hands-free assistance, smart home integration, accessible customer support |
| Accessibility | Text-based, suitable for most users | Text-based, suitable for detailed interactions | Voice-based, accessible for visually impaired and hands-free users |
| Ease of Integration | Integrated with websites and apps | Integrated with various customer service platforms | Integrated with smart devices and IoT ecosystems |

*Source: https://www.researchgate.net/figure/Comparison-of-the-features-and-capabilities-of-chatbots-virtual-assistants-and-voice_tbl2_381224987.*

#### *3.2.2.2.1. Chatbots*

Automated conversational agents, or chatbots, are made to interact with consumers in real time and respond to frequently asked questions right away. They are frequently incorporated into messaging apps, mobile apps, and websites, guaranteeing a widespread presence across various digital interfaces. The ability of chatbots to provide prompt responses, handle several queries at once, and significantly reduce customer wait times is one of their main benefits. This quick availability ensures that clients get help when they need it, improving their experience in general.

The fact that chatbots are available around-the-clock is another important advantage. Because chatbots can work around the clock, clients can get help whenever they need it, regardless of time zones or business hours. This continuous availability eliminates the need for human agents to be available at odd hours and is particularly crucial for multinational corporations that serve clients from various geographical areas.

Chatbots also provide cost-effectiveness. They free up human agents to concentrate on more complex and valuable interactions by automating repetitive tasks and answering commonly asked questions. In addition to lowering operating costs, this automation increases the customer support team's overall productivity.

#### *3.2.2.2.2. Virtual Assistants*

Beyond chatbots, virtual assistants are a huge step forward because they can handle complex interactions and provide individualized support. This is made possible by the application of machine learning and natural language processing, which improves their ability to understand and respond to consumer questions. The ability of virtual assistants to provide customized interactions is one of their main advantages. Virtual assistants can improve the user experience and build stronger customer relationships by using customer data to tailor their recommendations and responses for specific users. Virtual assistants are excellent at managing multi-step tasks, answering complex questions in-depth, and even interacting with users proactively based on their behavior. By resolving possible problems before they become more serious and providing assistance before clients specifically ask for it, this proactive strategy can greatly increase customer satisfaction. Additionally, through their interactions, virtual assistants are always learning and changing. Virtual assistants use machine learning to improve their responses over time, increasing their accuracy and efficacy with every interaction, in contrast to rule-based systems that require manual updates for new queries.

### *3.2.2.2.3. Voice Assistants*

As a component of customer interaction technologies, voice assistants enable voice-based customer support interactions, offering convenience and accessibility without the need for hands-on assistance. They improve accessibility by accommodating people who are visually impaired and those who would rather communicate verbally rather than through text. Additionally, by reacting to natural language and producing captivating customer experiences, voice assistants provide a human-like interaction experience that raises customer satisfaction. Furthermore, their seamless multi-channel support made possible by their integration with smart devices enables customers to interact with customer service via a variety of preferred devices, including smartphones, smart speakers, and other Internet of Things devices. All things considered, customer interaction technologies—which include chatbots, virtual assistants, and voice assistants—make a substantial contribution to contemporary customer service by providing prompt, individualized, and easily accessible assistance.

### ***3.2.2.3. Automation Tools***

Workflows are optimized, repetitive tasks are streamlined, and overall efficiency is increased when automation tools are integrated into customer service operations. By eliminating manual labor, these tools enable human agents to concentrate on more difficult and worthwhile tasks. AI Routing Algorithms, AI Workflow Engines, and Robotic Process Automation are important parts of automation tools for customer service. The primary capabilities of each of these technologies are described in Table 3.3.

**Table 3.3.** *Comparison of Automation Tools in Customer Service*

| **Feature** | **Feature** | **AI Workflow Engines** | **AI Routing Algorithms** |
|---|---|---|---|
| Primary Function | Automates repetitive and rule-based tasks | Manages and optimizes service workflows | Routes customer inquiries to the appropriate resource |
| Complexity of Tasks | Low to medium | Medium to high | Medium to high, involves decision-making |
| Adaptability | Limited to pre-defined tasks | Highly adaptable to changing workflows and circumstances | Highly adaptable, using real-time data for routing |
| Implemen-tation Time | Relatively quick to deploy | Requires significant setup and configuration | Requires setup but can quickly adjust to changing needs |
| Scalability | Scales easily with additional bots | Scales with increased work-flow management capabilities | Scales with improved rout-ing algorithms and resources |

*Source: https://www.researchgate.net/figure/Comparison-of-Automation-Tools-in-Customer-Service_tbl3_381224987.*

### *3.2.2.4. Personalization Technologies*

Customer service personalization technologies are intended to tailor recommendations and interactions to each individual customer's needs, preferences, and behaviors. By giving users a more personalized and interesting experience, these technologies are crucial for raising customer satisfaction and fostering loyalty. The two main components of customer service personalization technologies are collaborative filtering and recommender systems.

#### *3.2.2.4.1. Recommender Systems*

Recommender systems are algorithms created to suggest goods, services, or content to users based on their past preferences and interactions. To offer tailored recommendations, these systems examine data from multiple sources, including browsing history, demographic data, and past purchases.

By assisting users in finding goods or services they might find interesting, recommender systems improve the user experience and raise customer satisfaction and engagement. They are frequently utilized in streaming services, e-commerce, and other platforms where user engagement and sales can be increased by personalized recommendations.

Recommender systems have several advantages, such as better engagement by maintaining customers' interest, higher conversion rates by making relevant product or service recommendations, and enhanced customer satisfaction through personalized experiences.

#### *3.2.2.4.2. Collaborative Filtering*

A popular method in recommender systems for filtering data and predicting user preferences by looking at other users' preferences is called collaborative filtering. This technique works by finding commonalities between users or objects and using that information to produce suggestions. Item-based and user-based collaborative filtering are the two main types.

Finding users with similar tastes and recommending products that these users have favored are the components of user-based collaborative filtering. Items that User A has bought and enjoyed will be suggested to User B when their purchase histories are similar.

On the other hand, item-based collaborative filtering finds similarities between items and suggests items that are similar to those that a user finds appealing. For instance, the system will suggest other books that are in the same genre or have similar content to a customer who has enjoyed a specific book. Collaborative filtering enhances personalization by leveraging the collective tastes of a user group to provide more accurate and relevant suggestions. This method is widely utilized in various sectors, such as retail, entertainment, and digital services, to boost user interaction and contentment (Figure 3.1).

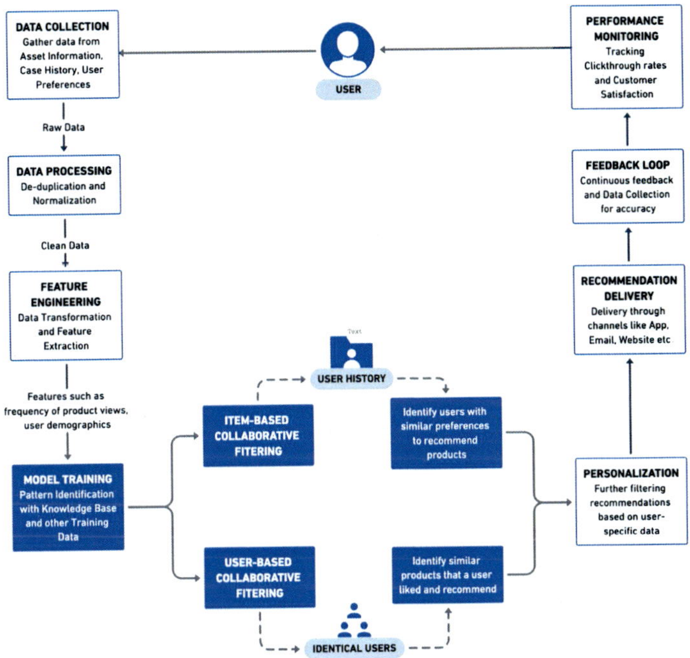


**Figure 3.1.** *Product recommendation workflow leveraging personalization technologies.*

*Source: https://www.researchgate.net/figure/Product-recommendation-workflow-leveraging-personalization-technologies_fig3_381224987.*

Collaborative filtering offers several benefits, including the ability to reveal hidden patterns and relationships between users and items, as well as more accurate and diverse recommendations as the system gains experience from a large dataset of user preferences. Collaborative filtering, for instance, is used by e-commerce websites to suggest goods and services to users based on shared interests, resulting in a tailored and pleasurable shopping experience.

### *3.2.2.5. Analytical and Predictive Technologies*

Utilizing analytical and predictive technologies in customer service entails combining machine learning and data analysis to predict customer needs, assess customer sentiment, and extract useful insights from large datasets. By enabling proactive customer service strategies, these technologies enable companies to anticipate problems and tailor interactions based on predictive analysis. Text analytics, sentiment analysis, and predictive analytics are essential components of analytical and predictive technologies used in customer service (Table 3.4).

**Table 3.4.** *Comparison of Analytical and Predictive Technologies*

| **Feature** | **Predictive Analytics** | **Sentiment Analysis** | **Text Analytics** |
|---|---|---|---|
| Primary Function | Forecasts future customer behavior and needs | Analyzes customer emotions and opinions from text data | Extracts meaningful information from unstructured text data |
| Data Sources | Historical data, real-time data, transaction records | Social media posts, customer reviews, case history | Case history, chat logs, and customer feedback |
| Key Benefits | Anticipates customer needs, proactive service, optimized resource allocation | Real-time sentiment understanding, identifies areas for improvement, tailored responses | Uncovers patterns and trends, improved decision-making, targeted service improvements |
| Use Cases | Forecasting customer churn, predicting maintenance needs | Monitoring social media sentiment, analyzing customer reviews | Analyzing support tickets, identifying common issues |
| Complexity | High, involves advanced statistical and machine learning models | Medium, involves NLP and machine learning for sentiment detection | Medium, involves text mining and NLP techniques |

*Source: https://www.researchgate.net/figure/Comparison-of-Analytical-and-Predictive-Technologies_tbl4_381224987.*

### *3.2.2.5.1. Predictive Analytics*

Statistical algorithms, machine learning techniques, and historical data are all used in predictive analytics to forecast possible future outcomes based on historical data. Predictive analytics is essential to customer service because it helps predict customer behavior, anticipate possible problems, and allocate resources as efficiently as possible.

Businesses can improve customer satisfaction by anticipating and addressing customer needs by incorporating predictive analytics into customer service operations. In order to reduce customer dissatisfaction and increase customer trust, proactive support can be given by precisely anticipating when customers might need help or when products might need maintenance.

Predictive analytics offers several benefits, such as the ability to anticipate customer needs, improve customer satisfaction by providing proactive service, and optimize resource allocation by identifying patterns in demand. Predictive analytics, for example, can be used by a telecom company to anticipate and take proactive measures to address network failures, which would reduce downtime and guarantee a smooth customer experience.

### *3.2.2.5.2. Sentiment Analysis*

Sentiment analysis analyzes and interprets customer sentiments and opinions as expressed in textual data by utilizing NLP and machine learning techniques. This technology makes it possible to evaluate customer sentiment from a variety of sources, such as support requests, social media posts, and customer reviews.

Companies can learn more about how consumers view their goods, services, and brand as a whole by using sentiment analysis. Organizations can adjust their strategies to address customer feedback, improve service quality, and raise overall customer satisfaction by identifying positive, negative, or neutral sentiments.

The benefits of sentiment analysis include understanding customer sentiment in real time, pinpointing areas for improvement, and enabling tailored customer interactions. An e-commerce company, for example, might use sentiment analysis to track customer opinions on social media, allowing for prompt resolution of any unfavorable comments and ultimately enhancing the overall customer experience.

### *3.2.2.5.3. Text Analytics*

Text analytics is the process of using techniques like text mining, information retrieval, and natural language processing to extract useful insights from unstructured text data. Text analytics examines customer feedback, chat logs, and support tickets in customer service to identify common problems, trends, and areas for improvement.

By providing a thorough understanding of customer interactions, identifying common pain points, and enabling data-informed decision-making to raise service standards, text analytics helps to improve customer service. For example, reviewing customer service tickets can reveal common problems, allowing businesses to create more effective solutions. One of text analytics' most important benefits is that it can reveal hidden patterns and trends in customer interactions, improve decision-making processes with data-driven insights, and predict service quality with targeted improvements. For example, a software company could use text analytics to examine support tickets and identify recurrent technical issues, which would allow for the creation of better troubleshooting resources and increased customer satisfaction.

## 3.3. AI-BASED TECHNOLOGIES EMPOWERING THE CUSTOMER EXPERIENCE

Modern methods to enhance the customer experience are driven by AI and include data science, extended reality, robots, recommender systems, the internet of things (IoT), conversational agents, and other new technologies. For a long-term competitive edge, the majority of businesses use AI-based customer experience tools. We discuss six cutting-edge AI-powered innovations that have the potential to revolutionize the consumer experience (Figure 3.2).

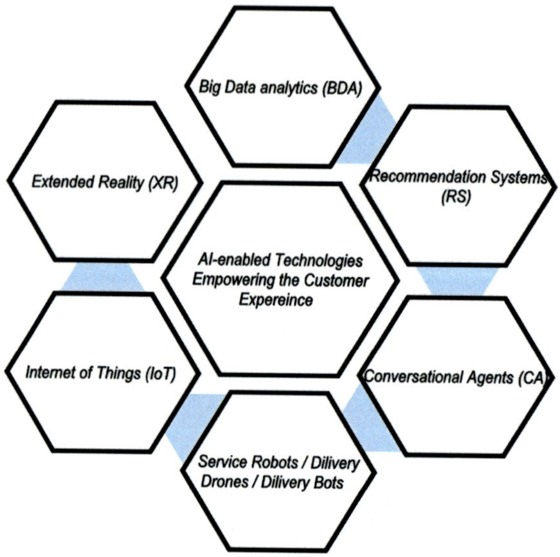


**Figure 3.2.** *AI-enabled technologies empowering the customer experience.*

*Source: https://cmr.berkeley.edu/2022/03/artificial-intelligence-driven-customer-experience-overcoming-the-challenges/.*

### 3.3.1. BIG DATA ANALYTICS (BDA)

Big data, including customer health, transaction, location, preference, choice, likes, dislikes, GPS signals, and feedback, has become a wealth of information due to the increasing popularity of digital marketing and online shopping. Big data continues to grow, offering a wealth of consumer insights to improve services and goods. In the world of the internet, data velocity and speed are crucial. Prominent companies are interested in real-time information, like GPS location for online order tracking. A wealth of unprocessed data transformed into insightful forecasts that predict consumer behavior, demand, the next purchase, etc.

Through descriptive, predictive, and prescriptive analytics, big data analytics assists managers with forecasting, decision-making, and other management tasks. Amazon surprises customers with products they might consider purchasing in the future through its anticipatory shipping. Businesses that describe themselves as data-driven are outperforming their competitors in financial operations and objective metrics. Leading companies like Amazon and Google use BDA-based competitive advantage in the era of intense analytics competition.

### 3.3.2. Recommendation Systems (RS)

E-commerce provides a plethora of options and information; nonetheless, having too much information at one's disposal can cause information overload and lead to poor decision making. In order to address this issue, recommender systems driven by AI assist users in making informed decisions by suggesting appropriate goods and services. Recommender systems compile user recommendations as input and route them to the right seekers. Different versions of the recommender system exist, depending on the underlying algorithms. Collaborative recommender systems, for instance, use community historical data to make recommendations, while content-based recommender systems use behavioral data. Hybrid recommender systems optimize recommendations by combining various combinations of algorithms.

### 3.3.3. Conversational Agents (CA)

Conversational agents are another AI-driven technology that has completely changed the industry (CA). CA is a novel mode of communication that involves a digital/voice assistant interacting with customers on behalf of brands. Conversational commerce is what happens when customers use a digital assistant to make purchases. Customers use digital assistants for everyday tasks like placing food orders, making purchases, and contemplating, according to a PWC report. Intelligent personal assistants like Google Assistant, Amazon's Alexa, Microsoft's Cortana, Apple's Siri, and Amazon's Assistant help users have a better and more convenient experience. Furthermore, contingent on the situation, digital assistants can function as a friend or companion, a home or workplace assistant, etc.

### 3.3.4. Service Robots/Delivery Drones/Delivery Bots

Cutting-edge technologies have enormous potential to enhance the customer experience, including image processing, biometrics, and service robots with built-in AI features. In the future, service robots may exist in virtual or physical forms in addition to physical embodiments. Hologram-based service robots, for instance, could be installed in retail centers, hospitals, hotels, airports, train, and metro stations, etc. to help customers with common inquiries. Holograms don't require expensive hardware or take up any floor space. Similar to this, delivery drones and bots can reach consumers' doorsteps quickly with packages of food or lightweight goods. This delivery method would be economical, environmentally beneficial, and user-friendly.

### 3.3.5. Internet of Things (IoT)

IoT stands for the Internet of Things, which is a network of interconnected objects, people, and devices. Future gadgets and household appliances, like air conditioners, microwaves, refrigerators, washing machines, and televisions, will function automatically thanks to sophisticated sensors. Imagine if your refrigerator placed online orders for bread, butter, eggs, fruits, milk, and vegetables based on the amount of each item still in its designated containers. The internet of things would soon make all devices more sophisticated and intelligent. The potential for IoT to revolutionize the shopping experience is enormous. With the aid of the Internet of Things, a product's price, usage, manufacturing date, specifications, expiration date, and other details could be shown by wearables or smartphones.

### 3.3.6. Extended Reality (XR)

Extended reality refers to technologies that improve our perception of the real world, such as augmented reality (AR), virtual reality (VR), and mixed reality (MR). AR uses computer-generated information to enhance the real world. Applications such as Instagram filters, Lenscart 3D mirrors, and IKEA are excellent examples of AR. VR creates a virtual world on a 3D wearable frame, replacing the user's view. VR has many uses, including gaming and entertainment, and its use in training, education, and healthcare services is steadily growing. VR has also opened up new opportunities for the travel and tourism sector because it allows for in-home tours. MR projects a virtual reality environment into a natural setting, fusing the real and virtual worlds. Consider a scenario in which consumers walk into a vegetable store and are thrust into a surreal farm environment. They have the ability to harvest produce from trees and crops that are merely artificial environments with mixed reality.

The technologies mentioned above present countless opportunities to improve the customer experience throughout the customer journey. To give their customers an amazing experience, businesses must create an AI-driven customer journey.

## 3.4. AI-DRIVEN CUSTOMER JOURNEY

Given that the journey shapes the customer experience, ratings of customer satisfaction may be high for a specific touchpoint and low for the entire experience. For businesses to create an AI-driven process, a significant capital investment and change management are necessary. Therefore, it is always a good idea to start by identifying the key journeys and customer pain points (Figure 3.3).

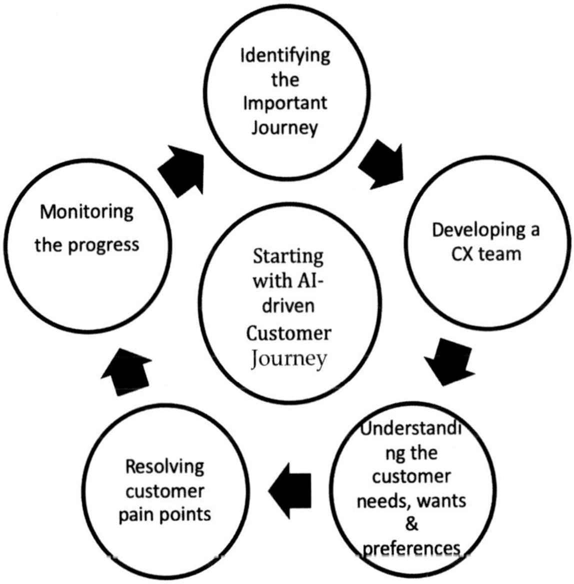


**Figure 3.3.** *Starting with AI-driven customer journey.*

*Source: https://cmr.berkeley.edu/2022/03/artificial-intelligence-driven-customer-experience-overcoming-the-challenges/.*

### 3.4.1. Identifying the Important Journey

It is possible to categorize isolated processes into fair sets of complete customer journeys. Regional transport offices, for instance, provide a range of services, such as granting driver's licenses, registering cars, transferring vehicle ownership, etc. Each service is linked to a distinct customer journey because of its distinct goals.

Only four journeys are found to contribute to customer satisfaction in McKinsey's annual customer-experience survey conducted in North America. Therefore, not all journeys are equally important. These include handling energy use, handling billing and payment processes, and handling outages.

Payment experiences can be improved in a number of ways. First, biometric checkout processes—like those at Amazon Go stores and quick tag services—can be made better for customers. Secondly, by utilizing real-time chargebacks to extend the post-purchase period. Third, customer data-driven online lending and insurance. Analyzing the customer journey can help pinpoint the primary source of satisfaction. For instance, customer satisfaction is improved by live order tracking on smartphones far more than by any other change to the customer journey.

### 3.4.2. Developing a CX (Customer Experience) Team

A cross-functional team made up of domain experts, business managers, data scientists, process engineers, and technology specialists is needed for transformation. The CX team is in charge of interpreting real-time consumer behavior and taking appropriate action to improve the process's strength, agility, and personalization. Monitoring each customer's unique journey can make their experience smoother. If there are any difficulties encountered during the trip, customers can benefit from a positive experience by receiving some compensation. For instance, a study conducted on a well-known fast-food restaurant reveals that when food items fall off the table while being eaten, it is viewed as a serious incident in the customer journey, and the staff responds by serving the customer another dish without adding to the bill. These restaurants place greater emphasis on the individual journey, and their patrons are thrilled to have a wonderful, unforgettable dining experience.

### 3.4.3. Understanding the Customer Behavior, Needs, Wants, and Preferences

A customer-centric perspective and improved comprehension of customer behavior can lead to personalization throughout the customer journey. For instance, CIBIL scores, transaction histories, and other similar data can be used by banks to offer a variety of policies. Additional components include automated voice agents for customer engagement and instant alerts and reminders based on previous transactions via messaging. For instance, automated calls and messages from telecommunications companies alert users when their validity is about to expire. There are sophisticated techniques for comprehending the CX. As was previously mentioned, businesses don't need to ask consumers directly about their preferences through surveys in order to obtain a variety of data from the internet. Prominent online retailers and travel agencies, for instance, examine client feedback on their websites and across various social media channels.

### 3.4.3.1. Resolving the Personalization-Privacy Paradox

As per a BCG survey report, a mere 29% of consumers acknowledge that data leads to improved services, while 75% express apprehension about their privacy and refrain from disclosing any personal information online. The personalization–privacy paradox refers to the dilemma where customers trade their privacy for personalization. The following matrix is proposed to solve this paradox (Figure 3.4).

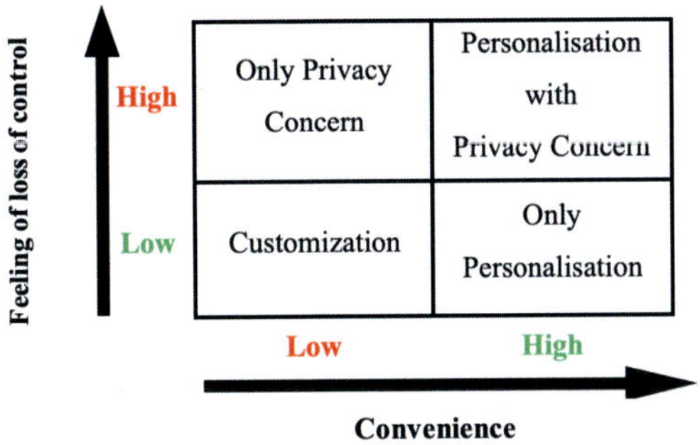


**Figure 3.4.** *Personalization-privacy paradox.*

*Source: https://cmr.berkeley.edu/2022/03/artificial-intelligence-driven-customer-experience-overcoming-the-challenges/.*

Privacy assurance reduces the feeling of loss of control as this entails privacy promises such as "we will not collect your data without your permission," "we will not disclose your data to any third party," "we will protect and secure your personal information," etc. Customers are more willing to share information if they are guaranteed security and control, which can allay feelings of loss of control and increase the usefulness of the services. Marketers use personalization because it offers benefits like efficiency, individualization, and convenience.

The privacy paradox is a planning tool that connects convenience with a sense of losing control in order to create a safe and customer-focused service strategy. In a 2x2 matrix, it offers four different outcomes of using customer data. The matrix has two dimensions: convenience (low or high) and feeling of loss of control (high or low). The sequence of consequences of using customer data are as follows:

1. **Only Privacy Concern:** Companies that combine a high degree of control loss with minimal convenience diminish the value of their services. Customers are not able to see any personalization from these services; instead, they are only left with the privacy concern. Customers exchange their information for convenience, which

explains why. Diminished comfort will be perceived as a privacy threat.

2. **Personalization with Privacy Concern:** This appears to be a frequent outcome of using client information. Businesses frequently use personal data, including past purchase history, transaction details, preferences, search history, etc., to give customers greater and better convenience. Because of the personalization that results, most customers eventually stop disclosing any private information online. Thus, regardless of the personalization feature provided, the loss of control over information breeds mistrust or insecurity towards their privacy.
3. **Customization:** Customization is the process by which companies provide particular product or service specifications that meet the needs of their clients. Over time, this strategy of customizing products or services has gained significant importance. When a product is personalized, no user effort is needed; however, when it is customized, customers must alter the design to meet their needs. Customization can be applied to this scenario with low convenience and low loss of control.
4. **Only Personalization:** While using personalized services, customers typically feel uneasy about their privacy, but this isn't always the case. Yes! Interestingly, customers may not worry about the misuse or leakage of their personal information if adequate privacy assurance is given to them, which can help to resolve the personalization-privacy paradox.

### *3.4.3.2. Framework to Reduce Customer Churn Using Data Analytics*

In order to give managers 360-degree, customer-centric insights, companies need to search for a real-time customer feedback system throughout the process. For instance, if a consumer enters a company's customer journey map with multiple touch points, they may encounter service failure at any time during the journey, starting from the first and ending at the last. The employees at the following touch points will be informed by the continuous feedback system to provide the specific customer with some compensation. Only journey mapping analytics can be used to operate this sophisticated customer service.

The company can lower customer attrition by using customer profiles. Using customer data, machine learning algorithms can forecast customer attrition, the cause of attrition, and retention strategies.

Now that the customers have been divided into red, yellow, and green groups, their subsequent journeys may be completely different. Moving customers from red and yellow boxes to green boxes is the aim of customer segmentation. In order to preserve their relationship, businesses can identify clients who have experienced service failure or delays and compensate them, as one of the top airlines does.

### 3.4.4. Resolving Customer Pain Points

While there may be numerous pain points along the way, figuring out and fixing the job is likely the most important one. For instance, banks noticed that their patrons were getting impatient while waiting in line, so they offered them a digital token system that allowed them to skip the line altogether. By looking at every touch point along the customer journey—from the pre-purchase to the purchase and finally the post-purchase phases—pain points can be found. AI agents can expedite and remove customer care service bottlenecks by booking, resolving, receiving, and canceling complaints.

### 3.4.5. Monitoring the Progress

A big data analytics-enabled continuous feedback system improves the system's journey mapping and monitoring. These days, businesses use AI and machine learning to automate the controls and monitoring procedures. Businesses can offer smooth and engaging customer experiences by enhancing customer journeys through real-time operation monitoring.

## 3.5. THEORETICAL FRAMEWORKS THAT CAN BE USED TO ANALYZE THE ROLE OF AI IN CUSTOMER EXPERIENCE

Theoretical frameworks are employed to examine how AI affects customer experience and offer insights into how AI-powered solutions can improve customer satisfaction and spur company expansion. There are several theoretical frameworks that can be used to analyze the role of AI in customer experience, including:

- Service Dominant Logic (SDL);
- Technology Acceptance Model (TAM);
- Social Exchange Theory (SET).

### *3.5.1. Service Dominant Logic (SDL)*

The significance of relationships between businesses and their customers is emphasized by Service Dominant Logic. According to this framework, a business's success is determined by both its capacity to build and preserve enduring relationships with its clients as well as its capacity to sell goods and services. SDL contends that value is not produced solely by the business but rather by the customer working together. According to the SDL framework, businesses should put more effort into comprehending and meeting the needs of their clients than just marketing goods and services.

Regarding AI in customer experience, SDL can be used to examine how AI-powered solutions can improve customer experience and co-create value. In this sense, a business's success is determined by its capacity to build and preserve enduring relationships with its clients in addition to its capacity to sell goods and services.

### 3.5.2. Technology Acceptance Model (TAM)

The TAM model, as its name suggests that perceived efficacy and apparent usability are key factors in determining user acceptance and adoption of technology. Regarding AI in customer experience, TAM can be used to comprehend how users embrace the practicality and usability of AI-powered tools, including mobile apps, information systems, chatbots, and virtual assistants. According to TAM, perceived utility and perceived ease of use are the two primary factors that affect users' acceptance of technology. While perceived ease of use refers to the user's perception that a technology is simple to use, perceived usefulness refers to the user's belief that a technology will enable them to complete a task more successfully. TAM states that people are more likely to adopt and use a technology if they believe it to be practical and user-friendly. It also suggests that other elements, such as individual norms, perceived behavioral control, and system usage, affect user acceptance.

### 3.5.3. Social Exchange Theory (SET)

A give and take policy forms the basis of every business in some way. When the advantages of social relationships outweigh the disadvantages, people are more inclined to form them. However, the kind of relationship, the cultural setting, and personal traits like personality and values can all affect the kind and degree of benefits and costs. When it comes to AI in customer experience, SET can be used to examine the advantages that AI-powered solutions can offer clients, like tailored suggestions and effective support, and the effects that these things have on the client and their relationship with the business. Regarding consumer behavior, SET forecasts and offers insightful knowledge. Assess the stability and quality of social ties. It has to do with weighing the advantages and disadvantages of a relationship.

The SET is used by marketers to create more successful advertising campaigns that emphasize the advantages of a specific good or service. The SET is a tool used by counselors to assist clients in weighing the advantages and disadvantages of various actions or relationship decisions.

## 3.6. CHALLENGES OF IMPLEMENTING AI-DRIVEN CUSTOMER SERVICE

While integrating AI into customer service has the potential to significantly improve the industry, there are a number of risks that must be carefully considered.

### 3.6.1. Humanizing Customer Interactions

AI in customer service frequently lacks the human touch and empathy that human agents offer. Customer trust may be impacted by interactions that seem robotic and impersonal as a result. Consumers usually want individualized experiences that acknowledge and cater to their specific needs as well as their emotional cues. The inability of current AI systems to fully mimic these human characteristics leads to a discrepancy between customer expectations and the provision of services.

Future research might focus on creating AI systems that mimic human empathy and interaction in order to overcome this difficulty. Putting in place hybrid systems—which combine AI and human support—can assist in handling routine questions while elevating difficult or delicate exchanges with human agents. AI that is enhanced by cutting-edge natural language processing methods may be better able to recognize and react to emotional cues. AI models can be trained on extensive human interaction datasets to acquire the subtleties of compassionate communication. Furthermore, the quality of AI-driven customer service can be greatly improved by consistently leveraging user feedback to hone and improve AI interactions.

### 3.6.2. Navigating Complex Customer Issues

While AI systems perform well on routine customer service tasks, they have trouble answering intricate or subtle questions. These problems require a deeper comprehension and contextual knowledge that AI does not yet possess. Consumers with complicated issues might favor human agents who can offer more thorough solutions, which could have an effect on customer satisfaction and the dependability of AI-powered customer support. Future directions for addressing this challenge include creating AI systems with improved contextual awareness and problem-solving skills. By incorporating cutting-edge machine learning algorithms, AI can learn from complicated situations and become more adept at handling complex problems. Using advanced AI decision-making frameworks can also aid in more efficiently answering challenging questions. Customer service can also be improved by developing dynamic AI systems that work in real-time with human agents. To maintain high standards of customer service, iterative learning based on feedback from complex interactions is crucial for continuous improvement.

### 3.6.3. Balancing Efficiency and Personalization

In customer service, AI systems are frequently built for efficiency, which can occasionally mean sacrificing personalization. While standardized procedures and automated answers can quickly handle large volumes of inquiries, they might not be able to give each customer the personalized attention they value. Customers may feel undervalued and unsatisfied as a result of this trade-off since they are deprived of the personalized interactions that human agents usually provide. However, an excessive emphasis on personalization can hinder productivity, leading to longer response times and increased operating expenses. Personalized service and operational efficiency must coexist in harmony if client loyalty and satisfaction are to be sustained.

Future directions for tackling this issue include applying cutting-edge AI algorithms to evaluate real-time customer data and provide customized responses, preserving a personal touch while guaranteeing prompt service.

By utilizing customer history and behavior data, AI integration with CRM systems can expedite interactions. Additionally, creating AI systems that adapt their degree of personalization according to the interaction's context can help keep routine queries efficient while giving complex problems individualized attention. By using these tactics, companies can improve the overall customer experience by striking a balance between efficiency and personalization (McCarthy et al., 1956).

### 3.6.4. Mitigating Algorithmic Bias

Customer service AI systems may reinforce biases found in their training data, producing unfair or discriminatory results. These prejudices can take many different forms, such as preferring particular groups of people over others on the basis of socioeconomic class, gender, or race. This compromises not just the AI system's fairness but also the confidence of customers and the reputation of the brand. In order to guarantee fair and reliable AI-driven customer support, algorithmic bias must be addressed.

Future approaches to this problem must take corrective as well as preventive action into account. In order to prevent biases from encoding from the beginning, preventative measures entail building AI models with input from stakeholders and scientists. Corrective actions include identifying bias, evaluating previous research, choosing relevant variables, and creating accountable models. To reduce biases over time, AI systems must be continuously monitored and updated based on fresh information and user feedback. Furthermore, using a variety of datasets that more accurately reflect the whole client base can aid in the development of more balanced AI models. Fairness can be further improved and customer trust can be increased by guaranteeing transparency in AI decision-making processes and routinely auditing AI systems for bias.

### 3.6.5. Reliance on Comprehensive Knowledge Base

For AI customer service systems to function effectively, a current and accurate knowledge base is essential. Incomplete or out-of-date data may cause the AI to give inaccurate answers, which would reduce customer satisfaction. The caliber of the knowledge that the AI has access to directly affects the caliber of its output.

Future directions entail enhancing the procedures for updating and maintaining knowledge bases in order to address this challenge. To facilitate ongoing enhancement and growth of the knowledge base, one approach is to implement self-learning knowledge management systems that make use of AI techniques like text clustering, natural language processing, and classification rule learning.

The information can be kept up to date and relevant with regular checks and updates. Incorporating user feedback mechanisms and collaborative filtering can also aid in identifying and filling knowledge base gaps, ensuring that the AI system has access to accurate and thorough data.

### 3.6.6. Building Trust through Ethical AI Implementation Using

Significant ethical and transparency issues are raised by AI in customer service. Consumers are concerned about the fairness of AI decision-making, the use of their data, and the general transparency of AI operations. Resolving these issues is essential to preserving client confidence.

A number of crucial methods will be used in future plans to address these issues of ethics and transparency. First and foremost, it is imperative to create Explainable AI systems that offer concise, intelligible justifications for their suggestions and actions. Consumers usually find it difficult to understand how

AI systems make decisions, which breeds mistrust. AI interactions become more transparent and reliable when algorithms are used that can explain the reasoning behind their choices.

Second, strong bias detection and mitigation techniques must be put into place. AI systems have the potential to reinforce preexisting biases in their training data, which could result in unfair outcomes. As a result, it is crucial to use a variety of training datasets, conduct routine bias audits on AI systems, and create algorithms that can detect and address biases instantly. To guarantee equity in AI-powered customer support, these actions are essential (Martin et al., 2017).

Lastly, it is critical to preserve data usage transparency by outlining the protocols for managing and protecting client data. It makes sense that customers are concerned about how their personal data is collected, used, and protected. These worries can be allayed by following strict ethical guidelines in the creation and application of AI, such as getting express consent from customers for data use and making sure relevant data protection laws are followed.

## REFERENCES


1. Adam, M., Wessel, M., & Benlian, A. (2020). AI-based chatbots in customer service and their effects on user compliance. *Electronic Markets, 30*(2), 427–445.
2. Campbell, M., Hoane Jr, A. J., & Hsu, F. H. (2002). Deep Blue. *Artificial Intelligence, 134*(1, 2), 57–83.
3. Chatterjee, S., Ghosh, S. K., Chaudhuri, R., & Nguyen, B. (2019). Are CRM systems ready for AI integration? A conceptual framework of organizational readiness for effective AI-CRM integration. *The Bottom Line, 32*(2), 144–157.
4. Chung, M., Ko, E., Joung, H., & Kim, S. J. (2020). Chatbot e-service and customer satisfaction regarding luxury brands. *Journal of Business Research, 117*, 587–595.
5. Cortes, C., & Vapnik, V. (1995). Support-vector networks. *Machine Learning, 20*(3), 273–297.
6. Davenport, T. H., Guha, A., Grewal, D., & Bressgott, T. (2020). How artificial intelligence will change the future of marketing. *Journal of the Academy of Marketing Science, 48*(1), 24–42.
7. Dwivedi, Y. K., Hughes, L., Ismagilova, E., Aarts, G., Coombs, C., Crick, T., et al. (2021). Artificial intelligence (AI): Multidisciplinary perspectives on emerging challenges, opportunities, and agenda for research, practice, and policy. *International Journal of Information Management, 57*, 101994.
8. Ferrucci, D., Brown, E., Chu-Carroll, J., Fan, J., Gondek, D., Kalyanpur, A. A., Lally, A., Murdock, J. W., Nyberg, E., Prager, J., Schlaefer, N., & Welty, C. (2010). Building Watson: An overview of the DeepQA project. *AI Magazine, 31*(3), 59–79.
9. Gensler, S., Völckner, F., Liu-Thompkins, Y., & Wiertz, C. (2013). Managing brands in the social media environment. *Journal of Interactive Marketing, 27*(4), 242–256.
10. Homburg, C., Jozić, D., & Kuehnl, C. (2017). Customer experience management: Toward implementing an evolving marketing concept. *Journal of the Academy of Marketing Science, 45*(3), 377–401.
11. Huang, M. H., & Rust, R. T. (2018). Artificial intelligence in service. *Journal of Service Research, 21*(2), 155–172.
12. Jiang, J., Luo, B., & Kulemeka, O. (2020). Examining factors influencing consumer adoption of mobile voice assistants: A trust-transfer perspective. *International Journal of Human-Computer Interaction, 36*(7), 661–672.

13. Kunz, W., & Wirtz, J. (2023). AI in customer services–A service revolution in the making. In J. Sheth, V. Jain, E. Mogaji, & A. Ambika (Eds.), *Artificial Intelligence in Customer Service: Next Frontier to Personalized Engagement* (pp. 11–20). Palgrave.
14. Lu, L., Cai, R., & Gursoy, D. (2019). Developing and validating a service robot integration willingness scale. *International Journal of Hospitality Management, 82*, 324–335.
15. Martin, K. D., & Murphy, P. E. (2017). The role of data privacy in marketing. *Journal of the Academy of Marketing Science, 45*(2), 135–155.
16. McCarthy, J., Minsky, M. L., Rochester, N., & Shannon, C. E. (1956). A proposal for the Dartmouth summer research project on artificial intelligence. *AI Magazine, 27*(4), 12–14.
17. McColl-Kennedy, J. R., Zaki, M., Lemon, K. N., Urmetzer, F., & Neely, A. (2019). Gaining customer experience insights that matter. *Journal of Service Research, 22*(1), 8–26.
18. Pansari, A., & Kumar, V. (2017). Customer engagement: The construct, antecedents, and consequences. *Journal of the Academy of Marketing Science, 45*(3), 294–311.
19. Paszke, A., Gross, S., Massa, F., Lerer, A., Bradbury, J., Chanan, G., Killeen, T., Lin, Z., Gimelshein, N., Antiga, L., Desmaison, A., Kopf, A., Yang, E., DeVito, Z., Raison, M., Tejani, A., Chilamkurthy, S., Steiner, B., Fang, L., Bai, J., & Chintala, S. (2019). PyTorch: An imperative style, high-performance deep learning library. *Advances in Neural Information Processing Systems, 32*, 8026–8037.
20. Rabiner, L. R. (1989). A tutorial on hidden Markov models and selected applications in speech recognition. *Proceedings of the IEEE, 77*(2), 257–286.
21. Rumelhart, D. E., Hinton, G. E., & Williams, R. J. (1986). Learning representations by backpropagating errors. *Nature, 323*(6088), 533–536.
22. Samuel, A. L. (1959). Some studies in machine learning using the game of checkers. *IBM Journal of Research and Development, 3*(3), 210–229.
23. Silver, D., Huang, A., Maddison, C. J., Guez, A., Sifre, L., van den Driessche, G., Schrittwieser, J., Antonoglou, I., Panneershelvam, V., Lanctot, M., Dieleman, S., Grewe, D., Nham, J., Kalchbrenner, N., Sutskever, I., Lillicrap, T., Leach, M., Kavukcuoglu, K., Graepel, T., & Hassabis, D. (2016). Mastering the game of Go with deep neural networks and tree search. *Nature, 529*(7587), 484–489.

24. Tarafdar, M., Beath, C. M., & Ross, J. W. (2019). Using AI to enhance business operations. *MIT Sloan Management Review, 60*(4), 6–23.
25. Turing, A. M. (1950). Computing machinery and intelligence. *Mind, 59*(236), 433–460.
26. Weizenbaum, J. (1966). ELIZA—A computer program for the study of natural language communication between man and machine. *Communications of the ACM, 9*(1), 36–45.
27. Wirtz, J., Kunz, W., & Paluch, S. (2021). The service revolution, intelligent automation, and service robots. *European Business Review, 29*(5), 909.
28. Wirtz, J., So, K. K. F., Mody, M. A., Liu, S. Q., & Chun, H. H. (2019). Platforms in the peer-to-peer sharing economy. *Journal of Service Management, 30*(4), 452–483.
29. Wirtz, J., Tarbit, J. J., Hartley, N., & Kunz, W. (2022). Corporate digital responsibility: Dealing with ethical, privacy, and fairness challenges of AI. *Journal of AI, Robotics & Workplace Automation, 1*(4), 325–328.
30. Xu, Y., Shieh, C. H., van Esch, P., & Ling, I. (2020). AI customer service: Task complexity, problem-solving ability, and usage intention. *Australasian Marketing Journal, 28*, 189–199.

CHAPTER 4

# AI IN OPERATIONS AND SUPPLY CHAIN

## Contents

# INTRODUCTION

Artificial intelligence (AI) has the potential to completely transform supply chain operations, including production, management, planning, and optimization. AI has the potential to enhance supply chain decision-making and operational efficiency through its ability to process large volumes of data, forecast trends, and execute intricate tasks instantly. Lately, this technology has become more and more popular as tools like chatbots and generative AI have taken off and demonstrated how useful the systems can be for supply chain management. Meanwhile, the COVID-19 pandemic demonstrated the vulnerability of the global supply chain and the need for improved management tools.

Machine learning (ML), a subset of AI is the process by which a system learns from data sets rather than being preprogrammed with preprogrammed instructions. ML is capable of much more than traditional software. It can predict consumer demand, identify trends, predict the market, decipher written and spoken language, and evaluate a wide range of variables that can improve the efficiency of a supply chain. There are now more use cases than ever before. Adopting AI is vital, but before implementing a new system in a supply chain, it's crucial to comprehend all of its potential advantages and disadvantages. In addition to realizing that such a large-scale optimization may require time and resources, manufacturers, and logistics companies should take the required actions to get their supply chains ready for AI systems. Particularly for manufacturers who frequently depend on their partners to ship their goods in a timely and organized manner, a supply chain can become complex. Unlike a conventional non-AI system, AI can identify patterns and relationships to maintain equilibrium across all components of a supply chain. From the warehouse to the cargo freighters to the distribution centers, these patterns can aid in the optimization of logistics networks. Given the size of today's supply chains, careful monitoring is necessary to prevent needless interruptions. Demand planning and the ability to forecast production and warehouse capacity based on customer demand are two examples of how AI systems can help with forecasting. Some are employing AI to extract insights from a larger dataset gathered from Internet of Things (IoT) devices placed throughout the supply chain. Supply chain operations can also use AI to monitor market trends and inventory levels. AI can improve supply chain visibility in inventory management, automate physical goods documentation, and intelligently enter data whenever items are transferred. It can give useful information to all supply chain participants and aid in the manufacturer's transparency. The increased supply chain transparency brought about by AI offers unparalleled time and cost savings. Additionally, it assists businesses in meeting sustainability and ethical standards, which have historically been costly and time-consuming.

## 4.1. AI IN SUPPLY CHAIN

Companies employ AI more effectively than traditional software to manage and optimize supply chain operations, including tracking product quality, maintaining inventory levels, and determining the most fuel-efficient delivery routes. Applications that mimic human intelligence and carry out intricate tasks are collectively referred to as artificial intelligence (AI). One of its subfields is machine learning (ML), where systems learn by ingesting large volumes of data instead of being explicitly programmed with instructions. AI systems can now perform tasks like decoding information from video feeds, interpreting written and spoken text, forecasting future market behavior, making decisions in complex scenarios, and uncovering insights hidden in massive data sets better than traditional software because of this learning process. Workflows in practically every link in the supply chain are being managed and optimized with the help of these kinds of capabilities. For instance, supply chain systems that use ML algorithms can find patterns and connections in data sets that are frequently invisible to non-AI or human systems. This allows them to predict customer demand more precisely, which results in more cost-effective inventory management. AI is also capable of analyzing weather and traffic data to suggest alternate shipping routes, which lowers the possibility of unforeseen delays and speeds up delivery. It can keep an eye on work areas to identify ineffective quality control practices as well as health and safety infractions. Additionally, as supply chain experts keep experimenting with the technology, new use cases keep coming up.

### 4.1.1. AI in Supply Chain Explained

AI systems are being used by businesses in their supply chains to improve warehouse productivity, optimize factory workflows, and more. Finished goods manufacturers frequently depend on hundreds or even thousands of components to be shipped from partners across the world and arrive at their assembly facilities on time. Large data sets contain relationships and patterns that AI is beginning to uncover, helping to optimize these logistics networks—which include distribution centers, warehouses, delivery trucks, and cargo freighters—in an efficient manner. In order to optimize the supply chain, tangible goods must be tracked each time they change hands. Here, AI can help maintain the integrity of multiparty transactions by automating documentation through its ability to intelligently enter, extract, and classify data embedded in text files.

Utilizing AI for forecasting, a few manufacturers are able to anticipate production capacity and optimize warehouse capacity in response to customer demand. Some are using AI to identify possible equipment failures and delays before they become a production issue. Some are utilizing AI to extract operational insights from massive data streams originating from the increasing number of Internet of Things (IoT) devices and sensors integrated throughout their transportation and storage infrastructure. Even though AI has a lot of potential advantages for the supply chain, putting the technology into practice can be costly and challenging. Powerful computing systems, such as cloud-based instances or on-premises edge servers, are necessary to run intelligent applications in production. These systems usually need to receive data from integrated sensors and field-deployed devices as part of an Industry 4.0 approach. Training machine learning models on their own data sets, which is an even more computationally and data-dependent process, usually yields the biggest benefits for businesses.

### 4.1.2. End-to-End Supply Chain Transparency with AI

Manufacturers find it difficult to keep an end-to-end track of the flow of materials and goods arriving at their facilities due to the complexity, entanglement, and expansion of modern supply chains. The inner workings of even the most intricate logistics networks can be revealed by AI's exceptional capacity to analyze large data sets quickly. Intelligent algorithms trained through machine learning frequently uncover important insights when ingesting massive streams of logged data and other logistics signals. These insights may include reasons for variability or strategies to increase capacity for processes with fixed and variable time elements that cause bottlenecks. Furthermore, supply chain management (SCM) tools driven by AI outperform conventional systems in tracking large volumes of supplies in real time as they move through intermediate manufacturing and distribution partners to become final goods. Manufacturers may be able to identify suppliers who may be breaking ethical sourcing or quality standards with the aid of this improved visibility and traceability.AI can save time and money by improving supply chain transparency; we'll go into more detail later. Additionally, it can assist manufacturers in meeting the ethical, quality, and sustainability standards that many consumers and regulators expect them to meet when sourcing the components used to create their products. Analytics tools integrated into AI-enabled supply chain applications can spot trends that point to fraudulent or unethical sourcing, and businesses simply cannot afford to work with suppliers—even those located abroad—who violate labor, good governance, or environmental regulations.

### 4.1.3. Advantages of AI in Supply Chain Management

Nearly every process can be improved by using AI in supply chain and logistics. It could lower expenses, boost operational effectiveness, and even enhance worker safety. How precisely? Let's examine each chain link in more detail.

### 4.1.3.1. Boosted Warehouse Efficiency

According to Forbes, warehouses that use AI solutions can experience improvements like up to 99.9% inventory accuracy, a minimum of 20% reduction in worker travel time, and a minimum of 15% increase in order fulfillment speeds. Supply chain and logistics organizations should think about putting the following AI-driven solutions into practice to get comparable results:

- **Warehouse Management Systems (WMS):** AI features in WMS generate insights on how to optimize storage space, modify loading operations, and enhance the workflow of manual processes, in addition to keeping all processes in one system.
- **Robotic Process Automation (RPA):** Robots can totally change tasks like picking, packing, sorting, and other operations that previously required human labor. They can also complete it more quickly and precisely.
- **Predictive Maintenance:** AI is able to gather information from equipment sensors while accounting for a number of parameters, including pressure, temperature, vibration, and more. This data provides insights into the condition of the machinery and potential maintenance procedures.

### *4.1.3.2. Lowered Operational Costs*

One of the primary motivations for businesses to begin evaluating AI tools is typically the chance to reduce operating expenses. More than half of survey participants reported that their companies had experienced supply chain cost reductions of 10–20% in 2021, according to Statista. The following are just a few of the cost-cutting opportunities that AI presents:

- **Resource Optimization:** Supply chain businesses can more effectively allocate human labor and equipment to complete tasks by using data analytics driven by artificial intelligence. Additionally, these analytics aid in the sustainable distribution of raw materials along the supply chain.
- **Energy Management:** Data-driven decision-making regarding the amount of energy required for specific tasks within a given timeframe can result from the application of AI to energy systems.
- **Cost-Efficient Procurement:** AI assists supply chain companies in negotiating prices and identifying cost-effective strategies by evaluating data on contracts with suppliers, distributors, and vendors.

#### *4.1.3.3. Minimization of Errors and Waste*

Supply chain management and artificial intelligence work well together to cut down on waste and human error. Organizations can minimize defects and waste by utilizing automation, data analytics, demand forecasting, and anomaly detection. These can help in the following ways:

- **Process Automation:** AI can reduce labor requirements for manual tasks and eliminate human error in a variety of operations, including document processing and logistics.
- **Quality Control:** Products can be inspected for flaws using AI tools equipped with anomaly detection. They can offer data on anomalies in real time to facilitate prompt problem solving.
- **Effective Resource Allocation:** AI-powered supply chain solutions can minimize material waste by producing data-driven decisions regarding the quantity of resources needed for particular tasks.

#### *4.1.3.4. Enhanced Inventory Management*

According to McKinsey, supply chain management companies have improved inventory levels by 35% since integrating AI. In fact, sophisticated analytics-equipped intelligent systems are able to gather, process, and evaluate historical data in order to produce predictions about possible product orders and distribution. More specifically, AI is capable of the following:

- **Demand Prediction:** Artificial intelligence algorithms examine past sales data and market trends to predict demand and offer advice on how to keep the right amount of inventory on hand.
- **Inventory Tracking:** IoT device sensors are able to track inventory metrics and notify staff members when there are stock level issues that need to be fixed.
- **Stock Replenishment:** AI systems have the ability to automate reordering, which includes negotiating prices and calculating delivery times. This ensures that stock replenishment is completed on schedule.

#### *4.1.3.5. Simulation-Based Operational Optimization*

AI can help with the creation of computer models that simulate various conditions in supply chain management, logistics procedures, and manufacturing processes. With the following AI capabilities, businesses can determine the most practical and effective ways to optimize their processes:

- **Scenario Analysis:** AI can simulate various scenarios to determine whether supply chain disruptions are possible because it can predict them. AI can also assist in creating backup plans and make recommendations about how those disruptions might affect the supply chain.
- **Capacity Planning:** AI models can be used by supply chain solutions to forecast whether logistics can meet demand and search for workable backup plans in the event that results fall short of expectations.

### *4.1.3.6. Safer Work Environment and Material Handling*

AI and computer vision-enabled IoT devices can greatly enhance safety conditions in warehouses, production settings, and transit. Furthermore, workers can depend on robots to handle hazardous jobs involving chemicals or large machinery, reducing the possibility of accidents and increasing operational effectiveness. You can accomplish those by:

- **Hazard Detection:** AI in supply chain management, in conjunction with cameras and sensors, allows for the real-time detection of spills and risky lifting practices, alerting staff members to potential mishaps before they happen.
- **Automated Handling:** AI automates risky jobs (e.g., using large gear in warehouses), which lowers the possibility of worker casualties.

### *4.1.3.7. Faster Deliveries and Better Customer Experience*

According to a survey, almost 17% of customers in the US said they had a great experience using artificial intelligence. At the same time, nearly 18% of those surveyed said they were completely satisfied with robotic automation. AI does, in fact, enhance customer service in a variety of ways. These are the most typical:

- **Route Optimization:** By identifying the most efficient routes that reduce the amount of time customers must wait for their orders, AI-driven deliveries become more efficient than ever.
- **Real-Time Tracking:** A variety of sensors mounted on delivery trucks can give clients up-to-date information on the status of their orders.
- **Customer Service:** AI chatbots have shown to be successful in providing prompt answers to customer service inquiries. As a result, customers have a great experience and develop enduring relationships with brands.

Furthermore, when it comes to optimizing operational procedures, chatbots are incredibly beneficial for companies and their tech support staff. For example, we provided a chatbot for one of our projects that responded to 99% of customer inquiries in less than ten seconds using pre-trained machine learning models for data embedding and natural language processing. The support staff could focus on projects that called for greater creativity at the same time.

#### *4.1.3.8. Greater Supply Chain Sustainability*

Supply chain management with AI can steer a business toward greener practices. The company's brand image will benefit from it as well as the planet since customers are increasingly choosing eco-friendly lifestyles. According to a McKinsey survey, 43% of participants from businesses that had implemented AI said that the technology improved their sustainability initiatives. These efforts may include:

- **Sustainable Sourcing:** AI can analyze supplier data to determine whether a supplier employs sustainable practices and assist businesses in determining whether to work with them.
- **Waste Management:** Businesses can sort their waste more quickly and effectively with AI-powered robots. Robots can guarantee appropriate recycling and disposal procedures, which is especially useful in the food sector.

#### *4.1.3.9. Precise Demand Prediction*

45% of businesses currently use AI to forecast demand, and 43% intend to do so in the upcoming years, according to a Gartner study that demonstrates a change in how businesses anticipate what consumers will want to buy. This demonstrates how artificial intelligence is swiftly taking the place of other supply chain planning tools. Here are some of the reasons why businesses decide to use AI for supply management:

- **Predictive Analytics:** AI-powered systems are able to make precise predictions about what customers will be searching for in stores by analyzing market trends and historical data.
- **Seasonal Adjustments:** AI systems are able to analyze demand during specific times of the year, such as holidays or special occasions, and recommend marketing tactics like sales, exclusive deals, or personalized goods.
- **Market Insights:** Using machine learning and NLP to improve businesses enables the processing of customer sentiment in reviews, social media trends, or news analysis to forecast changes in consumer behavior.

### 4.1.4. The Challenges of Developing an AI-Enabled Supply Chain Ecosystem

Adopting AI in supply chain management is not always simple, despite the fact that it has the potential to completely transform the industry and boost operational efficiency. Businesses report a number of challenges with this kind of digital transformation. Let us go over a few of them.

#### *4.1.4.1. Numerous and Complex Integrations*

It is crucial to add sensors or other Internet of things devices to the equipment because every link in a supply chain frequently depends on transportation or machinery. But in order to connect all the devices that transmit data to the entire ecosystem, this requires intricate software integrations. It goes without saying that adopters of AI have a lot of work ahead of them. All of these components must be able to communicate with one another, share the same protocols and data formats, and function together harmoniously at the same time. Although it will take a lot of work, it will be well worth it. Your company will have complete supply chain visibility and knowledge of the entire supply chain network once this entire ecosystem is put up.

#### *4.1.4.2. Complex ML Models*

Choosing the appropriate algorithms, modifying hyperparameters, and training the models on sizable datasets are all necessary to produce machine learning models with excellent accuracy and dependability. This process requires the expertise of data scientists and machine learning engineers, who not only understand machine learning techniques but also know how to interpret and apply them to specific supply chain requirements. The shortage of highly qualified AI/ML professionals can further complicate the development process.

#### *4.1.4.3. Potentially High Upfront Costs*

AI and supply chains are a potent but costly combination, particularly when it comes to initial adoption. Enterprises may need to invest in cutting-edge hardware, such as IoT devices and high-performance computer systems.

They'll need to invest in infrastructure and multiple software licenses. The creation and integration of specialized AI systems created especially for your company's needs, however, is the costliest component. You will also need to set aside extra money for your AI-enabled systems' ongoing maintenance and updates.

#### *4.1.4.4. Interoperability with Existing Systems*

The infrastructure and software that was purchased a few years ago may still be used by numerous businesses. But because technology is developing at an exponential rate, businesses must constantly update their systems. There is a chance that integrating AI technologies with a company's legacy system will cause compatibility problems. It will probably take a long time, require specialized knowledge, and call for middleware and customization to implement AI systems with legacy platforms.

#### *4.1.4.5. Real-Time Decision-Making*

When using AI for real-time decision-making, it can be challenging to achieve robust, fast data processing and a reliable network infrastructure. Making decisions instantly requires processing large amounts of data as quickly as possible, which necessitates sophisticated computing power and well-thought-out data pipelines. Low-latency communication across the network is a critical component that businesses must consider in order to provide prompt insights and answers. Only by making a significant investment in cutting-edge hardware and software, along with constant system tuning and monitoring, can this level of performance be reached.

### 4.1.5. Examples of AI in Supply Chain

Consider a fictitious American automaker that uses its Michigan plant to assemble three well-known models. The majority of the tens of thousands of parts and components, including steel, tires, spark plugs, and gauge needles, come from mills and manufacturing facilities located in 12 US states, as well as Canada, China, Germany, Japan, and Mexico. The company owns and runs facilities where some components are made, while others are purchased from outside distributors.

Massive deliveries, some from overseas on cargo freighters and others trucked from out of state or across North American borders, are routinely received by our fictitious auto company. At the Michigan plant, these components must eventually come together for final assembly into a sedan, truck, or SUV. However, they must first be ordered, paid for, tracked, received, and stored in the company's sizable, constrained warehouses near the plant.

As if managing a supply chain this size and intricate wasn't difficult enough, the automaker also has to deal with rising energy prices that reduce their profit margins and inflation that makes it more expensive to buy supplies. Increasing the cost of completed cars might be beneficial, but their sales executives think that would reduce consumer demand. Additionally, following the pandemic, the business has to comply with new rules governing factory work environments, such as those requiring the use of personal protective equipment (PPE). Executives who are worried inquire of technology consultants whether and where in the supply chain they stand to gain from artificial intelligence. Yes, they say, and practically everywhere.

To begin with, AI can forecast sales for each type of vehicle based on trends better than the company's basic software. Additionally, it can predict sales effects more precisely in the event of unanticipated market penetration for electric vehicles or increases in gas prices. For supply chain planners, those insightful forecasts are a blessing because they enable them to order just enough goods to meet demand without going over budget, piling up inventory, or overstocking their warehouses. Additionally, the forecasts provide planners with the assurance they need to staff production lines appropriately and invest in opening new lines or save money by closing existing ones.

To ensure that employees adhere to safety and environmental regulations, cameras linked to AI-powered visual models can keep an eye on the automaker's production lines and distribution centers. Additional machine learning-trained models can evaluate logistics data to optimize warehouse operations, cargo loads, and shipping routes, increasing on-time delivery. Last but not least, AI and decision-making models can automate tedious tasks related to managing tangible supplies as well as keeping the transaction and inventory records required to guarantee that everyone in the supply chain is paid promptly and fairly. In practically every aspect of their supply chain operations, actual automakers are saving money by increasing accounting accuracy, decreasing errors, redeploying staff to better support business needs, and improving efficiency. Take Mazda Motor Logistics, which increases on-time deliveries by using Oracle Transportation Management to help determine the best carrier, route, and service level for distributing automobiles and auto parts throughout Europe.

## 4.1.6. Preparing Your Supply Chain for AI-Driven Change

There are never any shortage of challenges when you are about to change the way your business is run. But if you approach this change in the right way, those difficulties won't frighten you or your staff. Here are some pointers for integrating AI into your supply chain.

### *4.1.6.1. Mapping Current Processes*

A thorough supply chain link visualization must be the first step in a well-organized AI transformation. You must consider not only the procedures but also the roles and responsibilities of every worker in the supply chain, from production and procurement to distribution and delivery. The document that will act as a guide for implementing AI should compile all of this data.

#### *4.1.6.2. Evaluating Existing Systems and Data*

Without assessing the condition of the current technological infrastructure, which includes hardware, software, and network capabilities, it is impossible to integrate the newest technologies. Businesses must determine whether changes are necessary in order to integrate AI technologies in the future. Logistics and supply chain firms also have to worry about the accuracy and accessibility of their data. To identify any gaps, the sources and formats must be examined. This stage suggests that data enrichment, cleansing, or the implementation of new data management strategies are required to ensure that the data can effectively drive AI models and algorithms.

#### *4.1.6.3. Pinpointing AI Integration Opportunities*

According to McKinsey, 75% of supply chain executives believe that their goals do not coincide with those of the system integrator. You must pinpoint particular domains where AI can be most useful, such as automation, demand forecasting, or predictive maintenance, if you want to use AI integrations to meet your business objectives. However, since they are prime candidates for AI-driven optimization, organizations should also look for processes that need a lot of data, are prone to errors, or are highly repetitive.

Additionally, examining operational challenges and pain points may reveal areas where AI could improve accuracy or productivity. This stage necessitates a strategic approach to ensure AI projects align with overall business goals and target the most significant supply chain segments.

#### *4.1.6.4. Prioritizing Use Cases*

Prioritizing which use cases you want to concentrate on first and which ones can wait until the next iterations is crucial after identifying possible AI integration opportunities.

Prioritization criteria could include feasibility, alignment with strategic goals, and possible return on investment. Planning the integration of AI into your supply chain systems in this way helps you focus resources and efforts on projects that will maximize benefits and minimize risks. The intricacy of implementation, the preparedness of current systems, and the anticipated effect on operational performance are all taken into account.

### *4.1.6.5. Partnering with a Tech Vendor*

One must evaluate potential partners based on their technological capabilities, experience, and track record of providing artificial intelligence solutions to the supply chain sector in order to select the best vendor. A trustworthy tech company can provide useful data, state-of-the-art tools, and ongoing support during the AI implementation process. We would be pleased to assist you in resolving any issues related to the deployment of AI. From initial planning to full-scale deployment and support, we are prepared to provide technical assistance and guidance because we have experience with both supply chain management specifics and AI/ML integration.

With AI, supply chain management gains significant power. AI is useful when supply chains and logistics face difficulties due to natural disasters, shifting geopolitical conditions, or changing work environments. Excellent inventory and warehouse efficiency is made possible by this technology, which also reduces human error through automation, makes workplaces safer, permits real-time decision-making, and offers demand forecasting.

Even though AI can help businesses navigate complex markets, individual businesses may face challenges in adopting it. These may include a large number of integrations, the creation of complex machine learning models, exorbitant expenses, or links to legacy systems. However, by developing a thorough adoption plan, assessing your current system, and formulating strategies for tackling the most demanding areas of your business first, you can overcome those bottlenecks with the right vendor.

## 4.2. AUTOMATION IN SUPPLY CHAINS

In a time of rapid change and technological innovation, the supply chain sector is poised for a significant transformation. A paradigm shift that promises to completely transform the flow of goods from producers to consumers is being driven by automation. The supply chain's automation journey is a decades-long continuum rather than a recent occurrence. The supply chain industry has undergone a remarkable evolution, from the modest beginnings of mechanized processes to the integration of cutting-edge technologies today. These days, advanced algorithms, AI, and RPA are leading the way in changing the conventional supply chain environment. As we go further, we will examine the background of automation, its slow development, and the combination of robotics and artificial intelligence, laying the groundwork for a thorough comprehension of its revolutionary possibilities.

In light of this, it is essential to examine the numerous advantages that automation offers the supply chain. Among the benefits that companies can take advantage of are increased productivity, lower expenses, and better data analytics. In addition to promoting operational excellence, these advantages enable businesses to make data-driven choices, giving them a competitive advantage in an increasingly interconnected world.

### 4.2.1. The Evolution of Automation in Supply Chain

Supply chain automation has a long history and has seen many notable advancements over time. To fully appreciate supply chain automation's current state and transformative potential, it is imperative to comprehend this evolution.

#### *4.2.1.1. Early Stages of Automation in Supply Chain*

The origins of supply chain automation can be traced to the introduction of basic mechanization in the early 1900s. In factories and warehouses, processes were streamlined with the use of conveyor belts and crude sorting systems. Even though the scope of these early automation technologies was constrained, they set the stage for later developments.

#### *4.2.1.2. Historical Milestones in Supply Chain Automation*

The advent of computer-based systems for order processing and inventory management in the middle of the 20th century was a major turning point. The advent of Material Requirements Planning (MRP) systems during this time period made it possible to better manage production scheduling and inventory. It was an important step toward efficiency driven by automation.

#### *4.2.1.3. Emergence of AI and Robotics in the Supply Chain*

The supply chain sector has undergone a technological revolution in recent decades. Automation has reached new heights thanks to the development of robotics and AI. These days, sophisticated robotics can perform complex jobs like picking and packing in warehouses. Delivery trucks' routes are optimized by AI-powered algorithms, leading to quicker and more economical deliveries.

#### *4.2.1.4. Technological Advancements Over the Years*

Automation technology has kept advancing quickly. Automated systems in modern warehouses track products, manage inventory, and fill orders with amazing accuracy. Proactive decision-making is now possible due to real-time visibility into supply chain operations brought about by the integration of sensors, IoT devices, and cloud computing.

#### 4.2.1.5. *Impact of Automation on Supply Chain Efficiency*

It is impossible to overestimate the effect of automation on supply chain effectiveness. Automation has become essential for guaranteeing on-time delivery, cutting down on errors, and optimizing inventory levels as supply chains have grown increasingly intricate and worldwide. Supply chain management is now a streamlined, data-driven operation instead of a labor-intensive, manual process thanks to it.

### 4.2.2. Benefits of Automation in Supply Chain

#### 4.2.2.1. *Improved Efficiency and Productivity*

Efficiency and productivity in the supply chain are greatly increased by automation. Businesses can now process orders, track inventory, and enter data more quickly and accurately than ever before by automating repetitive and routine tasks. The least amount of human error occurs, which not only saves time but also gets rid of expensive errors that can happen in manual processes. Moreover, automation makes it possible for operations to run continuously and nonstop. Because machines and software don't need to sleep or take breaks, essential supply chain operations can be carried out around-the-clock. Improved performance overall, shorter lead times, and quicker order fulfillment are all results of this increased operational efficiency.

#### 4.2.2.2. *Cost Reduction and Savings*

One of the main advantages of supply chain automation is cost reduction. Businesses can save a significant amount of money when procedures become more streamlined and error rates decline.

The use of manual labor, which can be highly expensive in supply chain operations, is reduced by automation. Because labor expenses are lower, workers can be assigned to more strategically important jobs like process optimization and quality control. Automation also optimizes the use of resources. By ensuring that resources like cars, machinery, and warehouses are used effectively, it lowers operating costs. Automation also makes predictive maintenance possible, which reduces costs by averting expensive malfunctions and guaranteeing that equipment is utilized to its maximum capacity.

#### 4.2.2.3. *Enhanced Data Analytics and Decision-Making*

A multitude of data is produced by automation, which can be used to improve data analytics and decision-making. Real-time supply chain performance insights enable organizations to take well-informed, data-driven decisions. Large volumes of data can be processed and analyzed by advanced analytics tools, which can then be used to find opportunities, trends, and patterns that would be difficult to find through manual analysis. This data-driven methodology encompasses supplier relationship management, inventory control, and demand forecasting. Automation makes it possible to continuously track important metrics and KPIs, giving your insight into the whole ecosystem of the supply chain. Businesses can react swiftly to changes in the market, act quickly when making decisions, and improve their supply chain strategies for increased competitiveness when they have access to accurate and current information.

#### *4.2.2.4. Streamlined Inventory Management*

One of the most important aspects of supply chain operations is inventory management, which is optimized in large part by automation. Real-time inventory tracking by automated systems guarantees that stock levels are neither excessively high nor low.

This lowers carrying costs and lowers the possibility of overstock or stockout scenarios. Automation also makes intelligent demand forecasting possible. Automated systems can forecast future demand with accuracy by examining past data and present trends. This enables businesses to modify their inventory levels appropriately. Better capital allocation and inventory turnover rates are the outcomes of this.

#### *4.2.2.5. Increased Customer Satisfaction and Service Quality*

Any business must prioritize customer satisfaction, and automation plays a big part in reaching this objective. Automation improves customer satisfaction by increasing productivity, decreasing errors, and guaranteeing on-time delivery. Customers receive precise information about their shipments, orders are processed more quickly, and deliveries are more dependable. Additionally, automation makes it easier to communicate with clients. Transparency and real-time order status updates are provided by automated notifications, tracking systems, and customer portals. In addition to lowering customer inquiries, this increases confidence in the supply chain procedure.

### 4.2.3. Robotic Process Automation in Supply Chain

In the supply chain sector, RPA has become a game-changing technology that is redefining how companies oversee and maximize their operations. We will delve into the many aspects of RPA in the supply chain in this section, starting with an overview of this innovative technology.

### *4.2.3.1. Introduction to Robotic Process Automation (RPA)*

RPA stands for robotic process automation, which is the process of automating repetitive, rule-based tasks within business processes using software robots, or "bots." These automated programs are made to simulate human tasks like data entry, data extraction, and interacting with other online platforms. RPA is a useful tool in supply chain management because of its high accuracy and efficiency.

### *4.2.3.2. Key Applications of RPA in Supply Chain*

RPA is widely used in many supply chain operations and provides significant advantages to businesses. The automation of order processing is one of its main uses. RPA bots can update inventory records in real-time, validate customer information, and process incoming orders quickly and accurately. This improves customer satisfaction by lowering errors and guaranteeing timely order fulfillment.

Demand forecasting and inventory management are two more critical areas where RPA is used. Accurate demand forecasts can be produced by RPA software by analyzing previous sales data, market trends, and other pertinent variables. By lowering excess stock and lowering the chance of stockouts, these forecasts assist businesses in optimizing their inventory levels. Consequently, businesses are able to keep their supply chains running smoothly and with lower carrying costs.

### *4.2.3.3. RPA's Role in Optimizing Supply Chain Processes*

By increasing productivity and lowering operating expenses, RPA is essential to supply chain process optimization. Invoicing is one prominent area where RPA shines. Bots are capable of automatically pulling information from invoices, cross-referencing it with purchase orders, and starting payment procedures. This decreases manual labor and the chance of error in addition to quickening the payment cycle. RPA can also expedite supplier communication and onboarding. Bots have the ability to gather and authenticate supplier data, guarantee adherence to contractual terms, and even enable automated correspondence between the company and its vendors. As a result, there is less administrative overhead in the supply chain and better collaboration.

### *4.2.3.4. Integration of RPA with Existing Systems*

RPA's ability to easily integrate with current software programs and systems is one of its benefits. Among other things, RPA bots can be used in conjunction with customer relationship management (CRM) software, warehouse management systems (WMS), and enterprise resource planning (ERP) systems. A coherent and synchronized supply chain ecosystem is made possible by this integration. Real-time data sharing and decision-making are also made possible by the integration. An RPA bot, for instance, can initiate order processing, update inventory levels in the ERP system, and send shipment information to the WMS when a customer places an order. Lead times are shortened, supply chain visibility is improved, and manual interventions are minimized with this degree of automation and integration.

### 4.2.4. Automation in Logistics and Supply Chain Management

In order to improve supply chain management and logistics' efficacy and efficiency, automation is essential. The importance of logistics in the larger supply chain context, the smooth integration of automation into logistics procedures, the benefits of real-time tracking and monitoring, the function of automation in transportation optimization, and the revolutionary effects of warehouse automation on supply chain management will all be covered in this section.

#### *4.2.4.1. The Significance of Logistics in the Supply Chain*

Logistics, which includes the procedures involved in moving, storing, and managing goods from the point of origin to the final destination, forms the core of the supply chain. Transportation, warehousing, inventory control, and order fulfillment are all coordinated in this process. A vital element in ensuring that goods are delivered to customers quickly and effectively is logistics. Logistics acts as a link between suppliers, manufacturers, distributors, and customers in the supply chain. Logistics automation can reduce lead times, minimize errors, and ultimately improve customer satisfaction by streamlining these intricate operations.

#### *4.2.4.2. Integration of Automation into Logistics Processes*

The application of technology-driven solutions to optimize different facets of transportation and warehousing is required for the integration of automation into logistics processes. Automated systems are capable of processing orders quickly and accurately, as well as planning routes and optimizing loads. For example, robotics can automate warehouse tasks like palletizing and depalletizing, while machine learning algorithms can analyze historical transportation data to determine the most economical routes. Increased overall efficiency, reduced operating costs, and smoother operations are guaranteed by the seamless integration of automation technologies.

#### *4.2.4.3. Benefits of Real-Time Tracking and Monitoring*

Modern logistics operations rely heavily on real-time tracking and monitoring. Automation makes it possible to keep an eye on the flow and condition of goods at every point of the supply chain.

Businesses are able to track the location, condition, and estimated time of arrival (ETA) of their products thanks to real-time visibility into shipments made possible by GPS tracking, RFID (Radio-Frequency Identification), and IoT (Internet of Things) sensors. Proactive decision-making is made possible by this degree of transparency, which also improves supply chain visibility. Real-time data minimizes possible bottlenecks by enabling prompt responses and rerouting in the event of delays or disruptions.

#### *4.2.4.4. Automation's Role in Optimizing Transportation*

An essential part of supply chain management and logistics is transportation. Drones and driverless cars are just two examples of the many technologies that fall under the umbrella of transportation automation. Autonomous cars with AI-powered navigation systems can speed up deliveries, cut down on fuel use, and optimize routes.

Last-mile deliveries can be made with drones, especially in cities where traffic is an issue. In addition to increasing efficiency, automation in transportation lowers costs and promotes environmental sustainability.

#### *4.2.4.5. Warehouse Automation and Its Impact on Supply Chain Management*

One revolutionary development in supply chain management is warehouse automation. Robotic systems in automated warehouses are capable of performing picking, packing, and sorting duties. By assisting human employees, these robots improve order fulfillment's accuracy and speed. Furthermore, automation in warehouses makes inventory management more effective and lowers the possibility of overstocking and stockouts. Automation of warehouses leads to more efficient operations, lower labor costs, and better supply chain performance overall.

### 4.2.5. Challenges in Implementing Automation

Although supply chain automation has a lot of potential, there are drawbacks as well. This section examines five significant obstacles that businesses frequently run into when automating their supply chain operations.

### *4.2.5.1. Resistance to Change in Traditional Supply Chain Processes*

Opposition to change within established procedures is one of the biggest obstacles to supply chain automation. Numerous well-established supply chain procedures and systems have existed for years or even decades. Workers may be used to manual processes, so the idea of switching to automated systems may cause them to become uneasy and resist. Organizations must spend money on change management techniques that highlight the advantages of automation, include staff members in the transition, and offer sufficient assistance and training in order to overcome this obstacle.

### *4.2.5.2. Initial Investment and Cost of Automation Technology*

There is no doubting that the initial investment needed can be significant, even though automation promises long-term cost savings and efficiency improvements. A company's budget may be strained by the acquisition and deployment of automation technologies like robotics, AI-driven software, and Internet of Things devices. It could be difficult for smaller companies in particular to set aside money for automation. Organizations should prioritize automation projects that yield the highest return on investment, investigate financing options, and perform a comprehensive cost-benefit analysis in order to overcome this obstacle.

### *4.2.5.2. Data Security and Cybersecurity Concerns*

Data is essential to supply chain automation, and as digital and innovative technologies are used more frequently, worries about data security and cybersecurity have grown. One of the main priorities is safeguarding private supply chain information from online dangers like ransomware attacks and data breaches. Strong cybersecurity measures, such as encryption, access controls, and frequent security audits, must be put in place by organizations. To protect their automated systems and sensitive data, they should also follow best practices and remain current on the most recent cybersecurity threats.

### *4.2.5.3. Training and Upskilling the Workforce*

The workforce must change in response to the increasing prevalence of automation technologies. For automated systems to be operated and managed efficiently, workers who have operated manually in the past might require training. A seamless transition requires upskilling the workforce in automation understanding and management. For workers to be prepared to collaborate with automated technologies, companies need to provide them with extensive training programs, workshops, and opportunities for ongoing education. This reduces resistance while also raising job satisfaction and employee engagement.

#### *4.2.5.4. Balancing Automation with Human Expertise*

Finding the ideal ratio between automation and human knowledge is a difficult task. While automation can increase productivity, increase accuracy, and streamline procedures, human judgment, creativity, and adaptability are still needed in some aspects of the supply chain. Excessive automation may result in inflexible procedures that are not equipped to manage unforeseen circumstances or specific client requirements. Organizations must carefully examine their supply chain procedures to identify the areas where automation is most helpful and the ones where human knowledge is essential in order to address this challenge. Finding the ideal balance guarantees that automation enhances human abilities, making the supply chain more responsive and agile.

### 4.2.6. Future Trends in Supply Chain Automation

#### *4.2.6.1. Predictive Analytics and Demand Forecasting*

Demand forecasting and predictive analytics are key components of supply chain automation's future. Data powers modern supply chains, and predictive analytics uses both historical and current data to forecast future demand trends. Businesses are able to predict customer preferences, product demand, and inventory levels with precision thanks to sophisticated algorithms and machine learning. This optimizes production schedules and logistics routes in addition to lowering the risk of stockouts or overstocking. By delivering goods when and where they are needed, businesses can improve customer satisfaction, reduce expenses, and streamline operations.

#### *4.2.6.2. Autonomous Vehicles and Drones in Logistics*

Drones and driverless car integration with logistics has the potential to completely transform the supply chain's transportation system. Delivery trucks and other autonomous vehicles can run effectively around-the-clock with less assistance from humans. To ensure the prompt and safe delivery of goods, they are outfitted with sensors, cameras, and cutting-edge software that allows them to navigate and react to traffic conditions. Drones are also being used for aerial surveillance of warehouse operations, last-mile delivery in urban areas, and reaching remote locations. This makes supply chains more sustainable by cutting down on the environmental impact of traditional delivery methods while also speeding up delivery times.

#### *4.2.6.3. Blockchain Technology in Supply Chain Transparency*

The supply chain's traceability and transparency will be improved by blockchain technology. Blockchain makes sure that every transaction and movement of goods is recorded and can be tracked back to its source by establishing an immutable and decentralized ledger. This degree of openness is crucial for guaranteeing product authenticity, stopping counterfeits, and handling problems like food safety and recalls. Real-time information about the origin, path, and state of products is accessible to suppliers, manufacturers, and consumers, promoting accountability and trust throughout the supply chain. Additionally, blockchain has the ability to cut down on paperwork, expedite customs procedures, and lessen fraud, all of which could save money.

#### *4.2.6.4. The Role of the Internet of Things (IoT) in Automation*

Automation of supply chain operations is greatly aided by the IoT. Real-time data collection and transmission can be facilitated by integrating IoT devices, like sensors and RFID tags, into transportation vehicles, packaging, and products. With the unmatched supply chain visibility provided by this data, proactive decision-making and effective resource allocation are made possible. For instance, while GPS tracking offers exact location data, temperature sensors in refrigerated trucks can guarantee the preservation of perishable goods. Automation powered by IoT makes it possible for companies to adapt to changing circumstances, plan the best routes, and keep an eye on the state of their inventory, all of which improve customer satisfaction and supply chain efficiency.

#### *4.2.6.5. Sustainability and Eco-Friendly Automation Practices*

Supply chain management is becoming more and more concerned with sustainability, and automation can help implement eco-friendly practices. Automated systems can minimize carbon emissions, cut waste, and optimize energy use. Energy savings can be achieved, for example, by using smart warehouse management systems to optimize HVAC and lighting based on occupancy. Furthermore, by monitoring the environmental impact of raw materials and selecting suppliers with eco-friendly policies, automation can facilitate sustainable sourcing. Automation-driven sustainable packaging solutions can lessen a product's environmental impact. In general, adopting automation to promote sustainability is in line with the global movement toward environmentally friendly supply chains, which is advantageous for a business's standing as well as the environment.

## 4.2.7. Human-Machine Collaboration

A new era in supply chain management has been brought about by automation, which has an impact on both processes and the roles that human workers play in these automated supply chains. It is essential to comprehend how human workers' roles are changing in this situation.

### *4.2.7.1. The Evolving Role of Human Workers in Automated Supply Chains*

The roles that human workers play in supply chain operations have changed significantly as a result of automation. Automation has changed the emphasis from the manual and repetitive nature of many supply chain tasks in the past. Human employees are now managing automated systems rather than just carrying out repetitive tasks.

These days, human workers are in charge of monitoring data analytics, supervising automated process performance, and formulating strategic decisions based on the insights these automated systems produce. This change from manual execution to decision-making emphasizes how important it is to retrain and upskill the workforce.

### *4.2.7.2. Upskilling and Reskilling the Workforce for Automation*

Investing in retraining and upskilling employees is essential for success in an automated supply chain environment. Routine tasks are being replaced by automation, and in order for human workers to effectively operate and manage automated systems, they must learn new skills.

Upskilling is improving current abilities, like problem-solving and data analysis, to meet the demands of automation. Conversely, reskilling entails giving employees whole new skill sets, frequently in the areas of technology and data management. To help with this transition, educational and training initiatives are crucial. Prioritizing upskilling and reskilling puts businesses in a better position to take advantage of automation's full potential while holding onto a workforce that is knowledgeable and flexible.

### *4.2.7.3. Ensuring a Balance Between Automation and Human Involvement*

Even though automation has many benefits, it's important to balance it with human involvement in supply chain operations. Over-automation can result in a loss of adaptability and flexibility when dealing with unforeseen difficulties. Human laborers contribute creativity, critical thinking, and problem-solving skills. A thorough grasp of the unique requirements and difficulties presented by every supply chain operation is necessary to strike this balance, as is meticulous planning. Optimizing overall efficiency and effectiveness requires determining which tasks are best suited for automation and which ones need human judgment.

### *4.2.7.4. Collaborative Robots (Cobots) and Their Use in Supply Chain*

One of the best examples of how human-machine collaboration can be achieved in the supply chain is collaborative robots, or cobots. Cobots, as opposed to conventional industrial robots, are made to work alongside humans, enhancing rather than substituting for their labor.

Human workers provide their adaptability and problem-solving abilities, while cobots perform exceptionally well in tasks requiring precision and repeatability. Cobots are used in supply chain operations for pick-and-place, packaging, and quality control tasks. Their capacity to cooperate with human laborers increases output while preserving efficiency and safety.

### *4.2.7.5. Strategies for Harmonious Human-Machine Collaboration*

In the supply chain, harmonious cooperation between humans and machines is a strategic necessity rather than merely an ideal. To make sure this cooperation goes smoothly, a few tactics can be used:

- **Education and Training:** Offer thorough training courses to give employees the abilities they need to work with automated systems.
- **Clear Communication:** To guarantee that tasks are coordinated effectively, create efficient channels of communication between human workers and machines.
- **Feedback Loops:** Set up systems that let employees offer suggestions for improving automated procedures in order to continuously improve them.
- **Adaptive Workflows:** Create adaptable processes that can handle demand variations or unplanned interruptions, in which case human involvement might be necessary.
- **Continuous Improvement:** Encourage a culture of continuous improvement in which people and machines collaborate to find opportunities for optimization.

## 4.2.8. Sustainability and Green Supply Chains

All industries now prioritize sustainability, and the supply chain industry is no different. Automation is essential for achieving sustainability objectives, improving the environmental impact of supply chains, and making them more eco-friendly.

### *4.2.8.1. Automation's Contribution to Sustainable Supply Chains*

The development of sustainable supply chains is greatly aided by automation in a number of ways. Automation aids in the preservation of important resources like energy and raw materials by streamlining procedures and cutting down on resource waste. By ensuring that resources are used wisely, automated systems can operate at maximum efficiency and help to lessen the environmental impact of supply chain operations. Automation also makes it easier to implement circular supply chain models. Automated systems, for example, can make it possible to recycle and refurbish materials and products more effectively, which can lessen the need to extract new resources. Because circularity reduces waste and encourages responsible resource management, it is consistent with sustainability goals.

### *4.2.8.2. Reducing Carbon Footprint Through Automation*

The decrease in carbon footprint is one of the main sustainability advantages of supply chain automation. Transportation and logistics systems that are automated can optimize routes, saving fuel and reducing greenhouse gas emissions. AI-driven autonomous cars can select the most fuel-efficient routes and cut down on idle time to further reduce emissions. Automation also makes accurate inventory management possible. This implies that businesses can cut back on excess inventory, which will reduce the amount of energy needed for transportation and storage. Automation reduces the carbon footprint that comes from hurried logistics operations by eliminating the need for expedited shipping or rush orders.

### *4.2.8.3. Ethical Considerations in Supply Chain Automation*

Even though automation has many advantages, moral issues should not be disregarded. There may be issues with job displacement for the workforce as supply chain operations grow more automated. A dedication to workforce development and transitioning is a necessary component of ethical automation practices. To ensure a fair transition, this entails giving employees whose jobs are affected by automation training and upskilling opportunities. Transparency in algorithms used for making decisions is another aspect of ethical automation. Automation and AI systems should be designed with moral principles in mind, steering clear of prejudices that might lead to unjust treatment. Supply chain operations need to preserve trust and moral integrity, which requires transparency in the decision-making process surrounding automation.

#### *4.2.8.4. Sustainable Packaging and Distribution Practices*

Automation has an impact on distribution and packaging procedures as well. Automated optimization of sustainable packaging materials can minimize waste and protect the environment. Precision packaging is made possible by automation, which ensures that the appropriate boxes or containers are used for each product and cuts down on extra packaging material. Moreover, automated distribution centers can be placed in a way that reduces transportation distances and emissions. Businesses may identify the most environmentally friendly distribution routes and techniques by using automation and data analytics, which will improve the sustainability and greenness of the supply chain.

#### *4.2.8.5. The Role of Automation in Reducing Waste and Energy Consumption*

A key element of sustainability is waste reduction, and automation is essential to cutting waste in the supply chain. Automation systems can precisely monitor and regulate processes, lowering the possibility of flaws or mistakes that could result in product waste. Automation also makes predictive maintenance possible, which guarantees that equipment runs as efficiently as possible while using less energy. Real-time detection of inefficiencies or malfunctions by automated sensors enables proactive maintenance that reduces energy waste.

## 4.3. AI-DRIVEN DEMAND FORECASTING, INVENTORY OPTIMIZATION, AND LOGISTICS

AI-driven logistics, inventory control, and demand forecasting may help companies increase productivity, cut expenses, and improve customer satisfaction.

### 4.3.1. Demand Forecasting

In the contemporary business landscape characterized by rapidity and intense competition, logistics enterprises perpetually explore avenues to enhance productivity, curtail expenses, and furnish superior customer services. Precise demand forecasting is a crucial component that can aid in accomplishing these objectives. The process of projecting future demand for goods or services using past data and other pertinent variables is known as demand forecasting. Businesses can more effectively plan their inventory, shipping, warehousing, and other logistical operations by accurately forecasting demand. In addition to lowering needless expenses related to stockouts or excess inventory, this raises customer satisfaction levels all around.

Historically, statistical models and other conventional forecasting techniques have been used in logistics to forecast demand. But thanks to technological advancements, particularly in the area of AI, businesses now have access to more potent instruments and methods that can greatly increase the precision and effectiveness of demand forecasting.

Demand forecasting in the logistics sector has been completely transformed by AI, especially machine learning algorithms. With great accuracy, these algorithms can forecast future demand by analyzing large volumes of data, such as market trends, seasonality, past sales data, and other external factors. AI-powered demand forecasting systems are able to adjust to shifting market conditions and produce more accurate forecasts by continuously learning from fresh data and refining their predictions.

There are many advantages to using AI in logistics for demand forecasting. The following are some of the main advantages:

- **Increased Forecast Accuracy:** Complex patterns in data that traditional forecasting techniques might miss can be analyzed by AI algorithms. As a result, there is less chance of overstocking or stockouts due to more precise demand projections.
- **Real-time Forecasting:** AI-driven demand forecasting systems can offer businesses real-time insights into demand variations, enabling them to swiftly modify their transportation and inventory schedules in response to shifting demand.
- **Cost Savings:** Businesses can optimize their inventory levels, cut expenses associated with excess inventory, and reduce stockouts by accurately forecasting demand. Significant cost savings and increased profitability result from this.
- **Improved Customer Service:** By ensuring that products are available when customers need them, companies can improve customer satisfaction and loyalty through accurate demand forecasting.

Numerous logistics industry sectors are utilizing AI-powered demand forecasting solutions to enhance operational effectiveness and customer service. Typical uses of AI in logistics demand forecasting include the following:

- **Inventory Management:** By forecasting demand for various goods and regions, AI algorithms can assist businesses in optimizing their stock levels. Businesses can lower holding costs and increase supply chain efficiency by making sure the appropriate quantity of stock is available at the appropriate time and location.
- **Transportation Planning:** By using demand patterns, logistics companies can anticipate future transportation requirements with the aid of AI-powered demand forecasting solutions. This makes it possible for businesses to improve delivery times, cut fuel expenses, and optimize their transportation routes.
- **Warehouse Operations:** By forecasting demand for various products and locations, AI algorithms can optimize warehouse operations. This enhances overall warehouse efficiency by lowering stockouts and picking errors.
- **Supply Chain Management:** By offering useful insights into demand patterns throughout the whole supply chain, AI-powered demand forecasting solutions can help businesses plan their manufacturing, distribution, and procurement procedures more effectively.

All things considered, there is no denying the advantages of using AI to logistics demand forecasting. Businesses can gain a competitive edge by increasing operational efficiency, cutting costs, and offering better customer services when they implement AI-powered demand forecasting solutions. We anticipate seeing even more cutting-edge uses of AI in logistics demand forecasting in the future as the technology develops. Early adopters of these technologies will be well-positioned to prosper in the dynamic and fast-paced logistics sector.

Businesses need to continuously monitor and modify their forecasts in response to shifting customer demand if they want to stay competitive and increase the accuracy of demand forecasting. Forecasting accuracy can be improved by putting best practices into practice. It is also advised to collaborate with a knowledgeable third-party logistics (3PL) provider that specializes in advanced analytics and machine learning technologies. Leading 3PL TVS Supply Chain Solutions provides clients with a wealth of experience and knowledge to help them create scalable and effective supply chains.

### 4.3.2. Inventory Optimization

In the business sector, AI has become a game-changer, transforming many facets of operations and decision-making. Inventory management is among the fields where artificial intelligence is having a big influence. Effective inventory control is essential for any company that deals with tangible products to succeed. It keeps customers happy, reduces expenses, and guarantees that products are available when needed. However, businesses have long struggled with inventory management issues, ranging from supply chain optimization to demand forecasting.

### *4.3.2.1. The Role of AI in Inventory Management*

Businesses are always searching for methods to enhance their operations and obtain a competitive advantage. In this endeavor, artificial intelligence has become a potent ally, providing creative answers to enduring inventory management problems. Artificial intelligence is a range of capabilities that allow machines to mimic human intelligence, such as learning from data, making predictions, and automating tasks. It is not a single, monolithic technology.

AI can enhance inventory management in a number of ways, from automated decision-making to real-time data analysis. This technology is a vital tool for inventory optimization because it can process enormous volumes of data fast, accurately, and without fatigue. Numerous industries, including manufacturing, logistics, e-commerce, and retail, can benefit from the use of AI for inventory management:

- **Retail:** AI-driven retail inventory systems assist in forecasting customer demand, enabling companies to keep the right amount of inventory on hand and prevent shortages or overstock.
- **Manufacturing:** By streamlining the supply of components and raw materials, AI can improve production scheduling.
- **Logistics:** AI in logistics can simplify route optimization, resulting in lower costs and on-time delivery.

Employing AI for inventory management in the industries mentioned comes with many advantages, including:

- **Accuracy:** AI can easily process large datasets and produce highly accurate predictions, which lowers forecasting errors and ensures that the correct products are available.
- **Real-Time Data Analysis:** AI systems are able to make proactive decisions by continuously monitoring sales patterns, inventory levels, and other pertinent data.
- **Automation:** Employees can concentrate on more strategic tasks by automating routine inventory tasks like placing and reordering orders.

- **Cost Reduction:** Businesses can save a lot of money by minimizing resource waste and streamlining operations and inventory levels.
- **Increased Customer Satisfaction:** AI helps companies satisfy consumer demand by guaranteeing that goods are available when needed, which raises customer satisfaction.

As you can see, AI is more than just a catchphrase when used properly. This innovative technology is changing the way companies handle their inventory, which will ultimately increase productivity and profitability.

## *4.3.2.2. Key AI Techniques for Inventory Management*

The function of AI in inventory management and its possible benefits were discussed in the previous section. Let's now explore the particular AI methods and algorithms that are at the core of revolutionizing conventional inventory management procedures.

### *4.3.2.2.1. Inventory Forecasting*

Using machine learning algorithms for inventory forecasting is one of the most important uses of AI in inventory management. Machine learning models make remarkably accurate predictions about future demand by analyzing past sales data, consumer trends, and outside variables. As more data becomes available, these algorithms can adjust and get better over time, becoming more accurate. Forecasting based on machine learning reduces overstock and stockout scenarios, which eventually saves companies money and guarantees customer satisfaction.

### *4.3.2.2.2. Demand Prediction*

One essential tool for comprehending consumer demand is predictive analytics. It offers a thorough understanding of demand patterns by fusing historical data, current information, and market trends. Businesses can anticipate changes in demand and take proactive measures to address them by modifying supply chain operations, production schedules, or inventory levels with the aid of AI-driven predictive analytics.

### *4.3.2.2.3. Inventory Segmentation*

Businesses can classify their products according to a number of criteria, such as demand trends, shelf life, and profitability, by using inventory segmentation techniques like ABC inventory. Targeted management strategies are made possible by this segmentation. Slow-moving, long-lasting items like furniture require different management strategies than high-demand, short-shelf-life products like perishables. AI can save time and money by ensuring that the appropriate products get the right attention. Many companies combine these AI techniques to create a comprehensive inventory management solution that meets their unique needs because they are not mutually exclusive. The end product is a flexible and dynamic system that changes to accommodate shifting consumer tastes and market conditions.

### *4.3.2.3. Benefits of AI in Inventory Management*

There are numerous advantages to using AI in inventory management, which not only improve operational efficiency but also affect a company's financial performance. Let's take a closer look at these.

#### *4.3.2.3.1. Cost Reduction*

The potential for large cost savings is one of the strongest arguments for companies to use AI in inventory management. AI-driven inventory optimization makes sure companies have the proper amount of goods on hand, which reduces holding costs. AI can assist in mitigating the costly issues of stockouts and overstocking. Businesses can increase profitability, lower storage costs, and more efficiently allocate resources when inventory levels are optimized.

#### *4.3.2.3.2. Improved Customer Satisfaction*

Customers expect products to be available instantly when they want them in this day and age, driven by the unending supply of humorous cat videos on TikTok and Amazone Prime's guaranteed one-day shipping. Inventory management with AI makes sure of that. Reducing out-of-stock situations through precise demand forecasting and real-time monitoring keeps customers loyal to the brand and stops them from switching to competitors.

#### *4.3.2.3.3. Enhanced Decision-making*

Massive volumes of data are processed and analyzed in real time by AI-powered systems, which then offer insightful analysis and suggestions. Based on these insights, businesses can make wise decisions, such as:

- Optimizing reorder points;
- Managing supplier relationships;
- Adjusting pricing strategies.

The result is smarter, data-driven decision-making that contributes to overall business success.

#### *4.3.2.3.4. Efficient Resource Allocation*

Because AI can automate repetitive inventory tasks like placing orders and reordering, businesses can allocate their human resources more effectively. While AI manages the daily inventory operations, staff members can concentrate on strategic tasks like marketing, customer service, and supplier negotiations.

#### *4.3.2.3.5. Inventory Accuracy and Reduction in Errors*

When applied appropriately, AI systems are incredibly accurate and dependable, which lowers the possibility of error in inventory management. Precise product tracking, fewer data entry mistakes, and fewer differences between recorded and physical inventory are all results of this accuracy.

#### *4.3.2.3.6. Scalability and Adaptability*

Inventory management systems powered by AI can grow with a company. AI is able to adjust to new products and shifting demand patterns as operations grow. These systems' adaptability guarantees that they will always be useful and efficient, regardless of how big or small a business is.

### *4.3.2.4. Challenges of AI for Inventory Management*

Although there are many advantages to using artificial intelligence in inventory management, it's crucial to recognize the difficulties as well. Businesses looking to incorporate AI into their inventory management procedures must have a thorough understanding of these factors.

#### *4.3.2.4.1. Data Quality and Availability*

Data is essential to AI systems. Data that is out-of-date, inaccurate, or incomplete can result in poor forecasts and less-than-ideal choices. Companies face the challenge of maintaining data quality, which frequently calls for data integration, cleansing, and regular updates. Furthermore, some companies might not have the historical data needed for precise forecasting powered by AI.

#### *4.3.2.4.2. Implementation Costs*

The cost of putting AI solutions into practice can be high. The expenses cover hiring staff to operate and maintain the systems as well as purchasing the required hardware and software. These expenses might be too much for smaller companies, even though cloud-based AI solutions are now more widely accessible.

#### *4.3.2.4.3. Skilled Personnel*

AI in inventory management frequently requires personnel with specialized skills for successful implementation. Experts in AI, machine learning, and data science are highly sought after. For some businesses, hiring new hires or upgrading the skills of current staff to handle AI systems can be difficult.

#### *4.3.2.4.4. Integration with Existing Systems*

There are numerous companies that have already set up inventory management systems. It can be difficult to integrate AI solutions with these legacy systems and may call for specialized development. Creating a smooth transition between AI and current procedures is essential.

#### *4.3.2.4.5. Security and Privacy*

Handling sensitive data when using AI raises security and privacy issues. It is crucial to make sure that AI systems are resilient to cyberattacks and that client and company data is secure.

While these challenges may seem daunting, they should not deter businesses from exploring AI for inventory management. Instead, they serve as points of awareness and preparation.

## 4.3.3. Logistics

The logistics sector is rapidly changing due to a technology called AI. It refers to the automation and optimization of a variety of logistics processes through the use of algorithms and machine learning. Artificial intelligence is especially well-suited for logistics because of the vast networks within the sector, and it is already being used to automate repetitive tasks and provide insights that were previously unattainable. AI can forecast future production and transportation volumes by analyzing data, which will result in more effective use of available resources. As a result, tasks are increasingly being assigned to digital systems that can learn on their own.

### *4.3.3.1. Applications of AI in the Logistics Industry*

Significant improvements in a variety of logistics operations are brought about by artificial intelligence. AI has already been embraced by numerous businesses to meet particular needs. Let's examine some of the most notable instances of AI application in this sector.

#### *4.3.3.1.1. Route Optimization*

AI-powered route planning software is used by DHL, a global logistics service provider, to enhance its shipping procedure. The delivery points on a route are analyzed by the company's system, which prioritizes them according to urgency—for example, urgent medical deliveries or those that must be made before 9 a.m. To generate the most effective route sequence, it also takes the distance between stops into account. DHL emphasizes that their customers gain from more precise delivery time windows and that AI allows for faster deliveries while using less fuel.

#### *4.3.3.1.2. Proactive Maintenance Predictions*

In order to anticipate truck repairs before they cause traffic jams, Paccar, an American company that designs and produces large trucks for the transportation sector, uses machine learning for predictive maintenance. The business outfits trucks with hardware and software to harness the potential of their data for quality assurance. This enables them to anticipate and resolve possible problems through proactive maintenance. With the ability to make well-informed operational decisions, businesses can now guarantee that their trucks remain on the road and that their deliveries arrive on schedule.

#### *4.3.3.1.3. Automated Warehousing Processes*

The AI-powered robotic order picking and sorting system was developed by Honeywell, a company that creates safety and productivity solutions. The solution lowers human error and improves warehouse process accuracy and efficiency for logistics service providers. This is accomplished by employing shuttles to manage more than 20,000 SKUs and making the most of floor space. The company highlights that this technology allows warehouses to optimize labor allocation by delivering a 40% increase in throughput. This helps to drastically reduce operating expenses and minimize manual processes.

#### *4.3.3.1.4. Supply Chain Management*

With AI, Unilever can guarantee a more intelligent and sustainable supply chain. Data scientists and machine learning engineers at the company adjust AI algorithms to verify real-time information from vendors, producers, and merchants. This multinational FMCG company thus obtains a comprehensive understanding of their supply chain. This AI-driven strategy has several advantages, including the ability to stabilize prices, mitigate potential disruptions, and provide substitute ingredients for products. This increases the supply chain's overall resilience for the company. Furthermore, the incorporation of AI into Unilever's system facilitates the creation of more environmentally friendly product formulas. This personal care and food production company minimized its environmental impact and optimized its manufacturing processes by eliminating superfluous ingredients.

#### *4.3.3.1.5. Fraudulent Activity Detection*

UPS and their Delivery Defense system are among the most well-known instances of fraud prevention in the logistics industry. By analyzing past data, the global delivery company's machine learning algorithms assign a delivery confidence score to each location.

This score considers a number of variables, including previous delivery attempts, the time of day, the features of the location, and even the weather. An anomaly detection feature driven by machine learning is included in such a fraud detection system. This indicates that the system keeps an eye out for changes to the pre-established patterns in incoming data.

#### *4.3.3.1.6. Customer Support and Chatbot Implementation*

A chatbot that can respond to queries from customers and determine their preferences was created by the retail company Lowe's. Chatbots provide tailored product recommendations in this manner. This improves customer satisfaction while also raising the possibility of pertinent cross- and up-selling and up-selling opportunities.

#### *4.3.3.1.7. Real-Time Vehicle Monitoring*

FedEx, one of the most well-known logistics service providers, uses sensors and AI/ML to collect data on autonomous cargo shipping and uses predictive analytics to extract insights from the data.

Their AI system provides real-time tracking of shipments by retrieving data every two seconds. FedEx and its clients benefit from a more transparent and predictable supply chain, which is made possible by the company's use of machine learning to process massive amounts of data.

### ***4.3.3.2. Advantages of Integrating AI in Logistics***

AI is completely changing the way businesses operate in logistics. Logistics service providers are changing the global logistics landscape by introducing artificial intelligence into their operations and reaping numerous benefits. A closer look at some of the main benefits is provided below.

#### *4.3.3.2.1. Enhanced Operational Efficiency*

A survey conducted in 2022 found that 60% of businesses globally anticipate RPA to revolutionize supply chains by 2025, according to Statista. This technology can help logistics companies by automating repetitive, rule-based tasks and enabling them to mimic human actions. AI-powered robots can relieve human workers of tasks like these:

- **Warehouse Management:** robots pick and pack orders, transport goods, and optimize storage layouts based on product characteristics and access frequency;
- **Quality Control:** vision systems can perform automated quality checks the accuracy of completing different processes;
- **Predictive Maintenance:** robots' sensors can continuously monitor equipment health;
- **Inventory Management:** robots equipped with sensors and AI can monitor inventory levels, identify low stock, and generate automatic purchase orders.

#### *4.3.3.2.2. Expense Minimization*

As previously mentioned, routine processes can be automated by artificial intelligence. This implies that logistics firms can achieve significant cost savings by streamlining their operations. This is supported by the McKinsey Global Survey, which shows that 44% of executives whose businesses have used AI said that the technology has cut costs.

AI assists businesses in achieving the following goals to ensure cost reduction:

- Reduced fuel consumption by optimizing delivery routes based on weather, historical traffic patterns, and real-time road congestion analysis;
- Prompt equipment maintenance by anticipating possible supply chain issues based on vehicle sensor data analysis;
- Supplying in accordance with demand by learning about client behavior patterns, market trends, and historical sales data; and
- Reduced issues by automating repetitive tasks that are prone to human error.

#### *4.3.3.2.3. Improved Eco-Friendliness*

Product transportation requires a significant amount of fuel. Accenture asserts, however, that air pollution and greenhouse gas emissions can be reduced

-through AI-driven data analysis. More specifically, businesses can optimize routes and supply processes to lower fuel consumption in the transportation and logistics sector by utilizing data from supply chains, weather patterns, and even consumer behavior.

By forecasting demand to have enough stock to meet customer needs and prevent needless resupply, the companies can optimize fuel consumption and thereby improve their environmental friendliness predicting weather-related disruptions because AI can recommend alternate routes or modify delivery schedules to reduce delays brought on by disruptions. Because precise demand projections reduce the need for last-minute expedited deliveries, unnecessary shipments can be eliminated.

### 4.3.3.2.4. Elevated Customer Service

Personalization is one of the most potent features AI provides for customer service. In particular, by comprehending contextual information, identifying customer sentiment, and producing organic dialogues, NLP, and machine learning enhance communication between companies and their clients. With these technologies, companies can develop chatbots that provide relevant information in response to customer inquiries around-the-clock.

Additionally, artificial intelligence transforms customer service for logistics companies with:

- Real-time tracking with accurate estimated time of arrival (ETA) to keep customers informed;
- Automated notifications about potential delays or disruptions;
- Predictive issue resolution based on data about customers, shipments, delays, etc.

### 4.3.3.2.5. Optimized Labor Schedules

AI cannot take the place of human labor in logistics. Rather, it gives them more power. According to McKinsey, AI has increased schedulers' and field workers' productivity by 10–20% and 20%–30%, respectively. Efficient and equitable labor planning is facilitated by intelligent scheduling. AI systems give logistics companies a standardized method for handling employee productivity.

This can be achieved thanks to:

- Elimination of human bias, when AI creates objective schedules that distribute workloads according to responsibilities;
- Automated analysis of such factors as employee skills, workload demands, and even traffic patterns for delivery drivers.

- Proactive response to disruptions as AI analyzes real-time data on traffic delays, weather events, or even equipment issues for allocating additional human resources.

### 4.3.3.3. Obstacles in Embracing AI for the Logistics Industry

Although artificial intelligence offers a potent toolkit for revolutionizing logistics firms, adoption may be hampered by major obstacles. Let's examine a few potential obstacles.

#### 4.3.3.3.1. Challenges Regarding Data Quality and Accessibility

AI requires high-quality data to function. But getting one isn't always feasible. According to reports, only 35% of CDOs believe they have adequate resources to gather clean, pertinent data. Inconsistent data formats, where information from suppliers, warehouses, or transportation providers is not standardized, can be a problem for logistics companies and prevent smooth integration. Incomplete datasets, such as missing data, present another difficulty since they may produce erroneous AI models and untrustworthy outcomes.

#### 4.3.3.3.2. Significant Implementation Expenses

Global spending on AI systems was projected to reach 154 billion U.S. dollars in 2023. S. dollars in all sectors of the economy. These figures suggest that a significant initial investment is needed for AI infrastructure and technology. The biggest challenge might be for smaller logistics firms because of their tighter budgets. Implementing changes gradually can assist in solving this issue. Before expanding, businesses can begin with simpler, smaller AI projects to show their worth. Utilizing cloud-based platforms that provide pay-as-you-go options is also crucial for cutting initial costs.

#### 4.3.3.3.3. Integrating with Current Systems and Scalability Issues

It can be challenging to integrate AI with legacy systems. Due to technological incompatibilities, it will not only take a lot of time, but it will also be complicated. Additionally, there is a chance that the system won't grow to support the operations of the expanding business. To ensure sufficient capacity to process data, such a shift might necessitate moving your system to cloud platforms or looking for AI solutions made for modular integration. Our specialty is creating AI-enabled, scalable systems for businesses looking to grow. SPD Technology produced a solution that manages increasing data volumes without compromising functionality.

#### *4.3.3.3.4. Proficient Talent Shortage*

AI implementation and management in logistics calls for qualified experts with knowledge of data science, machine learning, and operations unique to the sector. However, according to reports, 68% of executives have trouble finding qualified candidates. For logistics companies to assist their employees in developing AI/ML skills, training programs are therefore essential. Hiring outside experts is another way to address this issue. We at SPD Technologies have finished several logistics projects, and we can use our industry knowledge and AI/ML expertise to assist you in resolving particular system complexity.

### ***4.3.3.4. How Logistics Companies Can Start Embracing AI Innovation Step-by-Step***

Businesses may be deterred from implementing AI in logistics by obstacles. Nonetheless, there is a successful method for combining AI capabilities with business systems. The following actions can therefore simplify this digital transformation if you are prepared to go through it.

#### *4.3.3.4.1. Recognizing Primary Obstacles*

Prior to adopting AI innovation, a logistics company needs to identify any potential obstacles. These include a lack of funds, outdated systems, a lack of skill, or a rigid resistance to change. If cost is your top priority, look into more affordable options or begin with a partial digital transformation rather than converting every process to AI-driven right away. Invest in AI training for current employees to close skill gaps, or contract with outside specialists to handle AI development work. If employees are resistant to the shift to AI, it can be useful to communicate clearly and highlight the advantages. Explaining how AI can streamline manual processes and lessen workload can make the shift to operations powered by AI simpler. Furthermore, if a legacy system is your biggest barrier, consider either modernizing IT systems to guarantee AI compatibility or looking into cloud-based AI solutions that reduce reliance on infrastructure.

#### *4.3.3.4.2. Assessing and Choosing Resolutions*

After deciding which issue to tackle, look into your logistics processes to find areas where AI can produce noticeable outcomes. For instance, implementing predictive capabilities, optimizing warehouses, and managing inventories are some of the most popular places to start when implementing logistics AI. Once you have decided which aspect of your business you are willing to alter, investigate, and contrast various AI solutions, taking into account aspects like cost, scalability, functionality, and features. Next, create your pilot AI project as a proof-of-concept (POC). This will assist you in evaluating the solution's suitability, efficacy, and alignment with your unique requirements.

#### *4.3.3.4.3. Planning AI Integration Strategies*

A clear plan is essential for a successful AI implementation. A phased approach turns out to be the most effective and risk-averse in this case. As previously stated, before expanding the solution to all company processes, it would be wise to begin with a pilot project in a particular area to test the AI functionalities and their effect on business. Data is another crucial factor to take into account. To guarantee data security and quality for AI algorithms, this is where data governance comes into play.

#### *4.3.3.4.4. Gradual Implementation with Vendor Support*

You must assess the performance of the selected AI solution in light of the POC results. This will assist you in determining which areas require improvement or perform as anticipated. Furthermore, in order to determine the necessary improvements, make sure that monitoring procedures are followed and set important metrics (e.g., efficiency increases, client happiness, and cost savings) for assessment. And keep in mind that it never hurts to have assistance from an experienced team if you are new to AI. Seek partnerships with seasoned AI solution suppliers who can navigate the logistics industry's knowledge and provide implementation expertise.

## 4.4. ETHICAL CONSIDERATIONS IN AI-DRIVEN SUPPLY CHAIN OPERATIONS

AI's incorporation into supply chain decision-making has completely changed how companies function by providing data-driven insights that improve customer experiences, cut expenses, and optimize operations. To guarantee responsible and sustainable technology use, however, the adoption of AI also brings up difficult ethical issues that must be resolved. Large volumes of data are processed by AI algorithms to manage inventory, forecast demand, expedite logistics, and improve production schedules. Businesses can use this technology to make well-informed decisions instantly, which increases operational effectiveness and decreases waste.

### 4.4.1. Transparency and Explainability of AI Decisions

The lack of transparency in AI decision-making processes is one of the main ethical issues. It gets harder to comprehend how and why a certain decision was made as AI systems get more complex. To maintain accountability and foster trust, it is imperative to create systems that offer concise justifications for recommendations produced by AI.

### 4.4.2. Fairness and Bias in AI Algorithms

The objectivity of AI algorithms depends on the quality of the data they are trained on. The AI system may reinforce biases, such as racial or gender biases, if historical data exhibits them, producing unfair results. To detect and address bias in algorithms, ethical AI design necessitates ongoing attention to detail.

### 4.4.3. Data Privacy and Security Concerns

Supply chains enabled by AI rely largely on data, which raises questions regarding the security and privacy of sensitive data. Preventing breaches and upholding consumer trust necessitates the implementation of encryption, secure storage, and compliant data sharing measures.

### 4.4.4. Unemployment and Job Displacement

As routine tasks are automated, the use of AI may raise concerns about job displacement. But by upskilling workers to work with AI systems and developing new positions that call for distinctly human abilities, a balance can be achieved.

### 4.4.5. Social and Environmental Implications

AI may have an effect on the environment and nearby communities. Delivery route optimization, for example, may lower emissions, but it may also have an effect on nearby companies. Making ethical decisions requires taking these wider societal ramifications into account.

### 4.4.6. Accountability and Responsibility in AI Decisions

It can be difficult to assign blame for decisions made by AI. It is crucial to define distinct lines of accountability and comprehend the functions of both humans and machines in the decision-making process.

### 4.4.7. Balancing Automation with Human Judgment

AI is faster and more efficient than humans, but it lacks human empathy and intuition. Achieving ethical results requires striking the correct balance between human judgment and automated decision-making.

### 4.4.8. Ethical Frameworks for AI-Enabled Supply Chains

A number of ethical frameworks, including accountability, transparency, and fairness, can direct the creation and application of AI systems in supply chains. Following these guidelines aids in reducing potential dangers and damages.

### 4.4.9. Building Ethical AI Systems

Integrating fairness, transparency, and privacy principles throughout the development process is essential to designing ethical AI. To guarantee continued compliance with ethical standards, audits, and assessments on a regular basis are necessary.

### 4.4.10. The Need for Continuous Monitoring and Adaptation

Systems with ethical AI must adapt to changing conditions. As the business and societal landscapes change, AI algorithms are continuously monitored and adjusted to ensure that they stay in line with ethical considerations.

### 4.4.11. Stakeholder Engagement and Collaboration

Diverse viewpoints from stakeholders, including workers, clients, and local communities, must be taken into account in order to recognize and resolve any potential ethical issues with AI-enabled supply chains.

### 4.4.12. Regulatory and Legal Considerations

The establishment of norms and guidelines for AI ethics is largely the responsibility of governments and regulatory agencies. It's critical to strike the correct balance between innovation and protection.

Decision-making processes need to prioritize ethical considerations as artificial intelligence continues to transform the supply chain industry. Collaboration, fairness, accountability, and transparency are essential for creating AI-enabled supply chains that maximize value and efficiency while adhering to moral standards.

# REFERENCES

1. Allen, M. K. (1986). *The Development of An Artificial Intelligence System for Inventory Management*. Doctoral Dissertation, Ohio State University, Council of Logistics Management.

2. Andersen, L. A., Britt, F. E., & Donovan, J. F. (1997). The seven principles of supply chain management. *Supply Chain Management Review*. Spring 1997. http://www.manufacturing.net/magazine/logistics/pointpgs/webex.htm (accessed on 1 November 2024).

3. Ansam, A., & Modarres, B. (1990). *Just in Time Purchasing*. The Free Press, Colliers McMillan.

4. Balasubramanian, S., & Norrie, D. H. (n.d.). A multi-agent intelligent design system integrating manufacturing and shop-floor control. University of Calgary. http://ksi.cpsc.ucalgary.ca/projects/Mediator/ (accessed on 1 November 2024).

5. Bamfield, J. A. N. (1994). Implementing EDI: Problems in managing retail/supplier relationships by technology. *Logistics Information Management, 7*(1), 10.

CHAPTER 5

# AI IN MARKETING AND SALES

## Contents

# INTRODUCTION

AI is an effective marketing tool. In a procedure known as "lookalike modeling," the technology identifies the traits and attributes that your best clients have in common. This puts you one step closer to focusing on clients who share your characteristics and are probably interested in your goods or services. AI can assist in gathering the data you require if you don't already have it by improving your data collection techniques and sifting through enormous volumes of data to identify important trends and insights. These features can assist your team in creating effective marketing plans. Marketing teams get better at expressing particular requests or prompts the more they engage with natural language prompts because AI systems are made to be easy to use. The potential audience reach increases with prompt output effectiveness. As customized content improves, a wider range of consumers will emerge. Additionally, you can reach customers with a variety of interests and backgrounds by using generative AI. AI in marketing, for instance, can assist you in producing content that represents various cultural viewpoints, thereby expanding the reach and inclusivity of your messaging. You have a better chance of comprehending and reflecting the preferences of your distinct customer segments when you use generative AI. AI is also beneficial for retargeting, which is the process of repeatedly engaging a customer with better messaging. By employing artificial intelligence (AI) for automatic retargeting, you can continuously learn from every consumer interaction and conversion, improving future content and marketing strategies in light of the insights. Learning and adapting processes make sure that the information is interesting and relevant. It is expected that generative AI will advance to the point where it can create images, videos, and music with even more nuance. Because the output will resonate with the target audiences of the marketers, this shift in content creation will help improve customer engagement.

## 5.1. ARTIFICIAL INTELLIGENCE (AI) IN MARKETING

Artificial Intelligence has become so ingrained in our daily lives that it is nearly hard for us to envision a world without it. Businesses have adopted AI at a rate of over 270% growth in the last four years, according to Gartner. According to Fortune Business Insights, 2020, the global AI market is projected to reach $267 billion by 2027. With the AI market valued at $27.23 billion in 2019, there has been a ten-fold increase in just eight years. The majority of widely used products in use today are driven by AI systems. Even if the company in question isn't in the technology sector, AI systems may be able to support many of its operations and customer service-related tasks. Because they are inherently quick to adopt new technologies, marketers frequently use artificial intelligence (AI) to map customer journeys and gain insight into their target audience. In its most basic form, artificial intelligence is defined as "the science of making machines smart." Thus, AI marketing would bring marketing intelligence one step closer.

- **Audience Targeting:** It matters to whom you show your advertisement. If your targeting is ridiculous, you can't hope for much. It is not the best idea to show your advertisements to police in the Manhattan area when you are trying to reach Ohio dentists. Among the most popular platforms you use are Quora, Facebook, Instagram, Snapchat, Reddit, and Google possess a wealth of information that can be utilized to easily segment customers. Manually completing all of this is not feasible. AI examines your previous audiences, the effectiveness of your advertisements for that specific audience, and other data. It finds audiences who are more likely to make a purchase by taking into account the KPIs you use and your performance data. AI tools for advertising: AI aids in both the creation and performance and spend optimization of the advertisements.
  - **Tools:** The most widely used AI tools for advertising include Phrasee, WordStream, Adobe, IBM, GumGum, Pathmatics, and Albert.
- **Lead Generation:** Based on the data you already have, such as the characteristics of your ideal clients and customers, etc. when it comes to becoming your customers, the AI system will be able to provide you with a list of leads. In accordance with predetermined criteria, it will even score the lead. A solution like yours is what the leads with the highest score are searching for. They'll be able to receive a solution from your salespeople more quickly and with greater competence. It cuts down on the time needed for manual lead sifting from several sources. In addition to being exhausting, the majority of lead generation techniques are also not very successful. You may refocus your attention on more crucial duties that will directly improve the bottom line of the business by developing an AI lead generation system. LinkedIn's Sales Navigator Tool is an AI-powered tool for lead generation that assists in locating leads. An app like Node does the same thing by recommending new users based on metadata. In order to produce leads, HubSpot's Growthbot connects its AI with CRM platforms.
  - **Tools:** With the help of an AI tool called Conversica, salespeople can obtain real-time information by having conversations with potential leads.

- **Personalization:** You can close deals by providing your prospects with content that is tailored to their needs. These days, customers expect the moon, and it's okay because you can use AI to provide a solution. They anticipate that you will know what they want and be able to demonstrate it to them. You will be able to provide the visitor with a personalized and relevant experience with the aid of AI and ML. Your offers to potential clients should be accessible through a number of different channels. If not, they'll become perplexed and go work for your rival. Online merchants should collect data in a matter of seconds in order to offer such an experience. Is it feasible to do it by hand? Obviously not. Here, AI and ML work together to deliver offers and contextual content that will turn leads into sales. Everstring reports that 71% of marketers are considering using AI in their campaigns primarily for the purpose of personalization.
  - **AI Personalization Tools:** Curata, Scripted, Skyword, etc. aids in scaling your content. Acrolinx reads all of your content using natural language processing and makes improvement suggestions. To boost engagement, Atomic Reach advises the company to edit its content. Boomtrain identifies the content that has the highest chance of making a user feel "engaged." OneSpot uses website interaction data and machine learning to match content to the user's preferences.
- **Deep Understanding of Customers:** Nothing ever said in a business, "We know enough about our customers now, let's not spend more time collecting their data, let's make some sales." All businesses are aware that consumers are constantly shifting their preferences and searching for the newest and greatest thing. Therefore, you have to continuously improving your understanding of potential customers if you want to hold their attention. Prior to preparing any marketing campaign, one of the most important things you should do is identify buyer personas. After you have your product's personas, you can produce content that is tailored to what each persona wants to consume.
  - **Tools:** The AI-based persona creation tool Persona by Delve AI leverages first-party data (e.g., Google Analytics) and openly accessible data sources (e.g., G. voice of the consumer information from social media, review sites, communities, and forums) to automatically build personas for your company. With the use of information from over 20 sources, it provides amazing insights into the needs and preferences of potential

clients. It even takes things a step further and divides up your audience. The personas are automatically updated on a regular basis, so you don't have to worry about customers' expectations and behaviors changing over time.

- **Behavioral Analysis:** Because AI and ML enable customer segmentation and product offerings based on analysis and understanding of their purchasing patterns, retailers adore these technologies. Individualized interactions are what customers seek, and mere personalization falls short. It suggests a special offer for the specific client, not just because they belong to a certain customer group. Is it even humanly possible for a company to serve thousands of customers every day? Fortunately, an AI system exists that can do just that.
  - **Tools:** The estimated transaction value, likelihood of a purchase, brand affinity, and other information will be provided by AI/ML analytics tools. According to a Salesforce report, over 62% of consumers are open to letting AI enhance their user experience.
- **Competitor Insights:** It is imperative that you are aware of what your rivals are up to. Never. Anything your rival does could teach you a valuable lesson or be something your company needs to implement. A number of the world's most prosperous businesses have always made it a point to observe and learn from their rivals. No, obtaining competitive insights won't get you in trouble with the law; otherwise, why would corporate espionage exist? We're talking about employing tools designed expressly to analyze website traffic, content production, tool usage, and other aspects of your rival's business.
  - **Tools:** The Delve AI tool Competitor Persona assists you in learning specifics about your rivals' advertising tactics. The tool will automatically create personas of your competitors' users if you enter the domain of their website. It will provide you with a wealth of ideas about what your rivals are working on and assist you with competitor keyword research and market analysis. Manually reviewing all of your competitors' pages, social media accounts, content on various platforms, etc. may not be the best course of action.
- **PPC Advertising:** Both manual and automatic bidding, placement, and other options are available when setting up a PPC campaign. AI handles the latter. Even though PPC needs AI, a human is still

necessary for it to work. AI systems are excellent at enhancing campaigns, but they have only been able to replace repetitive PPC management tasks. It helps you optimize your ads, find the most relevant keywords for you, change your bidding value to help you reach your goal, and display different ads to users based on their browsing history, among other things.

  - **Tools:** Acquisio, Adzooma, and PPCHero are a few of the AI-powered tools that simplify PPC management.

- **Intelligent Advertising Design:** AI has made highly personalized design feasible, enabling the automatic personalization of numerous elements of advertising campaigns and marketing materials for specific audiences or even individuals. Even down to the color schemes and design aesthetics employed, algorithms can determine which elements of marketing campaigns are most likely to grab your audience's interest and inspire further participation. Algorithms can then assess how different combinations of audiences and design elements perform in order to pinpoint areas that could use improvement. Younger consumers, for example, are more responsive to highly visual marketing materials and ads, whereas older consumers prefer more textual or detailed descriptions of products and services. Advertising creatives would thus only need to produce a single version of their materials, which AI systems could then modify and automatically distribute to the appropriate target audiences.
  - **Tools:** Software like Persado, which creates customized sales copy using natural language processing algorithms, is currently used by advertisers. We benefit from AI's ability to recognize and categorize client segments at scale according to their behavioral patterns. Performance can then be optimized by monitoring the relative performance of different pieces of material.
- **Search Engine Optimization:** By using AI for SEO, you can develop a better strategy and use much better solutions that will improve your page rankings. Search engines are becoming more adept at spotting poor content, keyword stuffing, irrelevant backlinks, and other issues. Instead, marketers are utilizing AI to satisfy search engines' exacting requirements. An example of the kind of power AI has to improve SEO performance would be if you wanted to be able to check for mentions of your company without having to do it by hand. BuzzSumo and HubSpot are two examples of tools

that will alert you automatically. Research indicates that up to 85% of purchasing decisions originate on Google. As e-commerce has become more prevalent in our lives, the most effective strategies for ranking your website higher in search results may have changed. In fact, because algorithms are getting better at spotting attempts by marketers to manipulate the system, a number of strategies that used to yield great results, like link-building and keyword stuffing, may now result in your website being penalized. A key concept in SEO is search volume, which tells us how many people are using particular terms and phrases to find the products and services they need. Some of the most advanced SEO techniques available today use machine learning algorithms to better understand the intent behind term usage and search query content. It can also be used to investigate the SEO efforts of competitors in order to find any weaknesses in your own SEO strategy and produce SEO-friendly marketing content.

  – **Tools:** WordLift, Bright Edge, MarketBrew, Pave AI, Dialog Flow, and Albert.

- **Social Media Listening:** Customers' opinions about your company and its many facets, such as customer service, operations, order processing time, etc., reveal a lot about you. Their viewpoint should not only cause you to think, but it should also cause you to sit up and pay attention. AI has made it possible to gather this data instantly. It will assist you in identifying trends in their conversations. A subreddit may have a discussion about your product, a different customer may have used the same keyword on Twitter, and someone on Facebook may have made a similar statement. The AI system has realized by now that it is something you might find interesting. If you pay attention to what your clients and potential clients have to say about you, then you will be able to think of creative solutions and provide prompt resolution to their issues.
  – **Tools:** Lately, Genylabs, Synthesio, Socialbakers, Sprout Social, etc., are some of the tools that help businesses with understanding what your customers talk about you on the internet.
- **Email Marketing:** Businesses will pay thousands of dollars for the ability to write catchy subject lines that entice the recipient to open emails. Why? Because the return on investment (ROI) of email marketing is $42 for every dollar spent, and the more emails you send, the more likely it is that your prospects will become customers. The subject line is how your customers evaluate each email that

reaches them. They make a decision about whether or not to open it in the brief time it takes them to read the subject line. Subject lines are typically written at the end of a campaign, which indicates that companies don't always give them the consideration they merit. Considering the brand language, AI will use natural language technology to identify the most appropriate words that recipients are likely to respond to.

  - **Tools:** Two of the most widely used tools for businesses in this sector are Phrasee and Mizy.

- **Predictive Marketing:** Humans typically make irrational decisions, but there are trends in them. It requires a ton of data to arrive at; it cannot be done after looking through a few data sets. AI can analyze vast amounts of data to forecast the what, why, where, and how of a customer's purchase. It forecasts our behavior using a variety of attribute sets. By using text analysis, sentiment analysis, lead scoring based on a set of attributes, and other techniques, businesses can gain a deeper understanding of their clientele to do it correctly. You can be sure that a sale will go smoothly if a company can use the appropriate channel to provide a customer with the right product at the price they want.
  - **Tools:** Cortex, Crayon, IBM Watson, Google Cloud AI, are some of the tools that help with predictive marketing.
- **Chatbots:** Currently, one in four customer support companies use chatbots driven by AI. Chatbots have improved customer service beyond anything else that has been available. At first, it served as a location where clients or guests could obtain information based on a range of criteria. Chatbots with AI capabilities enable the systems to learn on their own. As a result, the system learns from each interaction and provides more accurate responses.
  - **Tools:** Thanks to chatbots like Siri, Alexa, Cortana, and Google Assistant, chatbots are already a big part of our daily lives.

According to the 2022 State of Marketing AI Report, AI-powered chatbots perform the following functions for you:

- Automatically solve common queries in real time;
- Answer a broad range of questions using the content on your website;
- Eliminate lead generation forms;
- Schedule sales calls.

The use of chatbots in intricate domains like law is also growing. It currently assists you in appealing traffic infractions. In the field of education, there are chatbots that grade essays. Woebot is a chatbot designed specifically for mental health. By enhancing customer service, enhancing your brand's charm, responding to inquiries, assisting customers in selecting the best products based on their suggestions, and more, they are transforming businesses and industries.

- Customer Support: With the help of Machine Learning and Natural Language Processing, customer support becomes a cakewalk for businesses. With its ability to multitask and handle multiple number of queries, AI generates responses with a speed and accuracy that humans cannot. By using tonnes of data, AI can do the following to enable customer support:
  - Understand the customer from the information collected;
  - Identify the issues that they are facing;
  - Analyze their behavior patterns;
  - Find out their decisions and preferences;
  - Create suitable solutions and products;
  - Respond to messages;
  - Offer personalized products and discounts;
  - Minimize the cart abandonment volume;
  - **Tools:** Solvvy, MonkeyLearn, Freshdesk, etc., are some of the AI-based tools for customer support. Gartner predicts that more than 15% of customer service interactions will be fully powered by AI by 2021.
- **Content Generation:** The use of AI in content creation is still in its infancy. It is known that certain programs, such as XLNET, GROVER, MarketMuse, and GPT-3, can produce content using only AI. However, these programs have not been able to generate content that is truly outstanding. On its blog, OkWrite, an AI content creation tool, states that although it can create content, it is unable to create an emotive atmosphere. They go on to say that the typical reader will be able to tell whether a piece of content was written by a human or an artificial intelligence system. While AI can't yet completely replace human content, it can be a big help when it comes to providing guidance for blog posts, conducting preliminary research, and even developing content marketing strategies. Using AI, The Washington Post created Heliograf, a writer who updated sentences using multiple data sources during the 2016 Rio Olympics.

Based on user requests, it could write about 850 stories. Though not longform content with a thorough analysis, these were stories meant to draw in pageviews.

- **Intelligent Website Audits:** More than ever, it is important to track the flow of traffic to your website and social media pages to spot any leaks that are making prospective customers back out before making a purchase. More recently, services powered by AI have the ability to automatically scan your website and alert you to any issues that may be influencing your conversion rate. In addition to potentially resulting in SEO penalties, large, inefficient images and videos or pages that load slowly can easily drive away visitors. Frequent audits usually require a skilled outside consultant and are very expensive and time-consuming to finish. But this is becoming easier to do thanks to automated AI tools, which will boost productivity and revenue.
- **Market Analysis:** Programs on computers can now see, or understand, visual data thanks to computer vision technologies. Marketers can scan the millions of photos that are posted to social media networks every day to gain a better understanding of how and where products or services are being used. This provides marketers with new approaches to assess factors such as market penetration and brand awareness. It can also be used to identify influencers who are already connected to your business, leading to more genuine exchanges. Trend analysis is an additional useful application. Here, AI can help you spot changing patterns of behavior and habits that could affect how your customers and prospective customers engage with vendors in your market. You can more easily assess the effectiveness of your competitors' visual marketing campaigns in addition to your own, and discover how different moods, color schemes, and settings affect your target audience. Image recognition can be used to automatically generate product descriptions for sales copy from product images in addition to the previously mentioned natural language processing. It can also be used to protect your brand by immediately alerting you to any possible theft of your creative IP, branding, or messaging.
- **Augmented Assistance:** Customers can view items in their homes to see how a new sofa or table would blend in with their current décor thanks to Ikea's augmented reality (AR) technologies, which overlay computer-generated images over real-world images. Here, AI is used to create realistic-looking composite images that the user

can view through the camera on their phone, usually in real-time. Cosmetic companies like L'Oreal also use the same technology to let customers try on makeup and other products to see how they look. Although this type of functionality has long been offered to clients by large corporations, websites such as wearfits.com are making it available as a service, allowing retailers of all sizes to use it.

### 5.1.1. Today's AI

These days, a lot of businesses use AI to help with broad tasks like improving prediction accuracy (think sales forecasts), handle narrow tasks like digital ad placement (also called "programmatic buying"), and support human efforts in structured tasks like customer service. Additionally, businesses use AI throughout the entire customer journey. AI will target advertisements to prospective buyers who are in the "consideration" stage of their product research and can assist in directing their search.

This is evident at Wayfair, an online furniture retailer that employs AI to identify which customers are most likely to be persuaded and selects which products to display to them based on their browsing history. Additionally, marketers can use AI-enabled bots from companies like Vee24 to better understand the needs of their customers, increase their search engagement, guide them toward a specific web page, and, if necessary, connect them to a human sales agent via chat, phone, video, or even "cobrowsing," which allows an agent to assist the customer in navigating a shared screen. By using incredibly detailed personal information, such as real-time geolocation data, to generate highly customized product or service offers, AI can expedite the sales process. AI helps with cross-selling and upselling later on in the journey, and it can lower the chance that customers will leave their online shopping carts empty. AI bots, for instance, can offer an encouraging review to help close a deal after a customer adds items to their cart, like "Excellent purchase! James from Vermont purchased the same mattress." Conversion rates can rise fivefold or more as a result of such initiatives.

AI-enabled service agents from companies like Amelia (formerly IPsoft) and Interactions are available around-the-clock to prioritize customer requests after the sale. They are more adept than human agents at handling varying service request volumes. Simple questions like delivery time or appointment scheduling can be handled by them, and more complicated problems can be forwarded to a human agent. In certain situations, AI helps human representatives by interpreting the tone of the customer and recommending different answers, advising agents on how to best meet the needs of the customer, or recommending supervisor intervention.

## 5.1.2. The Framework

Two factors can be used to categorize marketing AI: its level of intelligence and whether it operates independently or as a component of a larger platform. Certain technologies, like recommendation engines and chatbots, can fit into any of the categories; their classification is determined by how they are used in a particular application.

Let's look at the two types of intelligence first:

1. **Task Automation:** These programs carry out structured, repetitive tasks with comparatively low intelligence requirements. They are not capable of handling complex issues like subtle customer requests; instead, they are made to adhere to a set of rules or carry out a preset series of actions based on a given input. A system that automatically sends each new customer a welcome email would serve as an example. This category also includes more basic chatbots, like those offered by Facebook Messenger and other social media platforms. They can assist customers in basic interactions by guiding them through a predetermined decision tree, but they are unable to understand customers' intentions, provide tailored responses, or gain insight from interactions over time.
2. **Machine Learning:** Large amounts of data are used to train these algorithms, which then produce comparatively complex predictions and judgments. These models are able to segment customers, identify images, interpret text, and predict how they will react to different campaigns, like promotions. Programmatic buying in online advertising, e-commerce recommendation engines, and sales propensity models in customer relationship management (CRM) systems are already powered by machine learning. It and its more advanced version, deep learning, are the most popular AI technologies and are quickly emerging as effective marketing tools. However, it's crucial to make clear that current machine-learning applications still only carry out specific tasks and require extensive data for training. Let's now examine integrated versus stand-alone AI (Figure 5.1).
3. **Stand-Alone Applications:** The best way to conceptualize these is as distinct, or isolated, AI programs. They are distinct from the main avenues via which clients discover, purchase, or receive assistance for utilizing a business's products, as well as the avenues via which staff members advertise, sell, or provide support for those products. In other words, in order to use the AI, clients or staff must travel

outside of those channels. Take the color-discovery app developed by paint manufacturer Behr. Based on the mood customers want for their space, the application provides a number of customized Behr paint-color suggestions using IBM Watson's natural language processing and Tone Analyzer features, which can identify emotions in text. Customer's shortlist two or three colors for the room they want to paint using the app. Although the app does enable a connection to place a Home Depot order, the actual paint sale is then carried out outside of it.

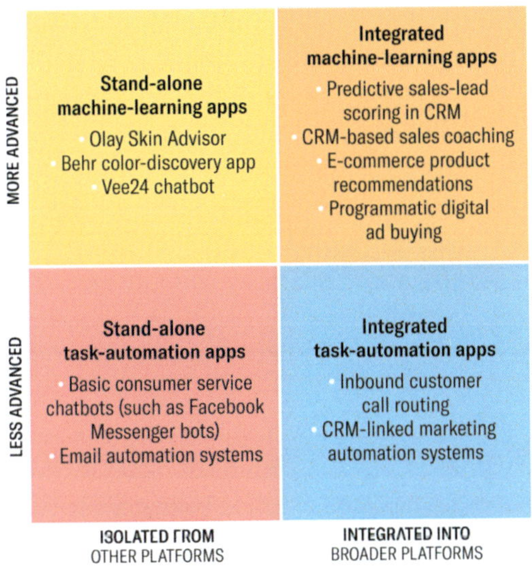


**Figure 5.1.** *The four kinds of marketing AI.*

*Source: https://hbr.org/resources/images/article_assets/2021/05/S21041_DAVENPORT_FOURKINDS.png.*

4. **Integrated Applications:** For consumers, marketers, and salespeople who use them, these AI applications that are integrated into pre-existing systems are frequently less noticeable than stand-alone ones. Machine learning, for instance, is integrated into platforms that manage the complete ad buying and placement process, making snap decisions about which digital ads to present to users. For over ten years, Netflix has been providing its users with video recommendations through its integrated machine learning; these recommendations merely show up in the menu of options that visitors see when they visit the website. They would need to use a specific app to ask for recommendations if the recommendation engine were standalone. More and more CRM system manufacturers

are incorporating machine learning into their products. An AI-based lead scoring system that automatically rates B2B customer leads according to their likelihood of purchase is one of the features of Salesforce's Sales Cloud Einstein suite. Salesforce's CRM system is integrated with the apps of vendors such as Cogito, which offers AI that trains call center salespeople.

### 5.1.3. Challenges for AI in Marketing

Even the most basic AI applications can be challenging to implement. Even with its lower technical complexity, stand-alone task-automation AI can still be challenging to configure for particular workflows and necessitates that businesses hire the right AI specialists. Any type of AI workflow must carefully combine human and machine tasks in order to ensure that the AI enhances human skills and isn't applied in ways that lead to issues. For example, less-capable chatbots can annoy customers, even though many businesses use rule-based chatbots to automate customer service. Instead of interacting with customers, it might be preferable to have these bots support human agents or advisers. There are additional factors to take into account when businesses implement more complex and integrated applications. It can be challenging to integrate AI into third-party platforms in particular. One example is Procter and Gamble's Olay Skin Advisor, which analyzes selfies taken by users, determines their age and skin type, and suggests products based on deep learning. It has increased conversion rates, bounce rates, and average basket sizes in some regions and is integrated into the Olay.com e-commerce and loyalty platform. But integrating it with Amazon and retail stores—third parties that make up a sizable portion of Olay's sales—has proven more difficult. Olay's ability to provide a flawless, AI-assisted customer experience on Amazon is hampered by the lack of The Skin Advisor on the company's expansive store site. Lastly, businesses need to prioritize the needs of their clients. Customers may be more concerned about privacy, security, and data ownership the more sophisticated and integrated AI applications are. Consumers may be wary of smart speakers that could be listening in on them or of applications that gather and share location data without the user's knowledge. Customers have generally demonstrated a willingness—even an eagerness—to give up some privacy and personal information in exchange for the benefits that cutting-edge apps can offer. The benefits of AI applications, such as Alexa, seem to outweigh any concerns. Therefore, the challenge facing marketers as they increase the sophistication and application of AI is to guarantee that its security and privacy measures are clear, that users have some control over the collection and use of their data, and that they receive just compensation from the company. CMOs should set up ethics and privacy review boards, comprising legal and marketing professionals, to ensure these safeguards are met and to ensure that customers remain trusting of AI projects. This is especially important for projects involving customer data or potentially biased algorithms, like credit scoring.

Despite the great potential that marketing AI has, we implore CMOs to be realistic about its current limitations. AI is still limited to specific tasks and cannot manage a full marketing function or process, despite all the hype. However, it is already providing marketers with significant advantages—in fact, it is indispensable in certain marketing endeavors—and its capabilities are expanding quickly. Though it will take decades, we think AI will eventually revolutionize marketing. Long-term focus on developing AI capabilities and mitigating associated risks will be required of the marketing function and the organizations that support it, especially IT. In order to capitalize on AI's potential and its current capabilities, we implore marketers to begin formulating a plan now. As per the Big Data and AI Executive Survey 2020, over 90% of leading companies have either made investments in AI or are about to invest in it. All businesses should adopt AI technology without fail, and they should do so aggressively. There are still problems with using AI for marketing, despite the fact that platforms with AI capabilities are more widespread than one may imagine. Some of the causes are as follows:

1. **Lack of Insufficient Infrastructure:** Make sure your IT infrastructure is already set up with high-performing hardware if you want AI to power your marketing engine. Due to the high setup costs of the computer systems needed, smaller businesses with tighter budgets may find it challenging to put up such an infrastructure. Fortunately, cloud-based solutions exist that are both less expensive and resource-intensive.
2. **Lack of Sufficient Data:** An artificial intelligence system needs a lot of data to make sense of it, in addition to high-quality data. The current datasets ought to be uncontaminated. The AI campaign's chances of success will be diminished if the data is of low quality since it is untrustworthy.
3. **Insufficient Budget:** There are no questions about the efficacy of AI systems adding a fillip to your marketing efforts. Having a tech stack and other martech tools can itself add a lot to your budget. The leadership team should be persuaded with details including highly relevant business data and forecasting to prove how good AI can be for your marketing.
4. **Lack of Skilled Professionals:** Due to a significant lack of AI expertise, only very large companies are considering developing

AI-based marketing strategies internally. The growth of AI talent is slower than that of other technology positions because AI demands specialized skill sets. Employees should receive enough training to handle and appropriately interpret the results, even for companies that use pre-made AI marketing tools. Although these are some of the issues that companies should think about before embracing "AI in marketing," there are always other options available. Companies need to make sure they use AI software sensibly. When determining whether you need AI systems for your marketing, bear in mind that the results will be exponential.

### *5.1.3.1. Trends and Technologies*

The field of marketing is expanding so quickly that if a marketer is not keeping up, every new development could sound like nonsense. Something that might have been useful two or three years ago might not be used anymore. Remember how many companies used to stuff articles with keywords? Even the largest companies no longer do it. AI is a relatively new trend that has a lot of applications in the marketing function alone, despite not having been thoroughly studied yet. Here are a few trends in AI marketing:

1. **Voice Assistance:** Voice search is going to become more and more important as smart homes become more and more popular. By 2023, there will be 8 billion voice assistants with AI capabilities. AI-powered voice assistants will help customers save time by eliminating the need to type lengthy questions, provide prompt solutions, increase sales and brand value, and enhance customer retention. In the US, 43% of voice-assisted device owners (aged 45 to 60) currently use their devices to make online purchases.
2. **AI Content:** No, artificial intelligence still lacks the sophistication to closely resemble the typical human brain. They can produce content using already-available data, but they might not be able to include humans in it just yet. AI is a huge asset for content strategy, which in turn helps with traffic growth and ranking well in search engine results.
3. **Personalized Recommendations:** The ability of artificial intelligence to make product recommendations based on historical data is one of its most widely used applications. It isn't even limited to a specific audience segment; it can generate personalized recommendations for every user, even if there are millions of them. Customizing your offerings will win you over to your customers' increasingly picky tastes.

4. **Hyper-Segmentation:** Prior to the development of AI, marketing campaigns relied more on conjecture than data. For the most part, the campaigns were either successful or unsuccessful. AI enables marketers to handle massive data sets. By analyzing vast amounts of data, machine learning algorithms can gain deeper insights into the target audience, establish correlations between individual data points, and generate highly focused and segmented groups.
5. **Persona Research:** A thorough grasp of the qualities of your customers can be obtained through hyper-segmenting your audience. This allows AI-powered software to create buyer personas that go beyond the standard attributes that are listed. By carefully examining every bit of data, you can build highly specific personas. After that, you can use them as highly targeted audience segments to offer them customized content. Lead scoring, lead qualification, targeted timing, micro moments, state-of-the-art predictive analytics, etc. are a few more examples of use cases.

### 5.1.4. Use AI in Marketing

Marketers can use AI to develop compelling offers that shorten the sales cycle, boost customer retention, and attract new clients. To put it simply, AI in marketing makes predictions about the actions of potential customers based on customer data, historical data, machine learning, and other computational data. What content do you need to show them before they are willing to part with their cash? What specifically are they looking for? What is the price range they are considering? What are the features of your product that appeal to them the most? And so on. Would they buy from you right away? If not, when would they buy it? You have the chance to make business decisions based on the responses to each of the aforementioned questions. That is the extent of AI's marketing power. Prior to joining a group, you should be clear about your goals. You must be fully aware of your strategic goals and know how artificial intelligence can support you in achieving them. Go ahead and use AI if there are currently available solutions that meet your needs. If your needs require you to develop a custom AI solution, you should talk to various stakeholders to determine whether you can afford it and what the opportunity cost would be of not doing so.

## 5.2. PREDICTIVE ANALYTICS IN MARKETING

The marketing industry has seen a significant transformation as a result of the convergence of AI and predictive analytics, which gives companies the ability to predict trends, improve advertising tactics, and increase the return on marketing expenditures. With the help of AI and ML algorithms, predictive analytics enables marketers to make proactive, data-driven decisions in addition to analyzing historical data. The capacity to predict trends with exceptional accuracy is one of AI's primary contributions to predictive analytics in marketing. Large datasets, such as social media trends, market dynamics, and consumer behavior, can be analyzed by these technologies to find patterns that might be difficult for humans to notice. AI and ML algorithms are able to forecast new trends and changes in customer preferences by identifying dependencies and correlations in the data. Because of this insight, marketers are able to stay ahead of the curve by modifying their approaches to take advantage of new opportunities and reduce risks brought on by shifting market conditions. Another crucial use of AI in marketing is the optimization of advertising campaigns. By examining various data sets to determine the traits of audiences with high conversion rates, these technologies improve targeting accuracy. Businesses can maximize the impact of their advertising messages and delivery channels by having a detailed understanding of customer segments. Real-time bidding strategy optimization by AI-driven algorithms guarantees that marketing funds are distributed effectively to campaigns and channels that provide the best returns on investment.

One of the main objectives for businesses is to increase the returns on marketing investments, and artificial intelligence is essential to this endeavor. By concentrating on campaigns that have a higher chance of connecting with their target audience, marketers can effectively allocate and prioritize their resources with the help of predictive analytics. AI algorithms have the ability to continuously learn from new data and analyze historical performance data to refine and adjust marketing strategies over time, optimizing for the channels and tactics that yield the best results. This iterative optimization process guarantees that marketing initiatives are both economical and flexible enough to adjust to the ever-changing needs of consumers. Additionally, AI supports targeted marketing campaigns by customizing messaging and content according to the tastes and actions of specific clients. Businesses may develop hyper-targeted campaigns that appeal to particular audience segments by utilizing predictive analytics. This will strengthen relationships with clients and raise engagement levels all around.

### 5.2.1. Supply Chain Optimization

AI is revolutionizing supply chain process optimization by providing companies with cutting-edge tools to boost productivity, cut expenses, and enhance supply chain management overall. Demand forecasting, inventory management, and logistics planning are three major domains where artificial intelligence algorithms are having a major impact such as:

1. **Demand Forecasting:** AI algorithms are highly skilled at evaluating past sales data, industry trends, and outside variables to forecast demand accurately in the future. These technologies uncover intricate patterns and dependencies in data that human analysts might miss, going beyond conventional forecasting techniques. AI -driven demand forecasting models provide more accurate and nuanced predictions by taking into account factors like economic indicators, promotions, and seasonal dynamics. In the end, this increases customer satisfaction by helping businesses meet customer demand more precisely, cut down on excess inventory, and optimize production schedules.
2. **Inventory Management:** By offering real-time insights into stock levels, demand fluctuations, and supply chain disruptions, AI greatly enhances inventory management optimization. Businesses can maintain ideal stock levels while reducing the costs associated with excess inventory by using these technologies, which enable dynamic and adaptive inventory control. To determine the ideal reorder points and quantities, machine learning algorithms can evaluate data from a variety of sources, including past sales, supplier performance, and outside variables like the weather or world events. By doing this, the possibility of stockouts is decreased as well as overstock scenarios are avoided, improving cash flow and lowering holding expenses.
3. **Logistics Planning:** A streamlined supply chain depends on effective logistics planning, and artificial intelligence is essential for streamlining the distribution and transportation of goods. To determine the most economical and timely logistics routes, machine learning algorithms can examine enormous datasets pertaining to shipping routes, transportation expenses, and delivery schedules. By rerouting shipments in real-time and anticipating possible disruptions, predictive analytics helps businesses ensure on-time deliveries and lessen the impact of unforeseen events. In line with sustainability objectives, AI-driven optimization algorithms also improve vehicle route planning by minimizing fuel consumption and lowering carbon emissions.

### 5.2.2. Fraud Detection and Cybersecurity

The financial industry needs AI to be strengthened against fraud and to improve cybersecurity protocols to protect sensitive data.

Combining these two technologies makes it possible for financial institutions to use cutting-edge instruments that can evaluate enormous volumes of data, spot trends, and identify anomalies, strengthening security and safeguarding the organizations and their customers.

1. **Fraud Detection in Financial Transactions:** AI continuously analyzes patterns and anomalies in real-time, which is helpful in identifying fraudulent activity within financial transactions. These technologies have the ability to evaluate transaction history in order to create a baseline of typical behavior for specific users and entities. With time, these systems learn and adjust, improving their ability to identify novel and developing patterns of fraudulent activity, such as account takeovers, identity theft, or unauthorized transactions. The precision of fraud detection systems is improved by the capacity to examine a broad range of transactional data, such as time, place, and spending trends.
2. **Anomaly Detection and Behavioral Analysis:** AI surpasses rule-based systems in anomaly detection and behavioral analysis. These technologies are better at differentiating between authentic and fraudulent activities because they comprehend and adjust to the dynamic changes in user behavior. An additional layer of security is added to the authentication process by behavioral biometrics, which include mouse movement patterns and keystroke dynamics.
3. **Enhanced Cybersecurity Measures:** AI improves authentication procedures, finds security flaws, and stops cyberattacks, all of which have a major positive impact on cybersecurity. When it comes to authentication, biometric technologies—like fingerprint scanning and facial recognition—offer reliable and easy-to-use ways to confirm identity while lowering the possibility of unwanted access. The algorithms can also scan network traffic for odd patterns or anomalies that could indicate a cyberattack. By foreseeing and averting attacks based on past data and new trends, predictive analytics in cybersecurity enables proactive threat mitigation.
4. **Fraud Prevention through Machine Learning Models:** Sophisticated fraud prevention systems are made using machine learning models, including supervised and unsupervised learning. Supervised learning models enable the system to learn and recognize patterns linked to fraudulent activity by using labeled datasets that contain examples of both legitimate and fraudulent behavior. Conversely, unsupervised learning models are especially useful for identifying intricate and new fraud patterns because they are able to recognize abnormalities even in the absence of predetermined labels.

5. **Continuous Learning and Adaptability:** The capacity of AI and ML to continuously learn and adjust to new threats is one of their advantages in the context of cybersecurity and fraud prevention. These technologies can instantly update their models and algorithms in response to changes in cybercriminal tactics, guaranteeing that defenses against new threats continue to be effective.

## 5.2.3. Financial Forecasting and Investment

The financial industry has seen the rise of AI as a potent tool that is changing the field of risk assessment, investment strategies, and predictive modeling. Increased efficiency and risk mitigation in a dynamic and complex financial environment have resulted from the integration of these technologies within financial institutions, which has also greatly improved financial forecasting and decision-making accuracy.

1. **Predictive Modeling:** Financial institutions use AI algorithms for predictive modeling, which forecasts a range of financial metrics. These models forecast future events, like stock prices, interest rates, or currency fluctuations, by examining past data, market trends, and a wide range of other variables. Financial institutions can make more informed decisions about market trends, asset valuations, and economic indicators thanks to algorithms' capacity to recognize intricate patterns and relationships in data.
2. **Risk Assessment:** A crucial component of financial management is risk assessment, and AI is essential to assessing and reducing risks. Large datasets can be analyzed by these technologies, which can also evaluate the possible effects of different risk factors on a financial institution or portfolio. By recognizing patterns linked to credit risk, market volatility, and operational risks, these algorithms offer a more thorough and nuanced comprehension of possible dangers. Financial institutions can reduce exposure and maximize risk-return profiles by taking proactive measures to better quantify and evaluate risks.
3. **Credit Scoring and Underwriting:** By utilizing a wider range of factors and data sources, artificial intelligence is revolutionizing the credit scoring and underwriting processes. While algorithms are able to evaluate alternative data, like social media activity or transaction history, to determine creditworthiness, traditional credit scoring models frequently depend on a restricted set of factors. This improves the accuracy of risk assessments and makes it possible for financial institutions to give credit to people or companies that conventional approaches might have missed.

4. **Algorithmic Trading and Investment Strategies:** In order to maximize portfolio management, AI algorithms are frequently utilized in algorithmic trading and investment strategies. Real-time market data analysis, trend detection, and trade execution at speeds well above human capacity are all made possible by these technologies. The algorithms have the ability to adjust trading strategies in response to shifting market conditions and lessons learned from past performance. This improves the performance of investment portfolios overall, lowers human biases, and increases the efficiency of investment processes.
5. **Fraud Detection and Compliance:** AI is utilized by financial institutions to improve their capacity to detect fraudulent activity. In order to detect potentially fraudulent activity in real-time, these technologies examine transaction patterns, user behavior, and anomalies. In order to lower the risk of non-compliance and the fines that come with it, AI is also used to automate monitoring and reporting procedures.
6. **Portfolio Optimization:** AI algorithms take a wider range of variables and factors into account, which helps with more complex portfolio optimization. These technologies create portfolios that optimize returns while lowering risk by analyzing past performance, market dynamics, and investor preferences.

## 5.2.4. Non-Marketing Use Cases

1. **Product Design:** Based on thousands of user sessions, AI systems are able to test the product or features just like a real user would. This allows them to identify bugs in the system that even a quality tester or product manager would have missed. An AI system can even recommend to the team how it can create better product designs if it is equipped with information about how users interact with a specific product. Even the suggested user flow can be analyzed by AI systems to predict whether or not a user will perform a desired action. It can save millions of dollars in research and development, for example, if we are discussing a manufacturing company.
2. **Sales Forecasting:** Salesforce reports that teams with a high level of AI usage are ten times more likely to have accurate sales pipelines and better forecasting. If manufacturers and retailers produce more than is necessary or less than is necessary, they will suffer significant losses. Humans can't possibly incorporate a large number of variables into a play and human forecasting only uses a few well-

honed formulas that haven't been used on millions of data sets. AI and ML are a boon to companies looking to predict revenue. To predict sales, it will examine previous opportunities, sales, triumphs, failures, win percentage, and so forth. The company only needs to produce the same number of products, according to the forecasts.

### 5.2.5. AI Marketing Analytics to Track

Marketers can quickly process and analyze datasets with the aid of AI-powered algorithms and machine learning techniques. Larger datasets can be handled and sorted in real time by AI analytics, in contrast to traditional analysis. It can also find intricate correlations and patterns in the data, revealing important relationships and trends. Marketers can monitor attribution modeling, performance insights, and customer insights by utilizing AI tools that are integrated into software platforms. By giving credit to different marketing touchpoints that lead to a desired result, AI attribution modeling provides insights into the efficacy of various marketing channels and campaigns. The efficacy of your marketing campaigns and strategies can be determined in-depth and practically with AI performance insights. AI customer insights evaluate consumer data, forecasting behaviors like inclination to purchase or churn, and recommending the best course of action for customized engagement and retention tactics. The capacity to handle sizable datasets aids in the data-driven decision-making of marketers and optimizes strategies for increased ROI and performance.

### 5.2.6. AI in Marketing ROI

Businesses can increase the size and reach of their audience by utilizing AI-driven insights and targeting capabilities. Additionally, we are aware that utilizing AI in marketing to provide tailored content and product recommendations can increase conversion rates. Similarly, audience retargeting uses AI to foster relationships through customized messaging. Furthermore, real-time and comprehensive insights into campaign performance are made possible by AI's sophisticated reporting and analytics capabilities. You can then use better data to inform your decisions. You can manage greater workloads without adding to your operational burden if you have the ability to automate tasks and streamline processes.

Automation frees up time for marketers to focus on innovation such as:

- Immersive technologies like augmented reality (AR) and virtual reality (VR);
- Voice search Optimisation and voice-based marketing strategies;
- Sustainable and ethical marketing practices;

- Influencer marketing and the development of targeted content for niche audiences;
- When marketers have the time to focus on strategy, their business is more likely to find repeat business and increased ROI.

### 5.2.7. Practices for AI in Marketing

Keep these 6 priorities in mind as you pave the way for AI in marketing at your company:

- Build an ethical, strategic, and technological foundation. This means using transparent data practices, ensuring data privacy compliance, and fostering a culture of ethical AI usage. For example, you can establish clear opt-in/opt-out mechanisms and communicate comprehensive data usage policies.
- Use AI capabilities to unify, democratize, and analyze your data. You learn more about your customers' preferences by integrating data using AI-powered tools. This holistic view of customer behavior helps create effective marketing.
- Plan how to optimize AI for audience segmentation and customer personalization. When you use AI-driven recommendation engines on e-commerce platforms, product suggestions are based on individual preferences and purchase history. The customer experience is vastly improved as a result.
- Train your team to use sophisticated prompt engineering for creating content. Providing training on how AI-driven natural language generation tools work will inspire you to craft compelling content at scale. You'll be able to generate Personalized email campaigns, product descriptions, and social media posts that resonate with target audiences.
- Automate monotonous tasks to speed up workflows. Using AI-powered automation tools for tasks such as data entry, report generation, and email scheduling to enable your team to focus on more strategic initiatives and creative campaign ideation.
- Brainstorm ways AI can track and improve campaign performance over time. AI-powered analytics platforms can provide real-time data on customer engagement and conversion rates. This means you can make data-driven decisions and adjust as necessary to optimize campaign performance and ROI.

### 5.2.8. What's Ahead for AI in Marketing?

The use of AI in marketing has enormous promise for the next two years. While there will undoubtedly be difficulties, AI will support businesses in their efforts to become more efficient while also meeting customer expectations for personalized content. AI will be used more often by marketers to make predictions based on unstructured data. In order to direct generative AI to generate outputs that are customer-focused and consistent with their brand, they will also learn to rely on first-party data. Security will come into sharper focus as technology advances. With 68% of consumers stating that trustworthy businesses are more important due to AI advancements, marketers have an opportunity to ensure that their privacy and security measures are strong. In order to guarantee that first-party data grounding is secure, reduces bias, and doesn't leak private information into publicly accessible platforms, brands will employ a trust layer. It's also feasible that the entire marketing process will be completely redesigned. As technology develops, AI solutions may be able to create campaign briefs with automatically generated content and journeys, giving humans control over the process while producing performance visibility and actionable insights.

## 5.3. ARTIFICIAL INTELLIGENCE (AI) IN SALES

The phrase "artificial intelligence" refers to a broad range of technologies, including deep learning, computer vision, machine learning, and natural language processing. Fundamentally, though, all of these technologies enable machines to carry out particular cognitive tasks on par with or even more effectively than humans. For example, AI-enabled computer vision systems in self-driving cars can recognize obstacles in the same way that humans can, enabling the machine to take control of the vehicle. Using AI, your preferred voice assistant, such as Alexa or Siri, comprehends what you say just like a human and then reacts appropriately. Using AI recommendation engines, Amazon and Netflix present movies and products you might enjoy based on presumptions about your tastes, much like a fellow movie or product enthusiast might. Even though there are many intricate details associated with various forms of artificial intelligence, for the time being all you really need to know is that artificial intelligence refers to a wide range of intelligent technology. Furthermore, a lot of these technologies have the potential to significantly affect your performance, career, and sales process. This is so even though AI may contain aspects of intelligent automation, it is more than just automation.

- ***AI Goes Much Further Than That:*** Large datasets are analyzed by these technologies. However, they do more than just calculate numbers. To glean insights from data, they employ cutting-edge computer science methodologies and enormous computational power. Decisions, suggestions, and predictions can then be made using these insights. The most remarkable capabilities in sales are powered by this kind of AI, machine learning. One kind of AI that finds patterns in big data sets is machine learning. These patterns are used by the machine to generate predictions. It then gradually improves those predictions by using an increasing amount of data.

- ***The Result?*** Machine learning-powered technology improves over time, frequently without human intervention. Compared to traditional software, this is very different. Your accounting software is an example of a typical non-AI system that depends on human input to function. Rules are hardcoded into the system by humans. It then precisely adheres to those guidelines to assist you with your taxes. Only when the system is enhanced by human programmers does it get better. However, machine learning tools are capable of self-improvement. A machine evaluating its own performance and fresh data is the source of this improvement. Furthermore, more advanced forms of AI, such as generative AI, can produce ever-better results that can help salespeople. An AI sales tool, for example, can create email subject lines for you. Humans use samples of a company's marketing copy to train the machine learning of the tool. The tool then creates its own subject lines for emails. Following split testing, the machine automatically determines what needs to be improved based on the outcomes. With minimal human intervention, the machine improves over time. This opens up potentially limitless performance possibilities. Imagine this power being applied to any data-driven marketing or sales technology. Ads, analytics, and content can all become more intelligent with AI. This implies that advanced AI is able to forecast outcomes, optimize pricing, identify which prospects are most likely to close, forecast results, and recommend the most crucial sales actions. Additionally, it means that more and more of the outputs you normally have to create manually for your sales work can be produced by generative AI tools.

## 5.3.1. AI for Sales Use Cases

Artificial intelligence systems exist that can predict or forecast outcomes using historical data to inform future results. Common predictions that sales AI systems can make include:

- Deals or prospects most likely to close.
- Deals or prospects to target next.
- New customers that may be interested in what you're selling.

Now, the quality of the data and the system being used determine how accurate those predictions are. But the truth is that AI can tell you who is most likely to make a purchase in the future if you give it the correct inputs from the past and present. Additionally, your sales team can benefit internally from predictive forecasting. Sales managers can use AI to predict their team's performance for the quarter well in advance, allowing them to take proactive measures based on the data.

#### *5.3.1.1. Summarize and Provide Action Items from Meetings and Calls*

Every salesperson calls both customers and prospects. Summarizing the topics covered in each sales call and then developing action items for sales teams based on the call's content takes a significant amount of time and effort. Humans should no longer perform this labor by hand. AI is now capable of accurately summarizing calls automatically, frequently just seconds after the call has ended. All participants can then automatically receive these summaries via email. These summaries can also be used by AI to automatically create next steps for each caller based on the topics covered. Even though these are simple tasks, hiring AI to do them saves a ton of human labor that could be put toward more valuable endeavors, like closing more deals.

#### *5.3.1.2. Analyze Sales Calls*

Furthermore, it goes beyond simple action items and summaries. Salespeople can learn a great deal from each call they make about a prospect or customer's perception of your offering, their problems, and the needs and desires that are important to them. However, manually obtaining all of this data on a case-by-case basis is difficult. For this reason, progressive salespeople are using AI to evaluate their calls. These days, artificial intelligence can tell you exactly what transpired during a call and what it means for closing the deal. In order to identify opportunities and challenges that affect whether the deal proceeds or closes, it can even comprehend the tone, sentiment, and mood of the calls.

#### *5.3.1.3. Recommend Next Actions for Sales Reps*

Being able to prioritize and know what to do next is a major obstacle to sales productivity. Your sales staff is overworked and handling numerous deals concurrently. They lose out on chances to close more deals if they don't accomplish the right things in the right order and prioritize. AI can be useful. AI can actually make real-time recommendations for each sales representative's next course of action based on all the data pertaining to that deal and its current stage. By directing representatives toward the precise actions required to attain optimal sales productivity, AI functions as an ever-present sales manager and coach.

#### 5.3.1.4. Generate Sales Emails and Subject Lines Automatically

Whether reaching out to outbound prospects or inbound leads, email outreach is an essential component of the work that most sales organizations do. Performing all of this outreach by hand becomes tiresome and repetitive. Additionally, it isn't as successful as it could be. Salespeople can create captivating email subject lines and copy from scratch in a matter of seconds with the aid of generative AI. This implies that you can use AI to significantly increase the reach of your emails, either by automating the creation of emails or by producing initial drafts and concentrating on refining and customizing them. Additionally, AI can instantly create hundreds or even thousands of captivating email subject lines, increasing the likelihood that your emails will be opened.

#### 5.3.1.5. Identify New In-Market Leads

AI can identify new leads that are in-market based on the criteria that are important to your company by scanning lead data for patterns using its large-scale data analysis capabilities. To find new individuals who are a perfect fit for the kinds of leads you're trying to generate, AI can first examine the characteristics of your current good-fit leads before examining third-party lead databases and platforms.

#### 5.3.1.6. Predict Likelihood to Close

AI can estimate the likelihood that leads in your database will close with ever-increasing accuracy by using its predictive capabilities. AI can determine which lead types have a higher chance of closing and when by evaluating enormous volumes of historical and market data. As a result, your sales pipeline gains a whole new degree of predictability and efficacy.

#### 5.3.1.7. Predict Readiness to Buy

Using past data and behavioral indicators, AI can also forecast when leads are prepared to make a purchase. This implies that you can start working on the leads that are most likely to be purchased and effectively prioritizing them, which will greatly increase your close rate. It also implies that you don't pass up leads who are prepared and eager to pay you, provided you have a sales conversation with them.

#### *5.3.1.8. Prioritize Leads Automatically*

AI has given you access to a multitude of forecasts regarding their propensity to close and their level of purchase readiness. In order to increase sales and efficiently move leads through your pipeline, AI can then use these signals to prioritize which leads you should be working on and when.

#### *5.3.1.9. Score Leads Automatically*

Lead scoring by hand is undoubtedly beneficial. Even more beneficial is automating a lead score you developed. However, this procedure is still largely static and necessitates some effort, assessment, and upkeep to guarantee that leads are being scored appropriately. AI can relieve you of some of your workload. AI is now able to score leads automatically as soon as they are received, using your scoring criteria, lead data, and behavioral factors. Furthermore, AI is able to instantly modify scoring criteria in response to fresh data, updated close rates, and new insights into the signals that suggest a lead is a good fit.

#### *5.3.1.10. Monitor Competitors Automatically with AI-Powered Intel*

Every salesperson in the world dedicates some amount of time to research. Researching the competition in particular. A significant amount of your sales strategy, including which actions to prioritize and deprioritize, is determined by what your competitors are doing on any given day. However, you frequently spend so much time manually researching the competition that you neglect to actually win them over. AI makes competitive analysis more efficient. These days, AI tools can automatically uncover the crucial information you require by monitoring competitor activity online in real time. This significantly cuts down on the time you need to obtain a comprehensive understanding of what the competition is doing, allowing you to reallocate your day to outperform them.

### 5.3.2. AI Tools for Sales

Now that you know what you can do with AI in sales, you might be wondering what solutions out there actually do it. There are plenty of quality sales AI vendors in the space that serve organizations of various sizes. Here are just a handful that are worth exploring to get you started:

1. **Crayon:** Crayon is a platform for AI competitive intelligence. It provides you with a comprehensive view of a rival company's online presence by tracking competitor activity in real-time across millions of online data sources. Crayon uses AI to score the significance

of competitive intelligence items, summarize news stories about competitors, and automatically surface these insights in your inbox every day. AI will eliminate the need for manual competitor research.

2. **Drift:** Salespeople can greatly benefit from the extremely intelligent conversational AI chatbots that Drift offers. You can automatically interact with, educate, and qualify incoming leads by using Drift's AI. This is so that no quality lead is lost because you don't have a human representative monitoring chat; instead, Drift's chatbots interact with leads around-the-clock and assign scores based on their quality. Drift then transfers qualified leads to real salespeople at the appropriate moment for a cordial, high-touch interaction.
3. **Gong:** Gong turns all of your interactions with clients and prospects into intelligence that will help you close more deals by using AI to record and analyze all of your interactions. This entails bringing to light the important subjects and inquiries raised with clients and prospects, as well as the real interpersonal dynamics that are crucial to completing the sale. Then, reps can be trained on what works best by Gong's AI, which will increase the effectiveness of every single customer interaction that follows.
4. **Quantified:** Using AI-generated avatars, Quantified is a sales AI coaching tool that can perform roleplaying and sales coaching with your sales team at scale, around-the-clock. It accomplishes this by using realistic AI avatars to simulate sales calls, assisting representatives in practicing until they are flawlessly on-message and productive. In addition, Quantified evaluates vocal and visual rep skills, allowing for coaching and development even in the absence of a human trainer.
5. **Salesforce:** Salesforce, a market leader in sales software, has fully embraced AI integration into every facet of its platform, much like other top offerings. The business' AI assistant, Einstein Copilot, opens up enormous productivity and personalization possibilities for all of Salesforce's sales tools. Using it, you can do things like:

- Automate account and prospect research;
- Surface insights to quickly prepare for meetings;
- Automatically update CRM records;
- Generate sales emails;
- Summarize sales calls, etc.

6. **Trender.ai:** An AI tool for B2B contact intelligence is called Trender. AI. By providing your ICP to the tool's AI, sales professionals can

use Trender.ai to automate the process of locating top leads on social media. In order to help you close leads more successfully, the tool also offers AI-powered research capabilities that reveal deep insights about these leads.

7. **6sense:** Sales leaders can use 6sense, an AI-powered sales platform, to predict and identify in-market accounts. Additionally, 6sense will rank the most important ones according to their likelihood of making a purchase. In order to forecast when you should interact with these prospects, 6sense's AI can even identify third-party buying signals.

### 5.3.3. Will AI for Sales Replace Salespeople?

After all, these technologies are becoming more and more potent every day, so it's a legitimate worry. There are a lot of sales representatives in our audience here at Marketing AI Institute. We speak with and interview these experts on a regular basis. Additionally, we monitor thousands of AI tools used in marketing and sales. In general, we are not overly concerned that sales will be replaced by AI. AI will undoubtedly change the way sales teams operate. However, rather than taking the place of human salespeople, these tools frequently enhance them. In actuality, tasks that human salespeople lack the skills or time to complete are increasingly being replaced by AI tools. One of the tools listed below, for example, follows up with leads without the need for human intervention and even engages in two-way dialogue with them. All leads are contacted, nurtured, and qualified rather than slipping through the cracks, as they frequently do. The machine transfers the lead to a human representative when it is warm or requires human intervention. The majority of AI sales tools give you superpowers rather than automating your demise.

## 5.4. PRIVACY IN THE AGE OF AI

AI is being used more and more in many aspects of our lives as a result of technology's unprecedently rapid advancement. AI has the potential to completely change how we use technology, from smart home appliances that learn our preferences and habits to generative AI that can produce any content with a simple prompt. But with the exponential growth in the amount of data we create and share online, privacy issues are more urgent than ever. As a futurist, I believe it is crucial to investigate the issue of privacy in the era of artificial intelligence and examine the ways in which AI affects our personal information and privacy. We'll look at the possible privacy advantages and disadvantages of AI and talk about what people, businesses, and governments can do to safeguard our personal information in this new technological era.

### 5.4.1. Importance of Privacy in the Digital Era

Personal data has become a highly valuable commodity in the digital age. Businesses, governments, and organizations are now able to make better decisions and acquire new insights thanks to the massive volumes of data that are created and shared online every day. Sensitive information that people might not want to share or that organizations have used without their permission is also included in this data. Herein lies the role of privacy. The right to privacy is the protection of private data from unauthorized access. It is a fundamental human right that guarantees people have authority over the use of their personal information. Since more and more personal data is being gathered and analyzed, privacy is more crucial than ever. For many reasons, privacy is important. First of all, it shields people from dangers like fraud and identity theft. Additionally, it supports the preservation of personal autonomy and control over private data, both of which are necessary for respect and dignity. Additionally, privacy enables people to continue their professional and personal relationships without worrying about interference or surveillance. Last but not least, it safeguards our free will. If all of our data is made publicly accessible, toxic recommendation engines could analyze it and use it to influence people to make particular purchases. To guarantee that AI systems are not used to discriminate against or manipulate people based on their personal information, privacy is crucial in the context of AI. To make sure they are not making unfair or biased decisions, AI systems that use personal data for decision-making must be open and accountable. It is impossible to overestimate the significance of privacy in the digital age. It is a basic human right that is required for justice, safety, and individual liberty. As AI continues to permeate our daily lives, we must be vigilant in safeguarding our privacy to guarantee that technology is applied sensibly and morally.

### 5.4.2. Privacy Challenges in the Age of AI

The intricacy of the algorithms employed in AI systems poses a threat to both individuals' and organizations' privacy. As AI develops, it will be able to make decisions based on data patterns that are hard for humans to notice. This implies that people might not even be conscious that decisions affecting them are being made using their personal information. Let's examine each of these in more detail:

1. **The Issue of Violation of Privacy:** Even though AI technology has a lot of potential advantages, using it also presents a number of serious difficulties. The possibility of privacy violations due to AI is one of the main obstacles. Large volumes of (personal) data are needed for AI systems, and if this data ends up in the wrong hands, it could be used for evil things like identity theft or cyberbullying.

2. **The Issue of Bias and Discrimination:** The possibility of prejudice and discrimination is another issue raised by AI technology. Because AI systems are only as objective as the data they are trained on, biased data will result in biased AI systems. This may result in decisions that discriminate against people on the basis of socioeconomic status, gender, or race. To avoid bias, it is crucial to make sure AI systems are trained on a variety of data and undergo frequent audits. The connection between bias and discrimination in AI and privacy might not be immediately clear at first glance. After all, privacy is frequently viewed as a distinct issue that is connected to the right to privacy and the protection of personal data. But in actuality, the two problems are closely related, and here's why. First, it's crucial to remember that a lot of AI systems base their judgments on data. This information may originate from a number of sources, including public records, social media posts, and internet activity. Despite initially appearing harmless, this information can disclose a great deal about a person's background, including their gender, race, political views, and religion. Therefore, if an AI system is discriminatory or biased, it may use this data to reinforce its prejudices, which could result in unfair or even dangerous outcomes for people. Consider, for instance, an AI system that a hiring company uses to review job applications. Data about a candidate's gender or race may be used to unfairly exclude them from consideration if the system is biased against women or people of color. In addition to hurting the individual applicant, this maintains structural disparities in the labor market.
3. **The Issue of Job Displacements for Workers:** A third issue raised by AI technology is the possibility of economic disruption and job loss. The ability of AI systems to carry out tasks that were previously completed by humans is growing as they develop. Jobs may be lost as a result, some industries may experience economic disruption, and people may need to retrain for different positions. However, there are several significant connections between privacy and the problem of job loss. For starters, workers may experience greater financial insecurity as a result of the economic disruption brought on by AI technology. This can therefore result in a circumstance where people are compelled to give up their privacy in order to survive. Imagine, for instance, that automation has caused a worker to lose their job. They are compelled to turn to the gig economy in order to earn money because they are having difficulty making ends meet and paying their bills. They might be asked to give a platform personal

information, like their location, employment history, and reviews from prior customers, in order to find employment. Finding a job might require this, but it also poses major privacy issues because the information could be shared with outside parties or used to target advertisements. But the gig economy isn't the only factor affecting job loss and privacy. It has to do with how AI technology is applied during the hiring process as well. For instance, some businesses employ AI algorithms to evaluate job candidates, examining their online behavior or social media activity to determine whether they are qualified for a given position. Because job seekers might not be aware that this data is being gathered and used in this manner, this raises concerns regarding privacy and the accuracy of the data being used. In the end, the problem of AI-induced job loss and economic disruption is closely related to privacy since it may result in circumstances where people must give up their privacy in order to survive in a changing economy.

4. **The Issue of Data Abuse Practices:** The possibility of malicious actors abusing AI technology is yet another important concern. AI has the ability to produce convincingly fake photos and videos that can be used to disseminate false information or even sway public opinion. AI can also be used to create extremely sophisticated phishing attacks, which deceive people into disclosing personal information or clicking on harmful links. False image and video production and distribution can have detrimental effects on privacy. This is due to the fact that these made-up media frequently include actual people whose consent may not have been obtained for the use of their image. This may result in circumstances where people suffer as a result of fake media being shared, either because it is used to propagate inaccurate or harmful information about them or because it is used in a way that infringes their privacy. Think about a scenario where a bad actor uses artificial intelligence to fabricate a video that purports to show a politician acting unethically or illegally. Even if the video is obviously phony, it might still be extensively circulated on social media and seriously damage the politician's reputation. This could be harmful in the real world in addition to invading their privacy. In order to guarantee that artificial intelligence is applied morally and sensibly, a number of issues with the most recent technology need to be resolved. The fact that modern AI software frequently uses machine learning algorithms—which are trained on massive volumes of data—is one reason it has been linked to these difficulties. The algorithms will be biased if the data contains biases,

which could result in scenarios where AI reinforces discrimination and inequality already in place. In order to make sure that AI is used for the greater good rather than for evil intentions that compromise our right to privacy, we must be vigilant in addressing these issues as AI develops.

## 5.4.3. Underlying Privacy Issues in the Age of AI

Privacy has grown more complicated in the era of artificial intelligence. People's personal information is more vulnerable than ever due to the massive volume of data that governments and businesses are gathering and analyzing. Among these problems are intrusive surveillance, which can worsen power disparities and undermine personal autonomy, and unauthorized data collection, which can expose people to cyberattacks and compromise private information. The power of BigTech companies, which have access to enormous volumes of data and substantial control over its collection, analysis, and use, frequently makes these issues worse. Let's examine each of these issues' ramifications in more detail:

1. **The Power of Big Tech on Data:** Large tech firms have grown to be some of the most potent forces in the world, exerting tremendous influence over both the global economy and society at large. As AI develops and the metaverse becomes more prevalent, their influence will only grow. Due to their unprecedented access to data, Big Tech companies like Google, Amazon, and Meta are now able to shape the global economy and affect consumer behavior. Because they can affect public opinion and government policy, they are also becoming more and more involved in politics. BigTech companies are expected to grow even more powerful as we move toward the metaverse, where people will live, work, and interact in a virtual environment. Twenty times as much data will be used in the metaverse as there is now on the internet, giving BigTech businesses even more chances to use their data and influence. The metaverse will also give BigTech companies even more control over the user experience by enabling them to build whole new virtual ecosystems. BigTech businesses may be able to take advantage of new opportunities to profit from their platforms and further impact society as a result. But this authority also carries a lot of responsibility. BigTech businesses need to be open and honest about how they handle data and make sure that the information they gather is handled sensibly and morally. Instead of being dominated by a few influential players, they must also endeavor to make sure that their platforms are open and accessible to everyone. With the advent of BigTech, these businesses now have more power than ever

before, and as the internet becomes more immersive, their impact will only grow. Even though there are a lot of exciting opportunities here, Big Tech companies need to be proactive in making sure their influence is used sensibly and morally. They can create a future in which technology serves society as a whole, not just a chosen few, by doing this. Naturally, it might be naive to assume that Big Tech will do this on its own initiative; therefore, regulation will probably need to compel Big Tech to adopt a different strategy.

2. **Data Collection and Use by AI Technologies:** The way AI technology gathers and uses data is among its most notable effects. AI systems are made to analyze enormous volumes of data in order to learn and get better. Because of this, the volume of personal information gathered by AI systems keeps increasing, which raises privacy and data security concerns. We only need to examine the different generative AI tools, like ChatGPT, Stable Diffusion, or any other tool under development, to see how our data—articles, photos, videos, etc.—can be used are being utilized, frequently without our permission. More significantly, it's not always clear how AI systems use personal information. People may find it challenging to comprehend how their data is being used to make decisions that impact them due to the complexity of the algorithms used in AI systems. Unease and mistrust of AI systems can result from a lack of transparency. Organizations and businesses that use AI technology must take proactive steps to protect people's privacy in order to allay these worries. This entails putting in place robust data security procedures, making sure that data is only utilized for the intended purpose, and creating AI systems that follow moral guidelines. It goes without saying that openness is essential when it comes to how AI systems use personal information. People need to have the ability to control how their data is used and comprehend how it is being used. This includes the option to request the deletion of their data and to opt out of data collection. By doing this, we can create a future in which AI technologies are applied to advance society while safeguarding people's privacy and data.

3. **The Use of AI in Surveillance:** The use of AI in surveillance is among its most contentious applications. Though they also present serious threats to civil liberties and privacy, AI-based surveillance systems have the potential to completely transform security and law enforcement. AI -based surveillance systems analyze enormous volumes of data from various sources, such as cameras, social media,

and other online sources, using algorithms. This enables security organizations and law enforcement to keep an eye on people and anticipate criminal activity before it happens. AI-based surveillance systems raise privacy and civil liberties issues even though they may appear to be a useful weapon in the war on crime and terrorism. Opponents contend that by monitoring and controlling people, these systems may cause them to lose their freedom and civil liberties. Even worse, there are situations when the use of AI-based surveillance systems is opaque. It can be challenging for people to understand when or why they are being watched. People may become uneasy and lose faith in security and law enforcement organizations as a result of this lack of openness. The use of AI-based surveillance systems needs to be strictly regulated and supervised in order to allay these worries. This entails the creation of independent oversight and review mechanisms in addition to explicit policies and procedures for the use of these systems. The use of these systems by law enforcement and security organizations must be open and transparent, and people must have access to information about the collection and use of their data. There is no denying that law enforcement and security agencies have benefited greatly from the integration of AI-based surveillance systems. Nonetheless, it is imperative to recognize the possible threats these systems pose to our basic liberties and rights. Regulatory agencies must address a number of issues to guarantee the preservation of civil liberties and individual privacy, including the possibility of discrimination and a lack of transparency.

In order to create a future where AI technologies are used to benefit society without compromising individual rights and freedoms, it is imperative that stringent regulations and oversight mechanisms be put in place. To control the use of AI-based surveillance systems and guarantee transparency in their implementation, it's critical to set up explicit policies and procedures. In order to guarantee accountability, separate oversight and review procedures also need to be established. The European Union (EU) Parliament has recently made a major advancement in the defense of personal privacy in the AI era. The use of AI surveillance in public spaces is now prohibited, according to a proposal supported by the majority of the EU Parliament. This proposal would forbid the use of AI surveillance technologies, such as facial recognition, in public spaces unless there is a clear threat to public safety. The growing concern over the possibility that AI technology will be applied in a way that violates people's privacy and other fundamental rights is reflected in this decision. In order to guarantee that AI technology is developed and applied in a way that respects individual privacy and other ethical considerations, the EU Parliament has passed a ban on the use of AI surveillance in public spaces. The only way, in my opinion, that the use of AI technology for surveillance can be justified is if it is done so responsibly and ethically. Without compromising the principles that make us a free and democratic society, we can create a future in which AI technologies are used to improve security and safeguard society by placing a high priority on individual privacy and civil rights.

### 5.4.4. The Future of Privacy in the Age of AI

The development of AI technologies and their increasing integration into our daily lives have put the future of privacy at a critical crossroads. We must start thinking about how these technologies will affect the security and privacy of our data in the future as the metaverse grows and our data production increases. Future generations will be greatly impacted by the decisions we make today, so it is up to us to make sure that we create a future in which AI technologies are applied in a way that both respects and upholds individual liberties and rights and benefits society as a whole.

1. **The Need for Regulation:** The possibility of misusing and abusing AI technology increases as these systems get more complex and have the capacity to process and analyze enormous volumes of data. AI technology must be effectively regulated and supervised to guarantee that it is created and applied in a manner that respects people's rights and liberties. In addition to the data collection and utilization, this also covers the design and development of AI systems to guarantee their objectivity, transparency, and explainability. To effectively regulate AI technology, governments, business, and civil society must work together to create precise rules and regulations for its moral application. To make sure that these standards are maintained, continuous enforcement and monitoring will also be necessary. Without adequate regulation, there is a chance that the growing use of AI technology will exacerbate already-existing biases and inequalities in society and further erode civil liberties and privacy. Establishing a framework for regulations on AI will help guarantee that this potent technology is applied for the benefit of society while preserving individual liberties and rights.
2. **The Importance of Data Security and Encryption:** Cyberattacks and data breaches can have serious repercussions, including identity theft, monetary loss, and harm to one's reputation. A number of well-publicized data breaches in recent years have brought attention to the significance of data security, and using encryption to safeguard private data has grown in significance.

The process of transforming data into an unintelligible format in order to stop unauthorized access is called encryption. It offers a means of safeguarding information while it is being transmitted and stored. Protecting sensitive data, including trade secrets, financial information, and personal information, requires encryption. Strong data security and encryption are becoming even more important as AI technology develops. Security measures must be put in place to prevent data loss or theft because AI depends on such a large volume of data that any breach could have far-reaching effects. Take, for instance, a healthcare organization that analyzes patient data using AI technologies. Sensitive information like diagnoses, treatment plans, and medical histories may be included in this data. There could be severe repercussions for the patients involved if this data were stolen or obtained by unauthorized individuals. The healthcare organization can guarantee the confidentiality and security of this data by employing robust encryption. A financial institution that employs AI to analyze consumer data in order to detect fraud is another example. Account numbers, transaction histories, and other financial and personal data may be among the information gathered by the organization. This information might be used for identity theft or other fraudulent purposes if it ended up in the wrong hands. The financial institution can avoid unauthorized access and safeguard the information of its clients by employing encryption to protect this data. These two instances demonstrate the significance of encryption and data security. To safeguard the sensitive information they gather, AI-using organizations must take data security seriously and put strong encryption measures in place. Failing to do so could have detrimental effects on the organization as well as the people whose data was compromised.

3. **The Correlation with Quantum Computing:** Data security and encryption are seriously threatened by the emergence of quantum computing, which emphasizes the necessity of more funding for cutting-edge encryption methods. Currently, sensitive data, including financial transactions, medical records, and personal information, is secured by traditional encryption algorithms that can be broken by quantum computers. The reason for this is that quantum computers can decipher encryption keys and expose the underlying data because they can execute computations far more quickly than classical computers. In order to counter this threat, scientists and business professionals are creating new encryption methods that are especially made to withstand attacks using quantum computing.

Post-quantum cryptography, which employs mathematical problems thought to be impervious to quantum computers, and quantum key distribution, which permits the safe transfer of cryptographic keys across great distances, are two examples. As the technology of quantum computing advances, it is critical that governments and organizations take action to protect their sensitive data. To avoid unauthorized access and data breaches, this entails putting money into cutting-edge encryption methods created especially to withstand quantum computing attacks and putting strong data security measures in place.

4. **The Role of Consumers in Protecting their Privacy:** More than ever, we must protect our privacy. People are crucial in safeguarding their own privacy, even though laws and data security procedures can offer some degree of protection. Customers can protect their personal information in a number of ways. Understanding the type of data being collected and its intended use is crucial first. Typically, terms of service agreements and privacy policies contain this information. Before utilizing any goods or services that gather their data, consumers should take the time to read and comprehend these documents. Second, people can benefit from privacy settings and tools that are frequently found in social media and software. For instance, a lot of websites give users the choice to restrict data sharing with outside businesses or to opt out of targeted advertising. In a similar vein, social media sites frequently offer privacy settings to limit who can see or access private data. Finally, customers ought to be careful about what they do online and what they disclose. Personal information that could be used to violate privacy can be found through social media posts, online transactions, and even basic web searches. Personal privacy can be greatly enhanced by being conscious of the information being shared and taking action to restrict its spread.

## REFERENCES


1. Broekhuizen, T., Broekhuis, M., Bouwer, J., & Haaker, T. (2021). How artificial intelligence in service enhances customer engagement: A conceptual framework. *Journal of Service Management, 32*(3), 442–460.
2. Chen, H., Chiang, R. H. L., & Storey, V. C. (2012). Business intelligence and analytics: From big data to big impact. *MIS Quarterly, 36*(4), 1165–1188.
3. Davenport, T. H., Guha, A., Grewal, D., & Bressgott, T. (2020). How artificial intelligence will change the future of marketing. *Journal of the Academy of Marketing Science, 48*(1), 24–42.
4. De Bruyn, A., Viswanathan, V., Beh, Y. S., Brock, J. K. U., & von Wangenheim, F. (2020). Artificial intelligence and marketing: Pitfalls and opportunities. *Journal of Interactive Marketing, 51*, 91–105.
5. Edelman, D. C., & Singer, M. (2015). Competing on customer journeys. *Harvard Business Review, 93*(11), 88–100.
6. Gentsch, P. (2019). *AI in Marketing, Sales and Service: How Marketers Without a Data Science Degree can use AI, Big Data and Bots*. Palgrave Macmillan.
7. Kietzmann, J., Paschen, J., & Treen, E. (2018). Artificial intelligence in advertising: How marketers can leverage AI to reach digital natives. *Journal of Advertising Research, 58*(3), 263–267.
8. Kiron, D., & Unruh, G. (2018). AI is going to change marketing forever. *MIT Sloan Management Review, 60*(2), 1–6.
9. Kumar, V., & Gupta, S. (2021). How artificial intelligence will transform marketing. *Journal of the Academy of Marketing Science, 49*(1), 61–85.
10. Lee, I., & Shin, Y. J. (2020). Machine learning for enterprises: Applications, algorithm selection, and challenges. *Business Horizons, 63*(2), 157–170.
11. Ma, L., & Sun, B. (2020). Machine learning and AI in marketing–Connecting computing power to human insights. *International Journal of Research in Marketing, 37*(3), 481–504.
12. Ng, A. (2018). *AI Transformation Playbook: How to Lead Your Company into the Artificial Intelligence Era*. AI Transformation Playbook.
13. Paschen, J., Pitt, C., & Kietzmann, J. (2020). Artificial intelligence: Building blocks and an innovation typology. *Business Horizons, 63*(2), 147–155.
14. Puranam, D., Narayan, V., & Kadiyali, V. (2021). The role of artificial intelligence in customization: A strategic perspective. *Journal of Marketing, 85*(5), 145–167.

15. Rust, R. T., & Huang, M. H. (2021). The AI revolution in marketing. *Journal of Marketing, 85*(1), 24–42.
16. Syam, N., & Sharma, A. (2018). Waiting for a sales renaissance in the fourth industrial revolution: Machine learning and artificial intelligence in sales research and practice. *Industrial Marketing Management, 69*, 135–146.
17. Wirth, N. (2018). Hello marketing, what can artificial intelligence help you with? *International Journal of Market Research, 60*(5), 435–438.

CHAPTER 6

# AI IN HUMAN RESOURCES AND TALENT MANAGEMENT

## Contents

# INTRODUCTION

The manner in which businesses recruit, nurture, and maintain their workforce has been completely transformed by the incorporation of artificial intelligence (AI) into talent management and human resources (HR) procedures. Artificial intelligence (AI)-driven technologies provide unmatched capacity to optimize and streamline HR operations, leading to more effective, data-driven decision-making and enhanced employee experiences. Recruiting and candidate sourcing are two important areas where AI is being used in HR and talent management. In order to more successfully identify and attract top talent, AI algorithms can analyze massive volumes of data from a variety of sources, including resumes, social media profiles, and job boards. By matching candidates with job requirements based on skills, experience, and cultural fit, these algorithms can shorten the hiring process and increase the caliber of hires. AI-driven chatbots and virtual assistants can also interact with applicants, respond to inquiries, and offer immediate feedback, improving the applicant experience and building a favorable employer brand. AI is also very important for performance management and talent development. With the help of AI-driven learning platforms, training programs can be tailored to the requirements and preferences of specific employees, allowing for the timely delivery of content in the most appropriate format.

In order to facilitate ongoing skill development and career advancement, these platforms can also track employee progress and make recommendations for additional learning opportunities. AI-powered performance management systems can also analyze employee data to find areas for improvement, provide more insightful and accurate performance evaluations, and enable managers and employees to have more meaningful feedback conversations.

Furthermore, by helping businesses better understand and address the needs of their workforce, AI improves employee engagement and retention initiatives. In order to find trends and patterns in employee satisfaction and sentiment, sentiment analysis algorithms can examine employee feedback from surveys, reviews, and social media. This knowledge enables HR managers to proactively handle problems, carry out focused interventions, and establish a more encouraging and helpful workplace. Additionally, firms can use retention strategies and tailored incentives to keep top talent by using AI-driven predictive analytics to identify employees who are at risk of leaving.

AI adoption in HR and talent management is not without its difficulties, though. To maintain justice and legal compliance, ethical issues like algorithmic bias and data privacy need to be properly handled. Additionally, companies need to spend money on the infrastructure, expertise, and training needed to use AI technologies efficiently. Notwithstanding these obstacles, artificial intelligence

(AI) has significant potential benefits for HR and talent management, giving businesses a competitive edge in luring, nurturing, and keeping their most valuable resource—their employees.

## 6.1. ROLE OF AI IN HUMAN RESOURCE MANAGEMENT

Artificial Intelligence has become a vital component of human resource management in today's business world. Businesses are looking to AI-driven solutions to optimize their resources and streamline their operations in an effort to stay efficient and competitive. Artificial Intelligence (AI) is transforming HR departments worldwide, ranging from automated recruitment systems that detect exceptional talent to advanced training programs that offer tailored content.

We will discuss the function of AI in HRM in this blog post and how it can help businesses save costs and increase worker satisfaction. We'll go over the benefits of utilizing AI in learning and development programs, performance management, on boarding, recruitment, and the difficulties in putting it into practice. Organizations can make their HR processes more efficient and competitive in today's dynamic business environment by utilizing cutting-edge technologies like machine learning and natural language processing.

### 6.1.1. How Does AI Play a Role in Human Resource Management?

AI has become increasingly pervasive in human resource management. AI-driven solutions are being used to streamline many of the traditional processes associated with HR such as recruitment, onboarding, performance management, and learning and development initiatives.

Below is a list of six ways that AI plays a role in human resource management.

#### *6.1.1.1. Streamlining Recruitment and Selection*

AI can facilitate the human resources management process of recruiting and selection. AI-powered tools are used to find suitable applicants with the qualifications for a position fast. It can also be used to filter out applicants who don't fit specific requirements, ensuring that employers hire the most qualified person.

This guarantees that only the most qualified candidates are hired for each position while also saving time and money. Artificial intelligence can use sophisticated algorithms and machine learning capabilities to quickly and accurately analyze candidate data. Because of this, it can find the best applicants more quickly than recruiters. AI can use elements like language analysis, tone of voice, and facial expressions to reveal aspects of a candidate's personality and workplace behavior that a human recruiter might miss on a CV.

AI also helps recruiters analyze the labor needs of the future while taking organizational strategy, performance data, and market trends into account. AI can help in the precise and realistic creation of job descriptions by helping to identify the behaviors and competencies needed for each position. AI can also help you build your employer brand and reputation by showcasing your benefits, culture, and values across a range of channels and platforms. By using AI to draw in candidates, you can expand the audience and visibility of your business and draw in more qualified candidates. By using algorithms and natural language processing to scan resumes, cover letters, and portfolios, AI can also help you automate and enhance your screening process. AI may help you conduct pre-screening tests and assessments in gamified and interactive formats, such as assessments of cognitive ability, personality, and skills. By using AI to screen your prospects, you may reduce bias and errors while saving time and money.

### *6.1.1.2. Onboarding*

Employee onboarding can be streamlined by automating manual, time-consuming activities with AI. Automation technology frees up time for onboarding teams to focus on the human side of bringing on a new team member. Onboarding automation tasks can involve updating databases, implementing training programs, and reducing FAQs.

By automating administrative chores like filling out paperwork, setting up accounts, and delivering training, AI can assist to speed the onboarding process. This allows HR professionals to focus on more strategic parts of the onboarding process, such as developing connections with new workers and assimilating them into the organization's culture. AI may also deliver individualized onboarding experiences based on each new employee's unique requirements and preferences, which can enhance engagement and retention.

### *6.1.1.3. Learning and Development (L&D)*

AI plays an important role in helping companies constantly teach their employees new skills and knowledge. AI can help find the best ways to learn and understand things, as well as suggest activities that are tailored to each person's individual needs. This helps employees stay up-to-date with the ever-changing business environment.

Artificial intelligence is revolutionizing the entire learning and development process and can help L&D professionals deliver better and more engaging learning. With AI, organizations can save time and money while ensuring the most effective learning outcomes for their employees.

AI-powered learning and development solutions can automatically deliver adaptive learning experiences for employees. By leveraging data, AI-driven algorithms can also assess the knowledge, skills, and experiences of all employees and deliver targeted learning content tailored to individual needs, preferences, and learning styles. This allows employees to improve their skills quickly and effectively. This personalized approach not only leads to better learning outcomes but can also increase employee engagement and retention.

Furthermore, AI can provide employees with personalized coaching by analyzing their performance data and providing tailored feedback. For example, having an AI-led learning and development program can examine individual employee performance and suggest specific areas for improvement, along with actionable advice.

This personalized coaching can help employees develop their skills and achieve their career goals in an efficient manner that also keeps employees motivated and optimistic about their personal and professional growth.

In addition to that, AI can assist HR professionals in enhancing their L&D programs by providing data-driven insights. By analyzing employee data, such as performance metrics and engagement surveys, AI-powered tools can recognize skills gaps and areas that need improvement. This helps HR professionals to develop customized L&D programs that target the specific requirements of their workforce.

### *6.1.1.4. Increasing Performance Management*

Every employee has to attend a performance review meeting, which always takes place in a conference room. Any organization must have a clear performance management system in place. The impact of employees on the workplace can be measured with a strong performance management system. This system allows for the tracking of the training's impact on the organization.

Employees will find it easier to match their work performance with the aims and objectives of the company with the help of this framework. Setting the goal, completing a self-evaluation, getting feedback from supervisors, having a discussion, and signing off are all laborious steps in traditional performance management. AI can help with goal monitoring in real time and provide feedback on tasks completed and tasks left undone. AI also plays a role in eliminating any biases when it comes to comparing employee performance. This can be accomplished by establishing detailed and measurable goals. AI can also help in aligning underperforming employees with the necessary set of goals to increase performance levels. Furthermore, it can also assist in providing information on employees' potential and predicting which employees will perform well or poorly, all of which can be highly useful information for HR professionals in succession planning. HR professionals utilize AI to create goals, track team, and individual performance, learn about developments and changes, and save operational time. This leads to increased productivity and overall positive outcomes.

### *6.1.1.5. Employee Engagement*

The use of Artificial Intelligence can improve the way businesses and employees interact. AI can be utilized for various employee engagement tasks like conducting intelligent surveys, providing real-time feedback, and offering rewards and recognition.

Here are some examples of the role that AI plays in employee engagement

- **Personalization:** AI-powered tools can improve the employee experience by customizing learning and development programs and HR processes to meet the individual needs and preferences of every employee. This can increase employee satisfaction and engagement.
- **Responsiveness:** The use of AI-powered chatbots and virtual assistants can offer around-the-clock assistance to employees by promptly answering their queries and providing feedback. This can result in better employee engagement by fostering a responsive and encouraging work atmosphere.
- **Data-driven Insights:** With the help of AI, HR professionals can evaluate employee data such as engagement surveys and performance metrics. They can then use this data to identify any potential issues and gain insights into the workforce. The findings can be used to develop targeted engagement programs and initiatives that cater to the specific needs and concerns of employees.

Furthermore, AI can use natural language processing and sentiment analysis to discover how engaged and motivated employees are feeling. Additionally, AI can also be a powerful factor in determining appropriate team composition by analyzing employee motivation and leveraging outcomes. AI can also understand what factors will motivate certain employees and advise managers on how to effectively encourage their teams.

Moreover, AI technology allows employees to communicate more freely and openly about their ideas and concerns. It provides real-time feedback to both employees and HR professionals, which can be positive or negative. As a result, employees can express their feelings without the need for physical meetings or scheduling a specific time.

### *6.1.1.6. Employee Retention*

Retaining talents serve to be one of the greatest challenges in the industry globally. Organizations are constantly experimenting with new strategies and methods to keep their employees for as long as possible. Retention of employees is primarily the responsibility of human resource professionals. In this competitive environment, it can be challenging for HR professionals to keep their employees in the organization. HR attempts to address this issue by introducing several techniques inside the company. Therefore, AI can help with career progression planning by monitoring and evaluating employees' performance to identify any signs of stagnation or depression. This will assist strategists and managers in planning the implementation of new learning and development (L&D) programs as well as identifying new growth opportunities.

Below are a few bullet points explaining the role that AI plays in improving employee retention:

- **Career Planning:** One of the main reasons employees choose to stay at a company is the potential for career progression and new opportunities. AI can help with this by monitoring employee performance to identify when they may be getting stuck and not growing. With this information, managers can introduce new learning and development programs and identify new areas for growth.
- **Identifying Opportunities for Growth:** AI has various applications for employee assessment, including evaluation of engagement and work performance. It can also notify managers when an employee needs a new challenge or has outgrown their current role. Furthermore, AI-based performance management tools can suggest training opportunities for employees. Employers can also use AI-assisted approaches for employee development and retention of talent at risk of leaving the company.
- **Better Work-Life Balance:** Employee satisfaction heavily relies on work-life balance, in which employees now seek more control over their work schedule and time. Utilizing AI can provide employees with the desired autonomy, while also meeting work requirements and needs. AI does this by helping employees automate repetitive and mundane tasks that can be completed much faster, giving employees the time to work on other tasks that require their own

critical thinking and creativity whilst still getting their other tasks done on time.

- **Achievable Equitable Compensation:** In today's economy, businesses are aiming to stay competitive and prioritize equal pay for equal work. This raises the question of how to compensate employees effectively. AI has the capability to analyze extensive data sets, recognize patterns and assist employers in offering fair and personalized compensation packages to their employees. The solutions mentioned are capable of evaluating market conditions, employee performance, and business outcomes to enhance compensation and rewards. With the help of these solutions, companies can establish clearer objectives, monitor employee progress, and suggest new methods to achieve better outcomes. AI, therefore, plays a role in helping employers create more favorable working conditions for their employees, which would be beneficial for everyone.
- **Improving Productivity:** Using AI can boost productivity, which in turn can improve employee retention. This can be achieved by automating tasks that are repetitive and consume a lot of time, offering employees real-time feedback and coaching, and pinpointing areas that can from process improvement. AI also enhances job satisfaction and retention of top talent by improving employee efficiency, reducing errors, and optimizing operations, ultimately leading to a more fulfilling and rewarding work environment while maximizing workforce potential.

### 6.1.2. Advantages and Disadvantages of AI in Human Resource Management

The integration of AI into human resource management (HRM) brings a host of advantages and disadvantages, transforming traditional HR practices while also presenting new challenges and considerations (Table 6.1).

**Table 6.1.** *The Advantages and Disadvantages of AI in Human Resource Management*

| Advantages | Disadvantages |
|---|---|
| Increased efficiency and accuracy in administrative tasks | Potentially high costs associated with implementing and maintaining AI technology |
| Improvement in the screening and selection process of candidates | Potential for cyber-security risks and data breaches |

| | |
|---|---|
| Improved employee engagement and retention by providing personalized experiences and real-time feedback | Dependence on AI technology, leading to potential disruptions if the technology fails |
| Improved human resource management's ability to make informed decisions by analyzing data | It is important to have greater transparency in AI algorithms. HR professionals should strive to gain a deeper understanding of AI algorithms to make more informed decisions. They must ensure that these algorithms are transparent and can be explained to prevent errors and unintentional biases. |
| Ensure compliance with labor laws and regulations | No disadvantages |
| Streamlined, personalized, and effective learning and development | No disadvantages |
| Increased productivity through routine task automation | No disadvantages |
| Reduced bias associated with the screening process | No disadvantages |
| HR employees can dedicate more time and concentration to tasks that require human interaction such as building closer relationships with candidates and clients and advancing organizational strategies | No disadvantages |

*Source: https://www.retorio.com/blog/what-ai-in-human-resource-management.*

### 6.1.3. Artificial Intelligence and a new Era of Human Resources

A new era of human resource management, where data analytics, machine learning, and automation combine to save time and promote higher-quality results, can be brought about with the aid of AI. As AI technology advances from automation to augmentation, businesses might be considering how AI tools can improve the work that human resources (HR) does for both candidates and current employees. Not only is time savings important, but near real-time information, insights, and recommendations are also provided.

And that's only the introduction of AI to HR. These discussions are taking place at a time when there is a significant shift in the workforce. Executives polled for a global study by the IBM Institute for Business Value (IBV) predict that over the course of the next three years, implementing AI and automation will require reskilling 40% of their workforce. This change is seen as creating more job opportunities. Indeed, 87% of respondents think that generative AI will more likely augment employee roles than replace them, with the effects being contingent upon the nature of the job.

Over the next three years, the implementation of automation and artificial intelligence will require the workforce to reskill. This change is expected to increase employment opportunities. According to 87% of respondents, generative AI is more likely to enhance rather than replace employee roles, though the impact varies based on job function. These technologies are becoming innovative tools that enable team members to approach human resources more strategically while preserving a human touch.

### 6.1.4. How HR Departments are Using AI

AI use in HR refers to the deployment of machine learning (ML), natural language processing (NLP) and other AI technologies to automate human resources tasks and support decision-making. It enables a data-based approach to talent acquisition, employee advancement and retention that seeks to mitigate bias and enhance the job seekers' and employees' experiences.

AI tools have the capabilities to assist HR leaders in a wide range of areas, including the following:

- Employee records management;
- Recruitment and hiring processes;
- Payroll processing;
- Performance management and assessments;
- Benefits administration;
- Onboarding new employees;
- HR support or service desks.

Companies today have the potential to use artificial intelligence in HR functions and processes to inform decision-making, make interacting with HR easier for employees and free up time to make better hiring decisions and invest in employee satisfaction and retention.

These are some possible use cases:

- **Professional Learning and Development:** Where do workers see themselves in five years? AI has the potential to assist in recommending personalized training modules for career mobility. By analyzing data on each employee, such as their skills and preferences, AI could tailor their training according to personal goals. AI could also have the potential to help HR managers identify hidden talent or identify employees ready for promotion.

- **Candidate Sourcing and Hiring:** A common complaint about the hiring process is that it's slow. AI can help pick up the pace by helping managers nurture each potential hire automatically, and it allows them to receive notifications when a candidate applies for an open position.
- **Procurement of Short-Term Workers:** AI in HR can help organizations fill open positions quickly, including short-term and temp positions. By using NLP capabilities, AI tools for HR can automate manual procurement tasks, saving HR teams valuable time for planning strategic initiatives and meeting client needs. For example, AI tools can help managers compile requirements from stakeholders and then work within a vendor management system (VMS) system to open a request with suppliers to find potential contractors and schedule interviews with hiring managers.
- **Onboarding:** AI can make the process of collecting information smoother and more personalized. AI-powered chatbots can guide new employees through the onboarding process, answer questions, provide information and send reminders about key documents—reducing time-consuming tasks and enhancing the new hire experience.
- **Automating HR Service:** Responding to employee needs is key to improving engagement and productivity, but navigating through complex corporate policies and HR and IT support processes can leave employees struggling to find answers—causing frustration and wasting time. AI-powered HR chatbots can help empower employees with fast answers and self-service support.

There is no doubt that AI can benefit HR departments. Here are some of the key advantages.

### *6.1.4.1. Time Efficiency*

One of the main advantages of integrating automation and artificial intelligence into routine HR tasks is time efficiency. Time-consuming tasks can be aided by AI and automation solutions, freeing up HR professionals' time to concentrate on tasks that require both human and professional skills.

One excellent illustration of how AI and machine learning can greatly reduce time is the hiring process. AI-integrated software can sort and suggest applicants with the necessary skills and experience for a particular job opening, eliminating the need to manually go through mountains of applications from hundreds or thousands of applicants. Even though AI excels at processing vast volumes of data, human review and supervision are always advised for any AI-supported processes, particularly hiring decisions.

#### *6.1.4.2. Cost Effectiveness*

Tasks can be completed by AI tools in a fraction of the time that humans would need. In just a few seconds, it is possible to crunch and summarize vast amounts of data and find patterns. AI can identify the best places to locate top talent and provide you with guidance on where to concentrate your resources and efforts. AI can help businesses save money and better allocate their human and material resources by expediting tasks.

#### *6.1.4.3. Bias Reduction*

Lessening prejudice during the hiring process is another advantage of utilizing AI in HR. AI can facilitate a more inclusive hiring process by giving priority to credentials and skills. HR professionals can make decisions based only on qualifications by removing personal information from applications, such as address, gender, age, and other private data.

But there is still disagreement on the subject of bias in AI. According to studies, AI may exhibit biases during the hiring process, which could lead to less diverse teams as the system attempts to match candidates with the perfect profile. Diverse underlying theories exist regarding the causes of AI biases. The one involving the training data is arguably the most well-established. AI runs the risk of reproducing and maintaining biases in its decision-making processes if the training data contains them.

#### *6.1.4.4. Improved Employee Experience*

AI tools and solutions can be used to improve employee satisfaction and boost retention. Workers can gain new, relevant tech skills, delegate repetitive administrative tasks, and streamline their overall workload. In addition to improving employee wellbeing, time and money invested in the employee experience builds your employer brand and yields benefits that come with having a happy workforce.

### 6.1.5. Benefits of AI in HR

If companies begin to use AI in HR to achieve more strategic goals, they may be able to see advanced benefits as well. Here are some examples:

- **Enhanced Employee Support:** In 2022, one in four employees was experiencing burnout symptoms, according to a global survey from

McKinsey Health Institute. This poses a challenge to employers vested in worker satisfaction and performance. For teams that want to better understand their employees to improve job satisfaction and performance, AI can be a useful resource if used in a responsible way.

- **Increased Efficiency:** As noted above, automation and generative AI tools can save HR teams time by taking on routine task work. AI can also be a helpful source of data sets for reviewing processes and digging deeper into how HR staff can make more informed decisions or streamline work. For example, AI can help analyze the outcomes of recruiting efforts, allowing recruiters and hiring managers to identify and refine their most successful outreach strategies.
- **Enhanced Candidate Experiences:** Along each step of the recruitment process, from hiring to onboarding, AI can help managers save time and better reach top talent. For example, managers can prompt generative AI tools to create customized messages that are automatically sent to each candidate. These messages can encourage engagement and move candidates along in the hiring process.

### 6.1.6. Challenges of AI in HR

AI is a disruptive technology that comes with some challenges and things to keep in mind:

- **Reskilling:** AI and automation can eliminate certain types of work traditionally performed by people and could impact the roles of some employees. Tackle this challenge head on with a plan for reskilling talent and restructuring job roles in a way that's empathetic to employees undergoing these changes.
- **Employee Privacy:** Using AI to optimize processes and evaluate performance could raise concerns. Employee privacy should be taken seriously and addressed in a data management strategy before AI systems are used to collect and analyze personal data. Let employees know what data is being collected and used for AI systems. Creating or using an AI system founded on transparency is a first step towards helping to address privacy concerns.
- **Bumpy Rollouts:** Organizations should be prepared to evolve AI models and continue to optimize processes. Initial rollouts might result in less-than-desired employee experiences and require tweaking. Companies should have the flexibility to change and adjust as needed.

- **Cyber-Security:** AI is susceptible to hacking, especially during the training pipeline where ML algorithms are created. Data poisoning attacks seed malicious code or information in the training sets, potentially infecting countless ML model runs and, ultimately, the company network. Business leaders should work alongside IT and security operation centers (SOCs) to create plans that will keep AI projects secure throughout their entire lifecycle.

There are many considerations in introducing AI into HR processes, leaving business leaders faced with decision overload on how, when, and where to use it to benefit their workforce. From questions about where to start, confirming you have the necessary skills and technologies, and using quality data, the decision-making process can be complex, overwhelming, and confusing. Additionally, there is a lot of pressure to integrate AI into more and more use cases, improve productivity levels and create new business models.

To simplify and determine the best course of action; however, you should go back to the basics, focusing on your strategy, operating model and people to help assess your organization's AI readiness includes:

- **Establish a Clear and Actionable Plan:** This combines both the business and AI strategies. Create specific objectives and goals with defined measurements for success. Understand your existing workforce and identify any skills gaps. Plan for gaps by reskilling current talent, restructuring job roles to incorporate AI into human workflows, automating routine tasks, and leveraging ecosystem partners.
- **Evolve Your Operating Model:** By reimagining the experience of your workforce as well as your customers to inform new ways of working. Visualize end-to-end processes and identify opportunities to apply AI and gain new efficiencies. Determine if legacy systems will integrate and use AIOps to address any IT issues.
- **Invest in the Talent and Skills of Your People:** Create a culture of continuous learning. Success in the new AI era requires you put people, instead of technology, at the center of your strategy. Your human workforce is integral to the success of this digital transformation. Their expertise gives them unique insights into where automation and AI could augment performance. Foster an open communication forum for them to provide direct input and insights.
- **Be Prepared to Ask and Answer the Hard Questions:** Generative AI is transforming the way we work globally and there are many hard

questions HR leaders need to be able to answer to make sure people, processes, and technology work together to create business value, deliver on business strategy and improve operational efficiency.

Challenges can become less of an issue by first aligning your organization's overall business strategy with the generative AI strategy, defining end-to-end processes and workflows, and educating people and technologies on how everything will work together. No matter where you are in this process, IBM Consulting can help you answer the hard questions, implement AI applications into your existing HR systems, accelerate digital transformation, and unlock workforce potential.

### 6.1.7. HR and Talent in the Era of AI

At this critical juncture, the rise of generative AI and foundation models has completely changed how businesses across all industries conduct business. This is particularly true for the HR department, which has been thrust forward in the wake of the AI revolution. 36% of CEOs surveyed in a recent IBM IBV study titled "CEO decision-making in the age of AI" cited workforce and skills as the most significant factor affecting their company. Increasing the use of AI capabilities to support human labor in core HR functions such as hiring, onboarding, and skill development holds the potential to transform businesses and enable them to compete in a global marketplace.

### 6.1.8. The Future of HR and Talent with Generative AI

Numerous HR applications, processes, and technologies, such as resume parsing, sourcing, and screening, and candidate skill matching, have historically benefited from and been closely associated with automation and AI capabilities. But with targeted advisors in this new era, generative AI can deliver more, and its useful use cases will only grow. Work done by human workers on tasks like creating job descriptions and intelligent searches can now be enhanced with the help of generative AI and data-driven insights. This can improve business operations and revolutionize HR procedures. It also gives HR professionals more freedom to experiment and concentrate on higher-value projects. For instance, over the past six years, IBM's HR department has worked to enhance the capabilities of AskHR, its in-house AI-driven digital assistant, in order to automate over one hundred processes and manage over 1.5 million employee conversations annually. In addition to offering pertinent information to users, AskHR has started to notify staff members about impending travel, provide weather alerts, and help with other standard procedures. Human workers will be able to focus on more complex work and save time on repetitive tasks as AskHR learns more and gains more capabilities.

## 6.2. RECRUITMENT AND CANDIDATE SCREENING USING AI ALGORITHMS

The hiring process has undergone a significant evolution with the introduction of AI algorithms for candidate screening and recruitment. AI algorithms provide companies with a faster and more effective way to find and assess candidates, expedite the hiring process, and enhance hiring results.

Rapidly sorting through a large number of applications and resumes is one of the main benefits of using AI algorithms in recruitment. Conventional manual screening techniques can be laborious and prone to human error. Conversely, AI algorithms have the capacity to evaluate resumes and applications on a large scale, detecting essential experiences, skills, and qualifications that align with the job specifications. As a result, the initial screening process is expedited, freeing up recruiters' time to concentrate on applicants who are the most qualified for the position.

An impartial assessment of candidates is another benefit provided by AI algorithms. Biases may be unintentionally introduced into the hiring process by human recruiters, whether they are aware of it or not. When used correctly, AI algorithms can reduce these biases by evaluating applicants only on the basis of their experiences and qualifications, rather than on the basis of their gender, race, or ethnicity. This may result in a more equitable and inclusive hiring process, which would ultimately produce a workforce that is more diverse.

Furthermore, in order to offer more thorough insights into candidate suitability, AI algorithms can evaluate data from a variety of sources. Algorithms, for instance, can evaluate a candidate's professional networks, online portfolios, and social media accounts to acquire a more thorough picture of their qualifications. Using a comprehensive approach to candidate evaluation, recruiters can find important information that might not be apparent from a resume alone, enabling them to make better hiring decisions.

AI systems can help with candidate engagement and communication during the hiring process in addition to screening applicants. AI-powered chatbots can converse with applicants and inform them about the business, the position, and the hiring procedure. These chatbots can set up interviews, respond to frequently asked questions, and even carry out mock interviews or preliminary tests to evaluate applicants' qualifications for the position.

Although employing AI algorithms in hiring has many advantages, it's important to understand that there are drawbacks as well. Organizations using AI in hiring must take into account factors like ensuring the algorithms are free from biases, protecting data privacy and security, and addressing concerns about algorithmic transparency. Furthermore, human supervision and involvement are required to guarantee that the algorithms are efficiently supplementing the knowledge of hiring managers and recruiters, rather than taking their place.

An important development in HR is the incorporation of AI algorithms into the hiring and applicant screening procedures. AI algorithms have the potential to completely transform how businesses find and hire talent. By automating time-consuming tasks, eliminating biases, offering deeper insights, and improving candidate engagement, these algorithms can ultimately improve hiring outcomes and boost business success.

### 6.2.1. Transforming Human Resources: The Impact of Artificial Intelligence on Recruitment and Talent Management

In the dynamic realm of Human Resources, the integration of AI has sparked a revolution, fundamentally reshaping recruitment and talent management processes. This fusion of cutting-edge technology with traditional HR practices holds the promise of greater efficiency, objectivity, and strategic decision-making. In this article, we will explore the profound impact of AI on these crucial aspects of HR, delving into the opportunities it presents and the challenges it poses.

#### *6.2.1.1. Automated Resume Screening and Candidate Matching*

Screening resumes and matching candidates to job requirements is the first frontier where AI is making a lasting impact in the recruitment process. Machine learning-powered AI algorithms are able to quickly and reliably analyze large datasets. This helps find applicants whose qualifications and experiences closely match the job requirements while also speeding up the hiring process. Nevertheless, bias presents a significant obstacle.

The neutrality of the data used to train AI systems is essential to their efficacy. Should there be historical biases present in this data, the AI might unintentionally reinforce them. It is imperative for HR professionals to be vigilant in monitoring and optimizing these systems to guarantee equity in the hiring procedure.

#### *6.2.1.2. Predictive Analytics for Identifying Top Talent*

The predictive analytics powers of AI are revolutionizing the hiring process for HR departments. AI can forecast which applicants are most likely to succeed in a particular role by examining past data and seeing trends. In addition to streamlining the hiring process, this helps high-achieving teams come together.

But it's important to understand that human interaction is still invaluable. Although AI can offer insightful information, it cannot replace the human HR professional's subtle judgment and intuition. To fully realize the promise of this technology, the proper ratio of human decision-making to AI-driven analytics must be struck.

### *6.2.1.3. Addressing Bias and Promoting Diversity*

The possibility of bias is an inherent problem with AI-driven hiring. The AI system may reinforce and even worsen biases if the historical data used to train the models reflects them. By routinely auditing and improving AI algorithms, HR professionals can actively work to mitigate bias. Furthermore, the emergence of AI tools specifically created to support diversity in hiring attempts to guarantee that underrepresented groups are not passed over during the hiring process.

### *6.2.1.4. Employee Engagement and Performance Management:*

AI extends its influence into talent management by enhancing employee engagement and performance evaluation. The virtual assistants powered by AI can facilitate communication between employees and HR, providing quick responses to queries, feedback, and support. Furthermore, AI-driven performance analytics can help identify trends, patterns, and areas for improvement, fostering a more data-driven approach to talent development. However, maintaining a balance between data-driven insights and the human-centric aspects of employee relations is crucial to fostering a positive workplace culture.

### *6.2.1.5. The Future of AI in HR*

With AI's continued development, HR could see even more advanced applications in the future. The potential for innovation is enormous, ranging from AI-driven employee well-being initiatives to customized learning and development programs. But these developments also bring with them moral questions and the requirement for open and responsible AI procedures.

AI's incorporation into HR procedures is revolutionary, especially when it comes to hiring and talent management. Although it offers previously unheard-of levels of efficiency and objectivity, it also calls for a proactive strategy to overcome prejudices and preserve moral principles. In order to create a workplace that is not only effective but also diverse, inclusive, and supportive of employee development and success, human intuition and artificial intelligence must work in harmony. HR professionals must embrace AI's potential while maintaining the human element at the center of their strategic initiatives as they navigate this revolutionary journey.

## 6.2.2. AI-Driven Employee Performance Evaluation and Feedback

AI-driven systems for employee performance reviews and feedback have become effective resources for contemporary businesses looking to improve their HR procedures. These systems gather, analyze, and interpret data about employee performance using machine learning and artificial intelligence algorithms.

This allows for more precise evaluations and focused feedback. The capacity of AI-driven performance evaluation to offer unbiased, fact-based insights into employee performance is one of its main advantages. Conventional performance reviews frequently depend on managers' subjective judgments, which may be skewed by personal prejudices or a lack of insight into an employee's daily activities. However, AI algorithms possess the ability to examine a vast array of data sources, such as project results, productivity metrics, customer feedback, and peer reviews, in order to offer a more thorough and objective assessment of an employee's performance.

Furthermore, patterns and trends in employee performance that might not be immediately obvious to human observers can be found by AI-driven performance evaluation systems. These systems can identify subtle changes in an employee's behavior or performance indicators, like a decrease in productivity or an increase in errors, that may call for additional research or intervention by analyzing vast amounts of data over time.

The ability of AI-driven performance evaluation to give staff members timely, useful feedback is another benefit. Employees can get immediate feedback based on their continuous performance metrics instead of waiting for recurring performance reviews. Employees can instantly modify their work habits or behaviors thanks to this ongoing feedback loop, which promotes quicker progress and better results.

AI-powered performance review tools can also be used to pinpoint areas where staff members need to improve and receive training. These systems are able to identify areas where employees might be having difficulties or where further training might be helpful by evaluating performance data and comparing it to predetermined benchmarks or goals. By taking a focused approach to staff development, companies can make the most of their training funds and guarantee that workers have the abilities and know-how required to be successful in their positions. But it's important to understand that AI-powered performance review tools have drawbacks and restrictions. Organizations deploying AI-driven performance evaluation systems must take into account a number of crucial factors, including ensuring the dependability and correctness of the data these systems use, addressing privacy and security concerns regarding data, and minimizing potential biases in algorithmic decision-making.

AI-powered systems for employee performance reviews and feedback have many advantages for businesses trying to streamline their HR procedures. These systems can offer unbiased evaluations, pinpoint areas for development, and promptly provide employees with feedback by utilizing artificial intelligence and machine learning. In the end, this helps to promote improved performance and accomplish organizational objectives. Nonetheless, it is imperative to adopt a methodical and moral approach to the deployment of these systems, considering the possible hazards and constraints linked to AI-powered decision-making.

## 6.2.3. How Can AI be Used to Evaluate Employee Performance?

The measurement and management of employee performance is one of the many business aspects that AI is revolutionizing. AI can assist employers with more accurate, efficient, and objective staff evaluations as well as coaching and feedback. We will examine the advantages and difficulties of using AI to assess employee performance in a few different ways.

### *6.2.3.1. AI-Based Performance Metrics*

Developing and monitoring relevant, dependable, and consistent performance metrics is one of the primary uses of AI in performance assessment. AI is capable of analyzing data from a wide range of sources, including online activity, sales reports, customer reviews, productivity tools, and online activity, to assess employee output in terms of both volume and quality as well as its influence on organizational objectives. Natural language processing, or NLP, is another tool AI can use to evaluate the sentiment, tone, and clarity of workers' communication abilities. Employers can lessen subjectivity, bias, and human error by implementing AI-based performance metrics, which also give a more accurate and thorough picture of workers' performance.

### *6.2.3.2. Help Improve Contributions*

If you feel that a contribution is unnecessary or unrelated to the article, mark it as unhelpful. This is private to you and will not be disclosed to third parties.

The following, in my experience as an enterprise architect, are essential for having AI-based performance metrics: – Standardized data models that enable AI to process data with the same semantics – Responsible AI measures to understand the data that needs to be kept private or that can be processed by AI (gender, race, and religion are considered Most Confidential Information according to legislation like NIST).

Artificial intelligence is expected to enhance the areas of analysis, planning, measurement, and improvement. When the enterprise framework is solidly established, this can be accomplished. Strategically speaking, by ensuring that every worker is accomplishing their goals, AI can facilitate the effortless alignment of business objectives with initiatives. Artificial intelligence can be useful in highlighting aspects of capability analysis and change management, as the enterprise framework comprises numerous components, each requiring a variety of reports due to their multifaceted relationships.

### *6.2.3.3. AI-Based Performance Feedback*

Giving workers timely and individualized feedback is another way AI can be used to assess their work. AI is capable of producing reports, insights, and suggestions for staff members to enhance their abilities, conduct, and output based on the data from performance metrics. AI can also address questions and concerns from staff members in a conversational and interactive manner by using chatbots, voice assistants, or virtual coaches. Employers can promote a continuous improvement culture and increase employee engagement, motivation, and learning by implementing AI-based performance feedback. Because AI can decrease human error, provide real-time analysis, and guarantee objective, data-driven evaluations—all of which improve the assessment process's efficiency and fairness—we ought to take its performance feedback into consideration. But it's important to proceed cautiously by addressing any potential negatives. In order to prevent discrimination, balance quantitative data with qualitative human insights, and protect employee privacy, we must make sure AI systems are ethically programmed. AI can transform performance feedback while preserving the crucial human component by finding this balance. AI transforms employee performance evaluation by utilizing natural language processing, real-time monitoring, and advanced data analytics. With the help of automated data collection and analysis, this revolutionary approach provides thorough insights into work quality, productivity, and project completion rates. When evaluating performance reviews, AI shines at using NLP and sentiment analysis to provide insightful feedback. It also makes 360-degree feedback analysis, skill evaluations, and predictive analytics easier, allowing for the identification of skill gaps and performance trends. While AI improves the evaluation and feedback process, fair, and thorough assessments require a balanced strategy that takes human judgment and ethical considerations into account.

#### *6.2.3.4. AI-Based Performance Management*

Setting objectives, monitoring development, and rewarding success are all part of the performance management process, which is the third way AI can be utilized to assess worker performance. Based on their roles, abilities, and ambitions, AI can assist employers in creating and coordinating SMART (specific, measurable, achievable, relevant, and time-bound) goals for their workforce. Using data-driven dashboards and alerts, AI can assist employers in tracking and assessing their employees' progress toward their objectives. Employers can use gamification, incentives, and recognition systems to recognize and reward employees' performance with the aid of AI. Employers can improve employee accountability, retention, and satisfaction while coordinating performance with the organization's strategy by implementing AI-based performance management.

With AI being used more frequently and eventually becoming a necessity for reducing workloads, Performance Management could be improved by AI using established corporate goals and cascading down to SMART targets for each employee. There will always need to be human management, of course, but AI could offer the following: A) a starting point for ten on required and suggested goals for each employee; B) targeted performance and improvement ideas (using KPI data); and C) improved reward systems (imagine a sales team; imagine AI's ability to more evenly and accurately distribute bonus pools). My main question is: Can artificial intelligence be used to ensure a more equitable and comprehensive ecosystem for performance management? I think so, but only time will tell.

#### *6.2.3.5. Benefits of Using AI for Performance Evaluation*

There are a number of advantages that employers and employees can enjoy when using AI for performance reviews. It can shorten the time, expense, and labor involved in performance evaluation and feedback while increasing the precision, objectivity, and consistency of performance measurement and feedback. Additionally, this can improve learning, motivation, and employee engagement while promoting an innovative and continuous improvement culture. AI can also improve employee accountability, satisfaction, and retention while assisting in coordinating worker performance with company objectives and strategy.

Personalized goal-setting and career development support, continuous performance improvement through real-time feedback, data-driven, objective, and unbiased evaluation, effective management through quantitative progress tracking, and increased insight into employee behavior patterns and potential are a few of these. These components support enhanced worker motivation and peak performance across the board for the company.

#### *6.2.3.6. Challenges of Using AI for Performance Evaluation*

There are risks and challenges associated with using AI for performance evaluation as well. These include managing potential employee resistance, ensuring the quality, validity, and security of the data used, addressing ethical, legal, and social implications, balancing the role of AI and human judgment in evaluation and feedback, and providing sufficient training, support, and transparency to enable employees to use and comprehend AI.

To guarantee that AI is successfully implemented in performance evaluation, such factors are crucial. Given some of the well-known AI biases that have been observed, such as in the determination of jail bonds, etc., it is a little risky to rely on AI to assess human performance. The AI model needs to take into account every element of a trustworthy performance assessment in order to be accurate. The AI's inability to determine the validity of the factors it evaluates or the data for each factor is the problem. AIs should be verified against a recognized, trustworthy, and validated method, just like in psychometrics. Like statistics, AI can be misleading because it provides a very obvious response. However, the result won't be valid until it has been demonstrated that the answer and the associated algorithms take into account all necessary and sufficient factors that affect performance.

#### *6.2.3.7. Best Practices for Using AI for Performance Evaluation*

Employers should adhere to certain best practices in order to optimize the advantages of utilizing AI for performance evaluation. This entails establishing the goals, parameters, and criteria for using AI; selecting appropriate AI tools and platforms; integrating AI with current systems and procedures; making sure the data used is secure, accurate, and relevant; adhering to legal and ethical requirements; involving and consulting stakeholders and employees in the design and implementation of AI; clearly communicating with and educating employees about AI; and routinely reviewing and updating the AI tools.

## 6.3. EMPLOYEE RETENTION STRATEGIES WITH AI INSIGHTS

For businesses hoping to keep a skilled and motivated workforce, employee retention is a major concern. By identifying the main causes of employee turnover and offering practical solutions, utilizing AI insights can greatly improve retention strategies. Large volumes of data, such as employee demographics, performance indicators, engagement surveys, and exit interviews, can be analyzed by AI algorithms to find patterns and trends related to employee turnover. AI can identify areas that require improvement to improve employee retention by looking at things like leadership effectiveness, work-life balance, career development opportunities, job satisfaction, and pay.

The ability of AI to identify which employees are most likely to leave is one of the main advantages of utilizing it in retention strategies. AI algorithms can create predictive models to predict future turnover by examining historical data and finding traits or behaviors shared by workers who have previously quit. With the help of these insights, companies can take proactive measures to keep valuable employees from leaving, like providing opportunities for career advancement, modifying compensation packages, or enhancing working conditions.

AI can also tailor retention tactics to the requirements and preferences of specific employees. AI algorithms can customize retention initiatives to each employee's particular motivations and objectives by evaluating data on preferences, interests, and career goals. To improve job satisfaction and loyalty, AI-powered recommendation systems, for instance, can recommend tailored training courses, mentorship opportunities, or flexible work schedules to each employee's needs. AI can also assist businesses in real-time monitoring and assessment of the success of their retention strategies. AI algorithms can track employee engagement levels, turnover rates, and other pertinent metrics to provide continuous feedback on the effectiveness of retention programs. With the help of this feedback loop, businesses can adjust their plans as necessary and gradually improve their strategy to increase employee satisfaction and retention.

But using AI in retention strategies requires a responsible and ethical approach. Businesses need to make sure that decisions are made fairly and transparently and that AI algorithms are trained on objective data. Additionally, it is important to prioritize employee privacy and data security, putting in place clear policies and safeguards to protect confidential employee information.

AI insights provide useful chances to improve employee retention plans through risk factor identification, intervention personalization, and ongoing efficacy monitoring. Organizations can better understand and address the root causes of employee turnover by using AI algorithms to analyze data and generate actionable recommendations. This will ultimately lead to a more engaged and devoted workforce. Organizations must, however, carefully and responsibly implement AI-driven retention strategies, with an emphasis on equity, openness, and employee privacy.

### 6.3.1. The Role of AI in Personalized Employee Retention Strategies

With employee turnover posing serious problems and expenses for businesses worldwide, the fight to retain top talent has heated up. A new age of tailored employee retention tactics is being ushered in by the introduction of AI into human resource management. AI's capacity to analyze enormous datasets provides previously unheard-of insights into employee behavior, preferences, and satisfaction levels, allowing for customized interventions. Predictive analytics is used by AI-driven retention strategies to anticipate employee attrition and enable prompt engagement and retention measures.

By providing individualized career development opportunitics, improving onboarding experiences, and cultivating a culture of ongoing feedback and recognition, this creative approach goes beyond conventional retention strategies. Businesses can gain a deeper understanding of their workforce and develop more individualized and successful retention strategies by incorporating AI into various HR procedures.

Predictive analytics, customized learning and development initiatives, and improved employee engagement tools are just a few of the ways AI is revolutionizing employee retention. Adopting AI in customized employee retention strategies is a crucial investment in an organization's most valuable asset—its employees—as it attempts to manage the complexity of the modern workplace. In order to gain a competitive edge in the fiercely competitive talent market, this new paradigm promises to lower turnover rates and foster a more engaged, motivated, and satisfied workforce.

#### *6.3.1.1. Predictive Analytics for Early Intervention*

The foundation of early intervention in employee retention strategies is AI predictive analytics. This technology uses machine learning and data analysis to find trends and forecast which employees are most likely to leave the company. AI offers actionable insights by evaluating factors like engagement levels, job satisfaction, and individual circumstances, enabling businesses to resolve problems before they result in resignation. By taking a proactive approach, turnover rates can be considerably decreased by implementing tailored interventions, such as addressing issues related to career development, increasing job satisfaction, or promoting work-life balance. By converting conventional reactive measures into strategic, preventative actions, the use of predictive analytics in HR creates a more encouraging and stimulating work environment.

#### 6.3.1.2. Personalized Career Development Paths

AI-enabled personalized career development pathways present a ground-breaking method of staff retention. By utilizing AI, companies can create customized career paths for each employee that take into account their individual goals, talents, and performance information. By coordinating individual development with company objectives, this personalization raises employee engagement and creates a feeling of purpose and community. AI powered platforms evaluate enormous volumes of data to suggest relevant employment openings and educational materials, promoting internal mobility and ongoing professional development. This gives workers hope for their future with the company and inspires them to take on new challenges and development opportunities. Employers can greatly increase employee loyalty and job satisfaction by fostering a more engaged, dynamic workforce, lowering turnover rates, and offering individualized career pathways.

#### 6.3.1.3. Enhanced Onboarding Experiences

AI-powered improved onboarding processes completely change how new hires fit into a company. AI tools can generate personalized onboarding plans that cater to the distinct requirements, abilities, and learning preferences of every new hire by utilizing data-driven insights. This personalization guarantees that workers feel appreciated and understood right away, greatly enhancing their commitment to the business and level of engagement. AI-driven onboarding systems can make the transition easier and more effective by suggesting role-specific resources, establishing realistic goals, and providing real-time feedback. Businesses can boost productivity, retain more new hires, and create a solid foundation for enduring employee loyalty and happiness by offering a customized onboarding experience. This method improves the onboarding process for the person and synchronizes their personal aspirations with the organization's goals, creating a feeling of purpose and belonging right away.

#### 6.3.1.4. Real-Time Feedback and Performance Monitoring

AI-powered real-time feedback and performance tracking turn the conventional employee review process into a dynamic, continuous dialogue between staff and management. This strategy guarantees ongoing participation and growth, enabling prompt acknowledgment of accomplishments and prompt handling of any problems. AI tools evaluate performance data in real time, giving managers useful information to effectively lead their teams. These systems help set specific, attainable goals based on each employee's growth trajectory and enable a more responsive and customized feedback loop. This degree of focus greatly lowers the probability of employee discontent and turnover while also boosting employee motivation and creating a positive workplace culture. Businesses can sustain a high degree of employee engagement by utilizing AI for real-time performance tracking. This ensures that workers feel appreciated and understood, which increases overall productivity and retention rates.

#### 6.3.1.5. AI-powered HRMS (Human Resource Management Systems)

Human resource management systems (HRMS) with AI capabilities automate and improve a range of HR tasks, revolutionizing conventional HR procedures. These systems use data analytics and machine learning to make administrative tasks more efficient, enhance decision-making, and offer profound insights into the needs and behavior of employees.

By integrating AI, HRMS can monitor employee sentiment, anticipate possible problems, and recommend customized training initiatives, all of which increase employee retention rates. HR procedures become more effective and efficient when repetitive tasks are automated, allowing HR professionals to concentrate on strategic projects like employee engagement and talent management. AI-powered HRMS also provide data-driven decision-making and objective performance reviews, which support an open, equitable, and inspiring workplace. HRMS increases operational effectiveness and cultivates a contented and devoted workforce by utilizing AI.

#### 6.3.1.6. Talent Management and Succession Planning

The use of AI in succession planning and talent management greatly improves an organization's capacity to find, nurture, and retain high-potential personnel. AI tools evaluate employee performance, potential, and leadership role readiness by utilizing predictive analytics, which helps businesses build a strategic talent pipeline.

These insights guarantee that the right people are available for future leadership roles by assisting in the alignment of individual career paths with organizational objectives. AI-powered solutions enable tailored development plans, monitor advancement, and anticipate succession gaps, enabling prompt and well-informed decision-making. By providing employees with clear career paths and ensuring business continuity, this proactive approach improves employee retention. Organizations can gain a competitive edge by adequately preparing for future challenges while keeping and involving their key personnel by investing in AI for talent management and succession planning.

### 6.3.1.7. Customized Training and Development Programs

AI-powered customized training and development initiatives give staff members individualized learning opportunities that are tailored to their particular skill set, learning style, and career goals. By ensuring that training is interesting and pertinent, this strategy greatly improves learning outcomes and worker satisfaction. In order to create specialized training programs and development plans that facilitate effective and efficient skill acquisition, AI-driven platforms can analyze individual performance data and learning preferences. These customized programs encourage a sense of personal investment and commitment among employees by addressing particular skill gaps and career goals, which raises motivation and retention rates. Furthermore, tailored training can adjust to evolving technology and business requirements, keeping the workforce competitive and flexible. AI's application in developing these individualized learning pathways shows a dedication to staff development, which is essential for establishing a positive work atmosphere and lowering attrition.

### 6.3.1.8. Enhanced Employee Surveys and Exit Interviews

AI-powered exit interviews and employee surveys transform conventional feedback methods by offering more in-depth, useful information. Large volumes of data from employee responses can be analyzed by these AI-powered tools, which can identify sentiments and patterns that manual analysis might miss. They make real-time feedback possible, which enables businesses to take prompt action to resolve problems and make wise choices to enhance the working environment. AI can more accurately interpret open-ended responses by using natural language processing, which captures employees' genuine sentiment. As a result, retention tactics become more sophisticated, focused, and successful. Businesses can take proactive steps to increase engagement and lower attrition rates by using enhanced surveys and exit interviews to better understand the underlying causes of employee discontent and turnover. Organizations can use AI to turn these conventional procedures into strategic assets that will enhance employee retention and the general well-being of the company.

### 6.3.1.9. Addressing Pay and Promotion Concerns

In order to ensure fair and competitive compensation structures as well as transparent and equitable promotion pathways, addressing pay and promotion concerns with AI requires analyzing large amounts of data. AI is able to identify pay disparities and pinpoint workers who are at risk of quitting because they are not being paid enough or have few opportunities for promotion. Organizations can proactively modify salaries and find qualified candidates for promotions by utilizing predictive analytics, which will align with internal equity and market norms. This strategy lowers turnover brought on by unhappiness with compensation or a stall in career advancement by preserving employee motivation and satisfaction. Additionally, AI-powered solutions can provide tailored suggestions for each worker's professional development, making sure they feel appreciated and acknowledged for their efforts. Effectively addressing these issues promotes a happy workplace and upholds an open and equitable culture, both of which are essential for retaining employees over the long run.

### *6.3.1.10. Improving Work-Life Balance*

Using intelligent systems to monitor and manage workloads will help improve work-life balance by ensuring that employees are not overworked and have enough time for personal activities. AI can analyze work patterns and make recommendations for changes to avoid burnout, like suggesting the best work schedules or pointing out tasks that can be delegated or automated. Additionally, AI-powered wellness initiatives can provide tailored advice on stress reduction and healthy living, enhancing workers' general wellbeing. By offering resources and tools that promote a better balance between work and personal life, organizations can increase employee retention and job satisfaction. This proactive approach shows a dedication to workers' well-being, which is becoming more and more crucial in the hectic workplace of today. Employees gain from investing in AI solutions to enhance work-life balance, which results in a more engaged, devoted, and productive workforce.

## 6.4. ETHICAL IMPLICATIONS AND BIASES IN AI-BASED HR PRACTICES

Enhancements in hiring, performance reviews, and employee retention have resulted from the incorporation of AI into HR procedures. But in order to maintain justice, openness, and adherence to moral and legal norms, organizations must carefully navigate the ethical implications and biases that come with these advantages.

The potential for algorithmic bias is one of the main ethical issues with AI-based HR procedures. AI systems pick up knowledge from historical data, which may be biased due to societal preconceptions or historical discriminatory practices. For instance, if past hiring data indicates a preference for applicants from particular demographic groups, the AI algorithm may unintentionally reinforce these biases by giving preference to applicants who share these traits. Similar to this, biased language or evaluation standards in job descriptions or performance reviews can produce distorted results and strengthen structural disparities. Furthermore, ethical HR practices are challenged by the opacity of AI algorithms. A lot of AI algorithms function as "black boxes," which means that humans cannot readily understand or understand how they make decisions. This lack of transparency creates questions regarding accountability and fairness and makes it challenging to comprehend how AI-based HR systems reach their conclusions.

If candidates and employees are unable to comprehend the reasoning behind AI-driven decisions, they may become suspicious of them, which would undermine their trust in the HR procedure. Additionally, the collection and analysis of sensitive employee data raises privacy concerns when AI is used in HR. Large volumes of personal data, such as performance indicators, biometric information, and even social media activity, may be processed by AI algorithms, posing concerns about data security and individual privacy rights. Employers must make sure that they have clear policies and safeguards in place to prevent misuse or unauthorized access, and that they collect and use employee data responsibly.

It takes a proactive, multifaceted approach to address these ethical implications. To find and reduce sources of bias, organizations must first critically assess the data used to train AI algorithms. To identify and fix biased results, this may entail diversifying training datasets, auditing historical data for biases, and using methods like algorithmic auditing or fairness-aware algorithms.

In order to foster accountability and trust, businesses should also give top priority to AI-based HR systems' explainability and transparency. This entails giving concise explanations of the data that AI algorithms use, how they operate, and how decisions are made. In order to ensure that systems are viewed as just and equitable, employers should also involve workers in the development and implementation of AI-driven HR practices. They should also ask for feedback and address any concerns.

Furthermore, maintaining employee data security and respecting privacy rights are essential components of ethical HR practices. To ensure compliance with pertinent privacy regulations, such as the General Data Protection Regulation (GDPR) or the California Consumer Privacy Act (CCPA), organizations must establish strong data governance policies and procedures to govern the collection, storage, and use of employee data.

In order to promote a culture of trust and respect for individual privacy, employers should also be open and honest with their staff regarding their data rights and the ways in which their information is being used. Although AI-based HR practices have many advantages for businesses, there are also serious ethical concerns and biases that need to be taken into consideration. Organizations can guarantee the fairness, transparency, and ethics of their AI-driven HR practices by proactively identifying and mitigating sources of bias, emphasizing transparency and accountability, and protecting privacy rights. To effectively navigate the complex ethical landscape of AI in HR professionals, data scientists, legal experts, and other stakeholders must work together.

### 6.4.1. Ethical Considerations in AI and ML

The swift progression of AI and Machine Learning (ML) technologies has led to an increasing recognition of the ethical issues associated with their creation and application. As these technologies become more and more ingrained in society, ethical issues must be addressed to guarantee their responsible and fair use.

Transparency is one of the main ethical considerations. Understanding how AI and ML algorithms make decisions can often be difficult due to their complexity. To foster trust among users and stakeholders, it is imperative to guarantee transparency in these systems. Accountability requires transparent explanations of the data algorithms use, how they work, and the factors that affect their choices. Openness promotes understanding and gives people the ability to judge the reliability and fairness of AI and ML systems.

In AI and ML, fairness and bias mitigation are crucial ethical considerations. Since algorithms are trained on historical data, they may reinforce or even worsen prejudicial behaviors if the data contains biases or unfair practices. It is imperative to incorporate mechanisms that detect and alleviate bias in training datasets and algorithms in order to guarantee equitable results for a variety of user groups. Maintaining fairness necessitates constant attention to detail and a dedication to confronting new issues related to prejudice and discrimination.

As AI and ML systems depend more and more on enormous volumes of personal data for training and decision-making, privacy concerns surface. Keeping people's privacy safe is a basic ethical obligation. Strong privacy policies, such as data encryption, anonymization methods, and explicit consent procedures, must be implemented by organizations. Maintaining ethical standards requires finding the ideal balance between using data to spur innovation and defending people's right to privacy.

Accountability is another crucial ethical factor. As AI and ML systems make decisions on their own, it gets harder to assign blame when mistakes or unexpected outcomes occur. Organizations and developers are held accountable for the moral application and results of their technologies when clear lines of accountability are established. This entails establishing procedures for quickly addressing and fixing problems as well as determining who is responsible for biases, system malfunctions, and other ethical transgressions. In order to keep societal divisions from getting worse, it is morally necessary to ensure inclusivity. Language barriers, cultural variances, and accessibility requirements should all be taken into account when designing AI and ML technologies to serve a variety of user groups. Making inclusivity a top priority promotes fair access to the advantages and opportunities offered by these technologies while preventing the escalation of already-existing inequalities.

The dynamic field of AI and ML requires constant observation and adaptation, which brings up important ethical considerations. It is essential to reevaluate and update ethical standards and practices as new issues arise and societal values change. AI and ML technologies are guaranteed to conform to changing societal norms and values through the establishment of continuous ethical frameworks that adjust to changing conditions.

### 6.4.2. Transparency in Algorithmic Decision-Making

The ethical ramifications of opaque ML and AI algorithms are significant, posing questions regarding user trust, accountability, and the possibility of unforeseen consequences. Systems with complicated and difficult-to-understand decision-making processes are referred to as opaque algorithms. This makes it difficult to comprehend, examine, and hold them responsible for their actions. In order to address these ethical issues and promote the responsible and reliable use of these technologies, transparency in AI and ML is crucial.

1. **Accountability:** The difficulty of determining who is responsible for the choices made by opaque algorithms is one of the main ethical issues surrounding these systems. It becomes challenging to hold developers, organizations, or AI systems themselves responsible for any unfavorable results when users, stakeholders, or impacted individuals are unable to comprehend how and why a decision was made. In algorithmic decision-making, transparency is crucial for defining distinct lines of accountability and assisting in the prompt identification and resolution of mistakes, biases, or unforeseen consequences.

2. **User Trust:** Transparency is fundamental to building and maintaining user trust in AI and ML systems. When users cannot comprehend the reasoning behind algorithmic decisions, trust erodes, and skepticism arises. Understanding the decision-making process allows users to make informed choices, especially in applications that impact their lives, such as healthcare, finance, or autonomous vehicles. Transparent systems enhance user confidence by providing insights into how algorithms function, demonstrating accountability, and

ultimately fostering a positive perception of AI and ML technologies.

3. **Prevention of Unintended Consequences:** Opaque algorithms may lead to unintended consequences, such as reinforcing existing biases, discriminating against certain groups, or making decisions based on flawed data. Transparency is a crucial tool in identifying and addressing these unintended consequences. By allowing stakeholders to scrutinize the algorithms and identify potential issues, transparency helps developers uncover biases in training data, correct flawed models, and iteratively improve the system to align with ethical standards. Openness in the decision-making process facilitates a proactive approach to minimizing unintended negative impacts.
4. **Ethical Decision-Making:** Ethical considerations are at the core of AI and ML development, and transparency is central to ethical decision-making. When the inner workings of algorithms are transparent, developers can ensure that ethical principles are embedded in the design, training, and deployment stages. Transparent systems empower developers to assess and mitigate potential biases, adhere to fairness standards, and align the technology with ethical guidelines, thereby minimizing the risk of unethical outcomes.
5. **Public Understanding and Informed Consent:** For AI and ML technologies to be ethically deployed, it is essential for the public to have a basic understanding of how these systems operate. Transparency enables developers to communicate effectively with users, regulators, and the broader public about the capabilities, limitations, and ethical considerations associated with AI and ML applications. Informed consent becomes more meaningful when users can make decisions with a clear understanding of how their data will be used and how algorithms will impact their experiences.

## 6.4.3. Fairness and Bias Mitigation

The ethical challenges related to bias in AI and ML algorithms are a critical and complex aspect of technology development, emphasizing the pressing need for fairness, diversity, and inclusivity throughout the entire lifecycle of these technologies. As AI and ML systems are trained on historical data, biases present in that data can be perpetuated or even exacerbated, leading to discriminatory outcomes. Addressing these challenges is paramount for ensuring equitable and responsible AI applications.

- **Bias in Training Data:** The most foundational ethical challenge is the presence of biases in training data. If historical data used for training AI models reflects societal biases or systemic inequalities, the algorithms learn and reproduce these biases. This can result in discriminatory outcomes, reinforcing existing disparities in areas such as gender, race, or socioeconomic status. It is essential to critically examine and preprocess training data to mitigate biases and promote fairness.

- **Algorithmic Decision-Making and Discrimination:** AI and ML algorithms make decisions that impact individuals in various domains, including hiring, lending, and criminal justice. Biased algorithms can lead to discriminatory outcomes, such as unfairly favoring certain groups or disadvantaging others. The challenge lies in developing algorithms that are not only accurate but also fair, ensuring that decision-making processes do not perpetuate or amplify societal biases.
- **Fairness Metrics and Definitions:** Defining and measuring fairness in algorithms pose significant ethical challenges. Different stakeholders may have divergent perspectives on what constitutes fairness. Striking the right balance between competing notions of fairness, such as equality of opportunity, disparate impact, or individual fairness, requires careful consideration. The choice of fairness metrics influences the behavior of algorithms and necessitates transparent decision-making in defining fairness goals.
- **Lack of Diversity in Development Teams:** The composition of development teams plays a crucial role in addressing biases in AI and ML algorithms. A lack of diversity in these teams can result in the oversight of certain perspectives and experiences, leading to unintentional biases in algorithmic decision-making. Emphasizing diversity and inclusion within development teams is essential to ensure a comprehensive understanding of potential biases and to foster the creation of fair and unbiased technologies.
- **Inherent Bias in Models:** Certain ML models may inherently exhibit biases, especially when trained on specific types of data. For example, language models may reflect and propagate gender and cultural biases present in textual data. It is imperative to assess and address inherent biases in models to prevent unintentional harm and discrimination, requiring ongoing research and development efforts.
- **Explainability and Transparency:** The lack of transparency and explainability in AI and ML models contributes to the ethical challenges related to bias. Users, affected individuals, and regulators may struggle to understand how decisions are made, hindering

the ability to identify and address biases. Ensuring transparency in algorithmic decision-making is crucial for building trust and accountability.

- **Mitigation Strategies and Continuous Monitoring:** Implementing effective bias mitigation strategies is a persistent challenge. Bias detection tools, adversarial training, and re-evaluating models with diverse datasets are some approaches. However, the dynamic nature of biases requires continuous monitoring and adaptation. Ethical considerations involve not only addressing biases during development but also ensuring that algorithms evolve responsibly over time.
- **Regulatory and Policy Frameworks:** Developing comprehensive regulatory and policy frameworks to govern the ethical use of AI and ML is an ongoing challenge. Striking the right balance between fostering innovation and safeguarding against biased outcomes is essential. Effective regulation requires collaboration between policymakers, industry experts, and advocacy groups to create frameworks that protect individuals from discriminatory practices.

## 6.4.4. Privacy in the Age of AI

As technology continues to advance at an unprecedented rate, the use of AI has become increasingly prevalent in many areas of our lives. From generative AI that can create any content using a simple prompt to smart home devices that learn our habits and preferences, AI has the potential to revolutionize the way we interact with technology. However, as the amount of data we generate and share online grows exponentially, privacy concerns have become more pressing than ever before. Therefore, as a futurist, I think it is important to explore the topic of privacy in the age of AI and delve into how AI impacts our personal data and privacy. We will examine the potential benefits and risks associated with AI in regard to privacy and discuss what individuals, organizations, and governments can do to protect our personal data in this new age of technology.

### *6.4.4.1. Importance of Privacy in the Digital Era*

In the digital era, personal data has become an incredibly valuable commodity. The vast amounts of data generated and shared online daily have enabled businesses, governments, and organizations to gain new insights and make better decisions. However, this data also contains sensitive information that individuals may not want to share or organizations have used without their consent. That is where privacy comes in.

Privacy is the right to keep personal information confidential and free from unauthorized access. It is an essential human right that ensures individuals have control over their personal data and how it is used. Today, privacy is more important than ever as the amount of personal data collected and analyzed continues to grow. Privacy is crucial for a variety of reasons. For one, it protects individuals from harm, such as identity theft or fraud. It also helps to maintain individual autonomy and control over personal information, which is essential for personal dignity and respect. Furthermore, privacy allows individuals to maintain their personal and professional relationships without fear of surveillance or interference. Last but not least, it protects our free will; if all our data is publicly available, toxic recommendation engines will be able to analyze our data and use it to manipulate individuals into making certain (buying) decisions. In the context of AI, privacy is essential to ensure that AI systems are not used to manipulate individuals or discriminate against them based on their personal data. AI systems that rely on personal data to make decisions must be transparent and accountable to ensure that they are not making unfair or biased decisions. The importance of privacy in the digital era cannot be overstated. It is a fundamental human right that is necessary for personal autonomy, protection, and fairness. As AI continues to become more prevalent in our lives, we must remain vigilant in protecting our privacy to ensure that technology is used ethically and responsibly.

### *6.4.4.2. Privacy Challenges in the Age of AI*

AI presents a challenge to the privacy of individuals and organizations because of the complexity of the algorithms used in AI systems. As AI becomes more advanced, it can make decisions based on subtle patterns in data that are difficult for humans to discern. This means that individuals may not even be aware that their personal data is being used to make decisions that affect them.

#### *6.4.4.2.1. The Issue of Violation of Privacy*

While AI technology offers many potential benefits, there are also several significant challenges posed by its use. One of the primary challenges is the potential for AI to be used to violate privacy. AI systems require vast amounts of (personal) data, and if this data falls into the wrong hands it can be used for nefarious purposes, such as identity theft or cyberbullying.

#### *6.4.4.2.2. The Issue of Bias and Discrimination*

Another challenge posed by AI technology is the potential for bias and discrimination. AI systems are only as unbiased as the data they are trained on; if that data is biased, the resulting system will be too. This can lead to discriminatory decisions that affect individuals based on factors such as race, gender, or socioeconomic status. It is essential to ensure that AI systems are trained on diverse data and regularly audited to prevent bias.

At first glance, the link between bias and discrimination in AI and privacy may not be immediately apparent. After all, privacy is often thought of as a separate issue related to the protection of personal information and the right to be left alone. However, the reality is that the two issues are intimately connected, and here's why.

To start with, it is important to note that many AI systems rely on data to make decisions. This data can come from a variety of sources, such as online activity, social media posts, and public records. While this data may seem innocuous at first, it can reveal a lot about a person's life, including their race, gender, religion, and political beliefs. As a result, if an AI system is biased or discriminatory, it can use this data to perpetuate these biases, leading to unfair or even harmful outcomes for individuals.

For example, imagine an AI system used by a hiring company to screen job applications. If the system is biased against women or people of color, it may use data about a candidate's gender or race to unfairly exclude them from consideration. This harms the individual applicant and perpetuates systemic inequalities in the workforce.

#### *6.4.4.2.3. The Issue of Job Displacements for Workers*

A third challenge posed by AI technology is the potential for job loss and economic disruption. As AI systems become more advanced, they are increasingly capable of performing tasks that were previously done by humans. This can lead to job displacement, economic disruption in certain industries, and the need for individuals to retrain for new roles.

But the issue of job loss is also connected to privacy in a number of important ways. For one thing, the economic disruption caused by AI technology can lead to increased financial insecurity for workers. This, in turn, can lead to a situation where individuals are forced to sacrifice their privacy to make ends meet.

For example, imagine a worker has lost their job due to automation. They are struggling to pay their bills and make ends meet and are forced to turn to the gig economy to make money. In order to find work, they may be required to provide personal information to a platform, such as their location, work history, and ratings from previous clients. While this may be necessary to find work, it also raises serious concerns about privacy, as this data may be shared with third parties or used to target ads (Figure 6.1).

**Figure 6.1.** *Privacy challenges in the Age of AI.*

*Source: https://habrastorage.org/r/w1560/getpro/habr/upload_files/5c5/03c/e2c/5c503ce2c870c243c99f93ac2bc50023.png.*

However, the issue of privacy and job loss is not just about the gig economy. It also relates to the ways in which AI technology is used in the hiring process. For example, some companies use AI algorithms to screen job applicants, analyzing their social media activity or online behavior to make decisions about their suitability for a particular role. This raises concerns about the accuracy of the data being used and questions about privacy, as job applicants may not be aware that this data is being collected and used in this way.

Ultimately, the issue of job loss and economic disruption caused by AI technology is closely tied to privacy because it can lead to situations where individuals are forced to sacrifice their privacy in order to survive in a changing economy.

### *6.4.4.2.4. The Issue of Data Abuse Practices*

Finally, another significant challenge posed by AI technology is the potential for misuse by bad actors. AI can be used to create convincing fake images and videos, which can be used to spread misinformation or even manipulate public opinion. Additionally, AI can be used to create highly sophisticated phishing attacks, which can trick individuals into revealing sensitive information or clicking on malicious links. The creation and dissemination of fake videos and images can have serious privacy implications. This is because these fabricated media often feature real people who may not have consented to their image being used in this way. This can lead to situations where individuals are harmed by the dissemination of fake media, either because it is used to spread false or damaging information about them or because it is used in a way that violates their privacy. For example, consider a case in which an evil actor uses artificial intelligence to create a fake video showing a politician engaging in illegal or immoral behavior. Even if the video is clearly fake, it may still be shared widely on social media, leading to serious reputational harm for the politician in question. This not only violates their privacy but also has the potential to cause real-world harm.

The most recent AI technology presents many challenges that must be addressed to ensure that it is used ethically and responsibly. One reason why recent AI software has been associated with these challenges is that it often relies on machine learning algorithms, which are trained on large amounts of data. If that data contains biases, the algorithms will also be biased, leading to situations where AI perpetuates existing inequalities and discrimination. As AI continues to evolve, it is essential that we remain vigilant in addressing these challenges to ensure that AI is used for the greater good rather than for nefarious purposes that negatively affect our rights to privacy.

# REFERENCES

1. Brynjolfsson, E., & McAfee, A. (2014). *The Second Machine Age: Work, Progress, and Prosperity in a Time of Brilliant Technologies*. W. W. Norton & Company.
2. Chen, M., Mao, S., & Liu, Y. (2014). Big data: A survey. *Mobile Networks and Applications, 19*(2), 171–209.
3. Davenport, T. H., & Harris, J. (2017). *Competing on Analytics: Updated, with a New Introduction: The New Science of Winning*. Harvard Business Review Press.
4. James, G., Witten, D., Hastie, T., & Tibshirani, R. (2013). *An Introduction to Statistical Learning: With Applications in R*. Springer.
5. Jordan, M. I., & Mitchell, T. M. (2015). Machine learning: Trends, perspectives, and prospects. *Science, 349*(6245), 255–260.
6. Kiron, D., Prentice, P. K., & Ferguson, R. B. (2018). Closing the gap between AI ambition and execution. *MIT Sloan Management Review*.
7. LeCun, Y., Bengio, Y., & Hinton, G. (2015). Deep learning. *Nature, 521*(7553), 436–444.
8. Manyika, J., Chui, M., Brown, B., Bughin, J., Dobbs, R., Roxburgh, C., & Byers, A. H. (2011). *Big Data: The Next Frontier for Innovation, Competition, and Productivity*. McKinsey Global Institute.
9. McAfee, A., & Brynjolfsson, E. (2017). *Machine, Platform, Crowd: Harnessing our Digital Future*. W. W. Norton & Company.

# CHAPTER 7

# AI IN FINANCIAL SERVICES

## Contents

# INTRODUCTION

Artificial Intelligence (AI) is transforming the financial services sector by enhancing operational efficiency, improving decision-making, and providing innovative customer solutions. In financial services, AI encompasses technologies such as machine learning, natural language processing, and robotics, which automate processes, analyze large volumes of data, and make predictions with high accuracy. This has revolutionized areas like fraud detection, risk management, and investment strategies by enabling more sophisticated analytics and faster responses to market changes.

AI-powered algorithms are now used in personal finance management, offering tailored recommendations based on user behavior and preferences. Banks and financial institutions deploy AI to streamline customer service through chatbots and virtual assistants, which handle routine inquiries, freeing up human resources for more complex tasks. Additionally, AI in credit scoring helps in better risk assessment by analyzing non-traditional data points, increasing accessibility to loans for underserved populations.

The automation of back-office functions, such as compliance monitoring and transaction processing, further enhances cost-effectiveness and reduces human error. In asset management, AI-driven portfolio optimization and trading strategies enable the real-time analysis of global financial data, giving institutions a competitive edge in investment decisions. While AI offers immense potential, its integration also poses challenges, particularly in terms of data security, regulatory compliance, and ethical considerations regarding algorithmic biases and transparency. As AI continues to evolve, its role in financial services will become increasingly central to driving innovation and maintaining competitiveness in the industry.

## 7.1. AI IN FINANCE

In the finance industry, artificial intelligence pertains to the utilization of specific technologies, specifically machine learning algorithms. Financial services companies can now increase the productivity, accuracy, and speed of tasks like fraud detection, investment management, risk management, forecasting, data analytics, and customer service thanks to fintech. By automating formerly manual banking procedures, improving our understanding of financial markets, and developing customer engagement strategies that resemble human intelligence and interaction, artificial intelligence (AI) is revolutionizing the financial sector.

AI is driving startups and transforming the way financial institutions function. AI models use real-time market data to execute trades with previously unheard-of speed and accuracy, revealing deeper insights and determining where investments should be made. Financial firms can enhance risk management, including security, fraud, anti-money laundering (AML), know your customer (KYC), and compliance initiatives, by using AI solutions to analyze complex patterns in transaction data sets. By anticipating consumer behavior and comprehending their purchase preferences, artificial intelligence is also transforming how financial institutions interact with their clientele. This makes it possible for more individualized interactions, quicker, and more precise customer service, improvements to credit scoring, and the development of novel goods and services. Overall, the integration of AI in finance is creating a new era of data-driven decision-making, efficiency, security, and customer experience in the financial sector.

## 7.1.1. Benefits of AI in Finance

### *7.1.1.1. Automation*

AI has the potential to improve decision-making and service delivery, work independently and responsibly, and automate workflows and processes. AI, for instance, can assist a payments provider in automating cybersecurity processes by continuously observing and evaluating network traffic. Alternately, it could strengthen a bank's client-first strategy by offering more individualized, adaptable digital banking experiences that expedite and secure client needs.

### *7.1.1.2. Accuracy*

Through automation and algorithms that adhere to consistent workflows, AI can assist financial services organizations in managing human errors in data processing, analytics, document processing and onboarding, customer interactions, and other tasks.

### *7.1.1.3. Efficiency*

People can concentrate on more strategic activities when AI handles monotonous tasks. AI bots are frequently used to carry out routine or low-touch tasks in place of a human. Examples of these tasks include verifying or summarizing documents, transcribing phone calls, and responding to customer inquiries like "what time do you close?"

### *7.1.1.4. Speed*

AI is faster than a human at processing information and is able to identify patterns and relationships in data that a human might overlook. Faster insights to support trading communications, risk modeling, compliance management, and other processes will result from this.

#### *7.1.1.5. Availability*

With AI, you can assist your clients with financial tasks, goal-solving, and money management from anywhere at any time. AI and ML can work on their designated tasks continuously when operating in the cloud.

#### *7.1.1.6. Innovation*

Analyzing substantial data quantities at high speed can give rise to distinctive and pioneering product and service ideas that surpass competitors. For instance, AI has been employed in predictive analytics to upgrade insurance customer encounters, maintaining the essential human touch.

### 7.1.2. Why Are Fintech Companies Opting for AI?

Fintech companies are turning to AI for several reasons. Here are some specific ways that Artificial Intelligence development services can benefit businesses in the financial sector (Figure 7.1).

**Figure 7.1.** *Artificial Intelligence development services can benefit businesses in the financial sector.*

*Source: https://www.valuecoders.com/blog/technology-and-apps/what-is-the-role-of-artificial-intelligence-in-the-financial-sector/.*

#### *7.1.2.1. Data Analysis and Decision Making*

AI makes it possible to move massive volumes of data more quickly and effectively than humans can. This is critical since fintech businesses frequently depend on dynamic, ever-evolving data to inform their decisions.

#### 7.1.2.2. Enhanced Customer Experience

Fintech development companies can better cater to their individual customers' needs and preferences by leveraging AI Fintech businesses can therefore offer a more individualized experience, which is likely to increase client happiness and loyalty.

#### 7.1.2.3. Gain Competitive Edge

Artificial intelligence's role in the financial services sector can help your company stay one step ahead of the competition. Businesses that can leverage AI to obtain a competitive edge will probably succeed in the long run as more enter the fintech space.

#### 7.1.2.4. Fraud Detection and Security

Real-time fraud pattern detection is facilitated by AI algorithms. It lowers financial risk and improves security. AI and machine learning models examine vast amounts of data to find trends and flag questionable transactions.

#### 7.1.2.5. Scalability and Innovation

Fintech businesses can now swiftly create and implement new services thanks to AI, which boosts technological innovation. Your company can stay ahead of the competition and adjust to changing market demands by utilizing AI-driven insights.

#### 7.1.2.6. Reduced Costs

AI for financial operations lowers costs in a number of ways, including by automating tedious tasks and identifying and stopping fraud. For instance, banks use chatbots driven by AI to answer customer support questions, freeing up human staff to work on more difficult jobs.

#### 7.1.2.7. Improving Client Experience

Financial institutions use AI to enhance the customer experience in a number of ways, such as by using chatbots to communicate with customers via text or voice, automating advice and recommendation systems, and personalizing financial services based on each customer's needs.

#### 7.1.2.8. Enabling New Services

Financial institutions can innovate and produce new goods, services, and client solutions with the aid of AI. For instance, banks have used AI to create Robo-advisory platforms, which use algorithms to assist customers in managing their finances.

#### *7.1.2.9. Financial Planning and Analysis*

Financial institutions can increase productivity and concentrate on higher-value tasks by using AI to automate low-value and repetitive tasks. Additionally, the development of artificial intelligence can help with risk and opportunity identification, investment decision-making, and personalized advice.

#### *7.1.2.10. Improved Operational Efficiency*

AI technology has been swiftly embraced by the financial industry to increase operational effectiveness. AI can expedite the loan approval process, help find and highlight errors in financial documents, and automate customer support tasks.

AI is also used by financial institutions to stop money laundering and identify fraudulent activity. Financial institutions frequently depend on Workday developers to help with these AI implementations. These developers are capable of integrating AI technologies with Workday's current systems to guarantee smooth data transfer and effective processing.

#### *7.1.2.11. Increased Sales and Revenues*

It is in charge of overseeing and controlling the flow of capital and investments as well as offering both individuals and companies vital services. To stay ahead of the competition and satisfy the ever-evolving needs of its clients, the financial industry is continuously innovating and changing. It is understandable why so many fintech companies use AI in their operations given the aforementioned factors. As was mentioned, firms in the financial sector can gain a lot from AI, such as better decision-making, more productivity, and increased security.

### 7.1.3. Challenges and Limitations of AI in the Financial Industry

While AI in finance offers many benefits, it also faces challenges.

#### *7.1.3.1. Data Quality and Availability*

One of the foremost challenges for AI in the financial industry is data quality and availability. AI systems rely heavily on vast amounts of data to generate accurate predictions and insights. However, financial data is often fragmented, siloed, and stored in legacy systems, making it difficult to access and integrate into AI algorithms. In addition, data sets used to train AI models must be of high quality, meaning they need to be clean, complete, and accurate. Unfortunately, data errors, inconsistencies, and missing information are common issues in financial institutions, which can lead to unreliable or biased outcomes from AI systems.

Another layer of complexity arises from the competitive nature of the financial industry. Firms may be reluctant to share data, and regulations often restrict data exchange, further limiting the potential of AI. Incomplete or unrepresentative data can significantly affect the performance of AI models, particularly when attempting to make predictions or assess risk in diverse markets.

### *7.1.3.2. Ethical and Bias Concerns*

AI systems are only as good as the data they are trained on, and bias in these datasets can lead to unfair or unethical outcomes. The financial industry deals with sensitive issues such as credit scoring, loan approvals, and investment advice, all of which directly impact individuals' lives and livelihoods. If AI algorithms are trained on biased data, they may perpetuate or even exacerbate existing inequalities. For example, if historical data reflects discriminatory lending practices, AI models may continue to reject loan applications from certain demographics, even if those applicants are financially qualified.

Ethical concerns are also raised in areas such as transparency and accountability. AI systems, particularly those that rely on deep learning models, can be seen as "black boxes," where the decision-making process is opaque. This lack of transparency can make it difficult for financial institutions to explain AI-driven decisions to regulators or customers. Moreover, in cases where AI systems make incorrect or harmful predictions, determining accountability can be problematic. Should the blame fall on the developers of the AI model, the data providers, or the financial institution that deployed the technology?

### *7.1.3.3. Regulatory and Compliance Challenges*

The financial industry is one of the most heavily regulated sectors, and the use of AI introduces new challenges for compliance. Regulators are still grappling with how to manage AI applications in finance, as the technology evolves much faster than regulatory frameworks. Financial institutions must ensure that AI models comply with existing laws, such as those concerning data privacy (e.g., GDPR and AML). Additionally, regulators often require that financial institutions be able to explain and justify their decision-making processes, which can be difficult when using complex AI systems.

Another challenge is the potential for AI-driven systems to inadvertently violate regulations. For instance, an AI system designed to optimize trading strategies could unintentionally engage in market manipulation by exploiting small inefficiencies in the market. Regulators must be able to keep pace with AI developments to ensure that the technology is being used responsibly and that it does not undermine the stability of financial markets.

### *7.1.3.4. Cybersecurity Risks*

As AI becomes more deeply embedded in financial operations, it also becomes a more attractive target for cybercriminals. AI systems can be vulnerable to attacks that manipulate input data to produce false or malicious outcomes. This type of attack, known as adversarial machine learning, could have severe consequences in the financial industry, where even small discrepancies in data can lead to significant financial losses. For example, if attackers were able to manipulate AI systems that detect fraudulent transactions, they could enable large-scale fraud without triggering any alarms.

In addition, the use of AI can create new cybersecurity risks by increasing the complexity of systems. The more interconnected AI systems become with various financial operations, the larger the attack surface for potential breaches. Financial institutions must invest heavily in cybersecurity measures to protect AI systems from being compromised, which can be costly and resource-intensive.

### *7.1.3.5. Integration with Legacy Systems*

Many financial institutions rely on legacy systems that were built decades ago and are not easily compatible with modern AI technologies. The integration of AI with these outdated systems presents significant technical challenges. Often, financial firms must undergo expensive and time-consuming overhauls to update their infrastructure and make it compatible with AI solutions.

Moreover, even when AI is successfully integrated, the speed at which AI technologies evolve can quickly render previous systems obsolete. Financial institutions must constantly adapt to new developments, which can strain budgets and resources. This need for continuous updates can also slow down the adoption of AI, particularly for smaller firms that may not have the financial capacity to keep up with these technological shifts.

### *7.1.3.6. Over-Reliance on AI and Loss of Human Expertise*

While AI can improve efficiency and decision-making, there is a risk that financial institutions may become overly reliant on the technology at the expense of human expertise. AI systems are incredibly powerful at processing large amounts of data and identifying patterns, but they lack the human ability to understand context, emotions, and ethical nuances. In situations where judgment and experience are crucial, such as during a financial crisis or when dealing with unusual market conditions, AI systems may fail to provide appropriate solutions.

The automation of many tasks traditionally performed by humans also raises concerns about the loss of expertise within the workforce. As more functions, such as risk assessment and portfolio management, are handed over to AI systems, there is a danger that financial professionals may lose the skills necessary to intervene when AI systems go awry. Financial institutions must strike a balance between leveraging AI's capabilities and preserving human oversight.

## 7.2. REAL-TIME USE CASES OF AI IN FINANCE

Artificial Intelligence holds the capability to revolutionize the financial services sector in a positive manner. It can enhance productivity, reduce expenses, and simplify procedures for both customers and workforce. From chatbots and digital aides to fraud detection and risk administration, AI is optimizing numerous operations and making them more streamlined.

### 7.2.1. Algorithmic Trading

One of the major participants in the international financial markets is algorithmic trading (AT), also known as an automated trading system. When computerized trading systems were first implemented in the US financial markets in the 1970s, AT was born. AT is the process of integrating trading rules into an advanced program and then using it to trade, according to Cartea et al. (2015). AT has now put in place sophisticated AI systems that can act very quickly, enabling them to trade far more quickly than people. 50% to 70% of all equity market trades and 60% of futures trades are generated by HFT and computers. According to some estimates, this percentage is slightly lower in emerging markets like India (about 40%) and even higher in the US.

There are a number of reasons why AT is so widely used. These programs can, first and foremost, execute trades at the optimal price. Second, compared to a human, a computer is far less likely to make mistakes. The capacity to handle enormous amounts of data simultaneously and monitor several markets at once comes next. Last but not least, human emotions have no bearing on trading when using a computer, and they may even lessen irrational choices. The stock exchange should ideally have the lowest time delays and the highest level of automation and integration capabilities in order to use AT and HFT. Proprietary trading firms that deal in a variety of securities, including derivatives, index funds, ETFs, and stocks, dominate HTF trading. HTF is also frequently used by corporates, hedge funds, and bank proprietary trading desks.

These days, trades can be completed in milliseconds by AT and HFT systems. According to "The High-Frequency Trading Arms Race: Frequent Batch Auctions as a Market Response," HTF algorithms have the ability to recognize minute changes in the market and take advantage of them. The following graphs display the price changes of SPDR S&P 500 ETFs and E-mini S&P 500 futures (ES) at various time intervals, tick by tick. The price differences between the two securities are noticeable when we enlarge the graphs. They appear to be perfectly correlated at first glance. The more one zooms into the graphs, the more significant price differences between two securities are visible. From the standpoint of extremely quick AT bots, what appears to be perfectly correlated in this instance turns out to be highly profitable (Figure 7.2).

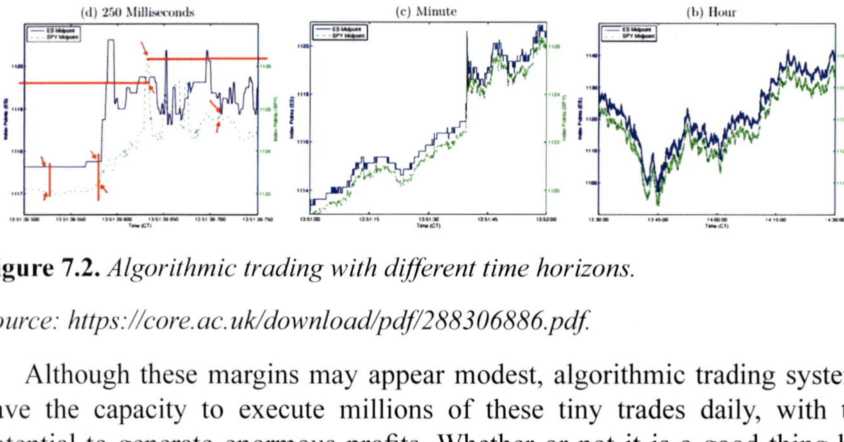


**Figure 7.2.** *Algorithmic trading with different time horizons.*

*Source: https://core.ac.uk/download/pdf/288306886.pdf.*

Although these margins may appear modest, algorithmic trading systems have the capacity to execute millions of these tiny trades daily, with the potential to generate enormous profits. Whether or not it is a good thing has been discussed on multiple occasions. Some contend that by increasing the trading market's liquidity, AT promotes price discovery and increases trading market efficiency. Additionally, they assert that the advancement of new AI and DL technologies will continue to transform the conventional field of market microstructure.

The financial sector currently uses AT for a number of additional purposes. The AT technique referred to as "news reader" is one of these technologies. This technology looks for stories and headlines related to news, and it is programmed to respond accordingly. The technology known as "pattern recognition" comes next, which gives machines the ability to recognize, understand, and respond to various patterns. The third is "signal processing," which is a sophisticated technical analysis expanded mathematically. With the use of signal processing technology, information is filtered to get rid of irrelevant data and identify trading patterns more accurately. Lastly, there is "market sentiment," where the computer needs data to learn about market activity. This type of AT aims to give the algorithm enough information to analyze and understand the psychology of the market (supply and demand).

Despite persistent doubts, a significant number of individuals remain skeptical toward AT, particularly traditional traders. This skepticism stems from several concerns, primarily the opaqueness of the system and the "black box" issues. The "black box" problem refers to potential complications that could arise within an IT system, such as cyber-attacks or hacking. Additional concerns include model risk and the possibility that the AT's performance may not perfectly align with the real-world situation as we perceive it. Moreover, some traders tend to replicate successful strategies without thoroughly evaluating the underlying value of the asset being traded. This practice is further complicated by the presence of confidential information that is not publicly accessible. AT systems, unfortunately, cannot anticipate or account for such information. Furthermore, AT has not been completely error-free and has been implicated in several instances, including the infamous "Flash Crash" at the S&P 500 in May 2010. During this incident, the index plunged more than 7% before swiftly recovering, marking the first market crash primarily triggered by automated trading.

## 7.2.2. Cyber Security

Cybersecurity is important. There are many different types of security, including protection for property, documents, and information. , and is always being enhanced by the modern era of technology. Furthermore, network technology underpins everything in our modern world, from governmental infrastructure to online banking. Therefore, data protection and cyber security are essential because they reduce the possibility of losing sensitive and priceless data. In fact, a 2014 CNBC report claimed that cybercrimes were costing the world economy $400 million annually. The human element is the weakest link in this situation and the primary cause of cyber security failures frequently. In the field of cyber security, automated systems like artificial intelligence apps are frequently employed to address this vulnerability.

As we've seen, AI has enormous potential in a variety of markets and industries. Similarly, using AI to build a more robust cyber security network can help organizations detect newer malware and protect them from online threats. In many situations, it is obvious to implement these security models since they can guarantee effective security standards and avoid errors. However, it's also critical to recognize that malware and spyware may be incorporated into future AI chips for a variety of reasons, including political motivations. Forbes claims that AI has multiple applications in cyber security; we will start by discussing biometric logins.

A few days prior to Black Friday in 2018, hackers gained access to thousands of customers' email addresses, credit card numbers, and personal information through a breach in Amazon's security network. Following the incident, representatives from Amazon advised users to reset their passwords to ensure that the hackers could not access their accounts. The use of AI was brought up multiple times, but numerous security experts made it plain that Amazon and other businesses needed to be more prepared for these kinds of attacks. In the modern world of technology, simply changing the password might not be enough because hackers are becoming increasingly skilled at cracking passwords and encrypted data. As a result, the use of AI in this field has led to the introduction of various biometric login methods for increased security. Facial recognition, palm, and retinal prints, and fingerprint scanners are a few of these AI applications. We are significantly raising the bar for hackers simply by adding these features to the standard password. It's important to note that the majority of smartphones available today already have these features, and there's a good chance that those of you reading this thesis will need to unlock your phone using either a face or fingerprint scan.

Advanced threat prevention is used by conventional cyber security systems to identify and stop cyberattacks. However, compared to 845 million in 2018, over 968 million malwares have been created so far this year. This highlights how crucial precautions are for people like you and me as well as businesses and government infrastructure. The exponential rise in malevolent malware can be attributed to the shortcomings of conventional cyber security systems in managing these novel threats. Thus, putting AI systems in place would reduce the amount of successful damage done as well as the growth of malware. Cyber security companies use a variety of data sets containing sophisticated algorithms and code to train AI systems to recognize viruses and other malicious software. In this manner, AI can perform pattern recognition, which aids in identifying malicious activity in data and software. Furthermore, machine learning (ML) is able to predict the routes that websites and software will take to direct you to infected domains. Similar to this, AI programs have the ability to identify harmful files—like web shells—and immediately cut you off from the system. In order to identify ransomware before it encrypts a system, AI can also be trained to analyze the minute behaviors of ransomware attacks. Last but not least, compared to a manual approach, the application of AI predictive analytics to AI-based alternatives will always make it far quicker and more efficient.

The potential of natural language processing, is the third and perhaps most important reason to use AI in the field of cyber security. By scanning publications, research, and news on cyberthreats, AI technology can quickly and automatically gather data for reference. Making it a huge benefit in managing the steadily rising quantity of malware and viruses. As previously said, natural language processing (NLP) is a technique that AI uses to scan and gather useful information from various texts, data, and websites. This information can assist us in reducing the likelihood of anomalies and cyberattacks and bolstering our preventative measures. We can then calculate risk, determine timescales, and gather insightful data to make accurate predictions by further analyzing this information. Because of our ability to predict and prepare, using AI in this field can therefore greatly aid in saving infrastructures, businesses, and sensitive data.

Finally, we have conditional access security. Authentication-based systems are typically used by businesses and organizations to protect sensitive information from unauthorized users. You can work from home with a lot of companies. The ability to remotely access sensitive data from the company's network is therefore crucial, and doing so increases the security system's vulnerability to hackers and cyberattacks. AI can be used to increase organizational flexibility and create a more dynamic, agile cyber security system that effectively compromises threats even when users are remote. MultiFactor Authentication systems can be used to create a global authentication system that modifies access privileges according to network and location. In order to modify a user's access privileges and create effective cyber security, even on distant networks, the AI system gathers user data in this manner and analyzes user behavior, applications, devices, networks, data, and locations.

Despite our ambition for robust networks shielding us from cyberattacks and harmful malware, it's crucial to remember that AI is still in its developmental stages. While it offers numerous advantages, it also comes with limitations. Premature implementation of AI might hinder widespread technology adoption. One of its drawbacks is the substantial requirement for resources, capacity, processing power, and data to maintain its systems. Companies must consistently address threats and furnish the AI with pertinent data about malware to ensure their systems remain updated. Moreover, the accuracy of the training data is pivotal; misinformation can lead to failure during a genuine attack. Additionally, just like ethical hackers and cybersecurity professionals, criminal hackers also have the capacity to educate their systems. This enables them to create more sophisticated code and malware resistant to AI. Utilizing their own principles, these hackers can surpass existing AI systems, making the digital realm a highly contaminated and hazardous environment for data storage and record-keeping. This underscores the importance of tenacity and precision in AI development before introducing the technology in critical online networks.

### 7.2.3. Fraud Detection

AI fraud detection is a technology-based method that uses machine learning to find fraudulent activity in big datasets. It entails teaching algorithms to identify trends and irregularities that point to potential fraud. These machine learning models get more skilled over time by constantly learning from fresh data, which increases their predictive accuracy and makes it possible for them to adjust to changing fraudulent strategies. This proactive defense mechanism gives companies an effective tool to ensure security and integrity of transactions.

#### *7.2.3.1. How does AI Fraud Detection Work?*

Machine learning algorithms that are intended to examine behaviors and identify irregularities suggestive of fraud are used in AI fraud detection. Establishing a baseline of typical user behaviors and transaction patterns is the first step. After that, the system keeps an eye on the data, searching for departures from the standard. The AI model adjusts its parameters in response to fresh and diverse data, improving its ability to distinguish between suspicious and legitimate activity.

The mechanisms behind AI fraud detection include the following:

- **Data Collection:** Aggregating vast amounts of transactional and behavioral data from various sources.
- Feature engineering. Identifying and selecting relevant attributes or features of the data that could indicate fraudulent behavior.
- **Model Training:** Using historical data to train the machine learning models to recognize fraud patterns.
- **Anomaly Detection:** Applying statistical techniques to identify outliers that diverge from standard patterns.
- **Continuous Learning:** Updating the model with new data, ensuring the system evolves with changing fraud tactics.
- **Alerting and Reporting:** Flagging suspicious activities and providing detailed reports for further investigation.

#### *7.2.3.2. AI Fraud Detection Use Cases*

According to a 2022 report, fraudulent activities cost an organization, on average, 5% of its annual revenue, with a median financial impact of $117,000 before the fraud is discovered. By using algorithms to identify anomalies and stop financial losses, AI fraud detection is revolutionizing how businesses fight fraud. Here are some instances of use cases from various industries.

#### *7.2.3.2.1. Banking and Financial Services*

AI algorithms in banking are responsible for the ongoing surveillance of accounts; they examine patterns of transactions to identify indications of fraudulent activity, like anomalously large withdrawals or atypical foreign transactions. In order to stop financial loss before it starts, sophisticated machine learning models examine credit and loan applications in order to identify irregularities that might point to fabricated identities. Because AI handles the initial detection workload, banks can operate more efficiently because human investigators can concentrate on thoroughly analyzing the highest-risk alerts.

#### *7.2.3.2.2. E-Commerce*

AI fraud detection assesses risk for e-commerce platforms by taking into account variables like transaction volume, frequency, and past customer purchases. By comparing shipping and billing data, it reduces the possibility of card-not-present fraud by spotting inconsistencies that might point to identity theft. The same AI systems are searching for trends in refund and return fraud, which are expensive problems for merchants. These systems safeguard the company's bottom line and guarantee a safe shopping experience, both of which are essential for retaining customers.

#### *7.2.3.2.3. Online Gaming and Virtual Economies*

Online gaming platforms and virtual economies are increasingly using AI to monitor for fraudulent transactions, such as the use of stolen credit cards to purchase in-game currency or the manipulation of game assets. AI algorithms can track transaction velocity, the geographic origin of transactions, and the transfer of in-game assets to identify patterns that deviate from the norm, which may indicate money laundering or account takeovers. This not only protects the game's revenue but also enhances player trust, as it ensures a level playing field and the legitimate use of in-game economies.

### *7.2.3.3. Benefits of AI Fraud Detection*

AI fraud detection systems offer a range of advantages for businesses looking to safeguard their operations from the ever-evolving threats. By harnessing the power of artificial intelligence, companies can improve security, efficiency, and customer service. Here are some advantages:

#### *7.2.3.3.1. Real-Time Detection And Prevention*

The ability of AI to monitor transactions 24/7 ensures that any suspicious activity is caught as it happens, allowing for immediate action. Speedy detection is critical in stopping fraudsters and minimizing potential losses. The immediacy of AI response provides businesses with a powerful tool to defend against fraud before it impacts their finances.

##### *7.2.3.3.2. Scalability*

As transaction volumes grow, AI fraud detection systems can expand their monitoring capabilities without the need for proportional increases in staffing. This scalability is essential for businesses experiencing growth, as it allows them to maintain high levels of fraud detection and prevention without significant additional costs.

AI systems can also handle the increased complexity that comes with larger datasets, ensuring that businesses remain protected as they evolve.

##### *7.2.3.3.3. Cost Reduction*

Using AI to detect fraud saves money by preventing fraud losses. It also reduces the financial burden on businesses by cutting down on the need for extensive manual review teams.

The automation of fraud detection tasks leads to a more resource-efficient operation, freeing up your team to focus on strategic tasks that require human expertise. Over time, the cost savings realized from using AI can be reinvested into other areas of the business—from building out your product roadmap to investing in marketing ideas.

##### *7.2.3.3.4. Increased Accuracy*

AI's capacity to analyze data with precision surpasses human capabilities, leading to more accurate identification of fraudulent transactions. These systems are less prone to the errors that can occur with manual reviews. AI algorithms also continuously learn and improve from new data, which means that the system becomes increasingly efficient at detecting fraud over time.

##### *7.2.3.3.5. Customer Trust And Satisfaction*

When customers feel secure in their transactions, they are more likely to remain loyal to a business. AI fraud detection helps maintain a safe environment for customers, heightening their trust and satisfaction with the company's services. A reputation for security can become a significant competitive advantage, attracting new customers who prioritize the safety of their personal and financial information.

## 7.2.3.4. Challenges of AI Fraud Detection

While AI fraud detection systems offer substantial benefits, they also come with a set of challenges that businesses must navigate. These obstacles can range from technical limitations to regulatory compliance issues. Here are challenges to consider:

### 7.2.3.4.1. Data Quality And Availability

For AI systems to effectively detect fraud, access to high-quality and relevant data is needed. However, data can sometimes be incomplete, outdated, or inaccurate, which can hinder the performance of AI algorithms. Additionally, privacy concerns and regulations may limit the availability of data, making it difficult for AI systems to learn from a comprehensive dataset. Ensuring data integrity and securing access to necessary data while respecting privacy laws is a delicate balance that must be maintained.

### 7.2.3.4.2. Integration with Existing Systems

Incorporating AI fraud detection into a business's existing infrastructure can be a complex task. Legacy systems may not be compatible with the latest AI business tools and machine learning technology, requiring significant upgrades or even complete overhauls. This integration process can be resource-intensive and disruptive, potentially leading to downtime or reduced functionality during the transition period. Businesses need to plan and execute the integration of AI systems thoughtfully to minimize these impacts.

### 7.2.3.4.3. False Positives And Customer Friction

AI systems can still generate false positives, where legitimate transactions are flagged as fraudulent. This can create friction for customers, leading to frustration and potentially damaging the customer-business relationship. Balancing sensitivity to fraud with the need to provide a smooth customer experience is an ongoing challenge. Continuous refinement of AI models is necessary to reduce the occurrence of false positives and maintain customer satisfaction.

### 7.2.3.4.4. Keeping Up With Evolving Threats

Fraudsters are constantly developing new tactics to circumvent detection systems. AI models, no matter how advanced, need regular updates to keep up with these evolving threats. This requires a commitment to ongoing training of the AI system with the latest data on fraudulent activities; AI systems cannot be static and must be part of an adaptive and proactive fraud prevention strategy.

#### *7.2.3.4.5. Regulatory Compliance and Ethical Considerations*

Businesses need to ensure that their AI fraud detection systems comply with all relevant regulations, including data protection and privacy laws like GDPR. The use of AI in decision-making processes also raises ethical considerations, such as the potential for bias in algorithms, which can lead to unfair treatment of certain customer segments. Companies must navigate these regulatory and ethical landscapes carefully to maintain compliance and uphold ethical standards.

### 7.2.4. Financial Forecasting and Planning

Data analysis has always been a key component of the financial industry's strategy planning, financial outcome forecasting, and market trend forecasting. The development of AI has greatly enhanced our capacity to evaluate large, complicated data sets and derive useful insights. By improving the accuracy, speed, and scalability of data-driven decisions, artificial intelligence has revolutionized financial forecasting and planning. Businesses' approaches to risk assessment, long-term strategic planning, and financial resource management are changing as a result of this shift.

#### *7.2.4.1. Enhanced Data Processing and Pattern Recognition*

One of AI's key contributions to financial forecasting is its ability to process massive volumes of data rapidly. Financial institutions generate a vast amount of data from transactions, market movements, and customer behavior. Traditional forecasting methods rely on historical data analysis and statistical models, which may struggle to process and interpret such high data volumes. AI-driven algorithms, particularly ML and deep learning, can process this data far more effectively. They can detect patterns, correlations, and anomalies that might go unnoticed using conventional methods.

For instance, in stock market forecasting, AI models can analyze historical prices, financial news, and even social media sentiment to predict price movements. Unlike traditional methods, which might require predefined rules, AI systems can "learn" from data and improve their predictions over time, enhancing accuracy in predicting stock performance or market crashes. This increased accuracy is vital for investment firms and traders who rely on precise forecasts to make quick decisions.

#### *7.2.4.2. Predictive Analytics and Scenario Planning*

Incorporating AI into financial planning enables the use of predictive analytics to forecast future trends and outcomes based on past data. Predictive models use

AI to estimate future financial metrics like sales growth, revenue, and expenses. The use of AI in predictive analytics extends beyond merely analyzing historical financial data; it includes external factors such as macroeconomic indicators, industry trends, and geopolitical events. By incorporating these diverse data points, AI systems can provide more comprehensive and accurate forecasts.

Scenario planning, another critical element in financial strategy, benefits from AI as well. AI-driven scenario planning allows financial planners to simulate various economic conditions, assess potential risks, and devise contingency plans. This approach gives organizations the ability to respond more effectively to unforeseen events such as economic downturns or regulatory changes. For example, an AI-based model could forecast the financial implications of a recession, enabling a company to adjust its spending or reallocate resources preemptively.

### *7.2.4.3. Automation and Efficiency Gains*

AI also plays a significant role in automating the financial forecasting process, which can lead to greater efficiency and reduced costs. Tasks that once took analysts weeks or months can now be performed by AI in a matter of hours or minutes. This shift enables finance professionals to focus more on strategic decision-making rather than routine data crunching. AI-powered software can automate the creation of financial reports, reduce human errors, and ensure consistent, reliable results. Moreover, automation through AI allows for real-time financial forecasting. Traditional forecasting methods rely on periodic updates, usually on a quarterly or annual basis. AI, on the other hand, can continuously monitor and analyze financial data, providing businesses with real-time insights. This capability is crucial for fast-paced industries such as trading, where market conditions can change in minutes. Real-time forecasting allows organizations to make timely adjustments to their strategies and stay ahead of potential risks.

### *7.2.4.4. Strategic Financial Planning*

AI's role in strategic financial planning goes beyond mere number crunching and risk assessment. It provides finance teams with deeper insights into long-term business strategies. AI systems can evaluate an organization's financial health, forecast future cash flows, and recommend strategies for growth or cost reduction. For instance, AI models can analyze expense trends and suggest where a company might reduce costs without sacrificing productivity or quality. These insights can be integrated into broader strategic decisions, such as expansion plans, mergers, or investments in new markets. Additionally, AI can optimize financial planning by improving cash flow management and capital allocation.

AI-powered tools can help businesses decide the best times to invest, save, or borrow money. By predicting cash flow needs more accurately, AI ensures that businesses have the necessary liquidity to meet their short-term and long-term goals.

### *7.2.4.5. Personalization and Customer-Centric Financial Planning*

AI is also revolutionizing personalized financial planning, especially for individual investors and clients of financial advisory firms. By analyzing personal financial data, AI can provide customized recommendations tailored to an individual's financial goals, risk tolerance, and investment preferences. Robo-advisors, which use AI algorithms, have emerged as a popular option for offering low-cost, personalized financial advice. These tools can analyze an individual's financial situation and recommend investment portfolios that align with their goals, adjusting strategies in real-time based on market conditions. Personalized financial planning extends to corporate clients as well. AI-powered financial planning systems can help businesses of all sizes make data-driven decisions tailored to their specific needs and market conditions. By using AI, businesses can receive recommendations that reflect their unique challenges, competitive landscape, and growth potential, ensuring a more customized and effective approach to financial planning.

### *7.2.4.6. Ethical Considerations and Limitations*

Despite the numerous advantages AI offers in financial forecasting and planning, it is essential to recognize its limitations and ethical considerations. One challenge is the "black box" nature of many AI models, particularly deep learning systems. These models can generate accurate forecasts, but their decision-making processes are often opaque, making it difficult for users to understand how they arrived at a particular conclusion. This lack of transparency can pose challenges in highly regulated industries like finance, where accountability and clarity are paramount. Another ethical consideration is data privacy. Financial institutions handle sensitive customer data, and the use of AI models necessitates strict data protection measures. Ensuring that AI systems comply with regulations such as the GDPR is crucial for maintaining consumer trust and avoiding legal repercussions.

## 7.2.5. Risk Management

Risk management is a critical function within the financial services industry, tasked with identifying, assessing, and mitigating potential risks that could adversely affect an organization's financial health and operational stability.

### 7.2.5.1. The Role of AI in Risk Identification

The first step in effective risk management is accurate risk identification. AI technologies, particularly machine learning algorithms, excel at processing large volumes of data from diverse sources to identify potential risks that might not be apparent through traditional methods. For instance, AI can analyze data from credit reports, transaction histories, market trends, and social media sentiment to identify credit risks associated with borrowers. By employing NLP, AI can also scan news articles, press releases, and online forums to detect emerging risks related to market volatility or company performance.

Moreover, AI systems can continuously learn and adapt from new data, allowing them to refine their risk identification processes over time. This adaptability is crucial in the fast-paced financial environment, where new risks can emerge suddenly due to economic shifts, regulatory changes, or technological advancements. By leveraging AI, financial institutions can enhance their ability to identify potential risks proactively, thereby positioning themselves to mitigate these risks before they materialize.

### 7.2.5.2. AI in Credit Risk Assessment

Credit risk assessment is one of the most critical areas in financial services, as it determines the likelihood of a borrower defaulting on a loan. Traditional credit scoring models often rely on historical data and predefined criteria, which may not adequately capture the complexities of an individual's financial situation. AI, with its ability to analyze vast amounts of data, offers a more nuanced approach to credit risk assessment.

Machine learning algorithms can analyze a multitude of variables, including a borrower's payment history, employment stability, income sources, and even behavioral data, such as spending habits and social media activity. By identifying patterns and correlations within this data, AI can generate more accurate credit scores and assess creditworthiness in real time. This not only improves the accuracy of credit risk assessments but also allows financial institutions to expand their lending to underserved populations who may not have traditional credit histories.

Furthermore, AI-driven credit risk assessment models can continuously learn from new data, allowing them to adapt to changing economic conditions and consumer behaviors. For example, during economic downturns, AI systems can quickly adjust their risk profiles to account for increased default rates, enabling financial institutions to make informed lending decisions that reflect the current market landscape.

#### *7.2.5.3. Market Risk Management with AI*

Market risk refers to the potential losses that financial institutions may face due to fluctuations in market prices, including interest rates, stock prices, and foreign exchange rates. Effective market risk management requires timely and accurate analysis of market data to predict potential price movements and mitigate risks accordingly. AI technologies have become invaluable tools in this regard.

AI algorithms can analyze vast amounts of market data in real time, including historical price movements, trading volumes, and macroeconomic indicators, to identify trends and predict future price fluctuations. By employing advanced statistical techniques and machine learning models, financial institutions can develop predictive models that enable them to make informed trading decisions and manage their exposure to market risks effectively.

Moreover, AI can enhance stress testing processes, which are essential for assessing an institution's resilience to adverse market conditions. Traditional stress testing methods often rely on static scenarios that may not accurately reflect real-world market dynamics. AI, on the other hand, can simulate a wide range of scenarios based on historical data and market trends, providing a more comprehensive understanding of potential vulnerabilities. By utilizing AI in market risk management, financial institutions can improve their ability to navigate volatile markets and make data-driven decisions that protect their portfolios.

### *7.2.5.4. Operational Risk Management*

Operational risk encompasses a wide range of potential risks arising from internal processes, systems, and human factors, including fraud, system failures, and regulatory compliance issues. The complexity and diversity of operational risks make them challenging to manage effectively. However, AI technologies can enhance operational risk management by automating processes, improving incident detection, and ensuring compliance.

AI-driven systems can monitor transactions in real time, flagging anomalies that may indicate fraudulent activities or operational errors. By leveraging machine learning algorithms, these systems can identify patterns of behavior associated with fraud, such as unusual transaction amounts or frequency, enabling financial institutions to respond promptly to potential threats. This proactive approach not only helps in preventing financial losses but also protects the institution's reputation.

Additionally, AI can facilitate compliance with regulatory requirements by automating data collection, reporting, and monitoring processes. Natural language processing can be employed to analyze regulatory texts and identify relevant compliance obligations, while machine learning algorithms can monitor transactions and flag potential violations. By streamlining compliance processes, AI reduces the burden on financial institutions and minimizes the risk of regulatory fines.

### *7.2.5.5. Liquidity Risk Management*

Liquidity risk refers to the potential inability of a financial institution to meet its short-term financial obligations due to an imbalance between its liquid assets and liabilities. Managing liquidity risk is crucial for maintaining financial stability, and AI technologies can significantly enhance liquidity risk management processes.

AI algorithms can analyze cash flow patterns, transaction histories, and market conditions to predict liquidity needs in real time. By employing advanced forecasting techniques, financial institutions can identify potential liquidity shortfalls and take proactive measures to address them. For instance, AI can help institutions optimize their funding strategies by identifying the most cost-effective sources of liquidity, whether through short-term borrowing, asset sales, or capital raising.

Moreover, AI-driven liquidity risk management models can continuously learn from new data, allowing them to adapt to changing market conditions and economic factors. This adaptability is essential in today's fast-paced financial environment, where sudden market shifts can significantly impact liquidity positions. By leveraging AI, financial institutions can enhance their ability to manage liquidity risks effectively, ensuring they can meet their obligations even in challenging market conditions.

### *7.2.5.6. AI in Regulatory Compliance and Reporting*

The financial services industry is subject to extensive regulatory oversight, making compliance a top priority for institutions. AI technologies are transforming compliance processes by automating data collection, monitoring, and reporting, thereby reducing the burden on compliance teams and enhancing accuracy.

AI systems can analyze vast amounts of data to identify potential compliance issues in real time. For example, machine learning algorithms can monitor transactions and flag those that deviate from established patterns, indicating potential money laundering or other illicit activities. By automating these monitoring processes, financial institutions can respond more quickly to potential compliance violations, reducing the risk of regulatory fines and reputational damage. Additionally, AI can streamline the reporting process by automatically generating compliance reports based on real-time data analysis. This reduces the time and effort required for manual reporting while ensuring that reports are accurate and up to date. By integrating AI into compliance processes, financial institutions can enhance their regulatory adherence and focus on more strategic initiatives.

#### *7.2.5.7. Challenges of Implementing AI in Risk Management*

While the benefits of AI in risk management are significant, financial institutions face several challenges in implementing these technologies effectively. One of the primary concerns is the lack of transparency in AI decision-making processes. Many AI algorithms, particularly deep learning models, operate as "black boxes," making it difficult for risk managers to understand how decisions are made. This lack of transparency can be problematic, especially in risk-sensitive areas such as credit assessment and fraud detection, where stakeholders need to understand the rationale behind AI-driven decisions.

Another challenge is the potential for bias in AI models. AI systems are trained on historical data, which may reflect existing biases in lending, hiring, or other decision-making processes. If not addressed, these biases can lead to discriminatory outcomes and reinforce existing inequalities. Financial institutions must be vigilant in monitoring their AI systems for bias and take proactive measures to ensure fair and equitable outcomes.

Data privacy and security are also critical concerns when implementing AI in risk management. AI systems require access to vast amounts of data, including sensitive customer information. Financial institutions must ensure that they comply with data protection regulations, such as the General Data Protection Regulation (GDPR), and implement robust data governance practices to protect customer data from breaches and unauthorized access.

Furthermore, the integration of AI into existing risk management frameworks requires significant investment in technology, talent, and training. Financial institutions must develop the necessary infrastructure to support AI technologies and invest in training their staff to effectively utilize these systems. This may require cultural shifts within organizations to foster a data-driven mindset and embrace AI as a core component of risk management.

### 7.2.6. Chatbots and Robotic Advisory Services

In an effort to increase business efficiency, financial services has begun implementing AI-based systems in recent years. Large financial institutions have historically had a large clientele, so they are using automated services like chatbots to improve the efficiency of their customer interactions. A chatbot can respond to consumers right away and provide round-the-clock support, seven days a week. 64% of people say they prefer interacting with chatbots because they are frequently safer and more efficient than speaking with a human. These chatbot interfaces can service millions of users while providing an excellent user experience for a relatively small price. According to a Juniper Research study, banks are using chatbots to handle each customer in an average of 4 minutes, saving them a significant amount of labor costs.

Since a robot is not included, the terms "chatbot" and "robotic advisory" are actually deceptive. Rather, a chatbot is a personalized conversational system that is built on NLP and ML algorithms. Algorithms used in robotic advisory systems are designed to determine a customer's ideal portfolio based on their objectives and risk tolerance. Due to the cost savings, chatbots are now practically a given for financial institutions with sizable user bases, like banks and insurance providers. This is just the beginning, given how comfortable millennials are interacting with AI systems. According to certain research, millennials would rather communicate with businesses via AI than face-to-face. On average, just 12% of respondents said they preferred speaking with someone.

A variety of AI applications are currently enhancing financial services. Clerkie is one of the robotic advisory apps that assists users in managing their savings and finances. With the use of your smartphone, Clerkie is a robotic advisor and chatbot that can manage all of your financial affairs. You can apply for loans from various banks, and the AI engine can analyze a customer's income and spending patterns to determine how much they should save and how much they can afford to spend. Additionally, they provide various investment options according to your time horizon and risk tolerance. You can also obtain your credit score through the app, which is required in order to apply for loans and open credit accounts in the US.

JP Morgan's latest AI application, named "COiN," stands out for its ability to scrutinize documents and pull out data at a pace surpassing that of a human. This technological marvel can process approximately 12,000 documents in a few seconds, a task that would consume over 360,000 human hours to complete if done manually.

### 7.2.7. Accounting and Auditing

The development of AI and data analytics is causing a fundamental shift in the accounting and auditing industry. According to the World Economic Forum's Deep Shift 2015 report, 816 senior executives from the communication and IT industries participated in a survey regarding technology tipping points and societal impact. According to their findings, 75% of participants concurred that by 2025, 30% of corporate audits conducted by AI will have been completed. AI's exceptional ability to match patterns is one of its best qualities, making it applicable to a wide range of industries and big businesses. The Deep Shift report makes it abundantly evident that robots and automated procedures will replace an increasing number of jobs in the upcoming years. Accounting and auditing fall under the category of "Management, Business, and Financial," as shown in the figure below. It is highly likely that a significant portion of these tasks will be automated in the next ten to twenty years. This solely considers the US economy. The changes will be much more pronounced when viewed on a global scale (Figure 7.3).

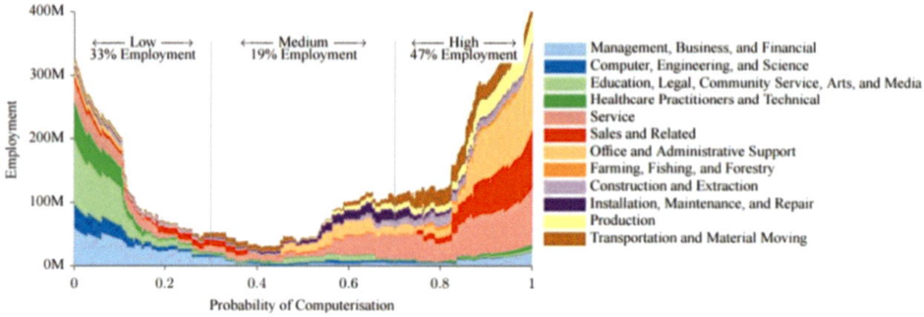


**Figure 7.3.** *Distribution of US occupational employment over computerization.*

*Source: https://core.ac.uk/download/pdf/288306886.pdf.*

Because it can be difficult to implement large volumes of both structured and unstructured data in order to gain insights into a company's financial and nonfinancial performance, auditing is particularly well suited for applications for artificial intelligence and business analytics. Additionally, working with AI can automate many of the repetitive and structured tasks that are part of auditing. We are aware that the four major consulting firms have substantial investments in AI, especially in auditing. To give an example of recent news, KPMG and IBM's Watson AI have partnered to develop AI auditing tools. Next up is PriceWaterhouseCoopers (PwC), the creator of the analytics platform Halo, which serves as a conduit for augmented reality and artificial intelligence products. Deloitte has also made significant investments in AI, developing Otix for data analytics and Argus for AI. Last but not least, EY has created its own AI platform with the aid of Microsoft Azure and has employed a large number of new tech professionals who will aid in the system's continued development and improvement.

AI can be used to automatically code account entries and, through the creation of complex machine learning code, to develop and enhance fraud detection models, to examine more specific cases. In the auditing industry, more sophisticated AI technologies, like deep learning (DL), are available that analyze both structured and unstructured data to generate reports and make accurate predictions. DL is capable of scanning a very wide variety of data, including emails, conference calls, audio files, and posts from social media. Contracts can be reviewed more thoroughly by allowing a larger amount of data to be scanned through the use of AI in accounting and audit.

In fact, this technology is currently being used by EY and other businesses to read and extract data from various lease contracts, which is significantly more effective and quicker than a manual assessment. One can optimize time and have more time to make human decisions to analyze the data by enabling auditors and accountants to use these analytical tools. Additionally, it helps them ask better questions and communicate more effectively with CFOs, audit committees, company boards, and other stakeholders to provide a better overall product for the client. Not to mention, the entire technological revolution in the accounting and auditing fields may help to make these fields' futures more fascinating and alluring.

## 7.2.8. Loan and Credit Underwriting

The financial services landscape has undergone a transformation in recent years due to the integration of AI in loan and credit underwriting. Underwriting procedures were formerly manual and mainly dependent on human judgment and historical data, which frequently resulted in biases, inefficiencies, and protracted decision-making periods. But thanks to developments in data analytics, machine learning, and natural language processing, AI has completely changed the underwriting industry by offering quicker, more precise, and impartial evaluations of creditworthiness.

### *7.2.8.1. The Traditional Underwriting Process*

Historically, loan and credit underwriting has been a time-consuming process involving the evaluation of a borrower's creditworthiness based on various factors, such as credit scores, income verification, and debt-to-income ratios. Underwriters would analyze financial documents, credit reports, and other relevant information to determine the risk associated with lending to a particular individual or entity. This process was not only tedious but also prone to human error and subjective bias, leading to inconsistencies in decision-making.

In addition, traditional underwriting practices often excluded potential borrowers with thin credit files or non-traditional financial backgrounds, such as freelancers or gig workers. These individuals may have stable incomes and a good ability to repay loans but lack the conventional credit history required by traditional lenders. As a result, many deserving applicants were denied credit, exacerbating financial inequalities and limiting access to financial services for a significant portion of the population.

### *7.2.8.2. The Rise of AI in Underwriting*

The advent of AI has significantly changed the underwriting landscape by introducing data-driven decision-making processes that enhance efficiency and accuracy. AI algorithms can analyze vast amounts of data from multiple sources in real-time, enabling lenders to evaluate creditworthiness more holistically. By leveraging machine learning models, AI can identify patterns and correlations that traditional underwriting methods might overlook, leading to more informed lending decisions.

One of the most notable advancements in AI-driven underwriting is the use of alternative data sources. These sources may include payment histories from utility bills, rent payments, and even social media activity. By incorporating alternative data, lenders can gain a more comprehensive understanding of a borrower's financial behavior and risk profile. This is particularly beneficial for individuals with limited credit histories, as it allows them to build a credit profile based on a broader range of financial activities.

## 7.2.9. AI in Insurance Claims Processing

Over time, AI has become more and more popular, and the insurance sector is no exception. Artificial Intelligence has many uses, one of which is the processing of insurance claims. As per CCC Information Services, out of all AI vendors, 46% offer solutions related to claims, and 43% deal with underwriting. This technology can boost productivity, shorten cycle times, and enhance client satisfaction.

Customers' dissatisfaction has cost insurance companies $170 billion in premiums over the next five years. Therefore, by enhancing customer experience through speed and accuracy, combining AI solutions with human intervention could help solve this challenge. Additionally, by streamlining the workflow, less time will be spent on administrative duties.

Because bots are trained to recognize various risk patterns, including fraudulent claims, and can identify suspicious activity, AI can also enhance fraud detection. AI solutions have already been used by Fukoku Mutual Life Insurance to identify fraudulent claims, leading to a cost-saving strategy that primarily involved lower labor expenses. Any insurer hoping to gain from more efficient claim processing within an organization must continue to integrate AI with humans. There is a lot of space for improvement once an insurer chooses to use these technologies. These improvements will affect internal operations as well as external stakeholders in the larger ecosystem, like partners or customers who collaborate with them to achieve shared objectives.

### 7.2.10. AI In Regulatory Compliance

AI is a revolutionary technology that could revolutionize financial regulatory compliance. AI has a significant application in AML and sanctions screening, where it can assist financial institutions in overcoming obstacles like significant fines for non-compliance. AI can improve screening procedures' efficacy and guarantee regulatory compliance by processing massive amounts of data quickly and accurately.

Another essential AI and ML use case for corporate finance is data governance. Financial firms can enhance their overall data quality by utilizing intelligent algorithms to manage data sources, detect missing or inaccurate information, minimize errors, and optimize decision-making processes. This can reduce operational risk and boost productivity.

The European Commission is expected to launch more comprehensive initiatives in 2023 that will impose fines of up to 6% of a company's annual revenue for noncompliance with AI regulations. As AI continues to drive regulatory compliance efforts in the finance industry, financial institutions will have the opportunity to innovate in a variety of areas, from risk management and alert management systems to fraud prevention.

There are several potential advantages, including streamlined procedures, lower operating costs from higher productivity and efficiency, and reduced risks from noncompliance and breaches. All of these advantages could result in a stricter system of checks and balances that benefits customers. There will undoubtedly be obstacles in the path of any revolutionary innovation, but it is evident that AI-driven developments are already improving the financial services industry, so these are truly exciting times.

## 7.3. THE FUTURE OF AI IN FINANCIAL SERVICES

AI's promising future in financial services is encouraging. Financial institutions are looking to adopt AI in a variety of ways to enhance their operations and provide better customer service in light of the technology's rapid development. Here are some of the ways AI is expected to impact financial services in the future (Figure 7.4).

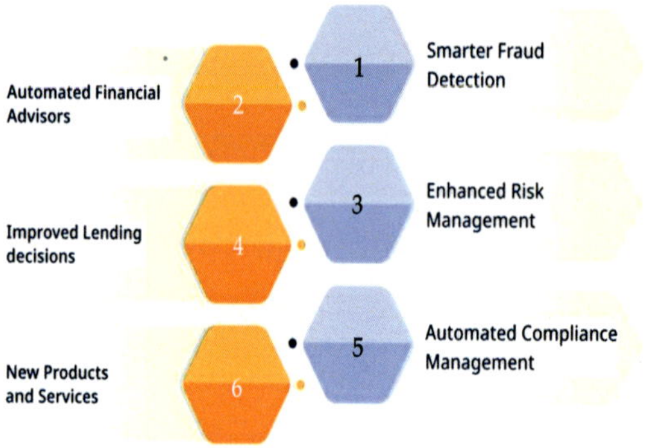


**Figure 7.4.** *The ways AI is expected to impact financial services in the future.*

*Source: https://www.valuecoders.com/blog/technology-and-apps/what-is-the-role-of-artificial-intelligence-in-the-financial-sector/.*

### 7.3.1. Smarter Fraud Detection

Financial institutions can more successfully identify and stop fraud with the aid of AI. For instance, patterns of fraudulent activity can be found using machine learning algorithms.

### 7.3.2. Automated Financial Advisors

Customers can receive automated financial advice via AI. For instance, robo-advisors can suggest a portfolio based on the investing objectives and risk tolerance of a client.

### 7.3.3. Enhanced Risk Management

AI has the potential to improve risk management for financial institutions. Algorithms that use machine learning, for instance, are able to instantly recognize possibilities and hazards.

### 7.3.4. Improved Lending Decisions

AI can assist financial institutions in improving their lending choices by evaluating a borrower's creditworthiness through data analysis.

### 7.3.5. Automated Compliance Management

AI can automatically track regulatory requirements and ensure compliance at all times.

### 7.3.6. New Products and Services

Lastly, over the coming years, it is anticipated that AI-powered products like chatbots, virtual bank tellers, Robo advice platforms, and smart advisors will upend the conventional banking industry.

## REFERENCES

1. Ai, H., & Yoon, S. J. (2021). AI in financial services: The new paradigm. *Journal of Business Research, 126,* 268–278.
2. Amilon, H. (2003). A neural network versus Black–Scholes: A comparison of pricing and hedging performances. *Journal of Forecasting, 22*(4), 317–335.
3. Arner, D. W., Barberis, J., & Buckley, R. P. (2016). Fintech: Evolution and regulation. *Journal of Banking Regulation, 17*(4), 223–228.
4. Athey, S. (2015). Machine learning and causal inference for policy evaluation. In *Proceedings of the 21st ACM SIGKDD International Conference on Knowledge Discovery and Data Mining* (pp. 5–6). ACM.
5. Athey, S., & Imbens, G. W. (2017). The state of applied econometrics: Causality and policy evaluation. *Journal of Economic Perspectives, 31*(2), 3–32.
6. Azad, M., & Khalil, A. (2021). Artificial intelligence applications in financial services. *International Journal of Financial Studies, 9*(2), 28.
7. Bălăceanu, C., & Rusu, L. (2021). Artificial intelligence in banking: Current applications and future trends. *Management and Marketing Journal, 19*(1), 15–30.
8. Bank for International Settlements. (2020). *The Future of Financial Services: Artificial Intelligence and Machine Learning.* BIS Papers No. 111.
9. Bao, Y., & Datta, A. (2014). Simultaneously discovering and quantifying risk types from textual risk disclosures. *Management Science, 60,* 1371–1391.
10. Barboza, F., Kimura, H., & Altman, E. (2017). Machine learning models and bankruptcy prediction. *Expert Systems with Applications, 83,* 405–417.
11. Bazot, G. (2013). Financial consumption and the cost of finance: Measuring financial efficiency in Europe (1950–2007). *Working Paper.* Paris School of Economics.
12. Bhanot, A., & Mukherjee, A. (2020). AI-powered financial services: Opportunities and challenges. *Journal of Business Research, 113,* 68–77.
13. Booth, A., Gerding, E., & McGroarty, F. (2014). Automated trading with performance weighted random forests and seasonality. *Expert Systems with Applications, 41*(8), 3651–3661.
14. Bougheas, S., & Gialamas, V. (2020). The role of AI in enhancing financial decision-making. *Expert Systems with Applications, 135,* 1–9.

15. Burges, C. J. (1998). A tutorial on support vector machines for pattern recognition. *Data Mining and Knowledge Discovery, 2*(2), 121–167.
16. Chaboud, A. P., Chiquoine, B., Hjalmarsson, E., & Vega, C. (2014). Rise of the machines: Algorithmic trading in the foreign exchange market. *The Journal of Finance, 69*(5), 2045–2084.
17. Chen, J., & McIntosh, K. (2020). Artificial intelligence and financial services: What's next? *Journal of Banking & Finance, 112,* 105355.
18. Chen, Y., & Xu, H. (2021). AI-driven credit scoring: A new paradigm. *Risk Analysis, 41*(5), 861–873.
19. Chishti, S., & Barberis, J. (2016). *The FINTECH Book: The Financial Technology Handbook for Investors, Entrepreneurs, and Finance Visionaries.* Wiley.
20. Cybenko, G. (1989). Approximation by superpositions of a sigmoidal function. *Mathematics of Control, Signals and Systems, 2*(4), 303–314.
21. Dietvorst, B. J., Simmons, J. P., & Massey, C. (2016). Overcoming algorithm aversion: People will use imperfect algorithms if they can (even slightly) modify them. *Management Science.*
22. Gao, L., & Hu, H. (2020). AI in financial services: New trends and challenges. *Journal of Financial Regulation and Compliance, 28*(3), 297–310.
23. Ghosh, S. (2020). Artificial intelligence and banking: A new era. *International Journal of Bank Marketing, 38*(5), 1–14.
24. Golmohammadi, K., & Zaiane, O. R. (2012). Data mining applications for fraud detection in securities market. In *Intelligence and Security Informatics Conference (EISIC), 2012 European* (pp. 107–114). IEEE.
25. Golmohammadi, K., & Zaiane, O. R. (2015). Time series contextual anomaly detection for detecting market manipulation in stock market. In *Data Science and Advanced Analytics (DSAA), 2015. 36678 2015. IEEE International Conference on* (pp. 1–10). IEEE.
26. Gozman, D., & Rudd, M. (2020). How artificial intelligence is reshaping financial services. *Business Horizons, 63*(4), 533–542.
27. Guo, L., Shi, F., & Tu, J. (2016). Textual analysis and machine learning: Crack unstructured data in finance and accounting. *The Journal of Finance and Data Science, 2*(3), 153–170.
28. Haffke, I., & Khan, H. (2020). The impact of AI on financial services: A systematic review. *Journal of Business Research, 121,* 497–507.

29. Hand, D. J., & Henley, W. E. (1997). Statistical classification methods in consumer credit scoring: A review. *Journal of the Royal Statistical Society: Series A (Statistics in Society), 160*(3), 523–541.
30. Hu, Y., & Zhao, Q. (2021). Artificial intelligence for wealth management: Opportunities and challenges. *International Review of Economics and Finance, 71,* 232–244.
31. Hutchinson, J. M., Lo, A. W., & Poggio, T. (1994). A nonparametric approach to pricing and hedging derivative securities via learning networks. *The Journal of Finance, 49*(3), 851–889.
32. Kauffman, R. J., & Wang, B. (2018). Artificial intelligence and the future of financial services. *Communications of the ACM, 61*(10), 32–35.
33. Khandani, A. E., Kim, A. J., & Lo, A. W. (2010). Consumer credit-risk models via machine-learning algorithms. *Journal of Banking & Finance, 34*(11), 2767–2787.
34. Koyuncugil, A. S., & Ozgulbas, N. (2012). Financial early warning system model and data mining application for risk detection. *Expert Systems with Applications, 39*(6), 6238–6253.
35. Lee, I., & Shin, Y. J. (2018). Fintech: Ecosystem, business models, investment decisions, and challenges. *Business Horizons, 61*(1), 17–24.
36. Lessmann, S., Baesens, B., Seow, H. V., & Thomas, L. C. (2015). Benchmarking state-of-the-art classification algorithms for credit scoring: An update of research. *European Journal of Operational Research, 247*(1), 124–136.
37. Lin, Y., & Zhang, Y. (2021). Artificial intelligence in risk management: A case study of financial services. *International Journal of Financial Engineering, 8*(3), 215–238.
38. Liu, Y., & Wang, J. (2020). AI and financial services: The next frontier. *Journal of Risk Finance, 21*(4), 331–345.
39. Loughran, T., & McDonald, B. (2011). When is a liability not a liability? Textual analysis, dictionaries, and 10 - Ks. *The Journal of Finance, 66*(1), 35–65.
40. Manela, A., & Moreira, A. (2017). News implied volatility and disaster concerns. *Journal of Financial Economics, 123*(1), 137–162.
41. McKinsey & Company. (2020). Artificial intelligence in banking: A North American perspective. *McKinsey Insights.*
42. Odom, M. D., & Sharda, R. (1990). A neural network model for bankruptcy prediction. In *Neural Networks, 1990.*, 1990 IJCNN International Joint Conference on (pp. 163–168). IEEE.

43. Perols, J. L., Bowen, R. M., Zimmermann, C., & Samba, B. (2017). Finding needles in a haystack: Using data analytics to improve fraud prediction. *Accounting Review, 92,* 221–245.

44. Sun, T., & Zhao, Y. (2021). The impact of artificial intelligence on financial services. *Financial Innovation, 7*(1), 1–18.

45. Tam, K. Y., & Kiang, M. Y. (1992). Managerial applications of neural networks: The case of bank failure predictions. *Management Science, 38*(7), 926–947.

46. Tang, J., & Yin, J. (2005). Developing an intelligent data discriminating system of anti-money laundering based on SVM. In *Machine Learning and Cybernetics, 2005. Proceedings of 2005 International Conference on* (Vol. 6, pp. 3453–3457). IEEE.

47. Tetlock, P. C., Saar - Tsechansky, M., & Macskassy, S. (2008). More than words: Quantifying language to measure firms' fundamentals. *The Journal of Finance, 63*(3), 1437–1467.

48. Utans, J., & Moody, J. (1991). Selecting neural network architectures via the prediction risk: Application to corporate bond rating prediction. In *Artificial Intelligence Applications on Wall Street, 1991. Proceedings., First International Conference on* (pp. 35–41). IEEE.

49. Verhoef, P. C., & Lentz, P. (2021). Artificial intelligence and the future of financial services. *Journal of Retailing and Consumer Services, 59,* 102305.

50. Wang, J., & Zhang, S. (2020). The role of artificial intelligence in financial services. *International Journal of Financial Studies, 8*(3), 31.

51. Yao, Y., & Wang, S. (2020). Big data and AI in financial services: Challenges and opportunities. *Journal of Financial Stability, 48,* 100733.

52. Zhang, R., & Liang, L. (2021). Fintech and artificial intelligence: The future of financial services. *Journal of Finance and Accountancy, 27*(1), 1–20.

53. Zhang, Y., & Kauffman, R. J. (2019). AI in finance: A review of current trends and future directions. *Journal of Management Information Systems, 36*(4), 957–995.

54. Zhang, Y., & Lee, J. (2020). AI-enabled financial services: Theoretical and practical implications. *Journal of Strategic Marketing, 28*(3), 233–245.

CHAPTER 8

# AI IN HEALTHCARE

## Contents

# INTRODUCTION

The application of artificial intelligence (AI) and related technologies is expanding across a range of domains and disciplines, and the healthcare industry is currently following suit. AI is being used successfully in many different contexts, including clinical laboratories, hospitals, and research methodologies. In addition to improved use in machinery, engines, etc. AI finds application in electronic health records (EHR) and in the advancement of life sciences and neurosciences. The diagnosis and treatment of illnesses is the fundamental or most notable application of AI in medicine. (Reddy et al., 2018).

AI, which deals with the computational understanding of intelligence or intelligent behavior and the creation of artifacts that impart such behaviors, is generally referred to as the "field of science" as well as engineering. (Alsheibani et al., 2018; Guan, 2019). Additionally, AI is the ability of a machine to mimic intelligent human behavior using specially designed computer software to complete tasks that require human brain intelligence faster and cheaper. Since creating systems that can think and behave like the human brain is the main goal of artificial intelligence, these systems are known as intelligent agents. The scientific study of what is commonly referred to as intelligent behavior and the development of intelligent agents that display such behaviors constitute the formal definition of AI. This could mean that a machine with human-like skills uses computers to carry out tasks that people have completed.

The intelligent agent concept is a credible way to infer AI theory. Thus, it incorporates the necessary characteristics to pass the Turing test (Reddy et al., 2018), which was administered by British mathematician Alan Turing, a key figure in the development of contemporary computer science and artificial intelligence. The Turing test evaluates computers based on their capacity to complete tasks similarly to humans (Alsheibani et al., 2018). Perception, practical reasoning, and task completion proficiency are necessary for an intelligent agent. (Reddy et al., 2018). "AI is used to address issues of understanding imitating intelligence and performing cognitive tasks with minimal human arbitrations because it is an interdisciplinary concept that embraces the foundations and tools of diverse areas like computation, mathematics, logic, and biology." Guan (2019). The success of AI systems in healthcare is attributed to sophisticated algorithms that can learn a wide range of traits from vast amounts of medical data, which aids in problem-solving and is accomplished at a rate and volume that is ineffective for humans. Autolearning can be added to the algorithms to increase accuracy and performance. AI systems are used to assist doctors with advanced medical knowledge regarding clinical papers and journals to inform medical textbooks and patient care in general. AI has the potential to reduce both therapeutic and diagnostic errors. It can use medical data, especially from patient populations, for the learning process. (Khanna, 2020). One type of intelligent agent used in AI systems is an infobot, which is a computational core with physical actuators and sensors angled like robots. If an advisory program is used in conjunction with human experts, it is referred to as a decision support system (Reddy et al., 2018). AI has many uses in medicine, including predicting disease risks, evaluating the effectiveness of treatments, managing treatment complexity, assisting with patient care, clinical research, and medication development (Arnold, 2021). Diagnosing diseases, conducting surgeries, and guiding researchers in creating costly clinical trial companions (Kiener, 2020).

## 8.1. THE ROLE OF ARTIFICIAL INTELLIGENCE IN HEALTHCARE

Artificial intelligence (AI) is a game-changing force that is changing the face of many industries, including finance, education, transportation, and more. Fundamentally, AI is the creation of computer systems that can carry out operations that usually call for human intelligence, like comprehending natural language, identifying patterns, coming to decisions, and picking up knowledge from past experiences (Dwivedi et al., 2021; Păvăloaia and Necula, 2023; Taj and Zaman, 2022). The healthcare industry has become one of the main beneficiaries of artificial intelligence's promise in recent years, using the technology to improve a range of patient care and administrative effectiveness. Due to the rapid expansion of healthcare data, increases in processing power, and important developments in machine learning algorithms, integrating AI technologies into healthcare is no longer only a vision for the future but a reality today (Dwivedi et al., 2021; Leone, Schiavone, Appio, and Chiao, 2021).

### 8.1.1. Importance of AI in Healthcare

It is impossible to exaggerate the importance of AI applications in healthcare. AI holds great promise for transforming the fields of disease diagnosis, personalized medicine, real-time health condition monitoring, and operational healthcare management. AI-driven diagnostic tools, for example, are able to accurately analyze medical images and frequently pick up on details that a human eye might miss. This accuracy results in earlier and more precise diagnoses, which has a substantial effect on patient outcomes. Similar to this, AI algorithms are making significant strides towards truly personalized medicine in the area of treatment personalization. They can comb through enormous datasets to find patterns and forecast which treatments will work best for particular patient profiles. AI is also used in patient monitoring, where wearable technology and remote monitoring systems provide ongoing patient health oversight, allowing for prompt interventions and a decrease in readmissions to hospitals. AI can improve efficiency and patient satisfaction in the delivery of healthcare by streamlining operations such as appointment scheduling and hospital workflow optimization (Alshamrani, 2022; Farid, Bello, Ahamed, and Hossain, 2023; Shaik et al., 2023).

### 8.1.2. Purpose and Scope of the Review

The goal of this systematic review is to carefully investigate the various applications and intrinsic difficulties of AI in the healthcare industry. This review offers a thorough overview of how AI technologies address healthcare challenges, improve patient care, and improve healthcare outcomes by methodically gathering and analyzing recent literature. This review will also critically evaluate the barriers and constraints that arise when incorporating AI into healthcare procedures, ranging from ethical and technical conundrums to implementation and regulatory challenges. The goal is to present a fair-minded viewpoint that acknowledges the advancements of AI in healthcare while also addressing the difficulties and complexities associated with its use. This review's scope, which covers a wide range of AI technologies and their applications in the healthcare industry, is purposefully broad but focused. Machine learning models, robotic process automation (RPA), natural language processing (NLP) tools, and AI-driven predictive analytics are a few examples of this. The review will examine these technologies in relation to public health initiatives, healthcare operations, patient monitoring and care, treatment personalization, and diagnostic support. Although AI has enormous potential in the healthcare industry, this review will also outline the limits of existing applications and critically assess the advantages and disadvantages of AI technologies in actual healthcare environments. By doing this, the review seeks to provide a comprehensive picture of the state of AI in healthcare today, highlighting promising areas, recurring difficulties, and possible directions for further study and application. All things considered, this introduction lays the groundwork for a comprehensive examination of the dynamic interactions between artificial intelligence and healthcare, highlighting the revolutionary potential of AI to improve patient outcomes and healthcare delivery while negotiating the many obstacles that come with integrating it into the healthcare ecosystem.

## 8.2. TYPES OF AI IN HEALTHCARE

Artificial Intelligence consists of multiple technologies rather than just one. Numerous technologies, each supporting specific mechanisms and tasks, are directly related to healthcare. Below is a summary of some significant AI healthcare technologies.

### 8.2.1. Machine Learning: Neural Networks and Deep Learning

Machine learning is one of the most widely used forms of AI. It is a statistical technique. Precision medicine is the common application of traditional machine learning. It is useful for determining the patient's precise condition based on their unique characteristics and medical history, and it approximates the course of treatment (Reddy et al., 2018; Davenport and Kalakota, 2019). The complex technology known as the neural network became possible after the 1960s. It has been validated in medical research for many years. It is used to predict a patient's propensity to contract a particular illness. It processes signals in a manner akin to that of a neuron, but it is less functional than the brain's processes (Reddy et al., 2018). Using radiology images, deep learning can be used to diagnose contusions and lacerations. Deep learning is essentially a kind of NLP and is increasingly being used for speech recognition (Reddy et al., 2018; Khanna, 2020).

### 8.2.2. Natural Language Processing

There are two types of data in the medical dataset: structured and unstructured. Unstructured medical data that is stored in electronic health record systems is used by NLP. NLP is used to transform data into a format that can be used and analyzed. NLP examines medical records to extract pertinent data, including prescriptions, treatment schedules, and health concerns. It can assess the quality of clients or examine social media trends. It has been attempting to use human language for text analysis and speech recognition. NLP algorithms for the collection and assimilation of clinical papers are developed using AI.

### 8.2.3. Rule-based Expert Systems

The primary objective of implementing rule-based expert systems in the medical field is to provide clinical decision assistance. This concept has been in practice for several decades and continues to be relevant today. These rule-sets originate from numerous electronic health records (EHR). Rule-based expert systems rely on data scientists and endeavor to make logical deductions akin to how humans reason (Davenport and Kalakota 2019; Kourou et al., 2021).

### 8.2.4. Physical Robots

They carry out meticulous tasks like lifting, shifting, welding, sorting items in warehouses and factories, and bringing supplies to hospitals. Robots and humans can now work together harmoniously, and they can be taught simple commands by following certain procedures. Surgical robots were certified in 2000, and they give surgeons a "superpower" by improving their vision, making clearer, less invasive incisions, stitching wounds, and many other tasks. Gynecologic, prostate, and head and neck surgery are all included in the robotic surgery protocol (Kalakota and Davenport, 2019).

### 8.2.5. Robotic Process Automation

When compared to other AI programs, it is transparent in operation, cheap, and simple to program. It is made up entirely of computer programs running on screens, not real robots. They are used in the healthcare industry for billing, updating patient records, and proceeding with endorsements. When combined with image recognition, they can also be used to extract data from a faxed image.

### 8.2.6. Artificial Neural Networking

Artificial neural networks (ANN) compute simulations inspired by the workings of the human brain. Voice, image, and robotics recognition are among the advances in ANN AI. The primary goals of artificial neural networks (ANNs) are to replicate the functions of human brain neurons by means of neural networks of algorithms and to preserve a correlation between a set of data, much like the human brain. For biological neurons, the response is instantaneous; however, because data processing is slower, the response takes longer. However, the benefit is that data processing is an ongoing activity. (Kourou et al., 2021; Alsheibani et al., 2018).

### 8.2.7. Clinical Decision Support System (CDSS)

The primary goal of CDSS is to use patient data from prior visits to make an accurate diagnosis of the illness. Clinicians can combine information from CDSS with their own expertise. CDSS uses web applications or interfaces with computerized provider order data (CPOE) and EHR systems. There are two categories for CDSS: knowledge-based and non-knowledge-based. In medicine, knowledge-based CDSS is used for AI, but it is unable to comprehend the logic that leads to problems with data availability. (Kourou et al., 2021; Amann et al., 2020).

### 8.2.8. Biomarkers

In order to identify molecular indicators of health and provide the patient with the best treatment possible, biomarkers testing, also referred to as molecular study, involves a number of complex tests. Biomarker discovery aided by machine learning is popular. A few hypotheses are evaluated by machine learning algorithms based on input features. The algorithms fall into two categories:

feature-based algorithms and classification algorithms. The algorithms are applied to gene expression data that were developed for human cell RNA sequencing data. Kourou et al., (2021).

### 8.2.9. Arterial Spin Labelling Imaging (ASL)

It is a method of measuring brain perfusion that is non-invasive. Its software functions in a multitude of ways to assess data and produce highly accurate diagnoses. It works well for keeping track of Alzheimer's patients. Kourou et al. (2021).

## 8.3. APPLICATIONS OF ARTIFICIAL INTELLIGENCE

AI in healthcare has created new opportunities to improve patient care, streamline operations, and advance public health programs. This section delves deeply into the essential uses of AI in a range of healthcare-related fields.

1. **Healthcare Drug Creation:** Algorithms for machine learning are used to speed up the drug discovery process. The parts of the discovery process that will benefit from AI use will be quicker, safer, and more affordable. It can help find novel compounds that could be used as potential medications to treat a condition. It can also be used to determine the intended use of compounds that have already undergone testing. For example, AI identified two medications for treating the Ebola outbreak in West Africa in a single day, whereas human identification might take months or even years. As a result, AI can be effectively combined with in-memory computing technology to be used in the development of new drugs, increasing the capacity to provide faster drug discovery and development. Khanna (2018).
2. **Treatment Design:** AI is capable of accurately recognizing and interpreting medical imaging images, including X-rays, CT, MRI, ultrasound, and PET scans, as well as their signs and symptoms. It facilitates quicker disease diagnosis. With the aid of medical assistant systems, AI is useful in gathering patient data, diagnosis records, testing procedures, and billing information organization. Thus, AI techniques can be applied to improve patient satisfaction and care design. Khanna (2018).
3. **Disease Progression:** AI aids in the documentation of disease progression at various stages through the use of biomarkers. AI is able to detect and store patient data in more efficient ways. All of

this is made possible by the application of artificial intelligence algorithms that create illness models. (Kourou et al., 2021).

4. **Diagnosis Aid:** AI can identify conditions like skin cancer with greater accuracy than a skilled medical professional. AI systems are automated; they incorporate all relevant data variables into the model and offer a diagnosis. (Reddy et al., 2018; Kourou et al., 2021).
5. **Health Monitoring:** Numerous fitness devices and wearables are capable of tracking a person's health. These devices use AI to track health, evaluate data, and give users information about their condition (Kourou et al., 2021).
6. **Managing Medical Data and Records:** AI plays a significant part in data management. AI facilitates the gathering, storing, transforming, and tracking of data sources. In healthcare, gathering and analyzing data are crucial processes, which is why artificial intelligence is used in this process. Khanna (2018).

### 8.3.1. Diagnostic Assistance

AI algorithms that use data from biometric sensors, genetic testing, and medical imaging have greatly increased the efficiency and accuracy of disease diagnosis. AI-driven technologies, for instance, analyze X-rays, MRI scans, and CT scans to identify anomalies like tumors, fractures, and indications of neurological disorders with an accuracy that frequently exceeds human capacity in the field of medical imaging. By using deep learning techniques, these systems can detect patterns and abnormalities that could point to the early stages of diseases like cancer and allow for timely intervention.

AI also shines in the analysis of genetic data, which provides information about a patient's susceptibility to specific illnesses and ailments. AI systems can forecast the likelihood of genetic illnesses by examining genetic variants and markers, allowing for early diagnosis and preventative measures based on a person's unique genetic composition. Analogously, wearable device data is processed by AI applications in biometric data analysis to track vital signs and identify deviations that might indicate health problems, allowing for early diagnosis and intervention (Abdallah et al., 2023; Alrefaei et al., 2022).

### 8.3.2. Treatment Personalization

AI plays a revolutionary role in personalizing care by facilitating the transition to precision medicine, in which patient-specific treatments are customized to meet their unique needs. To predict which treatment plans will work best for each patient, AI models examine large datasets that include genetic data, environmental factors, and patient history. This method decreases side effects, increases treatment efficacy, and lessens the trial-and-error process that is frequently involved in selecting the appropriate drug or therapy.

By forecasting the interactions between various chemical compounds and biological targets, AI speeds up the process of finding and testing new medications. This shortens the time and expense involved in introducing novel treatments to the market by accelerating the drug discovery process and raising the possibility of finding promising drug candidates (Gupta et al., 2021; Paul et al., 2021; Vatansever et al., 2021).

### 8.3.3. Patient Monitoring and Care

Wearable technology and remote monitoring systems are the primary ways that artificial intelligence has transformed patient monitoring and care. In order to provide real-time insights into the patient's health status, these AI-enabled devices continuously gather health data, including heart rate, blood pressure, glucose levels, and sleep patterns. This data is analyzed by sophisticated AI algorithms to find anomalies that might point to new health problems, allowing for timely medical intervention.

AI-powered solutions also provide tailored health advice and notifications, enhancing patient involvement in their care and enabling self-management of long-term illnesses. Patients are given more control over their health, hospital readmissions are decreased, and the quality of care is greatly improved by this proactive approach to patient monitoring (Ahmadi; B. Wang, Asan, and Zhang, 2024).

### 8.3.4. Healthcare Operations

AI applications improve efficiency, lower costs, and increase patient satisfaction by streamlining healthcare operations. Healthcare workers can concentrate on patient care by using AI tools to optimize workflows and automate administrative duties like appointment scheduling, patient triage, and billing. Algorithms for allocating resources maximize hospital beds and medical equipment. In addition, AI-powered patient flow management systems guarantee prompt treatment, cutting down on wait times and enhancing the quality of healthcare (Abidi, Rehman, Mian, Alkhalefah, and Usmani, 2024; Patil and Shankar, 2023).

### 8.3.5. Public Health and Epidemiology

AI plays a key role in epidemiology and public health by predicting outbreaks, analyzing disease trends, and guiding public health initiatives. To monitor and forecast the spread of diseases, AI systems analyze enormous volumes of data from multiple sources, such as social media, environmental sensors, and medical records. Public health officials can carry out focused interventions, distribute resources efficiently, and lessen the effects of outbreaks thanks to this real-time surveillance. Furthermore, by helping to comprehend intricate public health issues like how social determinants affect health outcomes, AI models support well-informed policymaking and intervention tactics (Schwalbe and Wahl, 2020; Zeng, Cao, and Neill, 2021). In summary, AI has a wide range of uses in healthcare, providing previously unheard-of chances to boost patient monitoring and care, improve diagnostic precision, customize treatment, streamline healthcare operations, and promote public health campaigns. As AI technologies advance, they have the potential to revolutionize the healthcare industry by improving patient outcomes worldwide and boosting the effectiveness of healthcare delivery.

## 8.3.6. Concerns in Healthcare

1. **Administrative Workflow:** There is a lot of paperwork in healthcare managed by doctors, nurses, and other healthcare employees. They also have to manage time consuming administrative tasks. The medical officers attending to patients under these circumstances may get exhausted and lose focus which can lead to misdiagnosis. So, AI should be employed for such repetitive tasks. (Kourou et al., 2021).
2. **Inadequate Nurses:** There are not adequate doctors and nurses for patient care. Patients have to wait for a longer period which causes anxiety that is harmful to them. Doctors and nurses are also under pressure to serve too many patients waiting in the queue within the limited time available. (Kourou et al., 2021).
3. **Surgery:** There are different forms of surgery such as minor, major, and non-invasive surgeries. The surgeries should be conducted efficiently. As surgeons take a long time for surgeries, they may get exhausted and lose focus in such a long time. (Kourou et al., 2021).
4. **Diagnosis:** Doctors and nurses utilize the symptoms observed in patients to diagnose the issue. They employ their knowledge from limited sources available around them. Therefore, fast and more adequate alternatives should also be taken into consideration for diagnosis. (Kourou et al., 2021).
5. **Health Monitoring:** Routine health monitoring needs patients' visits to the hospital to monitor their health status. This time-consuming process makes patients negligent towards their health status. They

only visit the hospital when their health issues severely increase. Thus, faster and more precise AI techniques should be incorporated to solve their issues (Kourou et al., 2021).

## 8.3.7. Advantages of Artificial Intelligence

1. **Expanded Healthcare Access:** The human body should be handled professionally to prevent misdiagnosis, mishandling, or wrong treatment. But developing and under-developed nations lack enough physicians. Therefore, these nations can utilize mechanisms based on AI algorithms for diagnosis. (Kourou et al., 2021).
2. **Improves Record-Keeping:** With the use of EHR in hospitals, storing and managing record data becomes easier. AI technologies like voice recognition and dictation further improve the documentation process. (Kourou et al., 2021).
3. **Advanced Immunotherapy:** In advancing immunotherapy for cancer treatment AI plays an important role. Since there is no particular cure for cancer, immunotherapy is being utilized for medication. But immunotherapy is not beneficial for all patients. Thence, AI is efficiently used for the identification of patients who can benefit from immunotherapy. (Kourou et al., 2021).
4. **Improves Quality of Services:** AI is beneficial in time-saving as machines utilized are faster than human beings. Therefore diagnosis, treatment, and record keeping becomes easy and can be done in less time, reduced labor employment. This leads to less treatment cost and offers improved quality of services. (Kourou et al., 2021).

## 8.3.8. Challenges of AI in Healthcare

### *8.3.8.1. Data Privacy and Security*

Managing data security and privacy is one of the main issues with using AI in healthcare. For AI systems to train algorithms and deliver individualized care, they need access to enormous volumes of private patient data.

This, however, brings up serious issues regarding the gathering, storing, and application of such data.

Maintaining the confidentiality and integrity of patient data is crucial because breaches may allow unauthorized access to private health information, which could put patients at risk for identity theft, discrimination, and other negative outcomes. Strict data protection laws, like the General Data Protection Regulation (GDPR) in Europe and the Health Insurance Portability and Accountability Act (HIPAA) in the US, must be followed by healthcare providers and AI developers. They also need to put strong security measures in place to protect patient data (Bradford, Aboy, and Liddell, 2020; Shuaib, Alam, and Nasir, 2021).

### 8.3.8.2. Ethical and Legal Considerations

There are several ethical and legal issues that are raised by the use of AI in healthcare. Algorithmic bias, in which AI systems display biases based on the data they were trained on, is one of the most urgent problems. This could result in disparate treatment outcomes for various demographic groups. Transparent algorithm design and ongoing oversight are necessary to address these biases and guarantee just and equal patient care. Furthermore, when AI systems are used in patient care, especially in cases of misdiagnosis or treatment errors, legal issues pertaining to liability and accountability surface. Determining responsibility—whether with the AI developer, the healthcare provider, or the technology itself—complicates the legal environment and calls for precise rules and regulations (McLennan et al., 2022; Naik et al., 2022).

### 8.3.8.3. Interoperability and Integration

Another major challenge is integrating AI technologies into current healthcare IT systems. The efficacy of AI applications is constrained by the fact that many healthcare systems are still running on antiquated platforms that might not be compatible with the newest AI solutions. Furthermore, the comprehensive, coordinated care that AI promises to improve depends on ensuring interoperability across various platforms and technologies, each of which has its own standards and protocols. To do this, technology developers, healthcare organizations, and regulatory agencies must work together to create and uphold universal standards that promote data exchange and interoperability (Dwivedi et al., 2021; Lee and Yoon, 2021).

### 8.3.8.4. Scalability and Accessibility

Another issue is the scalability of AI solutions in various healthcare contexts, particularly in settings with limited resources. Even though AI has the potential to greatly improve healthcare outcomes, underfunded clinics and hospitals may not be able to afford the infrastructure and technology needed to implement AI. Furthermore, socioeconomic differences may create a "digital divide" where only patients in well-funded healthcare systems gain from AI advancements, raising concerns about ensuring equitable access to AI-driven healthcare services. Creating affordable AI solutions and regulations that support technology access at all healthcare levels are necessary to address these problems (Krones and Walker, 2023; Lee and Yoon, 2021; Q. Wang, Su, Zhang, and Li, 2021).

### *8.3.8.5. Human-AI Interaction*

Lastly, there are significant issues raised by the dynamics of human-AI interaction in healthcare settings. For technology to be used effectively, patients and healthcare professionals must have faith in AI systems. But there are also serious concerns about over-reliance on AI, possible medical professional deskilling, and the necessity of meaningful oversight of AI decisions. For healthcare professionals to continue providing high-quality care and upholding their professional integrity, AI must be used as a supplement to human judgment rather than as a substitute. Healthcare workers must receive continual education and training in order to collaborate with AI technologies in an efficient manner, being aware of both their advantages and disadvantages.

In conclusion, even though AI has the potential to revolutionize healthcare, its full potential will only be realized if the issues of data privacy and security, ethical, and legal concerns, interoperability and integration, scalability and accessibility, and human-AI interaction are resolved. To overcome these obstacles and guarantee that AI technologies are applied in a way that is safe, moral, accessible, and improves healthcare for everyone, AI developers, healthcare providers, legislators, and the general public must work together.

## 8.4. THE ROLE OF AI IN MEDICAL IMAGING

While AI in medical imaging is a rapidly expanding field, it also presents a number of difficulties in terms of application and regulatory approval. Machine learning (ML) techniques based on artificial intelligence enable the application of routine and sophisticated workflows to 2D and 3D image data from CT and MRI scans, such as abnormality detection and segmentation of regions of anatomical interest (MRI). Ensuring that new technology is available for healthcare while maintaining accuracy and patient safety is one of the ongoing challenges for medical device companies and clinicians, especially when dealing with algorithms that change or adapt over time.

A revolutionary convergence of technology and healthcare is represented by AI in medical imaging. Beyond merely being a technological breakthrough, its incorporation into medical imaging represents a paradigm change that could completely alter treatment planning and diagnosis (Figure 8.1).

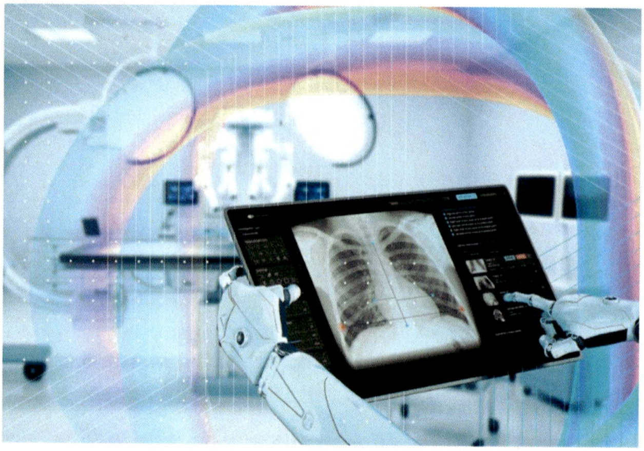

**Figure 8.1.** *AI in medical imaging.*

*Source: https://www.bgosoftware.com/blog/wp-content/uploads/2024/02/bgo-software-blog-post-size-Role-of-AI-no-title.png.*

It is impossible to overestimate the importance of AI in healthcare and medical imaging because it goes beyond simple enhancements in processing speed and image quality. For example, with an annual growth rate of 29.8% and a doubling time of roughly 2–7 years, the field of Radiology, Nuclear Magnetic Resonance, and Medical Imaging (RNMMI) has witnessed significant growth in AI and machine learning publications. This kind of expansion is not exclusive to radiology; AI's potential to improve personalized modern medicine and early disease detection has also revolutionized the field.

It's about saving lives with early intervention and customized treatment options, not just about quicker and clearer images. These developments have significant practical ramifications, especially in fields like neurology and oncology where prompt and precise diagnosis is essential. More precisely, it has been demonstrated to have the ability to significantly increase the daily number of patients scanned, highlighting not only better patient outcomes and safety but also increased productivity and cost-effectiveness. AI methods have a variety of effects on medical imaging. It is raising the bar for patient care by increasing diagnostic precision, lowering human error, and facilitating early disease detection.

### 8.4.1. The Potential of AI in Medical Imaging

When it comes to enhancing medical imaging, AI has many applications, but figuring out how to best incorporate it into your current system is not always simple (Figure 8.2).

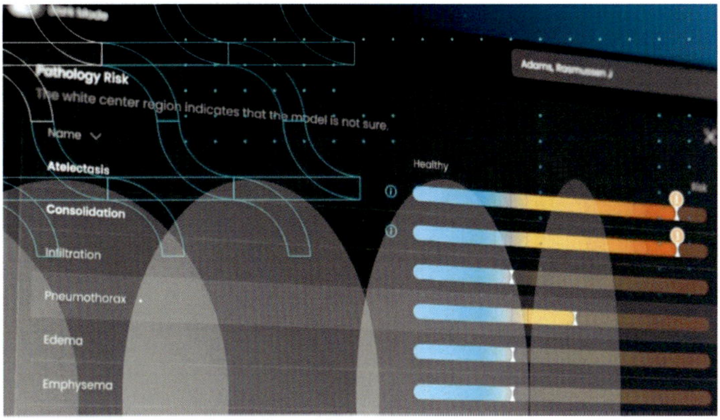


**Figure 8.2.** *The potential of AI in medical imaging.*

*Source: https://www.bgosoftware.com/blog/wp-content/uploads/2024/02/bgo-software-blog-post-in-article-simple-img-The-potential-of-AI.png.*

There are many ways to use AI to enhance medical imaging, but figuring out how to best incorporate it into your current system isn't always simple.

By skillfully applying machine learning and deep learning algorithms that let you be adaptable with your strategy, you can fully realize its potential. AI has begun to play a key role in improving medical imaging methods, which, when applied properly, can result in notable advancements in the four areas listed below. Enhancing the image quality is among the most noteworthy features. Large volumes of imaging data can be analyzed by AI algorithms that are trained to identify minute patterns and irregularities that the human eye would otherwise miss. More accurate diagnoses, such as the detection of fractures, have been made possible by the improved clarity and resolution of these images.

AI is also having a significant impact on processing speed for image production. Medical image analysis has historically taken a long time and frequently resulted in delays in diagnosis and treatment.

AI is significantly cutting down on the amount of time required for medical image analysis because of its rapid processing and analysis of large datasets. Consequently, AI systems can now analyze and produce complex images in a fraction of the time required for traditional methods, speeding up the diagnostic process. AI is then a useful tool for early disease detection and diagnosis since it can recognize patterns linked to particular diseases by incorporating deep learning algorithms. As a result, AI can greatly enhance many patients' experiences by detecting abnormalities like tumors early on through sophisticated image analysis.

For instance, Roche, Ibex Medical Analytics, and Amazon Web Services collaborated to improve digital pathology in October 2023. The partnership entails combining Roche's navify Digital Pathology software, which is hosted on Amazon's cloud platform, with Ibex's AI algorithms. By utilizing AI to increase workflow efficiency and speed up turnaround in pathology labs, this collaboration seeks to enhance the diagnostic procedures for breast and prostate cancer.

Another promising application of AI is in preventive healthcare and personalized medicine. AI can offer individualized diagnostic information by evaluating imaging data in conjunction with a patient's medical history. This opens the door to individualized treatment regimens.

This area of artificial intelligence has enormous promise for treating chronic illnesses and ailments, where early identification and individualized treatment regimens can have a big impact.

## 8.4.2. Current Applications of AI in Medical Imaging

Radiology, oncology, and neurology are among the fields that are greatly impacted by the current uses of AI in medical imaging. Medical professionals in these fields can improve the precision and effectiveness of numerous diagnoses and more effectively treat illnesses by utilizing AI (Figure 8.3).

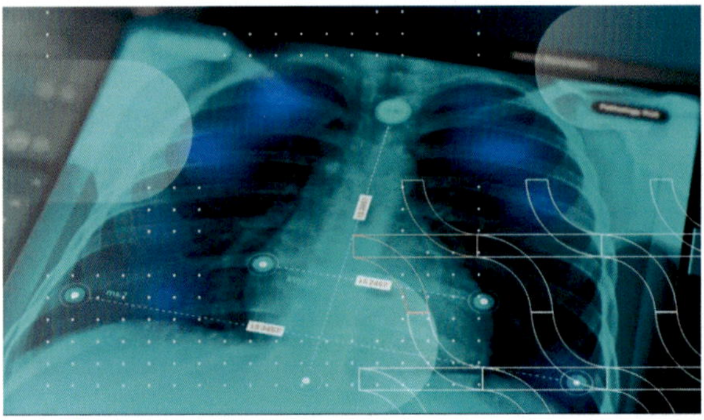

**Figure 8.3.** *Current applications of AI in medical imaging.*

*Source: https://www.bgosoftware.com/blog/wp-content/uploads/2024/02/bgo-software-blog-post-in-article-simple-img-Current-applications-of-AI.png.*

For instance, AI is primarily used in radiology to detect anomalies in imaging scans. AI algorithms can quickly recognize and segment regions of interest in brain, liver, and lung scans when they are applied to computed tomography (CT) and MRI images. The application of AI to the detection of pulmonary nodules in chest CT scans is a noteworthy example. AI greatly increases the detection rate of tiny nodules there, which are frequently overlooked by the human eye. It is especially important to note AI's role in oncology imaging. It increases the precision of breast cancer screenings by helping to identify and track malignant growths. For example, deep learning AI technology was utilized to analyze mammograms and accurately distinguish between benign and malignant lesions.

The AI-PHI's mammography studies, which eventually will comprise mammograms from more than 5 million women across five continents, are now centrally stored there. The prognosis of patients is greatly affected by early cancer detection, which is where this AI-driven method is crucial.

AI is improving neurology's ability to analyze brain images for diseases like brain tumors, Alzheimer's disease, and stroke. Early intervention and treatment are made possible by AI algorithms' ability to identify minute alterations in brain tissue. The use of AI in diffusion weighted imaging, a form of MRI, to quickly locate brain regions affected by stroke is an interesting example.

This AI model evaluated 6,716 cases from the national lung cancer screening trial and showed excellent performance, with an area under the curve of 94%. In a different, independent set of 1,139 clinical validation cases, it also retained comparable accuracy.

These three fields demonstrate how AI applications in medical imaging are expanding the field of personalized medicine while simultaneously improving existing diagnostic and therapeutic procedures. AI is proving to be a tremendous help in the healthcare sector, from increasing radiology diagnostic accuracy to assisting in the early detection of cancer cells and neurological disorders. In order for you to completely comprehend its potential, we must examine how it enhances diagnostic precision.

### 8.4.3. The Impact of AI on Diagnostic Accuracy

The accuracy of diagnosis has significantly increased with the use of AI in medical imaging analysis. In addition to improving early disease detection, it lowers human error. Precision medicine and medical imaging technology are changing as a result of this move toward AI-enhanced diagnostic techniques.

First off, AI algorithms have demonstrated a notable improvement in recognizing and diagnosing medical conditions due to their capacity to learn from large datasets. For example, when it comes to identifying illnesses like pneumonia in chest X-rays, AI can match or even exceed the accuracy of human body radiologists. This degree of precision is especially important in situations where early detection has a big impact on how well a medical intervention works.

AI's consistency in medical imaging is its second main advantage, as it significantly lowers human error. AI systems offer consistent analysis, in contrast to human radiologic technologists who might be swayed by subjective judgment or fatigue. AI support can improve the reliability of diagnoses by lowering diagnostic errors in mammograms used for breast cancer screening.

Effective treatment of diseases depends on early detection, and artificial intelligence is beginning to play a big part in this field. AI, for instance, has proven crucial in the early identification of diabetic retinopathy, a disorder that, if left untreated, can result in blindness. AI-based retinal image analysis could accurately identify this condition, frequently before the patient's body shows any symptoms. AI is improving patient care and opening the door for precision medicine breakthroughs by decreasing human error, increasing accuracy, and facilitating early disease detection.

### 8.4.4. Advancements in AI Technology for Medical Imaging

Significant progress in the field of medical imaging has been made thanks to the creation of new AI algorithms, improved machine learning techniques, and better hardware to support these developments. A timeline of these developments shows how AI in medical imaging has advanced quickly, with each new development building on the one before it to produce increasingly complex and useful tools. The use of machine learning techniques in medical imaging advanced quickly in the early 2010s. Since then, algorithms have advanced and are now able to process enormous volumes of imaging data more accurately. These developments in AI technology have been bolstered by concurrent hardware advancements in the latter half of the 2010s. The advancement of specialized AI processors and high-performance GPUs has made it possible to process complex algorithms more quickly, enabling real-time analysis of medical image registration. These hardware developments are now essential for meeting the processing demands of sophisticated AI applications in medical imaging.

By combining deep learning, cutting-edge machine learning methods, and potent hardware, artificial intelligence in medical imaging aims to deliver previously unheard-of levels of diagnostic efficiency and accuracy after 2020. AI models that are more interpretable, accurate, and able to shed light on intricate medical conditions are what the future holds.

AI Large Language Models are mainly used in medical imaging equipment to increase overall diagnostic process efficiency, improve diagnostic accuracy, and automate the interpretation of medical images. These models greatly facilitate disease detection and classification because of their prowess in processing large datasets, spotting complex patterns, and offering thorough insights.

## 8.4.5. Challenges in Adopting AI in Medical Imaging

Even though AI integration has many advantages, there are a number of obstacles preventing the industry from embracing it widely. These difficulties, which range from moral dilemmas to technological barriers, all have an effect on the healthcare sector in the ways listed below (Figure 8.4).

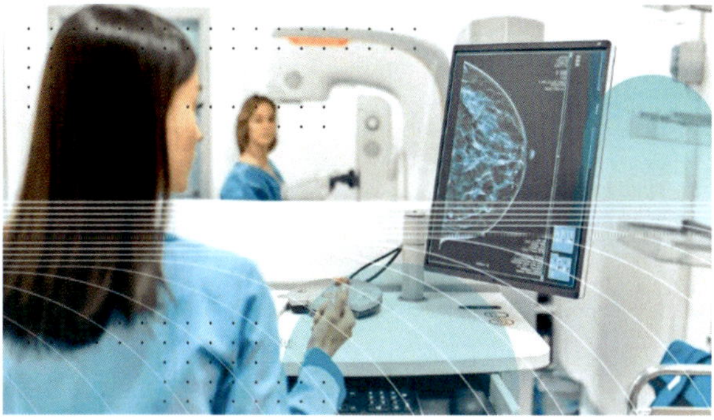

**Figure 8.4.** *Several challenges in adopting AI in medical imaging.*

*Source: https://www.bgosoftware.com/blog/wp-content/uploads/2024/02/bgo-software-blog-post-in-article-simple-img-Challenges-in-%D0%B0dopting-AI.png.*

The first issue that has the biggest impact on AI is data privacy. Large patient image datasets are necessary for AI systems to function, which poses serious privacy issues.

It is crucial to guarantee the security and privacy of this sensitive information. Strict data protection laws must be followed by healthcare organizations because it is crucial to guarantee the security and confidentiality of this sensitive information.

For instance, the HIPAA is the law most frequently used in the United States of America to protect patient data.

Another major obstacle is the expense of incorporating AI into currently used conventional imaging methods. Many healthcare facilities may find the cost of purchasing AI software and the required hardware upgrades to be unaffordable. If you are running a smaller medical practice, this process can be particularly challenging.

To lessen this, you might think about collaborating with a healthcare IT services provider, such as BGO Software, which will help you introduce AI gradually.

Successful AI implementation in medical imaging also necessitates specific training for medical personnel. In order to incorporate AI-generated results into their clinical decision-making processes, radiologists and technicians need to be trained in their interpretation. Comprehensive educational programs and workshops can help address this need for extra training and guarantee that your healthcare professionals are prepared to use AI in their practice. It's also critical to acknowledge that some medical professionals show resistance or skepticism toward AI. This frequently occurs as a result of worries about accuracy or a fear of technological replacement. It's critical to establish trust in AI systems, and you can do this by being open and honest with everyone you work with about AI's potential and constraints. Finally, technical issues like algorithm biases and data integration present serious difficulties. It can be difficult to integrate AI with current healthcare IT systems, and smooth interoperability is necessary. AI systems should be trained on inclusive, diverse datasets and rigorously validated to guarantee their accuracy and fairness in order to counteract this.

### 8.4.6. Regulatory and Legal Considerations

A complicated web of legal and regulatory issues arises when artificial intelligence is incorporated into medical imaging. To maintain compliance and safeguard patient interests, it is essential for developers and healthcare providers to comprehend this legal framework. The Food and Drug Administration's (FDA) regulation of AI in the US is the first important component of the legal framework. By emphasizing the security and efficacy of AI-based diagnostic tools, the FDA has taken an active role in establishing guidelines for AI in medical imaging. Clear regulatory pathways for AI applications are necessary, though, as evidenced by the FDA's changing approach to regulating AI in medical imaging. Another important legal factor is data protection. Adherence to data protection regulations such as the HIPAA in the US and the GDPR in Europe is crucial since AI systems handle enormous volumes of sensitive patient data. These laws guarantee patient data security and privacy by imposing stringent rules on data handling, storage, and sharing. The European Parliament and the Council of the European Union came to an agreement on the Artificial Intelligence Act, which is the first set of international regulations pertaining to AI, at the start of 2024. This ground-breaking law seeks to promote innovation and confidence in AI while guaranteeing its safe and legal application. The guidelines, which emphasize the transparent, traceable, and human-centric approach of high-risk AI systems, will be applied consistently across all member states. Nonetheless, the legal environment pertaining to AI in medical imaging is always changing. The swift progress of AI technologies is prompting the proposal of new regulations and the interpretation of current ones. As a result, there is a growing need for well-balanced laws that protect patient safety and privacy of data while also encouraging innovation.

### 8.4.7. Integration of AI with Traditional Medical Imaging Techniques

AI and conventional medical imaging methods have come together to form a synergistic relationship that improves the efficiency and accuracy of invasive and diagnostic procedures. The way medical imaging is carried out is being revolutionized by the combination of AI with well-established image modalities like MRI and CT. AI algorithms can significantly cut down on the amount of time needed for image reconstruction in MRI without sacrificing image quality. AI-based methods could speed up medical imaging procedures by drastically cutting down on scanning time and increasing patient throughput, according to a medical research article published in the Journal of Magnetic Resonance Imaging. AI and conventional imaging methods work together to produce a synergistic relationship in which each enhances the other. AI's ability to precisely evaluate enormous volumes of imaging data enhances radiologists' skills, resulting in more precise diagnoses and improved patient outcomes. As an illustration of the effectiveness of this synergistic approach, the use of AI in combination with conventional ultrasound wave techniques has increased the detection rate of advanced prostate and breast cancer.

## 8.5. AI IN DISEASE DIAGNOSIS AND PREDICTION

Many diseases use an AI-based disease detection system for different classification and pattern recognition tasks. AI and ML disease detection is specifically utilized for signal processing, imaging analysis, and multiple pathology identification. In addition to analyzing biomarkers and evaluating genetic markers for mutations, AI and machine learning can be used in disease detection. Below is the list of diseases that can be detected early with the help of AI and machine learning (Figure 8.5).

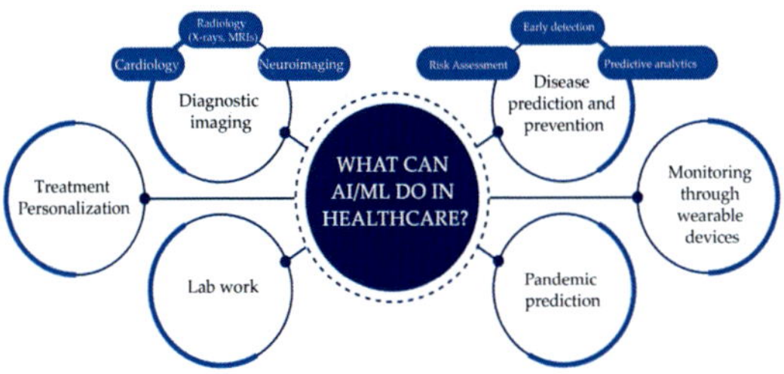


**Figure 8.5.** *List of diseases that can be detected early with the help of AI and machine learning.*

*Source: https://admin.binariks.com/storage/2023-09/bin-picture-080923-v03-main.webp.*

### 8.5.1. Cancer

The primary cause of death, according to the World Health Organization, is cancer. 10 million deaths worldwide are predicted to be related to it in 2020. Cancer is the second most common cause of death in the US. For cancer, early identification is crucial. ML helps AI analyze medical imaging data to aid in the early detection of cancers. For instance, the 5-year survival rate for malignant skin cancers, such as melanoma, is 32% for distant cancers and 99% for localized cancers. This illustrates how important early detection is for cancer patients.

AI-powered medical imaging analysis can also analyze blood to recommend the best treatment plan for a given patient. The disease detection algorithms for the various forms of cancer operate as follows.

- **Breast Cancer:** Algorithms can analyze mammogram images to detect tumors or abnormal patterns with 94% accuracy. Google's AI model for detecting breast cancer in mammograms showed a reduction of 5.7% in false positives and a reduction of 9.4% in false negatives compared to human radiologists.
- **Lung Cancer:** AI tools can examine CT scans to detect early-stage tumors. Like with breast cancer, the early stages of lung cancer were detected with 94 % accuracy.
- **Skin Cancer:** By analyzing skin images, disease detection algorithms can differentiate between benign moles and malignant melanomas. Datasets with hundreds of thousands of different images of skin lesions help detect signs of skin cancers early on.
- **Prostate Cancer:** MRI images and tissue biopsies can be analyzed to detect cancerous patterns.

### 8.5.2. Cardiovascular Diseases

Preventative health evaluations are very beneficial for cardiovascular diseases, which account for nearly 19 million deaths globally and are the leading cause of death. Machine learning can assist in the diagnosis of diseases by:

- Detecting arrhythmias from ECG data.
- Predicting heart failure based on patient health records and test results.
- Identifying atherosclerotic plaques in arterial images.
- Predicting the immediate and long-term risk of stroke and heart attacks with the help of wearable devices that monitor vital signs. For example, the prediction alert predicted the risk of stroke in 87, 6% of cases.

### 8.5.3. Neurological Diseases

Machine learning is used in medicine to diagnose neurological disorders such as Parkinson's and Alzheimer's. Even though they are incurable, early detection aids in timely planning and organization of high-quality care. For neurological diseases, the disease detection algorithm operates as follows:

- **Alzheimer's Disease:** ML can analyze brain imaging data to detect early signs of the disease. Currently, the technology is being adapted to demonstrate the early signs of decline before the symptoms become apparent.
- **Parkinson's Disease:** AI can analyze voice data, hand movements to detect early signs. The technologies to diagnose the disease before the symptoms become apparent are also relevant.

### 8.5.4. Diabetes

AI is transforming diabetes care, helping to improve outcomes and quality of life for people with diabetes. AI-based solutions can assist with monitoring blood sugar, adjusting insulin levels, predicting complications, and personalizing treatment plans. Here are some ways AI is advancing diabetes care:

*1.* *Continuous Glucose Monitoring (CGM) and Prediction*

- *Real-Time Monitoring*: AI algorithms analyze data from CGM devices, offering insights into blood glucose trends and alerting users about fluctuations.
- *Hypoglycemia and Hyperglycemia Prediction*: AI can predict dangerous blood sugar spikes or drops before they occur, providing real-time alerts to users and caregivers, which is especially valuable for people who experience unawareness of these shifts.
- *Automated Insulin Dosing*: Algorithms can adjust insulin doses in real time based on blood sugar levels, meals, and activity data.

*2.* *Personalized Diet and Activity Recommendations*

- *Smart Diet Tracking*: AI-powered diet apps can track food intake and give recommendations tailored to blood sugar patterns, helping patients make informed food choices.
- *Exercise and Lifestyle Insights*: AI can analyze activity data to give users insights on how exercise affects their glucose levels, providing personalized activity suggestions.

*3.* *Automated Insulin Delivery (AID) Systems*

- *Closed-Loop Systems*: AID systems, sometimes known as artificial pancreas systems, combine CGM and insulin pumps with AI algorithms that automatically adjust insulin delivery, making self-management easier and reducing risks of extreme highs and lows.

- *Learning Algorithms*: Some AID systems can "learn" from a user's daily patterns and adjust insulin delivery based on routine changes or life events.

4. *Early Detection and Prevention of Complications*

- *Retinopathy Screening*: AI can analyze retinal images for early signs of diabetic retinopathy, improving early detection rates.
- *Nephropathy and Neuropathy Prediction*: By analyzing health records and biomarkers, AI can help predict the risk of kidney damage or nerve damage, enabling preventive care.

5. *Behavioral Coaching and Mental Health Support*

- *Virtual Coaching*: AI-powered apps provide personalized coaching to support behavioral changes, from lifestyle habits to medication adherence.
- *Mental Health*: Diabetes can take an emotional toll, and AI tools can offer mental health resources and support, including AI-driven chatbots to offer encouragement and assistance in managing stress.

6. *Data Analytics and Population Health Management*

- *Personalized Treatment Plans*: AI models use health records to suggest treatment adjustments tailored to a patient's unique needs.
- *Public Health Insights*: At a population level, AI can identify trends and suggest interventions for groups at higher risk of diabetes complications, aiding in preventive healthcare efforts.

### 8.5.5. Eye Diseases

Disease detection driven by AI proved to be helpful for a number of eye conditions, including:

- **Glaucoma:** Analyzing eye scans for early detection.
- **Macular Degeneration:** Early signs can be detected in retinal images.

### 8.5.6. Infectious Diseases

Based on data from multiple sources, AI-based disease detection and machine learning for medical diagnosis have the potential to identify outbreaks and forecast the spread of diseases. Additionally, it is capable of predicting a virus's virulence or resistance patterns by analyzing its genetic sequence. AI disease detection algorithms, for instance, are helpful in the early detection of Covid-19.

### 8.5.7. Liver Diseases

It is possible to cure liver diseases if they are identified early. From MRI or ultrasound pictures, disease detection algorithms can identify fatty liver or fibrosis. They are also able to recognize possible outcomes and forecast the likelihood of developing severe liver disease.

### 8.5.8. Respiratory Diseases

Based on patterns in spirometry data or audio breathing analysis, AI and ML can be used in medical diagnosis to identify conditions like asthma or chronic obstructive pulmonary disease (COPD).

### 8.5.9. Bone and Joint Diseases

Using X-ray or MRI images, AI algorithms for disease detection can recognize the early indicators of osteoporosis or arthritis.

In addition to disease-specific detections, AI and ML can be employed for:

- **Genetic Disorder Predictions:** By analyzing genetic sequences to detect mutations that might lead to diseases.
- **Predicting Patient Deterioration:** Monitoring vital signs in real-time to detect and alert clinicians of potential adverse events in hospitalized patients.
- **Drug Interactions and Side Effects:** Predicting potential adverse drug reactions based on the patient's medical history and current medications.

### 8.5.10. AI/ML Algorithms for Disease Detection and Medical Diagnosis

The algorithms used in artificial intelligence and disease detection are different. Regarding their performance, each of these algorithms has particular advantages and disadvantages. For various data types and medical applications, different algorithms might be more appropriate. For optimal benefit, a combination of these algorithms is typically employed.

Let's look into some of the most popular disease-detection algorithms.

#### *8.5.10.1. Decision Tree*

A decision tree is a tree structure that resembles a flowchart, with each leaf node standing for an outcome, a branch for a decision rule, and an internal node for a feature. Applications include determining risk factors for conditions like diabetes or cardiovascular disorders and making a differential diagnosis based on the patient's symptoms and medical history. Finding co-occurrences is another excellent use for decision trees. Decision trees are simple to read and comprehend. Both numerical and categorical data are effectively handled by it. It is susceptible to overfitting, though, particularly for deep trees. Because of this, it might not be as accurate as other, more complex algorithms. Cardiovascular disorders, kidney disorders, and eye disorders are among the illnesses where decision trees show promise.

### *8.5.10.2. Support Vector Machine (SVM)*

SVM algorithms are applied to tasks involving regression and classification. They divide the dataset into classes by identifying the hyperplane that does so the best. SVMs are primarily used to categorize medical images in order to detect diseases like lung or breast cancer. In genetic testing and classification, they are also highly helpful for classifying protein sequences. SVMs are robust against outliers and efficient in high-dimensional spaces. Nevertheless, they are less interpretable than decision trees and necessitate careful kernel selection.

### *8.5.10.3. K-Nearest Neighbor (KNN)*

A new instance is classified using the majority class of its K closest models in the feature space by the instance-based KNN algorithm.

It categorizes patients with heart disease and forecasts disease outcomes based on symptom patterns. For regression analysis and classification, KNN is the most effective. KNN implementation is not too difficult. It is pricey and sensitive to superfluous or unnecessary features, though.

### *8.5.10.4. Logistic Regression*

Classification is done using logistic regression. It calculates the likelihood that a specific instance falls into a specific category. Based on a variety of metrics, this medical condition algorithm is used in the healthcare industry to diagnose diseases like diabetes and predict patient readmissions. Logistic regression yields not only classifications but also probabilities and is simple to use and understand. However, it is not appropriate for determining intricate connections among instances. It wouldn't be applied, for instance, to ascertain the risk of a disease.

### *8.5.10.5. Deep Learning*

Deep learning algorithms recognize complex patterns by employing multi-layered neural networks. They are employed in radiology to identify anomalies such as tumors and fractures through image recognition. Natural language processing for medical records is a completely different application of deep learning. Deep learning can automatically extract features and is very accurate at complex tasks. Nevertheless, it necessitates a significant amount of data and processing power.

#### *8.5.10.6. Convolutional Neural Network (CNN)*

A specific kind of neural network called a CNN is primarily used for image recognition. They are employed in the analysis of medical images, such as CT, MRI, and X-rays, for a variety of illnesses.

CNNS can automatically learn features and are very good at finding patterns in pictures. However, they are less interpretable and frequently regarded as a "black box," requiring sizable datasets for training. A healthcare professional finds it challenging to comprehend how the algorithm came to a specific conclusion.

Numerous studies in radiology, cardiology, and other medical specialties have shown the great promise and outstanding outcomes of disease detection powered by AI and ML today. The most important step in lowering mortality and improving outcomes for the majority of common diseases, such as diabetes, cancer, and cardiovascular disorders, is early, accurate diagnosis, which the AI/ ML disease detection system can provide. AI-powered disease detection will eventually cover more conditions and concentrate even more on individualized care. Given the advancements in the most prevalent diagnoses that contribute to global mortality, investing in ML and AI for disease detection is the best course of action for both healthcare organizations and individual patients.

## 8.6. AI IN PATIENT MANAGEMENT AND CARE

AI is quickly changing patient care and management by providing creative ways to enhance patient outcomes, lower medical expenses, and expedite clinical procedures. AI improves decision-making, enables individualized care, and supports ongoing patient monitoring through the use of machine learning algorithms, NLP, and data analytics. By making healthcare more patient-centered, predictive, and efficient, this technology has the potential to completely transform the industry.

### 8.6.1. Overview of AI in Patient Management

Coordinating care, monitoring patient progress, and making sure treatment plans are successfully adhered to are all part of patient management. This procedure has historically been time-consuming, requiring medical personnel to manually track patient information and plan treatment. But AI has become a potent tool that can automate a lot of this process, freeing up clinicians to work on more important projects while still guaranteeing that patients receive accurate and timely care.

In a number of crucial areas, such as virtual assistants, predictive analytics, remote monitoring, and individualized care, AI systems are being utilized to manage patients. Hospitals and clinics can lower errors, increase productivity, and provide a more seamless patient experience by incorporating AI into their healthcare systems.

### 8.6.2. AI in Remote Patient Monitoring

Remote patient monitoring (RPM) is one of the most significant applications of AI. Wearable technology and sensors with AI capabilities gather data on a patient's vital signs in real time, including blood pressure, heart rate, oxygen saturation, and glucose levels. These gadgets have the ability to continuously monitor patients, giving medical personnel up-to-date information on their condition.

In order to identify irregularities and anticipate possible health problems before they worsen, AI algorithms examine the data gathered from these devices. AI systems, for instance, can recognize early warning indicators of complications like hyperglycemia or heart failure in the treatment of chronic diseases like diabetes and heart disease. Early intervention is made possible, which lowers the need for hospital stays and enhances patient outcomes.

Additionally, patients can receive care from the convenience of their homes with AI-powered RPM systems, which eases the strain on medical facilities. Patients with chronic conditions who need regular monitoring but do not require frequent hospital visits will especially benefit from this. The value of remote monitoring was further highlighted during the COVID-19 pandemic, when AI systems reduced the risk of infection by reducing in-person visits while preserving high-quality care.

### 8.6.3. Predictive Analytics for Proactive Care

AI-powered predictive analytics is yet another game-changing instrument for patient care and management. In order to forecast the probability of specific health outcomes, predictive models employ machine learning algorithms to evaluate enormous volumes of patient data, such as genetics, medical histories, and environmental factors. Before symptoms appear or worsen, this proactive approach assists clinicians in identifying patients who are at risk and putting preventive measures in place.

AI models, for example, are able to forecast the chance of readmissions for patients suffering from long-term illnesses like asthma, COPD. AI can assist clinicians in customizing interventions to avoid expensive and potentially fatal hospital readmissions by evaluating patient histories, treatment plans, and social determinants of health. This degree of proactive care lowers healthcare costs and boosts the general effectiveness of healthcare systems in addition to improving patient outcomes.

AI-powered predictive analytics in oncology can assist in identifying patients who have a high chance of developing cancer again after treatment. AI can create individualized follow-up plans by evaluating clinical notes, imaging data, and molecular data. This enables oncologists to monitor and modify treatments according to each patient's unique risk profile.

Moreover, by examining trends in patient admissions, test results, and environmental data, AI can forecast disease outbreaks or the spread of infections within hospitals. This makes it possible for medical professionals to carry out early interventions to stop the spread of infectious diseases, like isolating patients or adding more staff.

### 8.6.4. AI-Powered Virtual Health Assistants

AI -driven virtual health assistants, or VHAs, are revolutionizing patient care by offering 24/7 assistance to patients and medical staff. These smart systems communicate with patients, respond to their inquiries, and help with activities like appointment scheduling, medication reminders, and symptom monitoring by utilizing NLP and machine learning.

VHAs are an important tool for patients to manage their health and adhere to their treatment plans. AI chatbots, for instance, can instantly respond to inquiries about prescription dosages, adverse effects, or health issues, negating the need for repeated phone conversations with medical professionals. To help patients adhere to their care plans and manage chronic diseases, VHAs can provide tailored reminders regarding medication adherence, exercise regimens, and dietary restrictions.

By automating repetitive processes like data entry, follow-up correspondence, and appointment scheduling, VHAs lessen the administrative load on healthcare providers. This gives clinicians more time to devote to providing direct patient care and making difficult decisions. By offering clinical decision support and making evidence-based recommendations for diagnosis and treatment options based on patient data, AI assistants can also help physicians.

Cognitive behavioral therapy (CBT) and other psychological interventions are being offered by AI-based virtual therapists in the field of mental health care. By talking with patients, evaluating their mental health, and providing therapeutic advice, these systems can increase access to mental health care, especially in underprivileged areas.

### 8.6.5. Personalized Patient Care

Artificial Intelligence has made personalized medicine a reality by analyzing large amounts of data and producing customized treatment plans. AI enables healthcare providers to customize treatments based on the individual characteristics of each patient, such as their genetics, lifestyle, and medical history, as opposed to the traditional practice of basing medical decisions on population averages.

For instance, AI is used in oncology to examine the genetic composition of tumors, allowing for the creation of customized cancer treatments. Oncologists can choose the best course of treatment, such as immunotherapies or targeted therapies, by using AI-driven systems to pinpoint the precise mutations causing a patient's cancer. This individualized approach lowers the risk of side effects while increasing the likelihood of successful treatment outcomes.

AI is also being used to help patients with chronic conditions like diabetes and hypertension have more individualized treatment regimens. AI can provide personalized lifestyle recommendations, medication adjustments, and dietary plans based on patient data analyzed from wearables, genetic profiles, and EHRs. Better long-term outcomes result from patient engagement and compliance being increased to this degree of personalization.

### 8.6.6. AI in Hospital Management Systems

AI is also having a big impact on how hospitals manage their facilities, how resources are allocated, and how patients are treated. In order to guarantee that patients receive timely and effective care, AI-powered systems can optimize staffing schedules, forecast patient demand, and streamline hospital workflows.

For example, AI can forecast future demand for hospital beds, operating rooms, or intensive care units (ICUs) by analyzing historical data on patient admissions, treatment durations, and seasonal trends. This makes it possible for hospital managers to more efficiently distribute resources, avoiding bottlenecks and guaranteeing that patients get the care they require on time.

Additionally, AI is being used to expedite the admission and discharge of patients, cutting down on wait times and enhancing the general patient experience. AI relieves hospital employees of administrative duties like data entry and billing, freeing them up to concentrate on patient care.

# 8.7. ETHICAL AND MEDICOLEGAL CONCERNS

## 8.7.1. Informed Consent

The relationship between a patient and a clinician is directly impacted by the use of AI in healthcare applications such as imaging, surgery, and diagnostics. Concerns remain regarding how AI is used conventionally to support patient interfaces and the circumstances in which informed consent is required. There ought to be rules governing the application of AI. Even clinicians find it challenging to comprehend the intricate black box testing algorithms used by some AI programs. They are therefore on the lookout for the application of AI in healthcare. Chatbots and health apps also make bioethicists think, particularly about user approval of informed consent. Because there is no in-person conversation as there is with traditional informed consent, informed content is typically disregarded when AI is used. The fact that chatbots are used to convey information to patients is a major worry regarding AI. It should be prohibited for professionals to provide certain medical declarations rather than allowing do-it-yourself applications. (Guan, 2019; Amann, 2020; Kourou et al., 2021).

## 8.7.2. Safety and Transparency

Prejudice should not exist in the healthcare industry, which prioritizes safety. AI is primarily used in the maintenance and evaluation of patient medical records, which results in the exploration of treatment options for the patients. Unsafe and inappropriate treatment recommendations result from algorithms that are imprecise or poorly trained. How to guarantee AI maintains the validity, dependability, and transparency of datasets is the ethical dilemma here. To guarantee dependable performance and legitimate results, these AI algorithms must be trained using high-quality data. To reduce cybersecurity risks, data sharing after analysis should be kept private. The kinds of data used and their limitations are declared through transparency. Transparency in this context is challenging because the majority of medical AI uses black box testing. (Guan, 2019; Amann, 2020; Kourou et al., 2021).

## 8.7.3. Algorithmic Fairness and Biases

By guaranteeing the globalization of healthcare, AI can improve overall standards of care. The coherence and authenticity of the algorithm are determined by the caliber of the trained data. Therefore, in addition to bias peculiarities like disabilities, AI creates the risk of bias imparting discrimination based on gender or skin coloration. Because of the complex and opaque algorithm, it is difficult to determine whether algorithms are biased. It gets trickier when black-box testing is applied. Despite all of these problems, AI in healthcare needs to be evaluated equally for positive results across all demographic groups. (Guan, 2019; Amann, 2020; Kourou et al., 2021).

### 8.7.4. Data Privacy

Patient health information should be kept private. The ethical issue with it is that governments and healthcare organizations may abuse it for their own gain and financial gain, frequently at the expense of the patient. AI trainers occasionally reach agreements with other partners to use patient data for algorithm testing and training. The type of data being used and the extent of privacy invasion are the other significant issues. (Guan, 2019; Amann, 2020; Kourou et al., 2021).

### 8.7.5. Medicolegal Issues

Who is responsible for harm caused to patients by the use of AI? Laws and regulations have not kept up with advances in technology and medical applications. Cohen and Price (2019). For the sake of the patients,' healthcare providers,' and the system's overall safety, artificial intelligence in healthcare must thus be taken into account within the pertinent legal framework.

## 8.8. FUTURE TRENDS OF AI IN HEALTHCARE

AI has the potential to revolutionize healthcare in ways that were previously unthinkable. AI technologies are already having an impact in fields like diagnostics and personalized medicine, but more ground-breaking developments are anticipated in the future. AI will revolutionize the way diseases are identified, treated, and managed in the healthcare industry, leading to more effective and individualized patient care. Here, we examine the probable advancements, prospects, and difficulties that could mold the healthcare sector in the upcoming years as we examine the future trends of AI.

### 8.8.1. AI and Precision Medicine

The development of precision medicine is one of the most exciting future trends in AI-powered healthcare. This method entails adjusting medical care to each patient's unique attributes, including their genetic composition, lifestyle, and surroundings. By evaluating enormous volumes of genomic, proteomic, and clinical data to find patterns and correlations that are invisible to human analysis, AI will be instrumental in advancing precision medicine.

The growing availability of genetic data combined with advancements in AI algorithms will allow medical professionals to provide extremely individualized treatment regimens. AI can assist in forecasting a patient's response to a given treatment, enabling more focused and efficient interventions. AI systems, for instance, are able to examine the genetic mutations present in cancer patients in order to suggest tailored treatments, like immunotherapies or targeted therapies, that are most likely to be effective given the patient's particular profile.

AI-driven precision medicine has the potential to improve patient outcomes and decrease adverse drug reactions by reducing the need for trial-and-error medical treatment as it becomes more widely used. The way medical professionals treat patients will continue to change as a result of AI's capacity to handle complicated datasets, enabling truly individualized care.

### 8.8.2. AI in Drug Discovery and Development

Traditionally, the process of finding and developing new drugs is drawn out, costly, and uncertain. However, by speeding up and cutting costs, AI is drastically altering this scene. In AI-driven drug discovery, biological data is analyzed, molecular behavior is predicted, and possible drug candidates are identified more quickly and effectively than with conventional techniques. This is accomplished by applying machine learning algorithms.

AI is probably going to become even more important in the future as it comes to transforming pharmaceutical research. Researchers can find potential drug candidates in a fraction of the time it takes with traditional laboratory methods thanks to AI models, which can simulate millions of chemical compounds and predict how they interact with human proteins. This will expedite the creation of novel medications and create opportunities for the discovery of cures for illnesses that were previously thought to be incurable.

AI-powered platforms will also make it easier to conduct virtual clinical trials, which simulate clinical trials using patient data from wearable technology and EHRs. By examining a variety of patient populations, this could lessen the need for expensive, conventional large-scale trials and improve the effectiveness and inclusivity of the drug development process.

### 8.8.3. AI in Healthcare Robotics

With AI's assistance, robotic systems in the medical field should advance dramatically, allowing for more accurate surgeries, the automation of tedious tasks, and better patient outcomes. Surgeons can already perform minimally invasive procedures with greater precision and less risk of complications, as well as faster recovery times, thanks to AI-powered surgical robots. AI will continue to progress robotic surgery in the future, allowing completely autonomous robotic systems that can carry out difficult operations without the need for human assistance. AI-driven robots will become more prevalent in patient care beyond surgery. Medication administration, vital sign monitoring, and daily activity assistance for elderly or disabled patients could be performed by robots. For instance, AI-enabled robots in assisted living facilities are able to keep an eye on residents' health and notify personnel of any emergencies. By automating repetitive tasks, these robots may also help alleviate the scarcity of healthcare workers by freeing up human caregivers to concentrate on more crucial aspects of patient care.

AI-driven prosthetics and exoskeletons are anticipated to develop into more intelligent and adaptable tools for rehabilitation, assisting patients in regaining their range of motion following neurological disorders or injuries. These gadgets can be tailored to the individual requirements of the patient and offer immediate feedback to enhance the healing process.

### 8.8.4. AI in Mental Health Care

The use of AI in mental health care is a developing field that has the potential to completely change the way that psychological disorders are identified, treated, and handled. AI-powered platforms are able to analyze speech, text, and behavioral patterns to identify indicators of mental health disorders like depression, anxiety, and schizophrenia. This is made possible by advances in NLP and machine learning.

In the future, voice assistants, smartphones, and wearables could all be used by AI systems to continuously monitor patients' mental health. These devices will have the capacity to identify early indicators of mental health decline and notify caregivers or medical professionals. Furthermore, chatbots and virtual therapists powered by AI are being developed to offer cognitive behavioral therapy (CBT) and other mental health interventions. This will increase accessibility to mental health care, particularly in underserved areas.

AI has the potential to help remove obstacles to mental health treatment by offering anonymous, on-demand support to people who are reluctant to seek care in conventional settings. AI can supplement human therapists, giving patients additional avenues for support, even though it won't replace them.

### 8.8.5. AI and the Internet of Medical Things (IoMT)

The future of healthcare will also be shaped by the convergence of AI and the Internet of Medical Things (IoMT), which is another significant trend. The IoMT is a network of interconnected sensors and medical devices that gather and share health data. AI combined with this data allows for real-time analysis, predictive care, and ongoing patient monitoring.

For example, wearable technology—such as fitness trackers or smartwatches—can provide data to AI algorithms that can be used to identify early indicators of conditions like irregular heartbeats, sleep apnea, or respiratory disorders. AI-powered IoMT devices will advance to even greater levels in the future, able to identify a greater variety of illnesses and anticipate possible health hazards before symptoms manifest. IoMT devices that are integrated with AI systems in hospitals will improve patient care by facilitating automated medication administration, real-time vital sign monitoring, and patient deterioration prediction. To lower the risk of bedsores, smart hospital beds with sensors can track patient movement and pressure points. AI systems will also be able to forecast patient outcomes, like recovery times or the possibility of complications, by analyzing data from IoMT devices.

## 8.8.6. AI in Healthcare Data Integration and Interoperability

Data integration and interoperability will be essential for ensuring that AI technologies are effectively used throughout the healthcare ecosystem as the volume of healthcare data continues to grow exponentially. At the moment, healthcare data is frequently fragmented among various organizations and systems, which makes it challenging for AI models to access and evaluate the entirety of patient data.

AI will be essential in the future for combining various data sources, including imaging, genomic data, EHRs, and patient-reported outcomes. Artificial Intelligence has the potential to facilitate more thorough analysis and provide physicians with timely, actionable insights by fostering a more cohesive and interoperable healthcare data ecosystem.

Additionally necessary to the success of population health management will be interoperability. AI-powered systems will be able to identify populations that are at-risk and suggest focused interventions by analyzing data from multiple sources, such as social determinants of health and public health records. This will make it possible for medical professionals to provide population-level preventive care, which will lessen the burden of chronic illnesses and enhance general public health outcomes.

## 8.8.7. AI and Quantum Computing in Healthcare

The combination of AI and quantum computing, though still in its infancy, has the potential to completely transform healthcare. With quantum computing's capacity to process massive volumes of data at previously unheard-of speeds, AI may be better able to find drugs, analyze genetic data, and solve challenging medical problems.

AI-powered quantum computers, for instance, might be able to simulate biological systems at the molecular level, enabling researchers to create new medications and treatments more quickly than in the past. Because quantum computing makes it possible for AI to analyze massive amounts of genomic and proteomic data more effectively, it may also hasten the development of personalized medicine.

As quantum computing technology advances, it may open up new avenues for AI applications in healthcare, facilitating advancements in fields that are presently inaccessible to classical computing.

## REFERENCES


1. Abdallah, S., Sharifa, M., Almadhoun, M. K. I. K., Khawar Sr, M. M., Shaikh, U., Balabel, K. M., & Ekomwereren, O. (2023). The impact of artificial intelligence on optimizing diagnosis and treatment plans for rare genetic disorders. *Cureus, 15*(10).
2. Abidi, M. H., Rehman, A. U., Mian, S. H., Alkhalefah, H., & Usmani, Y. S. (2024). The role of AI in elevating hospital service quality: Framework, development, and applications. In *Modern Healthcare Marketing in the Digital Era* (pp. 211–224). IGI Global.
3. Ahmadi, A. (2024). Digital health transformation: Leveraging AI for monitoring and disease management.
4. Alrefaei, A. F., Hawsawi, Y. M., Almaleki, D., Alafif, T., Alzahrani, F. A., & Bakhrebah, M. A. (2022). Genetic data sharing and artificial intelligence in the era of personalized medicine based on a cross - sectional analysis of the Saudi Human Genome Program. *Scientific Reports, 12*(1), 1405.
5. Alshamrani, M. (2022). IoT and artificial intelligence implementations for remote healthcare monitoring systems: A survey. *Journal of King Saud University–Computer and Information Sciences, 34*(8), 4687–4701.
6. Alsheibani, S., Cheung, Y., & Messom, C. (2018). Artificial intelligence adoption: AI readiness at firm level. In M. Tanabu & D. Senoo (Eds.), *Proceedings of PACIS2018: Pacific Asia Conference in Information Systems (PACIS)*. Association for Information Systems. https://aisel.aisnet.org/pacis2018/37/ (accessed on 1 November 2024).
7. Amann, J., Blasimme, A., Vayena, E., Frey, D., & Madai, V. I. (2020). Explainability for artificial intelligence in healthcare: A multidisciplinary perspective. *BMC Medical Informatics and Decision Making, 20*(1). https://doi.org/10.1186/s12911-020-01332-6.
8. Arnold, M. H. (2021). Teasing out artificial intelligence in medicine: An ethical critique of artificial intelligence and machine learning in medicine. *Journal of Bioethical Inquiry, 18*(1), 121–139. https://doi.org/10.1007/s11673-020-10080-1.
9. Bradford, L., Aboy, M., & Liddell, K. (2020). International transfers of health data between the EU and USA: A sector-specific approach for the USA to ensure an 'adequate' level of protection. *Journal of Law and the Biosciences, 7*(1), lsaa055.
10. Davenport, T., & Kalakota, R. (2019). The potential for artificial intelligence in healthcare. *Future Healthcare Journal, 6*(2), 94–98. https://doi.org/10.7861/futurehosp.6-2-94.

11. Dwivedi, Y. K., Hughes, L., Ismagilova, E., Aarts, G., Coombs, C., Crick, T., & Eirug, A. (2021). Artificial intelligence (AI): Multidisciplinary perspectives on emerging challenges, opportunities, and agenda for research, practice, and policy. *International Journal of Information Management, 57,* 101994.
12. Farid, F., Bello, A., Ahamed, F., & Hossain, F. (2023). The roles of AI technologies in reducing hospital readmission for chronic diseases: A comprehensive analysis.
13. Guan, (2019). Artificial intelligence in healthcare and medicine: Promises, ethical challenges, and governance. *Chinese Medical Sciences Journal, 0*(0), 99. https://doi.org/10.24920/003611.
14. Gupta, R., Srivastava, D., Sahu, M., Tiwari, S., Ambasta, R. K., & Kumar, P. (2021). Artificial intelligence to deep learning: Machine intelligence approach for drug discovery. *Molecular Diversity, 25,* 1315–1360.
15. Khanna, D. (2020). Use of artificial intelligence in healthcare and medicine. https://doi.org/10.31221/osf.io/eshm9.
16. Kiener, M. (2020). Artificial intelligence in medicine and the disclosure of risks. *AI & Society, 36*(3), 705–713. https://doi.org/10.1007/s00146-020-01085-w.
17. Kourou, K., Exarchos, K. P., Papaloukas, C., Sakaloglou, P., Exarchos, T., & Fotiadis, D. I. (2021). Applied machine learning in cancer research: A systematic review for patient diagnosis, classification, and prognosis. *Computational and Structural Biotechnology Journal, 19,* 5546–5555. https://doi.org/10.1016/j.csbj.2021.10.006.
18. Krones, F. H., & Walker, B. (2023). From theoretical models to practical deployment: A perspective and case study of opportunities and challenges in AI-driven healthcare research for low-income settings. *MedRxiv,* 2023.2012.2026.23300539.
19. Lee, D., & Yoon, S. N. (2021). Application of artificial intelligence-based technologies in the healthcare industry: Opportunities and challenges. *International Journal of Environmental Research and Public Health, 18*(1), 271.
20. Leone, D., Schiavone, F., Appio, F. P., & Chiao, B. (2021). How does artificial intelligence enable and enhance value co-creation in industrial markets? An exploratory case study in the healthcare ecosystem. *Journal of Business Research, 129,* 849–859.
21. McLennan, S., Fiske, A., Tigard, D., Müller, R., Haddadin, S., & Buyx, A. (2022). Embedded ethics: A proposal for integrating ethics into the development of medical AI. *BMC Medical Ethics, 23*(1), 6.

22. Naik, N., Hameed, B., Shetty, D. K., Swain, D., Shah, M., Paul, R., & Smriti, K. (2022). Legal and ethical considerations in artificial intelligence in healthcare: Who takes responsibility? *Frontiers in Surgery, 9,* 266.
23. Patil, S., & Shankar, H. (2023). Transforming healthcare: Harnessing the power of AI in the modern era. *International Journal of Multidisciplinary Sciences and Arts, 2*(1), 60–70.
24. Paul, D., Sanap, G., Shenoy, S., Kalyane, D., Kalia, K., & Tekade, R. K. (2021). Artificial intelligence in drug discovery and development. *Drug Discovery Today, 26*(1), 80.
25. Păvăloaia, V. D., & Necula, S. C. (2023). Artificial intelligence as a disruptive technology—A systematic literature review. *Electronics, 12*(5), 1102.
26. Price, W. N., & Cohen, I. G. (2019). Privacy in the age of medical big data. *Nature Medicine, 25*(1), 37–43. https://doi.org/10.1038/s41591-018-0272-7.
27. Reddy, S., Fox, J., & Purohit, M. P. (2018). Artificial intelligence-enabled healthcare delivery. *Journal of the Royal Society of Medicine, 112*(1), 22–28. https://doi.org/10.1177/0141076818815510.
28. Schwalbe, N., & Wahl, B. (2020). Artificial intelligence and the future of global health. *The Lancet, 395*(10236), 1579–1586.
29. Shaik, T., Tao, X., Higgins, N., Li, L., Gururajan, R., Zhou, X., & Acharya, U. R. (2023). Remote patient monitoring using artificial intelligence: Current state, applications, and challenges. *Wiley Interdisciplinary Reviews: Data Mining and Knowledge Discovery, 13*(2), e1485.
30. Shuaib, M., Alam, S., Alam, M. S., & Nasir, M. S. (2021). Compliance with HIPAA and GDPR in blockchain-based electronic health records. *Materials Today: Proceedings.*
31. Taj, I., & Zaman, N. (2022). Towards industrial revolution 5.0 and explainable artificial intelligence: Challenges and opportunities. *International Journal of Computing and Digital Systems, 12*(1), 295–320.
32. Vatansever, S., Schlessinger, A., Wacker, D., Kaniskan, H. Ü., Jin, J., Zhou, M. M., & Zhang, B. (2021). Artificial intelligence and machine learning - aided drug discovery in central nervous system diseases: State - of - the - arts and future directions. *Medicinal Research Reviews, 41*(3), 1427–1473.
33. Wang, B., Asan, O., & Zhang, Y. (2024). Shaping the future of chronic disease management: Insights into patient needs for AI-based homecare systems. *International Journal of Medical Informatics, 181,* 105301.

34. Wang, Q., Su, M., Zhang, M., & Li, R. (2021). Integrating digital technologies and public health to fight the Covid-19 pandemic: Key technologies, applications, challenges, and outlook of digital healthcare. *International Journal of Environmental Research and Public Health, 18*(11), 6053.

35. Zeng, D., Cao, Z., & Neill, D. B. (2021). Artificial intelligence–enabled public health surveillance: From local detection to global epidemic monitoring and control. In *Artificial Intelligence in Medicine* (pp. 437–453). Elsevier.

CHAPTER 9

# AI AND CYBERSECURITY

## Contents

## INTRODUCTION

Companies need to use cutting-edge technologies to keep ahead of malicious actors as cyberattacks get more complex. Presenting artificial intelligence (AI), a potent instrument that has revolutionized how businesses identify, control, and react to online threats. Cybersecurity teams can make quicker, more accurate decisions by automating time-consuming procedures and gaining important insights by integrating AI.

The 21st century is seeing a growing trend toward AI in a variety of application domains due to technology breakthroughs and the spread of automation systems. The potential of AI-centric implementations is highlighted by elements like the sharp increase in computing power, the pervasive integration of smart devices, and the quick evolution of businesses through datafication. But as we move through this age of AI-driven advancements, worries about the safety and well-being of human society also grow. Taking into account the variety of AI-related applications, this chapter focuses only on the growth, opportunity, and susceptibility of AI in the field of cyber security. Around the world, different organizations and standards have different definitions and purposes for cyber security. Cybersecurity is the process of protecting internet-connected systems, including hardware, software, and data, from cyberattacks, damage, or unauthorized access, according to ISO/IEC 27032:2023(en) Cybersecurity—Guidelines for Internet security. It includes a variety of procedures, tools, and safeguards intended to keep networks, computers, and information safe from online dangers. In this situation, safeguarding entails minimizing cyberthreats and preserving as many assets as you can. The goal of incorporating cybersecurity is not just to secure the perimeters but also to prioritize actions to build a defense-in-depth framework that guarantees service continuity, as well as to identify the value of the assets that are under threat and localize the threat.

Cyberattacks have been aimed at transport infrastructure systems, nuclear power plants, petrochemical facilities, and water supply in an effort to cause power outages and compromise private information. The combination of physical devices, networked software, and sensors, along with the growing threats, has made the technical system more complex as a result of the convergence of IT and OT. IEC advises using integrated strategies incorporating people, processes, and technologies like AI to build cyber resilience from such complexity and vulnerability. However, when combined with cyber security, AI-driven technologies have both advantages and disadvantages. AI supports cyber resilience in part, but it also supports infiltration in another way. Although there is a wide range of research being done on AI-based applications, security is a much bigger concern than safety precautions. The cyber defense survey revealed expectations about the use of AI to automate the system's analysis of the massive volume of data and carry out crucial inspections to spot cyber threats. Ten years after the study's recommendation that neural network models improve cyber resilience in military applications, researchers are still examining the advantages and disadvantages of applying automated AI.

## 9.1. AI IN CYBERSECURITY

Artificial intelligence (AI) in cybersecurity incorporates AI tools like neural networks and machine learning into security frameworks. With the help of these technologies, cybersecurity systems can now analyze enormous volumes of data, spot trends, and adjust to new and changing threats with little assistance from humans.

AI -driven systems learn from experience, which enables them to anticipate, detect, and respond to known and unknown threats more effectively than traditional cybersecurity tools, which rely on predefined rules to detect threats. AI enables businesses to improve their cybersecurity posture and lower the risk of breaches by doing this.

AI in cybersecurity refers to tools that can comprehend, learn from, and respond to data. There are three major phases in the evolution of AI:

- **Assisted Intelligence:** Enhances what people and organizations already do today.
- **Augmented Intelligence:** Enables new capabilities, allowing people to perform tasks they couldn't do before.
- **Autonomous Intelligence:** Future technology where machines will act independently, like self-driving cars.

### 9.1.1. Why Is AI in Cybersecurity Important?

It is impossible to exaggerate the significance of AI in cybersecurity. Conventional security systems require assistance to keep up with the increasingly sophisticated tactics used by cybercriminals. Modern networks generate enormous amounts of data, which makes it more difficult to identify threats and exposes many organizations to attack.

AI offers a solution to these challenges by:

- **Enhancing the Speed and Accuracy of Threat Detection:** AI can swiftly sort through enormous volumes of data to find irregularities and possible dangers, cutting down on the amount of time it takes to react to threats.

- **Automating Routine Tasks:** By automating time-consuming procedures like log analysis and vulnerability scanning, AI frees up security teams to concentrate on more strategic endeavors.
- **Predicting Future Attacks:** AI helps businesses stay one step ahead of cybercriminals by spotting trends in previous attacks and foreseeing emerging threats.

## 9.1.2. How Is AI Used in Cybersecurity?

AI has many uses in cybersecurity, ranging from threat detection to response automation. Three of the most popular applications of AI are listed below.

### *9.1.2.1. Threat Detection*

AI is particularly good at spotting dangers that humans would otherwise miss. Conventional security tools might miss irregularities or have trouble identifying zero-day threats. AI-powered systems, on the other hand, identify anomalous activity that might point to an attack by using pattern recognition and anomaly detection. AI-powered solutions can also automatically identify possible weak points by continuously scanning networks and systems for vulnerabilities.

### *9.1.2.2. Threat Management*

AI plays a critical role in automating the threat detection and management process. Organizations can prioritize addressing critical issues first and streamline patch management by using AI to rank vulnerabilities according to their potential impact. This entails ranking threats according to risk assessments and choosing the best course of action. AI can assist in real-time response coordination, reducing attack damage.

### *9.1.2.3. Threat Response*

AI can automate a lot of threat response tasks in addition to identifying and controlling threats. This entails performing tasks like creating incident reports, isolating impacted systems, and blocking malicious traffic. AI is a useful tool for reacting to new threats as they materialize because of its capacity for adaptation and evolution.

## 9.1.3. Top Benefits of AI in Cybersecurity

1. **Improved Threat Intelligence:** Through real-time analysis of massive datasets and the provision of predictive insights, AI improves threat intelligence. Because of this capability, cybersecurity teams

are able to foresee attacks before they happen and take preventative action.

2. **Faster Incident Response Times:** During a cyberattack, speed is essential, and AI improves incident response by automating threat detection, analysis, and mitigation. As a result, possible breach impacts are decreased and the time between detection and action is shortened. AI-powered solutions facilitate quick incident response, improve context for security alert prioritization, and pinpoint the underlying causes of vulnerabilities to minimize problems in the future.

3. **Better Vulnerability Management:** The capacity of AI to detect weaknesses in systems and networks is yet another important benefit. By prioritizing risks according to reachability, exploitability, and business criticality, AI-powered vulnerability scanners assist organizations in addressing the most urgent problems first. This lowers false positives and guarantees the effectiveness of security teams.

4. **More Accurate Breach Risk Predictions:** AI-based systems can forecast how and where you are most likely to be breached, taking into account threat exposure, security controls effectiveness, and IT asset inventory. This allows you to allocate resources and tools to areas of vulnerability. Prescriptive insights from AI analysis can assist you in setting up and improving procedures and controls to maximize the cyber resilience of your company.

5. **Automated Recommendations:** The explainability of analysis and recommendations is another essential component of using AI to support human infosec teams. Gaining support from stakeholders throughout the company, comprehending the effects of different infosec initiatives, and providing pertinent data to all parties involved—end users, security operations, CISO, auditors, CIO, CEO, and board of directors—are all made possible by doing this.

## 9.2. KEY AI TECHNOLOGIES IN CYBERSECURITY

1. **Machine Learning (ML):** A type of artificial intelligence called machine learning (ML) allows systems to learn from data and get better without the need for explicit programming. User and Entity Behavior Analytics (UEBA), which examines patterns and behaviors to identify threats, is a common use of machine learning in cybersecurity. By detecting irregularities in user behavior, such as

odd login times or locations, UEBA, for instance, can flag unusual login activity. This allows for quicker responses and may indicate a security breach. ML is particularly good at detecting abnormalities in network traffic and thwarting attacks by spotting strange activity before it gets out of control.

2. **Deep Learning:** A subset of machine learning called deep learning analyzes complex data using neural networks and is very good at spotting sophisticated cybersecurity risks like changing malware strains. Deep learning is used in cybersecurity to identify polymorphic malware, which is malware that continuously modifies its code to avoid detection by conventional techniques. Even when the code is different, deep learning models can identify underlying patterns in malware behavior by analyzing large amounts of data. Deep learning, for instance, can spot irregularities in the way files interact with a system, indicating malicious intent even in cases where the malware has never been seen before. Deep learning is crucial for staying ahead of sophisticated cyberattacks because of its capacity to learn from subtle behavioral patterns, which greatly enhances detection and response times to threats that were previously invisible.

3. **Neural Networks:** AI models called neural networks are modeled after the architecture of the human brain. They use weighted inputs for data processing by nodes. Every node assesses its input and modifies weights to increase precision. The total of these assessments serves as the basis for the outcome. Neural networks are a potent tool for threat detection in cybersecurity because they can analyze large volumes of data, like firewall logs, to find trends and anticipate possible threats.

4. **Large Language Models (LLMs):** GPT-4 and other large language models (LLMs) are important AI tools in cybersecurity. LLMs are very helpful for automating threat analysis and enhancing security responses because they specialize in processing and comprehending human language. In order to find possible threats and patterns that might indicate an attack, these models are able to sort through enormous volumes of text data, including threat reports, logs, and documentation. Additionally, LLMs assist with tasks like automating responses to security incidents, creating threat reports that are readable by humans, and detecting phishing. They can improve cybersecurity tools by comprehending language context, which will allow for quicker and more precise decision-making.

## 9.3. LATEST DEVELOPMENTS IN AI FOR CYBERSECURITY

1. **AI-Powered Remediation:** AI-powered remediation, which automates the real-time response to security incidents, is one of the most exciting developments as AI continues to advance. Manual investigation, decision-making, and intervention are common components of traditional incident response procedures, which cause delays that allow attackers more time to take advantage of weaknesses. By isolating compromised systems, preventing malicious traffic, or even restoring compromised systems to a secure state, AI-powered remediation, on the other hand, can respond to threats instantly.
2. **Generative AI for Enhanced Threat Intelligence:** More sophisticated threat intelligence tools are also produced by generative AI, which makes it possible to analyze new threats in real time and automatically produce security insights.
3. **AI-Powered Security Automation:** The efficiency of cybersecurity teams is being further increased by using AI to automate complicated security procedures like vendor questionnaires and incident response workflows.
4. **Advanced Threat Deception Tactics:** AI can now build dynamic environments that are intended to deceive and trap cybercriminals, giving organizations useful intelligence while eliminating threats thanks to advancements in threat deception.

## 9.4. OPPORTUNITIES AND ADVANCEMENTS

The broad use of AI methods in a variety of applications has enormous promise for solving a wide range of environmental and socioeconomic problems. However, it is crucial to give research efforts focused on securing these technologies top priority in order to fully realize this potential. Adversarial machine learning is one of the crucial fields attracting a lot of research interest. Since this field is essential to the dependable spread of revolutionary AI technologies, it requires constant and committed attention. The creation of reliable algorithms becomes increasingly crucial as AI continues to be incorporated into many aspects of human endeavors and daily life. In order to promote a future marked by innovation, safety, and security, these strong algorithms are not only desirable but also vital. Therefore, fostering developments in adversarial machine learning will strengthen the basis of AI, allowing its responsible and secure application to address urgent global issues while protecting people and organizations from possible threats. AI's contributions to threat detection, response, and prevention have significantly improved cybersecurity applications. Large datasets are analyzed using machine learning and deep learning algorithms, which help find patterns and anomalies for prompt threat detection. Additionally, AI-enabled systems enhance the automation sector's standard security tasks, giving cybersecurity operators the chance to focus their skills on more complex problems. AI-powered authentication techniques like biometrics and behavioral analysis are also used to implement strong security measures that successfully prevent unwanted access (Katina et al., 2022; Andrew et al., 2020).

Furthermore, AI demonstrates the ability to rigorously adjust to the constantly changing threat landscape, guaranteeing proactive measures in cybersecurity defense method improvisation, collectively strengthening cybersecurity protocols, and protecting vital data and infrastructure in the context of our increasingly interconnected digital world. Furthermore, because AI enables organizations to perform predictive analysis, which successfully identifies vulnerabilities and potential attack vectors, its impact on cybersecurity goes far beyond its conventional role in threat detection. Organizations can prevent security flaws by taking this proactive approach. AI-driven technologies also improve incident response, allowing businesses to quickly lessen the effects of cyberattacks. AI is not just useful for threat detection; it is also essential for analyzing user behavior, which makes it easier to spot insider threats and illegal activity in company networks. The ability to process vast amounts of data and produce insights that can be put to use has brought about a revolution in cybersecurity. This technical development improves flexibility and competence in protecting against ever-more-advanced cyberthreats. In today's linked digital world, artificial intelligence's function in protecting digital assets and guaranteeing privacy will only grow more important as it develops. The most popular solutions for addressing cybersecurity issues in practically every application domain are host-based and network-based intrusion detection systems. The contributions of different AI techniques to improving cybersecurity measures are categorized in the following sections, which also include information on how they were developed.

### 9.4.1. Anomaly Detection

Different statistical models are used to identify and mitigate deviation from normal behavior, which is defined by the particular organizations and resiliency requirements. These models' ability to recognize patterns in attack vectors aids security staff in making prompt, effective decisions. To understand the actual nature of the threat and handle the proactive analysis, the model is frequently combined with other techniques. For anomaly detection, a hybrid model incorporating a Gaussian mixture and decision tree model for network misuse detection was suggested. The model considers the discrepancies in the logs or dataset that may cause the detection mechanism to be misguided or, worse, to have high false rates. The conditional statement-based rules that distinguish the abnormal pattern from the typical ones are made easier by the decision tree.

The decision to isolate the pre-defined attack patterns and select the typical pattern is ultimately made using the best attributes from the decision tree model. Gaussian Mixture Models (GMM) are used to model each normal leaf in the decision tree. According to this method, observations come from a variety of Gaussian distributions, each of whose parameters are unknown. The Expectation Maximization (EM) algorithm is used to estimate these parameters. This technique is particularly effective at spotting attacks that resemble patterns of normal distribution. In order to better understand and analyze the normal pattern and spot attack patterns, the hybrid model divides the data's normal pattern into several subsets. The Advanced Metering Infrastructure (AMI) may become vulnerable as a result of the integration of IoT devices into smart grid systems. By eliminating the need for outside expertise and a preset threshold, the GMM-based detection mechanism can strengthen the system in situations where conventional techniques for protecting the AMI fall short (Xinyu et al., 2016). Malicious event detection is improved by GMM's ability to cluster historical data to define various ranges of typical patterns, independent of outside inputs and resilient to data fluctuations. GMM is much more resilient to frequent data fluctuations in detecting anomalous data than Hidden Markov Models (HMM) since it does not require specific training data or predefined knowledge (Chia-Mei et al., 2016).

A smart city with many ICT devices, cloud-connected data storage systems, and IoT communications can be developed by embedding AI-integrated models at different system levels to improve anomaly detection. The need for AI-based machine learning models to secure edge-to-cloud networks in smart cities is reflected in a hybrid model with a centralized to distributed architecture. The architecture uses cloud-based services and a facilitated ML-integrated SDN network to counteract attacks on distributed computing devices. SDN, multiple controllers, and machine learning techniques working together at the edge networks improve security against malicious or unusual data and detect compromised system resources. Expert system collaboration frequently improves detector performance by providing feedback from operators and system analysts on detection results and accuracy, allowing the AI model to learn from the human in the loop system. With the ExS for distributed systems, an ensemble tree-based method using an Isolation Forest anomaly detector was suggested. By decreasing false positives and improving accurate attack pattern identification, the model leverages expert feedback to improve comprehension of the attack patterns and the detection procedure. External data flow: AI-integrated models, such as Isolation Forest and GMM, are effective in identifying DDoS and Cache Pollution Attack (CPA) attacks in content delivery networks (Li et al., 2021). Although ML and statistical techniques combined with expert systems are widely used in cybersecurity, many anomaly tool detection and attack prevention techniques also use NN-based LSTM models.

### 9.4.2. Signature-based Detection

The use of signatures as an attribute for the detection mechanism is widely used in the literature to identify more prominent features in the data pattern with time-dependency and time-urgency. Signature-based models, which are separated into two mechanisms, use either a ruleset to protect the network from unidentified or unknown activity or patterns to separate instances of abnormal behavior from regular traffic. The predetermined set of rules in rule-based models determines how attacks and typical patterns in data are filtered; the most widely used tools for this purpose are Snort, Suricata, Zeek, and others. A fuzzy rule-based model for hazard identification in cross-country product pipeline systems is one of several rule-based techniques that have been developed in addition to these open-source IDS tools. In a complex and uncertain environment, such as a pipeline system with limited data, the model applies more nuanced and flexible risk analysis by addressing imprecise, uncertain, or subjective information using a Fuzzy Rule Base (FRB) approach with Grey Relations Theory (GRT). During pandemics, there has been a noticeable increase in ransomware, phishing, and business email exploitation.

The impact of possible threats and adversaries is reduced through the use of data mining techniques and rule-based fuzzy logic. The ability to identify even the smallest departure from appropriately addressing the pattern type is difficult, but it has been accomplished with various models, such as Absolute Median Deviation (AMD), for a more sophisticated detection and prevention process. Pattern-matching methods measure the deviation from normal and historical data. To make informed decisions on the unknown data in real time, a pattern recognition mechanism processes logs of various event categories, known attack patterns, and benign occurrences found in historical data. As explained in the creation of the Digital Forensics Face Pattern Recognition Using PCA, NN, and GA Integrated Model, pattern-matching techniques are also combined with a number of other approaches to incorporate the necessary analysis and improve the detection capability. In this federated model, NN and GA are used for optimal pattern matching following dimensionality reduction by PCA.

### 9.4.3. Cloud Security and Encryption

Secure authentication, resource access control, and privacy protection are critical components of cloud-based data communication in databases, various applications, and infrastructure. The EEIBDM framework is used to propose an energy-efficient industry-scale data management system in an Internet of Things setting. In order to improve cloud security, this framework combines federated learning and reinforcement techniques to enable a digital twin system that represents industrial IoT-based big data management virtually. The use of DNA-based Huffman coding in the encryption process was motivated by biological resilience and resulted in a more intricate and unpredictable data encoding technique. By using DNA-motivated Huffman coding to encrypt data instead of conventional binary coding, the suggested approach significantly increases the cloud's security and resilience. Sensors and traffic management systems, two interconnected components of the Internet of Vehicles (IoV), are particularly susceptible to data transmission attacks if improperly secured. To offer multilayer AI-driven defense against such cyberattacks, the effective encryption algorithm EAST is suggested, along with steganography to hide the encrypted data.

### 9.4.4. Incident Response and Mitigation

The next steps necessitate analyzing the threat encountered and fixing the vulnerability, while the detection and security monitoring techniques help identify the negative events. In contemporary technological infrastructures, artificial intelligence has not only aided in detection techniques but also in prevention and attack response systems. The security concerns that are successfully addressed by AI models such as statistical decision trees to arrive at the best optimal decision or NN models to automatically resolve anomalous events after detection are at the heart of the growing interest in and development of automated infrastructures. By continuously monitoring and evaluating events from endpoint devices for possible malicious activity or detected infiltration, AI can also improve endpoint security. By helping to promptly identify and fix vulnerabilities at the device level, such a preventive mechanism can lessen the threat's impact on the entire network.

Deep learning models are used in wireless sensor networks to detect possible threats, and then CNN-based prevention mechanisms are used to virtually completely stop sensor attacks. Phishing attacks that involve social engineering or interacting with malicious software can seriously harm a system or network. Giving operators AI-driven training and evaluations can significantly enhance the prevention mechanism and help avoid such adversity. The countermeasure would be just as effective as incorporating comparable AI technology to protect against sophisticated attacks, given that contemporary attackers are increasingly using AI to their advantage. In addition to these preventive analytics, AI technology helps with adaptive decision-making to create a more dynamic defense mechanism that can change to meet the ever-evolving tactics and attack vectors. To enforce risk management decision support for vital industrial infrastructures, an intelligent AI -based decision support system was proposed. To support intricate industrial installations, the decision model incorporates AI-based techniques like knowledge engineering, causal networks, and multi-criteria analysis. For possible complex cybersecurity issues, a model based on sensor and historical data aids in threat prevention, protection, and mitigation.

### 9.4.5. Threat Intelligence and Deception Technology

Modern security management systems frequently permit vulnerable areas within particular infrastructure components or tracking mechanisms within the system to capture the behavior or data flow from cybercriminals, moving away from active protection mechanisms and toward more proactive approaches. The "Honey Pot" approach to enticing the adversaries helps system analysts obtain crucial data about the attack signatures and strategies of the attackers. The Honey Pot analysis can also be used to model the intrusion detection system or even to reroute attacks away from critical targets. The Honeypot mechanism's data is a wealth of up-to-date threat intelligence. Security analysts and forensic experts can identify novel attack patterns, malware injection strategies, and exploitation trends by examining this data. Threat intelligence is essential for maintaining cyber resilience and staying ahead of attackers since security measures must be updated frequently to keep up with the modular attacks that are becoming more sophisticated. From unstructured Cyber Threat Intelligence (CTI) reports, the suggested AttackKG system automatically extracts and examines attack patterns. To modify the system's identification methods, the analysis is redirected to the knowledge graphs in order to generate templates and a revised graph alignment algorithm. The potential of AI to stop sophisticated cyberattacks is demonstrated by its ability to increase threat detection accuracy, decrease manual interventions, and work in an environment with a high volume of unstructured data.

## REFERENCES


1. Abebe, A. D., & Chilamkurti, N. (2018). Distributed attack detection scheme using deep learning approach for internet of things. *Future Generation Computer Systems, 82,* 761–768.
2. Bui, D. T., Tsangaratos, P., Nguyen, V. T., Liem, N. V., & Trinh, P. T. (2020). Comparing the prediction performance of a deep learning neural network model with conventional machine learning models in landslide susceptibility assessment. *Catena, 188,* 104426.
3. Chen, C. M., Guan, D. J., Huang, Y. Z., & Ou, Y. H. (2016). Anomaly network intrusion detection using hidden Markov model. *International Journal of Innovative Computing, Information and Control, 12,* 569–580.
4. Costa, P. C. G., Laskey, K. B., & Alghamdi, G. (2006). Bayesian ontologies in AI systems.
5. Kriegeskorte, N., & Golan, T. (2019). Neural network models and deep learning. *Current Biology, 29*(7), R231–R236.
6. Li, W. (2004). Using genetic algorithm for network intrusion detection. *Proceedings of the United States Department of Energy Cyber Security Group, 1*(1), 8.
7. Manikopoulos, C., & Papavassiliou, S. (2002). Network intrusion and fault detection: A statistical anomaly approach. *IEEE Communications Magazine, 40*(10), 76–82.
8. McCarthy, J. (1987). Generality in artificial intelligence. *Communications of the ACM, 30*(12), 1030–1035.
9. McStay, A. (2020). Emotional AI, soft biometrics, and the surveillance of emotional life: An unusual consensus on privacy. *Big Data & Society, 7*(1), 2053951720904386.
10. Michael, K., Abbas, R., Jayashree, P., Bandara, R. J., & Aloudat, A. (2022). Biometrics and AI bias. *IEEE Transactions on Technology and Society, 3*(1), 2–8.
11. Nourani, C. F., & Moudi, R. M. (2002). Intelligent cyberspace interfaces and WAP generic computing. *IKS,* St. Thomas, Virgin Islands.
12. Plêta, T., Tvaronavičienė, M., Della Casa, S., & Agafonov, K. (2020). Cyber-attacks to critical energy infrastructure and management issues: Overview of selected cases. *Insights into Regional Development, 2*(3).
13. Rieck, K., Trinius, P., Willems, C., & Holz, T. (2011). Automatic analysis of malware behavior using machine learning. *Journal of Computer Security, 19*(4), 639–668.

14. Sarker, I. H., Abushark, Y. B., Alsolami, F., & Khan, A. I. (2020). Intrudtree: A machine learning based cyber security intrusion detection model. *Symmetry, 12*(5), 754.
15. Seuba, X. (1982). Big data, AI and border enforcement of intellectual property rights. *Intelligence, 4,* 707–748.
16. Srinidhi, C. L., Ciga, O., & Martel, A. L. (2021). Deep neural network models for computational histopathology: A survey. *Medical Image Analysis, 67,* 101813.
17. Staudemeyer, R. C., & Morris, E. R. (2019). Understanding LSTM–A tutorial into long short-term memory recurrent neural networks. *arXiv preprint arXiv:1909.09586.*
18. Sultana, N., Chilamkurti, N., Peng, W., & Alhadad, R. (2019). Survey on SDN based network intrusion detection system using machine learning approaches. *Peer-to-Peer Networking and Applications, 12,* 493–501.
19. Turing, A. M. (2009). Computing machinery and intelligence. Springer.
20. Wu, Z., Zhang, H., Wang, P., & Sun, Z. (2022). RTIDS: A robust transformer-based approach for intrusion detection system. *IEEE Access, 10,* 64375–64387.
21. Yang, L., Moubayed, A., Shami, A., Heidari, P., Boukhtouta, A., Larabi, A., Brunner, R., Preda, S., & Migault, D. (2021). Multi-perspective content delivery networks security framework using optimized unsupervised anomaly detection. *IEEE Transactions on Network and Service Management, 19*(1), 686–705.
22. Yang, X., Zhao, P., Zhang, X., Lin, J., & Yu, W. (2016). Toward a Gaussian-mixture model-based detection scheme against data integrity attacks in the smart grid. *IEEE Internet of Things Journal, 4*(1), 147–161.

# INDEX

## C

## D



## E



## F

**G**



**H**



**I**



**K**



**L**

## M



## N



## O



## P

## Q



## R



## S

## T



## U



## V



## W